The Bı

MW01035521

By Walter E. Wilson *and* Gary L. McKay

James D. Bulloch: Secret Agent and Mastermind of the Confederate Navy (McFarland, 2012)

The Bulloch Belles

Three First Ladies, a Spy,
a President's Mother and Other
Women of a 19th Century
Georgia Family

WALTER E. WILSON

McFarland & Company, Inc., Publishers
Jefferson, North Carolina

Library of Congress Cataloguing-in-Publication Data

Wilson, Walter E., 1949– author.
    The Bulloch belles : three first ladies, a spy, a president's mother and
other women of a 19th century Georgia family / Walter E. Wilson.
        p.   cm.
    Includes bibliographical references and index.

    ISBN 978-0-7864-9993-9 (softcover : acid free paper) ∞
    ISBN 978-1-4766-2242-2 (ebook)

    1. Bullock family.   2. Women—Georgia—History—19th century.
3. Women—Georgia—Biography.   4. Roswell (Ga.)—Biography.
I. Title.

CS71.B936 2015
920.72—dc23   2015032222

British Library cataloguing data are available

On the cover: Mrs. Alice Hathaway Lee Roosevelt, photograph
taken between 1880 and 1884 (Library of Congress)

Printed in the United States of America

McFarland & Company, Inc., Publishers
  Box 611, Jefferson, North Carolina 28640
    www.mcfarlandpub.com

Table of Contents

Preface

The Bulloch women were part of a large, extended family of stepchildren, cousins, and those who befriended or married Bulloch men. They included three first ladies, a famous spy, and the mother of a president of the United States, but most were unknown to the general public. Regardless of their renown, the Bulloch women uniformly exemplified the ironclad strength and resilience of women whose roles and expectations were forever altered during and after the American Civil War. The private lives of these strong ladies unlocked the secrets of a mysterious Confederate agent, formed the character of one of America's greatest presidents, and embodied new ideals of femininity.

This is not a story about the well-known leaders who drove the events of the Civil War. Rather, it is the personal story, derived from primary source materials, of a particular group of women who operated in the shadows. These exceptional women were all connected to a single family, the Bullochs of Roswell, Georgia, by kinship or intimate friendship. The Bullochs came to Georgia from Scotland via South Carolina prior to the American Revolution. They settled in the fertile coastal region around Savannah and helped establish the small Presbyterian colony of Roswell, a few miles north of a railway junction that grew into Atlanta. Through fortuitous marriages that included other prominent Georgian families such as the Stewarts, Elliotts, and Dunwodys, the Bulloch family grew in numbers and influence. Later generations added the Caskies of Richmond and the Roosevelts of New York as integral members of the extended Bulloch clan.

During the great American tragedy that played out from 1861 to 1865, the Bulloch women were especially active, especially given the limitations placed upon their sex. In the United States, the most visible political, military, and business leaders were all males. The paternalistic society of the mid-nineteenth century considered all issues and events within the public domain as the sole responsibility of white males. This meant that almost every form of professional employment discouraged or excluded the participation of women, particularly in the South. With very few exceptions, females simply could not work outside the home in the political, business, financial, military, or religious arenas. Barring exceptional circumstances, even primary school teachers and hospital nursing positions had to be filled by males. These professions were by definition inappropriate occupations for a lady.

The realm of antebellum southern women was the household, particularly on the plantations. The circumstances of the Bulloch women helped create and exemplify a unique category of southern ladies. Although they were from the South, they were not plantation mistresses. They did not even live on plantations in the decade before the Civil War. They were well-educated and adept at moving in social circles far beyond the isolated boundaries of the rural South. This group of special ladies included close friends as well as family members. The Bulloch women were the individuals most responsible for shaping, influencing, tempting, and sustaining the family before, during, and after the war. Their roles grew in importance during the exciting and dangerous Civil War period. Afterwards, they became vital to the survival of their southern namesakes. These powerful and influential women (or their mothers) were all ladies of the antebellum South.

During the war, they remained southern belles with typical southern sympathies even though most were living north of the Mason-Dixon Line. They took full advantage of their privileged positions to support the cause of their native land. But those who lived in the North had to carefully avoid direct confrontations. Overt actions would have jeopardized the status of their men, their northern family members, and their own safety. The Bulloch women who survived the war formed a small cadre of ladies who remained of the South, even though they were not living in the South. Wealthy northern family ties allowed them to prosper in a world still defined by servants, first class travel, high society, and no unseemly requirement to seek wage-earning employment.

The personal stories of the Bulloch women illuminate the changing roles of women in the period from the mid-nineteenth to the early twentieth centuries. These women were all intimately connected to the extended Bulloch family. As the Bulloch men assumed important business, military, and political positions, they influenced the course of their regions and nations. The Bulloch ladies participated in these changes as they operated behind the scenes. More importantly, they were on the leading edge of a slower moving social upheaval that permanently altered the way men and women perceive their respective roles in society. Their previously untold stories provide insight into the forces behind the evolving roles of American women during the nineteenth century.

Special thanks are in order to Gwen Koehler, the education director, and the entire staff of Bulloch Hall in Roswell, Georgia. Gwen's knowledge, encouragement, and willingness to share information have been constant during the years I have invested in this project. Connie Huddleston, archeologist and historian, is an invaluable resource for information about Bulloch Hall, its people and events. They kindly shared insights gained from their book , *Mittie & Thee,* that highlights the early letters of Mittie Bulloch and Theodore Roosevelt, Sr.

Sharon McKusker Wilson, my wife and partner for over 45 years, was my navigator as we traveled to historic sites, and she helped refine the text. Dr. Brittany Wilson of Duke University provided helpful insights about modern and historical gender issues. Dr. Jim Elliott, of Perth, Australia, continued to share Bulloch family information related to his grandfather, Stuart Elliott (né Stuart Elliott Bulloch), and his father, James Elliott. Mr. Christopher "Kit" Collier helped direct me to information and solve part of the mystery surrounding the fate of the Bulloch family's servant Nancy Jackson.

The staff at numerous archive collections provided invaluable and timely assistance including: Lindsay Sheldon and Sherry Cortes with the Georgia Historical Society, Savannah; Susan Aprill, archivist, Kingston Public Library, Kingston, Massachusetts; Maria Paxi, librarian, History and Genealogy Unit, Connecticut State Library, Hartford; and Wallace Finley Dailey, former curator, Theodore Roosevelt Collection, Harvard College Library, Cambridge, Massachusetts.

I am extremely grateful to the following individuals and organizations for their assistance in obtaining photographs and illustrations that help bring the text to life: Stephen Bohlin, director, Andrew Low House, Savannah, Georgia; Heather Cole, curator of the Theodore Roosevelt Collection, Houghton Library, Harvard University, Cambridge, Massachusetts; Virginia Lewick, archivist, Franklin D. Roosevelt Presidential Library, Hyde Park, New York; and Graham Roberts, archivist, Dumfries and Galloway Libraries, Information and Archives, Dumfries, Scotland.

Robert "Bob" Jones (1940–2015), the legendary local historian and unofficial Confederate Navy tour guide of Liverpool, first excited my interest in the Bulloch family in 2007. He will be missed. Roy Rawlinson continues to inform and inspire Bulloch family and American Civil War historical research and preservation in Liverpool through his website When Liverpool Was Dixie and as part of the 290 Foundation. I owe Dr. Gary L. McKay a tremendous debt of gratitude for allowing me to be his co-author on our biography of James D. Bulloch. Finally, a special thanks to James "Hal" Hardaway for asking me to tag along with him during his travels to London, Liverpool, Crewe, and several stops in between.

Introduction

Before the American Civil War, the Bullochs were one of Georgia's most prominent families. The family history is replete with stories of brave and successful men. During colonial times, Georgia's first president and supreme military commander was a Bulloch. Afterwards, the Bullochs continued their tradition of political and military service through the Civil War era. The Bulloch women sometimes received a portion of the credit for these successes, most often as passive participants in the advantageous marriages that helped sustain the finances of the Bulloch men. At the turn of the twentieth century, the Roswell branch of the Bulloch surname disappeared as perspectives about the proper role women began to change. The family spirit and legacy continued to live on, however, through the Bulloch women, particularly those who became Roosevelts.

Three of the Bulloch men of Roswell, Georgia, were combatants in the Civil War. Two of the family's sons and one stepson fought for the Confederacy. Stepson Daniel Stuart Elliott served briefly as an army private and Irvine Stephens Bulloch became a well-traveled junior officer in the Confederate Navy. Easily the most prominent and influential wartime Bulloch male was Commander James Dunwoody Bulloch. His friends and family knew him as a dashing captain of a blockade-runner and the Confederacy's most effective overseas secret agent. His enemies, most particularly the anxious Union spies, knew him as the "most dangerous man" in Europe.[1]

A nephew by James' youngest sister, Mittie, was the first to remember him as Admiral Bulloch. Heavily influenced by his mother and her sisters, Teddy Roosevelt, the twenty-sixth president of the United States, elevated his Uncle Jimmie to the rank of "Admiral in the Confederate Navy" in his autobiography and political speeches.[2] Even Margaret Mitchell borrowed Teddy's "Admiral Bulloch" as an example of a loyal, honest officer in her novel *Gone With the Wind*.[3]

Bulloch, Elliott, Roosevelt Family Tree

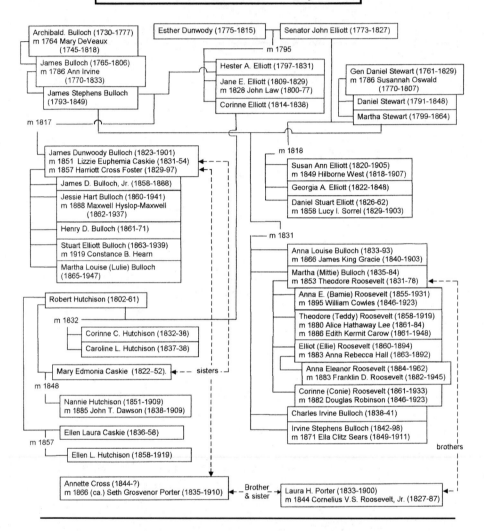

Often lost in the impressive litany of the Bulloch men's wartime achievements was the vital role that the Bulloch women played in those successes. Strong women shaped, assisted, and loved their men, before, during, and after the war. At the same time, wartime necessities and postwar consequences slowly altered the Bulloch families' expectations about gender roles in social, economic, and political contexts. The Bullochs spent little time overtly contemplating the role of women. That is, until new and uncomfortable realities about their men's inability to protect and provide for the family became apparent. Challenging post-war circumstances, family traditions, and fortunate female relations subtly shifted their perspectives. These changing attitudes were representative of a radical new paradigm that slowly but steadily enveloped twentieth century Western society.

The Bulloch women did not easily conform to the categories that recent scholars have used to describe nineteenth century women of the South. Although their family and friends certainly aligned their sentiments with the southern social elite, none of them were planters in the decade prior to the war. Most of them had, however, spent their childhood on plantations or in wealthy households with large household staffs. These experiences nurtured a firm identification with the plantation owners. Only the family's Civil War matriarch, Martha (Stewart) Bulloch, had briefly assumed the role of plantation mistress while she was married to Senator John Elliott.[4]

Due to a combination of circumstance and deliberate intent, the Bulloch ladies assumed roles and attitudes that were more complex than the stereotypical southern belle. Their families were merchants, commodity brokers and shippers, bankers, military officers, investors, speculators, and part of the governing class. These women assumed the role of an intelligent partner in these endeavors. Accordingly, parents and guardians paid for their daughters to attend the same primary schools as their boys. Afterwards, they financed each girl's schooling at the finest secondary and collegiate academies then available to young ladies of means. They did not limit themselves to the meager offerings available in Georgia or even the United States. Their schooling ranged from South Carolina, to Philadelphia and Hartford (Connecticut) and across the ocean to Paris, France, and the United Kingdom.[5]

In another fortunate distinction, most of the Bulloch women did not lose their fortunes or positions as a result of the Civil War. Their friends, neighbors, and more distant relatives were not as blessed. At the outbreak of the war, the women within the Bullochs' immediate family had already moved to the North. There, they met, loved and married northern men and became prominent members of northern society. After the war, they continued to prosper. The transplanted Bulloch ladies managed to maintain and elevate their status within the northern social elite.

Although they did not experience the same deprivations as their post-war southern counterparts, the Bulloch women were not completely insulated from the war's heartaches and unintended social changes. Young men within the extended family fought for both sides. Disease claimed one brother who wore Rebel gray, while another brother who donned Yankee blue died in combat. Their losses were but two of the 620,000 to 750,000 young American men who died during the war. With a national population of only 31 million in 1860, the twenty-first century casualty equivalent would have been almost 7.5 million deaths. Most of the casualties were mere boys. They were American sons, brothers, and husbands who died on American soil. Each loss was a very personal one that touched almost every home. In the case of the Bulloch ladies, even their men who did not bear arms were often absent for long periods. The absence of male "heads of household" through death or employment during and after the war became the new norm.[6]

The Bulloch ladies seldom questioned the racial, class, or sexual dogmas of southern society. Like most southern white women, they were not particularly frustrated by their lack of opportunity as compared to their male counterparts. The Bulloch ladies were content to allow their men to be the primary actors in the public arena. The women remained active, but silent, partners in these social welfare efforts. Socially elite, well-educated women like the Bullochs quietly opposed militant feminists such as the suffragettes. This anti-feminist stance reflected their sincerely held beliefs, but at the same time increased their credibility and influence among intimate male associates. These women achieved their aims out of public view through intelligent and subtle persuasion rather than confrontation.[7]

Their approach was a successful one. After the Civil War, women obtained the best traction for positive social change when they simultaneously advocated traditional values. Their public voice resonated with both male and female audiences when they acknowledged a subordinate, but not inferior, position to men. Men were generally willing to accept women's superior status in the domestic and spiritual realms in exchange for female deference in all others, especially political and public concerns.[8]

In their personal conduct, the Bulloch ladies continued to embody pre-war ideals of domestic perfection: chastity, piety, and purity. However, they did not pine for the antebellum days, for their post-war lives had remained quite comfortable. Theirs was a coherent era that valued the comfort and security of home life as a woman's crowning achievement. The Bulloch ladies, however, often delayed marriage rather than rushing into an unsuitable match. Even as "spinsters" they sustained powerful positions that allowed them to retain their sense of class distinctions and pursue their own personal and intellectual interests. For them, marriage was not a decision based primarily on necessity or social expectations; it was something they wanted to do.[9]

As displaced southern women, the Bulloch ladies also retained and passed on much of their antebellum heritage. They modeled new and more vibrant roles for women within the social fabric of the nation. These special women did not set out to be reformers and were never especially active in public feminist causes. Instead, they expected their Bulloch and Roosevelt father-figures to model benevolent social activism outside the home. The Bulloch women evolved and adapted according to their circumstances and new experiences, but held firm to their ideals. More importantly, they passed their expectations for social activism on to their daughters. They provided an unusual twist to the sense of the proper "place" of women in society and the definition of being a lady.

Some have argued that the white women of both the North and South soon lost the few feminist gains they had made during wartime. These observers note that southern women particularly clung to traditional definitions of feminine character and rarely pursued unconventional roles. These southern women had no interest in taking on the risks of radical gender-related issues, and remained loyal to their class and race. It was change without change.[10]

Contemporary understandings of proper social equity have typically colored judgments about the defects of nineteenth century interpretations of race and gender. It is relatively easy to analyze and understand the errant assumptions about race and gender and the "scientific" conclusions from that era. No rational twenty-first century social scientist would accept the validity of the limitations that the paternalistic nineteenth century society had institutionalized into every aspect of its cultural fiber. Although the entire country shared many of the same cultural assumptions about gender and race, only the agrarian south thrived on chattel slavery. Southern rationalizations of benign paternalism and the correctness of slavery was so clearly wrong that modern observers find it difficult to find any redeeming qualities of the people from that place and time.

Retrospective historical and cultural bias frequently prompts modern analysts to figuratively wag their fingers and cluck their tongues at the stupidity and immorality of their Confederate forebears. Similarly, contemporary analysts have concluded that since nineteenth century women never had a viable public voice, the Civil War had no lasting effect on a woman's power in society. However, the relative absence of women in public positions in the years after the Civil War did not mean that there had been no change in their roles or expectations. Such conclusions trivialize the influence of women on events and mask a slower moving, but fundamental shift in social norms.

Nineteenth century women in positions of social and economic power like the Bulloch ladies did not seek or desire remarkable change in their public roles. They were flexible in adapting to changed circumstances, but they did not abandon their long-standing definitions of feminine character. They refused to shed all of the old and suddenly become something entirely new. Instead, they blended some of the new with a lot of the old, particularly their southern ideas about what it meant to be a lady. The Bulloch women succeeded in their traditional nurturing roles as a mother and matriarch who managed the affairs of home and family. At the same time, they steadily and subtly assumed what had been purely masculine roles as social advocate, provider, and protector.[11]

1

Antebellum First Ladies

The Bulloch family ties were deep and they were complex. None more so than the romantic quadrangle that began when 20-year-old Hettie Hester ("Hettie") Amarintha Elliott married 24-year-old James Stephens Bulloch. The couple exchanged the traditional vows on the last day of 1817 in their rural family church at Midway, about 30 miles southwest of Savannah, Georgia. The Bulloch and Elliott families had known each other for generations. They were already connected through Hettie's uncle, John Dunwoody. John had married her husband James' older sister Jane nine years earlier. Both families were well known within Georgia's elite social and political circles. Hettie's grandfather, John Elliott, Jr., had been a colonel in the Georgia militia. Grandfather Elliott had inherited the nearby Laurel View plantation through his marriage to Rebecca Maxwell.[1]

John Elliott, Jr., received his education at Yale and became a prominent Georgia lawyer and politician. Like her father John, Hettie Elliott grew up at Laurel View. It was a relatively large rice and sea-island cotton plantation of 2500 acres that employed 170 slaves. The plantation home commanded a magnificent view of the Midway River. Perched on a high bank named Hester's Bluff, it was a beautiful location that inspired Hettie's given name.[2]

Not to be outdone, the Bulloch side of the family could point to Archibald Bulloch as the first president of colonial Georgia's Executive Council. He was an early advocate of independence from the United Kingdom and an associate of Benjamin Franklin and other revolutionary heroes. He married Mary DeVeaux, the aristocratic daughter of a member of the King of England's court. Archibald died suddenly and mysteriously after the legislature had elected him commander-in-chief of Georgia's militia. Archibald Bulloch had named one of his sons after his own father, a Presbyterian minister and planter. That son was James Bulloch, an ambitious, brave, and skilled leader of men. He joined the Revolutionary army at the age of 13 and rose to the rank of captain as a 17-year-old. Like his father, James married well and died young. It was James' namesake son who became the most accomplished of his progeny, but only after James Stephens Bulloch entered into a controversial and sometimes scandalous marital chain of events.[3]

The unusual circumstances of the tangled Bulloch–Elliott romance began two years after John Elliott's first wife, Esther Dunwody Elliott, died at their Laurel View plantation. Both he and his teenage daughter Hettie found themselves in the unusual situation of seeking a spouse at the same time. The pool of eligible and suitable candidates for marriage was decidedly limited in the Georgian society of 1817 and created overlapping social circles for father and daughter.

That fall, the 44-year-old John Elliott identified a likely young contender named Martha "Patsy" Stewart. John Elliott, however, was not the

Martha Stewart Elliott Bulloch (Theodore Roosevelt Collection, Houghton Library, Harvard University, TRC-PH-2 570.87m).

first of Martha's suitors. James Stephens Bulloch had noticed the inner and physical beauty that the lone surviving photograph of Martha failed to capture. James was young, handsome, and confident. The small community around Savannah was well-aware of his interest in the lovely Miss Stewart. However, when the much older but prosperous John Elliott entered the picture, he quickly turned Martha's head. Following strict courting protocol, John wrote to her father seeking permission to begin a formal courtship. Martha's father was 56-year-old General Daniel Stewart, Georgia's hero of the Revolutionary and Indian wars. In his letter, John revealed his "secret wishes" to marry the general's beautiful daughter. He followed up with a letter to the 18-year-old Martha declaring his love and requesting, "a personal interview to receive the all important answer to my future happiness."[4]

In an era when women had very few choices about significant matters, affairs of the heart were an important exception. Martha had her pick of the best and most likely candidates from the coastal counties of Georgia. In addition to being a war hero, her father was a former state senator, a selectman of the Midway Congregational Church (with John Elliott and John Dunwoody), and the owner of nearby Cedar Hill and Tranquil Hill Plantations. When Martha waivered in her affections, James Stephens Bulloch redirected his attentions to John Elliott's youngest daughter Hester Amarintha. Just shy of her twentieth birthday, "Hettie" was almost two years older than Martha.[5]

James S. Bulloch and Hettie Elliott had been friends and neighbors since childhood. They had also been schoolmates at nearby Sunbury Academy, the only public education available in Liberty County. Like all primary schools of that era, it was a privately funded school that operated under a state charter. Sunbury and nearby Chatham Academy in Savannah both commenced offering classes as state-authorized co-educational schools around 1788. The Bulloch and Elliott families shared an interest in the education of their children, both male and female. Hettie's grandfather was one of Sunbury's five founding commissioners. Its student body included about seventy boys and girls from affluent Georgia families. The challenging curriculum included reading, spelling, writing, geography, Latin, Greek, English grammar, and higher mathematics.[6]

The Reverend William McWhir was a fixture at Sunbury Academy, where he had been headmaster since 1791. His credentials were impeccable, having spent the previous ten years as principal of a similar school in Virginia. That academy counted George Washington as a trustee and his stepchildren were McWhir's students. Reverend McWhir promptly elevated the standards of Sunbury Academy until it became and remained the best preparatory school in the state for almost thirty years. The dour-looking Presbyterian headmaster was a "terror to all dolts and delinquents." Socially, however, he was cheerful, sincere, and friendly.[7]

In the ten years since Hettie and James had been students under his care, Rev. McWhir had developed a personal bond with the couple. Their former headmaster and teacher presided over the Elliott-Bulloch nuptials on New Year's Eve, 1817. The venue was the same Midway Congregational Church that both families had helped build and restore. One week later, the father of the bride, John Elliott, again donned his best formal attire and stood facing the assembled multitude that filled the familiar pew boxes and balcony benches at the Midway Church. This time, Mr. Elliott was the groom, as he and Martha Stewart exchanged vows on January 6, 1818.[8]

There was no apparent residual acrimony in their unusual familial courtships. John Elliott and his new son-in-law became frequent travelling companions. On one trip in June of 1818, they were on the Augusta Road outside of Savannah, when highwaymen attacked their carriage. The "villains" managed to detach John's trunk from the wagon, but he and his son-in-law were able to thwart the attempt. They chased the foiled robbers who escaped into the woods, leaving the men with an exciting tale to tell, but no injuries and all their property intact.[9]

The Bulloch-Elliott-Stewart combination proved advantageous for both couples in other ways. John Elliott's bride, the "lovely and charming" Martha, provided a boost to his aspiring political career. In addition to her personal qualities, she was the daughter of a popular and well-connected general. The family connections of Elliott's new son-in-law, James Stephens Bulloch, were also helpful. As the grandson of Archibald Bulloch, the respected first president and commander in chief of the state of Georgia, James S. Bulloch also had influential allies. This mix of family connections, plantation interests, and his superb professional qualifications as a Yale-educated lawyer cemented John's attractiveness as a political candidate.[10]

Later that year, John Elliott decided to make a run for a seat in the U.S. Senate. The result was a successful fall campaign and a seat in the U.S. capitol as a "Democratic-Republican." He took office on March 4, 1819, just over a year after he and Martha Stewart had married. Martha's journey to Washington, D.C., was the first time she had ever ventured out of the Deep South. The beautiful Martha naturally attracted attention as a 19-year-old senator's wife. Dealing with the subtle social mores in the nation's capitol might have been an intimidating prospect for a lesser teenage girl. Instead of suffocating in the rarified Washington air, it was Martha who took people's breath away. She seemed to welcome the attention. She wore stylish dresses that featured flamboyant ostrich feathers that "hung down to her belt." At formal balls, in church, and at home, the vivacious Martha and her distinguished husband seemed well suited as the "handsomest couple" on the Washington, D.C., social scene.[11]

As her many letters attest, Martha's vibrant personality could not be confused with shallowness or frivolity. She was an attractive and intelligent asset to her husband's political career as she moved comfortably in his circle of friends and constituents. Back in Georgia, Martha was also the mistress of her husband's moderately large Laurel View plantation. She was an insightful companion and became a loving, caring mother to her entire extended family. Martha soon delivered children of her own. She and John had five children at two year intervals, beginning with John Whitehead (1818) and then Susan Ann (1820), Georgia Amanda (1822), Charles Williams (1824) and finally Daniel Stuart (1826).[12]

Martha's responsibilities as household mistress and mother included buying, growing, and preparing the food; acquiring, mending and making clothes; cleaning and maintaining the home; tending to the sick, and instructing the young in basic academics and religion. Despite her confinement to the domestic sphere, her domain was expansive. She had charge of the moral, spiritual, and physical well-being of the entire plantation. That domain encompassed the big house, barnyard, slave cabins, and every inhabitant of the plantation, both black and white. This menagerie included Jane and Corinne, Senator Elliott's surviving children with his first wife, and the estate's 170 slaves.[13]

These broad duties challenged the young bride, but she was merely fulfilling the role she had come to expect. By all appearances, she had achieved the height of every antebellum southern woman's aspirations. She led a pampered life on a stately plantation as the wife of a prominent and wealthy man. The glamorous balls and receptions among the Nation's most powerful elite were an added delight. Still, Martha and John experienced their share of personal tragedy early in their marriage. Their first son, John, died (1820) while he was still a toddler. That same year, a tornado destroyed much of Laurel View, including its cotton gin where 30 blacks were severely injured and one was killed.[14]

Despite positive endorsements from powerful constituents, Senator Elliott served only one term in the capital. He chose not to run for a second term due to health concerns related to severe attacks of vertigo. At the end of his term, Martha and the children preceded him to Savannah. John finally returned to Georgia via New York City on June 20, 1826, reportedly "in improved health." Martha and the rest of the children had already taken up residence at Laurel View for she was four months pregnant with their fifth child. On November 20, Martha gave birth to Daniel Stewart Elliott, named after Martha's famous father. Most commonly known as "Stuart," he would be her only son with John Elliott to survive into adulthood. Like all the rest of their children, the proud parents presented Stuart for baptism at the same Midway Congregational church where they had been married almost nine years earlier.[15]

While Martha and John Elliott were living and serving in Washington, D.C., James S. and Hettie Bulloch had taken up residence on Broughton Street in the center of Savannah. They were only a few blocks from the

Savannah River. From their upstairs windows, the couple could see the masts of sailing vessels in the harbor. Their home provided an excellent vantage point to view the movements of staple commodities like cotton and rice out of the port and the import of finished goods from Europe and the northern states. James was an agent and broker who bought and sold these goods and arranged for their shipment to other ports, particularly New York City.[16]

When John Elliott began his campaign for the Senate in 1818, James was busy establishing the Building & Insurance Bank of Georgia. He and his fellow investors formed the bank out of the Savannah Marine and Fire Insurance Company. James was one of its first five commissioners. A year later, he entered into a "Factorage and Commission Business" partnership with George Sadler under the name of Bulloch & Sadler. The partners shipped "sundries" and booked passengers on small sailing vessels through the spring of 1820. James S. Bulloch had begun a pattern he would maintain throughout his life. His business interests were many, varied, and often short-lived.[17]

By 1821, James formed another mercantile partnership in Savannah with his brother-in-law, John Dunwoody. This partnership was more successful. The firm Bulloch & Dunwoody routinely sold or rented city homes, plantations, tracts of land, and cotton gins on behalf of their clients. Their primary business, however, remained as commission agents. They bought, sold, and shipped commodities such as cotton and rice, and booked passage for travelers. In short, they facilitated business for ships that plied Georgia's rivers and bays to Savannah, and on to Charleston and New York.[18]

James was always watchful for new and varied opportunities. He had been one of the founding directors of the Marine and Fire Insurance Co. In 1825, he was one of five elected port wardens. As a port warden, he conducted safety inspections and enforced compliance repairs on ships and their cargoes for a fee. James was also an investor and a director of the Savannah Steam Ship Company. The company financed the construction of the SS *Savannah*, the first steamship to cross the Atlantic. The project worked in association with the innovative Nicholas I. Roosevelt of New York. Roosevelt was a partner of Robert Fulton, the steamship inventor. Although the ship was a technical success, the enterprise was a financial disaster. Fortunately for the Bulloch family, theirs was a minority holding.[19]

James and Hettie were also very active socially. If John and Martha Elliott exemplified the paternalism of the southern family and plantation life, James and Hettie did the same for the urban society of Savannah.

They helped project southern hospitality into the entire community, which included those who were in need or required protection.

Examples of James' community activism were numerous. He was the board of health representative for his city ward along with his brother-in-law and partner, John Dunwoody. James and fourteen others received a public note of thanks from Savannah's Fire Company for extinguishing a fire in December of 1823. Later, he was the secretary of a committee for the relief of fire victims in both Augusta and Savanna. He twice served as a Savannah alderman (1817–1818 & 1823–1824). He volunteered for military service and rose in the ranks from sergeant to major in the local Chatham Artillery. James was also a founding member and the first chairman of the Savannah Temperance Society.[20]

Hettie's husband and her father represented the business and political aspects of the plantation economy. They were also the public face of moral crusades that advocated conservative values and Christian principles. As seen with James Stephens Bulloch's involvement with the temperance movement, southern men were often at the forefront of reform issues most often championed by northern middleclass women. In contrast, southern women usually played supportive roles. They encouraged these social justice movements, but their rural isolation and cultural expectations offered few opportunities for them to act beyond the comfort and security of home. Women of the southern mercantile class like Hettie were exceptions. These women lived in the cities and generally had a greater sense of community and communal service. They were able to carve out small roles of their own.[21]

As an active participant in Savannah society, Hettie Bulloch's interests went beyond social visits, cotillions, and caring for home and family. She served on the board of managers for the Savannah Female Asylum for fatherless orphans. The society operated an eight room boarding house "for the relief of Poor Widows with small Children, and destitute females." The society initially depended upon contributions from individuals and church congregations for their support. Hettie and her sister-in-law Mrs. Jane Bulloch Dunwoody, the spouse of James' business partner, were responsible for superintending the area from Savannah's Price Street to East Broad Street. Later, they participated in other fund raising initiatives such as lectures, concerts, and an annual Christmas fair where the society offered for sale, "every article useful and ornamental."[22]

On the home front, Hettie gave birth to a son within their first year of marriage. She named the boy John Elliott Bulloch after her own father. He was born within days of Hettie's stepmother Martha's first son, John

Whitehead Elliott. In a sad parallel with Martha's experience, Hettie's first son died suddenly while he was just a toddler. Unlike Martha, who continued to bear children at two year intervals, Hettie did not carry another full term child for another four years. Given the lack of nineteenth century birth control knowledge or methods, other than abstinence, it is likely that Hettie had health issues. Her condition would worsen over time, but not before she finally had a healthy baby boy in Savannah on June 25, 1823, after over five years of marriage.[23]

They named their son James Dunwoody Bulloch, after his father James and his Uncle John Dunwoody. Hettie and James continued the common practice of reflecting the family's maternal lineage through their children. In addition to Dunwoody, other given names from the Bulloch female line included Irvine, Elliott, and Stewart. Future generations would continue the tradition by adding Bulloch to the list of given names that honored the family's maternal ancestors.[24]

When Martha and John returned to Georgia from their political sojourn in Washington, the presence of James and Hettie in Savannah influenced their decision to live in town. Despite their long-standing ties to Laurel View, Senator Elliott made arrangements to sell his plantation to William Maxwell, a nephew by the senator's first wife, Rebecca. After spending most of the past six years in the city of Washington, life in rural Liberty County, located 40 miles from Savannah, never seemed more remote. To support his new life, John Elliott accepted a directorship with the Planter's Bank of Georgia in Savannah.

Unfortunately, the year that began on so many hopeful notes would be a trying one for Martha and the Elliott family. In short order, her second son, Charles William, died, as did the 55-year-old former senator. John Elliott had received word in Savannah that several of his plantation slaves were seriously ill. True to his caring nature and paternalistic responsibilities, he quickly returned to Laurel View to be with those who depended upon him. Unfortunately, he lingered there too long and "while administering to his sick slaves in Liberty Co., 12 of whom died of dysentery, [he] was seized with the same complaint." He died in August of 1827. Newspaper editors throughout the state and nation lamented his passing.[25]

John died just six days before Martha's 28th birthday. He left their three young children and his two daughters from his first marriage in her care. The young widow was now responsible for her own children Susan (8), Georgia (6), and Daniel Stuart (8 months), plus two teenage stepdaughters, Jane (18) and Corinne (13). Stepdaughter Jane Elliott married Dr. John Law seven months after John Elliott's death, leaving young Corinne as the only stepchild still at home with the widowed Martha. Predictably, Corinne became "devotedly attached to her Step-mother" Martha.[26]

John and Martha Elliott's only male heir was the infant Daniel. Even with the pending sale of Laurel View to the Maxwell family, Martha needed assistance with the business affairs of the estate. In the nineteenth century, a woman often had little to say about the disposal of her husband's estate unless she administered it herself. John had named their son-in-law, James Stephens Bulloch, as the executor of his will, but he proved to be a fortunate choice. Although family members customarily took widows under their wing, it was a sad, but privileged duty for James and Hettie that they were happy to perform.[27]

Through the years, the couple had remained close to Martha, thinking of her as more of a friend than a mother-in-law. Like their husbands, Martha and Hettie were regular travelling companions. In early March of 1828, they both sailed on the steamboat *Carolina* for its round trip between Augusta and Savannah. A year later, James and Hettie decided to sell their Savannah home. The motivation for this sale is unclear, but was probably connected to their stepmother, Martha Elliott. After the Bullochs sold their home, James shipped rice from "Bulloch's plantation" indicating that he and Hettie had relocated to Laurel View with Martha. As manager of John Elliott's estate on Martha's behalf, James then offered the Elliott's Savannah "dwelling house" for immediate sale. The home occupied two lots, had a favorable southeast frontage on Broughton Street, and included "all the furniture, &c." The home was "a great bargain" with credit available to a buyer for up to five years at no interest.[28]

The chain of events that drew the Elliott and Bulloch families even closer together continued when Martha's father, General Daniel Stewart, died in May of 1829. The General's second wife, Susannah Oswald (Martha's mother), had passed 22 years earlier and his third wife, Sarah Hines, was also in ill health and died just months after General Stewart. Martha's older brother Daniel McLochlan Stewart, the general's only surviving male heir, was the executor of the estate. Daniel auctioned off a portion of his father's goods and 27 slaves in 1832, but he retained the Cedar Hill and Tranquil Hill plantations on behalf of the family (at least through 1832). Martha's one fourth share of the goods and slaves from the estate were valued at $3959.50 (about $115,000 in 2015).[29]

Planters like General Stewart often wanted to keep their plantations intact. They did not believe that a woman could successfully manage one on her own. Accordingly, men sometimes bequeathed slaves rather than land to their daughters. In this case, however, Martha's brother, Daniel,

lived 80 miles away near Brunswick, Georgia. He was an aspiring politician, who served as a colonel in the state militia. He was also standing for
election as a congressman from Glynn County. Colonel Stewart clearly had
no interest in managing the plantations or properties in distant Chatham
and Liberty Counties. These happy circumstances allowed Martha to
receive a full share of the Cedar Hill plantation property in Liberty County,
where she would later take up residence. As a result of her inheritances,
Martha was a young, attractive, and wealthy widow, and highly eligible
for marriage.[30]

As spring turned to summer, the Elliotts and Bullochs considered
their next move. Beginning in the eighteenth century, well-to-do southerners had avoided the unhealthy coastal summer heat by sailing to the
cooler climates of the northern states. They typically migrated north in
May or June and returned in October or November. Hettie and James,
plus their young son, James Dunwoody, followed this tradition in the
tumultuous summer of 1829. They boarded the sailing ship *Florian* on the
morning of June 29. It was just over a month after the death of General
Stewart and six days after James Dunwoody Bulloch's sixth birthday. The
family celebrated the Fourth of July at sea before arriving in New York
City on the evening of July 6. Accompanying them on the voyage was their
stepmother-in-law, Martha, and her children Susan, Georgia, and Daniel
Elliott. Corinne Elliott (Martha's youngest stepchild), Jane Bulloch (the
daughter of James' deceased brother John Irvine), and a servant also sailed
with them.[31]

In addition to seeking cooler climes, there were other important factors that prompted these unusual travel arrangements. Martha's share of
her husband's and father's estates had not been completely settled, and she
probably felt the need to get away from the scene of her recent losses.
Although she was six years younger than James Stephens Bulloch and two
years younger than Hettie, Martha Stewart Elliott was technically their
stepmother. As the executor of John Elliott's estate, James had the added
paternal expectation of personally ensuring Martha's physical and financial
well-being.

James' other consuming concern was Hettie's health. As suggested
by her lack of children and confirmed by subsequent events, Hettie was
not well. Both she and her son, James Dunwoody, needed the nurturing
presence that Martha could provide. The Elliotts and Hettie's small family
remained in New York through October when they all returned to Savannah. There was one addition and one exception on the homeward journey.
Robert Hutchison joined the family for their five day voyage on the sailing

ship *Hamilton*. The 27-year-old Hutchison was a successful Savannah merchant who, like the Bulloch family, was from Scotland. Robert assisted James with his duties as executor of John Elliott's estate, and became a life-long family friend and benefactor. Robert also took an interest in the 15-year-old Corinne Elliott, a liaison that would eventually bring him into the family. The one person who did not make the return trip was a niece, identified as "Miss Bulloch." This was probably Jane Bulloch, who returned ten days later with Alexander Telfair and his nieces. The Misses Mary and Margaret Telfair had just completed the summer semester at a girls' boarding school in New York City.[32]

For mid-nineteenth century girls, formal or advanced educational opportunities depended primarily on the widely varied attitudes of their parents. For the Bullochs and Elliotts, the education of their children had long been a parental priority. The expectation for proper academic instruction extended to the family females. Senator Elliott had demonstrated his progressive attitude and leadership as one of the founders of the co-educational Sunbury Academy. Consistent with contemporary female education advocates, the academy maintained separate male and female spheres, but assumed all children had equal intellectual capabilities. The Bullochs and Elliotts were among those who believed that it was much preferable for a young lady to be considered dull and studious than vivacious and empty headed.[33]

When the Bullochs and Elliotts returned to Savannah, they were just in time to enroll their children in Chatham Academy, one of the two superb coeducational schools in Georgia that offered separate classes for boys and girls from wealthy families. The curriculum included the basics of reading, writing, spelling, and arithmetic, plus history, English grammar, oratory, U.S. Constitution, natural philosophy, geography, German, Greek, and Latin. The family's young scholars included Georgia (7) and Susan (9) Elliott and James Dunwoody Bulloch (6). They joined cousins John Dunwoody (the son of James S. Bulloch's partner) and Catharine Bulloch at the academy. James excelled at reading and geography and received commendations for his industry and good behavior. Martha's daughters Georgia and Susan Elliott also performed well. Susan excelled at reading and writing and received recognition for her industry and good behavior. For her part, Georgia did well at writing, spelling, and geography.[34]

By the end of the spring semester of 1830, major changes were in the wind for the Bulloch family. James and his brother-in-law, John Dunwoody, dissolved their partnership by mutual consent on October 2, 1830. The parting was amicable, but the two men were headed in different professional directions. John returned to his Arcadia Plantation in Liberty County, but he and James remained active in politics as members of the Union Party. Four years later they even collaborated on a resolution that declared, "The friends of the Union need fear nothing for Liberty County, as she was the first in the State to declare for the Union, she will be the last to desert it." James S. Bulloch continued operating the Savannah brokerage business under his own name, but his duties as Martha's executor and Hettie's husband were taking precedence. After his partnership disbanded, James' agent bookings dropped significantly. James made another bid to take one of the city alderman seats, but this time, his half-hearted election effort fell short.[35]

These setbacks were probably the result of a personal crisis that diverted his attention from professional pursuits. The extended summer trips to healthier climates and a husband's attentions had not been enough to avoid the ravages of disease. Young James Dunwoody Bulloch was just in his eighth year when his mother Hettie died on February 21 of 1831. Hers was a "painful and protracted illness" that she endured with "patience, mildness, and ... complete resignation."[36] Written records about the impact of this devastating loss were sparse during this sad period, but Hettie was probably buried in the Elliott family mausoleum at the Midway Church Cemetery. Her son, James Dunwoody Bulloch resolutely continued his studies at Chatham Academy. He performed with distinction in Latin grammar and once again in geography, but did not gain recognition for industry and good behavior as he had the previous year.[37]

Young James' father's year as a widower was also one of upheaval. On July 1, 1831, James S. Bulloch terminated the "Factorage and Commission" business that he had conducted with two different partners and on his own for the past 16 years. As a statement of the finality of his decision, James sold all of his office furnishings and equipment, including his "Counting Room Desks, Copying Machine, [and] Dearborne's Patent Balances."[38]

Knowing that his son needed motherly attentions after Hettie's death, the distraught widower moved in with his stepmother-in-law and former sweetheart Martha Stewart Elliott and her children. The two may have partially combined their Savannah households even prior to Hettie's death. James Stephens had already made arrangements to sell his own home two years earlier before the two families traveled to New York. He needed a place where he could tend to his wife when they returned in October. He probably took up residence in one of John Elliott's homes in Savannah as he continued to pursue his duties as the executor of Martha's husband's estate. Martha Elliott, now almost thirty years old, and her former suitor,

James Bulloch, found themselves free to wed and living under the same roof.[39]

Martha and James' physical and personal proximity rekindled their long dormant romance. It was an inevitable union of the heart. Martha had a second chance to reclaim the love that she had once lost. James and Martha set the wedding date for May 8, 1832, a respectable fourteen months after Hettie's death. The interval was socially acceptable, but the circumstances were not. As the ever-perceptive Mary Telfair observed in a letter written in Savannah on April 6, 1832, "propinquity" had produced a socially and morally dangerous situation for Martha and James.

> A very singular marriage is about to take place here in a few days. ... Mrs. John Elliott, a woman I understand of exalted piety—she married in the first instance a man old enough to be her father and no doubt sacrificed feeling to ambition. She made a most exemplary wife & (hardest of all duties) an excellent Step Mother.
>
> For four years she has acted the part of a dignified Widow ... and now she is about marrying her husband's daughter's husband—he has been living in the house ever since the death of his wife and I thought viewed by her with sisterly regard. I begin to think with Miss Edgeworth that propinquity is dangerous and, beyond the relationship of Brother and Sister, mutual dependence is apt to create sentiments more tender than platonic.
>
> The beautiful expression of the Psalmist "we are fearfully and wonderfully made" may be as well applied to the structure of the mind as the body. The imperfections of human nature as well as every day's experience and every view of our own hearts ought to teach us lessons of charity towards others, and constant humility and distrust of ourselves.[40]

Although Mary Telfair made an oblique, but scandalous assumption about Martha's pre-marital chastity, her observations about her motivation and personal circumstances rang true. Mary's reference to the nineteenth century novelist Maria Edgeworth described an unromantic vision of marriage. "Ask half the men you are acquainted with why they married, and their answer, if they speak truth, will be 'Because I met miss such-a-one at such a place, and we were continually together'—Propinquity! Propinquity!"[41]

Mary Telfair went on to describe the difficult social and family atmosphere that Martha and James' romance had created.

> I was told last evening that a very pious member of the church had remarked that the church would weep over such an act [James and Martha's marriage]. It does not strike me as a criminal connexion [sic], but one highly revolting to delicacy. I do not think our clergy will object to marry them.
>
> Mr. Elliott's daughter's feelings are very much outraged; she was devotedly attached to her Step Mother, but refuses to have an intercourse with her or her Brother in Law. It shows that the remembrance of a thousand acts of kind-

ness may be obliterated by one act inconsistent with the general character of
the individual.

I feel sorry for Mrs. Elliott, she had in her first marriage to practice an
Apprenticeship of self denial in order to conciliate the good will of daughters
as old as herself—by a noble and disinterested course of conduct she received
their confidence and affection and fulfilled her duties as a wife as faithfully as
if she had married from Love.[42]

The 19-year-old Corinne Elliott's outraged feelings were perhaps
understandable, but Corinne soon became reconciled to the union. She
had married Robert Hutchison a few months earlier. Corinne and Robert
had their own "propinquity" experience at sea four years earlier, and were
in no position to object to Martha's happiness. Ironically, of all young James
Dunwoody Bulloch's aunts, uncles and cousins, brothers and sisters, this
more distant relative would have the most direct impact on his own love
life and his long-term financial security. The attitudes of Savannah society
were another matter.

Martha Stewart Elliott Bulloch, young James' former stepgrandmother,
was now his new stepmother! If the youngster was conflicted by this
strange turn of events, he hid it well. Martha, who had lost her own mother
when she was just an eight-year-old, always treated her stepson James Dunwoody Bulloch as one of her own. For his part, James affectionately referred
to her as "mother" even when he was an adult. These mutual feelings continued even after the family grew to include a total of nine children, with
seven of them living at home. Martha's family included stepdaughters
Corinne and Jane, stepson James Dunwoody Bulloch, daughters Susan,
Georgia, and son Daniel (with John Elliott), and finally Anna Louisa,
Martha "Mittie," Charles Irvine, and Irvine Stephens with James Stephens
Bulloch.[43]

Less than a month after their marriage, James Stephens Bulloch
apparently concluded his duties as administrator of his father-in-law John
Elliott's estate. On June 5, 1832, he sold a Savannah City Lot with improvements from the estate. James had been the trustee for other estates and
was an effective administrator. At about the same time, Martha's brother,
Daniel McLochlan Stewart, made arrangements to sell additional real
estate belonging to their father, General Stewart. In late November of that
year, Daniel offered for sale the undeveloped pine timberland in Liberty
County and the Tranquil Hill plantation, near Riceboro, Georgia. By
December, Martha and James had moved to the General's former plantation at Cedar Hill in Liberty County.[44]

There, they worked with Robert Hutchison, who was now both a friend and step- uncle/brother-in-law by his marriage to Corinne Elliott. Robert and his partner, Andrew Low, were helping James liquidate the estate of John Elliott. Hutchison and Low offered for sale, "a small gang of prime Negroes." The slaves were "at present working on the plantation of the late Mr. Elliott near Sunbury, in Liberty County, from which they will be discharged on the first day of January 1833. An order to see the Negroes can be obtained from Mr. James S. Bulloch, residing at Cedar Hill plantation near Riceboro." James was acting as a caretaker of the plantation on Martha's behalf and was using her inherited assets (slaves) from John Elliott's former Laurel View plantation.[45]

In the antebellum South, a commission agent often had to auction off property to pay debts and distribute the inheritance. A large portion, and sometimes the largest portion, of those assets were usually slaves. John Elliott's estate was no exception. Consistent with the ideal of southern paternalism, the slaves at Laurel View had been relatively well treated. Obituaries for Senator Elliott were effusive in their praise of his management of the inherited "coloured population" on his estate. The papers described the Senator as "more their protector than their master ... no white man held the rod over his slaves. His overseer, one of themselves, held more a patriarchal than a magisterial sway."[46]

The Bullochs also had a good reputation among the African American community of Savannah. Georgia law stipulated that "free persons of color" needed a guardian to act on their behalf in legal and other matters just as if they were infant children. Individuals could select which white person they wanted to represent them. If the white person agreed, he became their guardian. The guardian could defend or prosecute the freedman's legal rights, request travel permits, obtain credit and guarantee payment of debts. Between the years 1828 and 1846, James Stephens Bulloch was the guardian for at least six different individuals, including two men who were ships' carpenters. Priscilla Boyd, a "wash woman," was the only female of the group. She was also the longest tenured, spending fifteen years as James' ward in Savannah.[47]

Martha had grown up with slaves on her father's plantation. Her husband John Elliott's households always had servants to assist with cooking, housework and tending to the children. For his part, James S. Bulloch owned seven household slaves as early as 1821, his third year of marriage to Hettie.[48] James did his best to play the part of paternalistic guardian and master to his slaves, and even to those who were not. As a commission agent, he sold slaves on behalf of his clients and their estates. Rather than sell them as individuals, he advertised them as family units: "A GANG of twenty-six prime NEGROES; they will be disposed of in families, to suit purchasers."[49]

A fundamental tenet of the Bullochs' antebellum world was the certainty that slavery was morally right, legally protected, and scientifically justified. Foreshadowing the coming bloody conflict, most protestant Christian denominations split over the question of slavery. The Presbyterians were first in line when they divided along regional lines over various issues in 1837. The split among the Presbyterians over the issue of slavery became official twenty years later. The Methodists (Methodist Episcopal Church South), separated in 1844 and the Southern Baptists followed suit in 1845.[50]

From a social and safety perspective, white southerners believed that slaves were prone to moral depravity. They feared that freedom for the slaves would gravely jeopardize public morals and the safety of their families, particularly in rural areas. Righteous southerners also held that it would be cruel to set the slaves free immediately. They believed slaves had limited mental capacity and they knew that their slaves lacked experience and skills in self-sufficiency. Many slave holders genuinely, but self-servingly, thought that if African Americans were truly freed, they would be unable to feed or clothe themselves or their families. James and Martha Bulloch would soon give public voice to these arguments when they found themselves in the midst of a political and legal cauldron during one of their extended stays in the North.[51]

The Bullochs had far-ranging motives for moving the family to Connecticut in 1835. First, they wanted to remove their family from the heat and unhealthy summer months of coastal Georgia. Martha had given birth to Anna Louisa, in September of 1833. Anna was her first child by James, but a second was on the way and infants were especially vulnerable to coastal diseases. Martha was eight months pregnant when she and her entourage boarded the sailing ship *Celia* on June 2, 1835, bound for New York City via Charleston. In addition to her husband James, the travelers included stepdaughter Corinne Hutchison and her new baby Corinne, (affectionately known as Conie or Connie), Martha's three children by John Elliott (Susan, Georgia, and Daniel), plus "Master J.D. Bullock [sic]." For extra company, Mary Telfair's nieces, Mary and Margaret, were also on their annual summer voyage to New York City. There was one other important member of the Bulloch household who made the trip: the 22-year-old slave and children's nursemaid, Nancy Jackson.[52]

The extended Bulloch family soon found their way to the Frederick and Mary Oakes Boarding house at 215 Main Street in Hartford, Connecticut. They arrived just in time for the July birth of Martha's namesake daughter, who became known throughout her life as "Mittie." They were only two blocks away from the First Congregational Church, where the learned but somber Rev. Joel Hawes presided. Making the acquaintance of Rev. Hawes was no coincident. He happened to be a trustee of the nearby Hartford Female Seminary as well as the Hartford Grammar School. The schooling of their older children Susan (15), Georgia (13), and Daniel Elliott (8), and James Dunwoody Bulloch (12) appears to have been the primary reason James and Martha temporarily relocated to the North. They selected Hartford as their residence where they would be closer to the girls. The boys went to local tutors and attended nearby boarding schools.[53]

The Reverend Charles Colcock Jones was the likely inspiration for the Bullochs' choice of a school for the girls. The Reverend and his family were longtime friends and relations of the Dunwoody's and Stewart's. Martha's former husband, Senator John Elliott, had even offered Rev. Jones an appointment to West Point before Charles decided to enter the ministry. While a student at Andover Theological Seminary in Massachusetts, Charles met Catharine Beecher, the daughter of a famous Presbyterian clergyman. Catharine was an early feminist reformer who believed that female education should be something more than ornamental and social. She wrote that girls should learn rationality along with persistence to develop their intellectual and moral character. Charles visited Miss Beecher in 1827 at the Hartford Female Seminary that she had founded four years earlier. Rev. Jones was reminded of the school's happy atmosphere and rigorous academic standards when he visited Catharine again in 1829.[54]

The Hartford Female Seminary was one of the first advanced educational institutions in the United States for young women aged twelve and older. Reform and innovation was a common family trait in the Beecher family. Like her father, Catharine's brother was a prominent Presbyterian minister who championed social and moral reform. He advocated the abolition of slavery, temperance, and women's suffrage. For her part, Catharine campaigned for equal educational opportunities for women and wrote extensively on the subject.[55]

Beecher's female academy was just the right place for the Bulloch girls. Although progressive for its time, the curriculum still emphasized conventional themes. Beecher taught that the home was the foundation of society and was fundamental to the well-being of women. The girls also learned that the strength and prosperity of American society depended not upon the equality, but "the superiority of their women." Females remained superior only if they retained and displayed the "manners of women." This logic held that a woman simply could not be a lady if she dared to enter the coarse world of politics. Despite its acceptance of a subservient position in the political arena, the Seminary expected women to have an equal interest in all social and civil issues. The consequence of that equity was a duty on the part of society and the individual to develop the innately equal intellect of females. The Bulloch girls absorbed Hartford Female Seminary's assumption that they should and would reach the same level of understanding as their male counterparts.[56]

Although Catharine Beecher had left Hartford by the time the Bullochs arrived in 1835, her imprint remained and the Seminary carried on as an institution run by and for women. The Bullochs were on the leading edge of nineteenth century thinking and practice when it came to the education of their daughters. Unfortunately, young Georgia Elliott was in poor health for a good portion of the fall semester of 1836, but she and Susan both attended classes there.[57]

James Stephens Bulloch left the family in Hartford for long periods between 1835 and 1837 when he twice returned to Savannah for business. Like a migratory bird, he spent about half his time in Georgia, returning to Hartford in the spring. His stepdaughters Georgia and Susan were completing their course of study in the spring of 1837 when the family began making plans to return to Georgia that fall. Nancy Jackson was the one member of the household who had second thoughts about going home. Nancy was the "servant" the Bullochs had brought with them as the nanny for young Anna and newborn Mittie. Nancy apparently confided her desire for freedom to the lady who washed the Bullochs' clothes at Miss Oakes' boarding house. Nancy's situation soon came to the attention of Edward R. Tyler, a resident of Hartford who was an ardent abolitionist writer and activist. Mr. Tyler had attended a Sunday service at the Talcott Street Congregational Church on May 20, 1837. After the service, one of the "colored" members of the church informed him of Nancy's desire for freedom.[58]

Mr. Tyler subsequently arranged a private meeting with Nancy and convinced her that rather than running away and eventually having to return to her master, she should attempt a legal challenge. Nancy agreed, leaving the details and expense to Mr. Tyler. He quickly went to work. To start the proceedings, Tyler met with the former slave James Mars, a deacon at the Talcott Street Church and the husband of the Bullochs' wash woman. Deacon Mars agreed "to make a strike for her [Nancy's] liberty" by signing a petition for a writ of habeas corpus. Mr. Tyler employed a law firm and had the writ served on James S. Bulloch on Wednesday afternoon, May 30.[59]

Edward Tyler personally knew "Major James S. Bullock [sic]" to be "a gentleman of fine mind, manners and character, (slavery excepted,) an elder in the Presbyterian church." Tyler had also spoken to "friends of Mr. Bullock [*sic*], who had frequently seen Nancy, and who had the highest esteem for Mr. B. as a gentleman and a Christian." Those friends of Mr. Bulloch told Edward Tyler that Nancy was, "too much attached to him [Mr. Bulloch] and his family to accept her freedom, if it should be offered her." Undeterred, Mr. Tyler knew that slaves were skilled at pleasing their masters and his friends. They would tell their owners only what they wanted to hear. Despite these testimonials, Tyler countered that Nancy had confided to an "intelligent colored person" her "strong desire for freedom." She reportedly had the "utmost dread of being carried back to Georgia." James S. Bulloch's purported authorship of a "pamphlet defending slavery by a wresting and blasphemy of the Bible" relieved Mr. Tyler of any qualms he may have had about his own actions.[60] The abolitionist saw no sin on his part for stealing Nancy away without compensation, for he categorized Mr. Bulloch as a sinning slave holder.

The summons from Chief Justice Thomas Scott Williams ordered Mr. J.S. Bulloch to appear with Nancy Jackson at Connecticut's Supreme Court of Errors the next morning at 8:00. When the summons arrived, however, Nancy was away from the Oakes boarding house with Anna and Mittie. Her absence forced Judge Williams to postpone the hearing until the next day. James Bulloch promptly retained a lawyer and obtained another delay until June 2. Mr. Bulloch had to sign a $400 appearance bond that guaranteed he would deliver Nancy to the hearing. This extra time gave the Bullochs an opportunity to prepare their defense and press Nancy about her loyalty to them and to her family in Georgia.

Nancy had spoken to Martha Bulloch once before about her desire to be free. Like most southerners, Martha saw herself as a benevolent protector and told Nancy that the very idea of freedom was foolish. She "could not support herself, or even earn her own clothes ... she must go back where she could be taken care of." Next, Mr. Bulloch confronted Nancy with his determination to retain her services. He was willing to spare no expense in the effort. Even if his lawyers were unsuccessful in court, he personally would appeal to Governor Schley of Georgia who was sure to demand her return. Next, he turned to a fellow lodger at Miss Oakes' Boarding House for assistance, the Rev. Cornelius C. Vanarsdalen, pastor of the South Congregational Church on Hartford's Main Street.[61]

Originally from New Jersey, Rev. Vanarsdalen challenged Nancy with selected passages from the Bible that, "exhort servants to obey their masters, and mankind to be contented with their lot."[62] The reverend was not alone in his pro-slavery understanding of the Bible. Advocates of slavery often turned to scripture to justify the South's peculiar institution. Popular extracts included: "Slaves, obey your earthly masters" (Ephesians 6:5), "submit yourselves to your masters" (1 Peter 2:18–20), and an admonition for slaves to be "subject to their masters in everything" (Titus 2: 9–10). Other popular Bible passages that seemed to endorse or condone slavery included the "Curse of Ham" (Genesis 9:25–27) and the story about a runaway slave (Philemon 1: 10–12; 15–16). In the letter to Philemon, the slave owner was obligated to treat his runaway slave as a brother in Christ, but the slave was equally obligated to return to his master and continue in service. The texts that Rev. Vanarsdalen used to pressure Nancy Jackson were typical antebellum references heard from pulpits, North and South. Pastors played an important role in helping to keep slaves peacefully in their place. They also assured slave owners that they were not, by definition, the damnable sinners that the abolitionists proclaimed them to be.[63]

After appealing to Nancy's sense of morality and obligation to her master, Rev. Vanarsdalen then took a more personal approach. She needed to consider, "her affection for her mother, brothers, and sisters in Georgia." By staying in Connecticut, she undoubtedly would never see her family again. Beaten down by these arguments, Nancy agreed that "she did not wish to be free and would not have sought it, if others had let her alone." When Mr. Tyler and his fellow abolition activist Theodore D. Weld saw Nancy on June 1, she refused to meet with them in private. While they stood on the sidewalk, she told them, "it would do no good to try to get free."[64]

Seeing that she was "nearly paralyzed with fear and despair," the two men urged her to not give up hope.[65] They believed she would win the case. If she did, the court would not allow the Governor of Georgia to intervene. Their encouragement revived Nancy's flagging spirits. That evening when she returned to Miss Oakes' Boarding House with the children, Martha Bulloch sent Nancy to her room with instructions to go straight to bed. Suspicious, she eavesdropped on Martha's conversation with her husband. She overheard Martha advising James to take Nancy with him early the next morning. She wanted him to leave for New York and, "never mind the bond ... send Nancy south." Alarmed, Nancy "went to the house of a colored man and stopped for the night."[66]

This unidentified "colored man" may have been the reason Nancy was so willing to risk so much. If she was in love, her only chance to be with him was to be set free. Another troubling possibility for her reluctance about returning to Georgia may have been fear. Based on a census report, Nancy was a "mulatto," the illegitimate daughter of a white father.

She might have worried that what had happened to her mother would happen to her if she left the relatively safe cocoon within the Bulloch family quarters in Hartford.[67]

That next morning, Friday, June 2, Nancy did not appear in court with her owner. Bulloch's lawyers claimed that James Mars had produced the writ without Nancy's knowledge and against her wishes. When Nancy was called to testify, James announced that the "abolitionists had wheedled her away from him the night before." Nancy's attorneys informed the court that "she had been to spend the night with a colored friend" and they soon produced her. Upon questioning, Nancy testified that she did indeed wish to proceed and disingenuously said that she had not been influenced by others to seek freedom. For Mr. Bulloch's part, the defense claimed that he had never denied freedom to a slave that wished it. In fact, "slavery administered by such a kind master as Mr. B. [Bulloch] is a very light burden, or no burden at all, so that a slave cannot desire to be set free, unless some impertinent abolitionist first interfere." His lawyers declared that Nancy had been "perfectly contented until the abolitionists tampered with her, and threatened to flog her if she would not sue for her freedom." Rev. Vanarsdalen's testimony supported these claims. The defense was convinced that these arguments and powerful laws that respected the rights of property would protect the Bullochs' interest.[68]

The abolitionists based their legal case on technicalities within two Connecticut anti-slavery laws. The first prohibited a slave from being "disposed of, left or sold" within the state. The other provided freedom for any permanent resident slave born after 1784 when they reached the age of 25. These laws were meant to gradually eradicate slavery in Connecticut, but they did not specifically apply to "sojourners" who intended to leave the State.[69] Aided by Mr. Tyler's friend Theodore Weld, Nancy's lawyers argued that Mr. Bulloch had departed the state twice during the two years that Nancy and his family remained in Hartford. Nancy had been left in the state with Mrs. Bulloch and the children, and was therefore abandoned and free.[70] However, a significant portion of their argument centered on the "evils of slavery" and the "immoral and anti–Christian tendency of the institution."[71]

Judge Williams understood the importance of the case and decided to confer with the four absent members of the court before delivering a judgement. He adjourned the hearing until it could be reconvened on June 15. This interval allowed Hartford citizens and northern newspaper editors an opportunity to express their opinions. Surprisingly, they were supportive of James S. Bulloch's position. Newspapers editorialized that arguments about the morality of slavery seemed "out of place in a discussion upon the simple question whether the law of Connecticut recognized the relation of Master and Slave." They pointed out that slavery had existed in Connecticut from pre-colonial days, and that it had never been abolished. Emancipation efforts were intended to be gradual and confined to persons born within the State.[72]

James Mars, who filed the original writ, felt the brunt of the community's sense of injustice for having raised the issue in the first place. Mars said, "I was frowned upon; I was blamed; I was told that I had done wrong; [that] the house where I lived would be pulled down; I should be mobbed; and all kinds of scarecrows were talked about, and this by men of wealth and standing." With the benefit of hindsight, this attitude is difficult to reconcile. Hartford was a center of advanced education and a northern state where the terms "Connecticut" and "Yankee" were nearly synonymous.[73]

Hartford was the place where Catharine Beecher's sister and aspiring writer, Harriet, had lived for eight years as a student and teacher at her Female Seminary. The change in popular attitudes toward slavery did not occur until about 14 years after the Nancy Jackson case. In fact, the tide of public opinion did not begin to shift until Harriet first issued her novel in serial form in 1851. The title of Miss Beecher's story was *Uncle Tom's Cabin,* published under her married name, Harriet Beecher Stowe. It became the second best-selling book of the nineteenth century, trailing only the Holy Bible.[74]

In the context of 1837, however, the attitudes that James Mars described were common even in the New England states. By late twentieth century standards, antebellum abolitionists were almost as racist as their pro-slavery counterparts. Well-educated persons in the United States, regardless of their gender or regional affinity, generally accepted the notion that there was a hierarchy of "races." It was a term that more broadly blended understandings of race and ethnic origin with culture. Contemporary textbooks written and published in New York, Philadelphia, and Hartford typically depicted the "African" race as uncivilized and lacking in intellectual capacity.

Geography books of the 1830s and 1840s included cultural and social topics that had numerous examples of this teaching. Roswell C. Smith published one of these popular school text books in numerous editions for many years. These standard texts would have been on the desks and in the homes of the Bulloch children as they studied their lessons in Georgia and Connecticut. Each edition stated that "the human race exhibits many varieties, not only in color, stature, but also in mental capacity and disposition."[75] The associated caption for this text depicted and ranked

"Races of Men" as "1. European, 2. Asiatic, 3. Malay, 4. [Native] American, [and] 5. African." All the men were pictured standing except the African who held a spear and sat at the feet of the European. Another popular text book example from the same antebellum period was Morse's *School Geography*. Sydney E. Morse, the brother of the famed inventor of the telegraph, reported that "Africa is noted for its burning climate, its vast deserts, and for the dark colour and degraded character of its inhabitants."[76]

Despite these near-universal racist attitudes and "scientific" understandings, a fundamental belief among the abolitionists was that slavery was morally wrong. They steadfastly held that no human should own or sell another. Even among southerners who conceded that there were inherent evils in their peculiar institution of slavery, a key point of conflict was the notion of immediate manumission, or freedom. The strident rhetoric of weekly abolitionist newspapers like Boston's *The Liberator* and New York City's *The Emancipator* placed even moderate southerners on the defensive. In the case of Jackson v. Bullock [*sic*] *The Liberator* reprinted Edward Tyler's long article from *The Emancipator* in its entirety and added its own supportive commentary.

When the five members of the Connecticut Supreme Court of Errors met on June 15th, four were evenly split in their opinions. They left Chief Justice Williams to deliver his deciding vote. Two days later, Judge Williams announced that he agreed with the complainant that Mr. Bulloch had left, or abandoned, his slave in the state of Connecticut. Nancy Jackson was, therefore, a free person. Moreover, the Judge held that as a person over 25 years of age (even though Nancy was probably only 24), she could not be held in slavery as a matter of fairness to other Connecticut citizens. He reasoned that if state residents could not own a slave who was over 25 years of age, neither should "sojourners" like Mr. Bulloch.[77]

Harriet Beecher Stowe by Francis Holl (D42120 © National Portrait Gallery, London).

James Mars, the former slave who had filed the original writ, saw the situation more simply and perhaps more clearly.

> The Judge said that slavery was tolerated in some of the States, but it was not now in this State; we all liked to be free. This girl would like to be free; he said she should be free,– the law of the State made her free, when brought here by her master. This made a change in the feelings of the people. I could pass along the streets in quiet.[78]

The case received a great deal of national attention. Consistent with popular attitudes, newspaper editors attributed the verdict to the "schemes of anti-slavery fanatics."[79] They were very supportive of James Stevens Bulloch: "We particularly regret that this attack should be made upon an individual whom all must respect for his intelligence, urbanity and irreproachable character."[80] Even the abolitionist instigator of the case, Edward Tyler professed kind feelings toward him, "I can assure Mr. Bullock [sic], that, in this whole transaction, we have entertained the kindest feelings towards him. It was not that we loved him less, but justice more."[81]

After the trial, *The Liberator* reported that Bulloch claimed to have convinced anti-slavery advocate Rev. Dr. Wayland, president of Brown University and fellow member of the West Point Board of Visitors of the righteousness of his position. The reverend reportedly agreed that, "under the circumstances in which Mr. Bullock held his slaves, such as kind treatment, a measure of instruction, difficulty of emancipation, &c., he was not sinning." Wayland's allusion to a "measure of instruction" referred to Bulloch's support of the Liberty County Association for the Religious Instruction of the Negroes. Rev. Charles Colcock Jones had initiated this association for the religious education of slaves and Bulloch was a founding member.[82]

Writing from Hartford in early August, James S. Bulloch responded to an article by the editor of the Savannah *Georgian*. He wanted to counter some of the bad feelings the Nancy Jackson case had generated. Under a headline of "Judicially Robbed" Mr. Bulloch was careful to inform his southern friends that the people of Connecticut had surrounded him with support and friendship. Mr. Bulloch said that it was only "some of the colored people" along with "Mr. E.B. Tyler, an agent of the New York Anti-Slavery Society" who had enticed, "my servant to leave me."[83]

Bulloch's main concern was the "reckless immediate Emancipationists." He cited two northern men who had southern roots as illustrative examples. One of these men had become rich in Georgia, sold his slaves, and moved to New York. Another who lived in Pennsylvania had inherited the proceeds from the auction of slaves from his father's estate in Georgia. James confessed that he too, had inherited a portion of the slaves from that same estate. He said that both of these former slave-holding men were now "declaiming him" as a sinner. He pointed out that neither proposed to refund the money that they had realized from the sale of their slaves. James' rhetorical question was, "How clean these hands! How pure these hearts! Judge ye!"[84]

Martha Bulloch's thoughts about slaves and slavery matched her husband's, but she did not of course, express them publicly. She did write to her stepdaughter Corinne Elliott Hutchison warning her to keep a close watch on her servant girl, Sarah. There were "abolitionists in N Port [Newport, RI] as well as Hartford." She also informed Corinne that her own two young daughters were well. She noted that her youngest, Mittie, was about to celebrate her second birthday. Referring to her as "Miss," she described Mittie as, "an arbitrary little thing, taking all of Anna's play things from her constantly." Anna and Mittie were too young to appreciate the specific issues at stake, but they certainly experienced the family's turmoil, their sense of being judicially robbed, and the hurt feelings from the personal and public attacks on their integrity and morality. The children and even their slave playmates wondered what became of Nancy, who "had been carried off by the Abolitionist." They hoped that she was not "suffering like the poor in England." Nancy's mother was most likely "Maum" Charlotte Mounar, who remained a faithful servant to the Bullochs in Georgia.[85]

Nancy Jackson's personal story faded with the trial and she quickly disappeared from public view. It was not until many years later that Mittie and Anna discovered what had happened to their former nursemaid. In the mid–1860s she and Nancy had a cordial reunion in New York City. As a free woman, Nancy had resumed her role as a nurse and domestic servant for white families in Connecticut and New York City. She was a long-time lady's maid and companion for the mother of Judge John Gray at their home on 709 Fifth Avenue in New York City.[86]

Nancy professed kind feelings toward the Bulloch family and her time spent as Anna and Mittie's nanny. For her part, Mittie did not harbor the feelings of betrayal that embittered so many southern ladies whose servants abandoned them. At Mittie's invitation, Nancy attended Anna Bulloch and James Gracie's wedding in 1866. Mittie even offered Nancy a job, but she was happy with her position with Mrs. Gray. Mittie's interactions with Nancy were friendly, but not purely social. Nancy was careful to respect her unchanged place within the elite Northern culture, just as she had in Georgia. Rather than just chatting over tea, Nancy polished Mittie's silver.[87]

There is no record that Nancy ever married, but contrary to Rev. Vanarsdalen's warnings, she eventually did make contact with her family. In her elderly years, she actively supported her family including nephews and nieces in Georgia and New York. She was living in Long Island with three of her nieces when she passed in 1906 at the age of ninety-four.[88]

In 1837, Nancy's case set a precedent that made any slave arriving in a Northern state subject to immediate emancipation. Those slaves who already resided in New England had to bide their time in bondage. Southerners like James Bulloch and the rest of his family focused on the hypocrisy of the abolitionists. It seemed that both sides found it easier to condemn evil when they saw it in someone else.

James S. and Martha Bulloch's children said very little about slavery and were never slave-owners themselves. However, they had lived in the same house with Nancy Jackson for over three years. The eldest at 14 years of age, James Dunwoody was mature enough to understand the dynamics at play. After the war, he expressed his own views about the role of slavery as a cause of the Civil War. His observations were consistent with contemporary British opinion, but they also reflected the clear stamp of his experience with Nancy Jackson in Connecticut. Brother Jimmie Bulloch concluded that slavery was "a national sin" that should have been "redressed by a common sacrifice" and not just the South. He noted that instead of entering into a constructive dialogue, "the North discarded or ignored all practical measures for emancipation, and confined their operations to oratory, preaching, sentimental poems, fiction, and invective." One of those practical ideas, of course, was the one his father and stepmother had broached: compensation for southern slave-owners who freed their slaves. Like his father, Commander Bulloch complained that abolitionists and newspapers like *The Liberator* dismissed such ideas as "unjust, wicked, monstrous, [and] damnable!"[89]

In the midst of the family's legal contretemps and preparations to depart for Georgia in the fall, the two boys, Daniel Stuart Elliott and James Dunwoody Bulloch, were immersed in their own preparations to remain behind in school. Daniel was in his 11th year and "doing well" 30 miles north in Hampton, Massachusetts, under the tutorial care of a clergyman. James was with the rest of the family in Hartford. He was studying French and Spanish under the guidance of a tutor and took voice lessons at a "singing school." His father believed that James was still too young for college at 14 years of age.[90]

After two years in Connecticut, and with the Nancy Jackson trial behind them, the Bulloch family prepared to go their separate ways before reuniting in Savannah. James Stephens Bulloch wrote his friend Robert Hutchison that he was undecided about which route his stepdaughter Georgia Elliott should take back to Savannah. She did not like to travel by steamboat, so he considered delivering her to Robert by train via a circuitous route north from Hartford and then west to join him at Saratoga Springs, NY. The other alternative was to have her join her cousins Jane and William Elliott Dunwoody in Philadelphia.[91]

The Dunwoody cousins were attending school in Philadelphia along with their older and similarly named cousins, Jane and William Gaston Bulloch. These two Bulloch cousins were the children of James Stephens's deceased brother, John Irvine Bulloch. James had assumed the father-figure role in their lives and maintained a frequent correspondence with his brother's children. He may have also been the executor of his brother's estate. His niece, Jane, was the same age as his own son, James Dunwoody Bulloch (14). Nephew William was 23 years of age and had graduated from Yale in the class of 1835. William was completing his medical studies at the University of Pennsylvania. The "2 Dunwody's" were scheduled to arrive in Saratoga Springs on July 17 and were staying at Union Hall, a luxury hotel that catered to the wealthy elite.[92]

The elder Bulloch's own son James and his stepson Daniel were set to enter a prep school in Middletown, 20 miles down the Connecticut River from Hartford. Informally known as Isaac Webb's Academy, its official name was Isaac Webb and Julius S. Shailer's Family School. Isaac Webb opened his boarding school in 1833 with enrollment limited to 20 students. He offered a rigorous education for boys who were intent on continuing their schooling at university. A single large building known as "Maple Grove" served as both classroom and dormitory. It was an imposing structure of formality and grace at the northeast corner of Middletown's High and William streets.[93]

In November, after most of the family had already returned to Georgia, "James D. Bulloch," entered the school as one of ten members in the class of 1837. The boys studied arithmetic, Latin and Greek, and French. The primary difference between Maple Grove and the Hartford Female Seminary was its emphasis on classical instruction, which was the most import element of nineteenth century university education. The boys' daily routine was to wake at 6:30 a.m., and take breakfast at 7:00 with prayers afterwards. School began at 9:00 with lunch from 12 until 1:00 pm. Mealtime provided an opportunity for the boys to reinforce their studies. Only French was spoken at the dinner table. Classes recommenced from 1:00 until 4:00, and again from 6:00 until 9:00 p.m. Like the girls' seminary,

Mr. Webb required regular attendance "upon public worship" and refused to admit or retain anyone "of known vicious habits" or who was "incorrigible." Tuition, including room and board, was $250 per annum, plus books and clothing.[94]

His stay at the boarding school was the first time that James had been away from the sheltering arms of his mother or stepmother. He seems to have thrived in the all-male environment. One of James' classmates at Maple Grove was a fellow Georgian from Savannah. James J. Law had been in the same class with Bulloch six years earlier at Chatham. Not coincidentally, their fathers, James Stephens Bulloch and William Law, also had been school mates at Sunbury Academy sixteen years earlier. The Honorable William Law was a Georgia State Judge of the Eastern District and a Director of the Bank of Georgia. Webb's Academy prominently mentioned both men as sponsors of the school.[95]

James' most accomplished classmate was Rutherford B. Hayes, who also began his studies at Webb's school in 1837. In the fall of 1838, Hayes went on to Kenyon College in Ohio and then to Harvard Law School. Even though Mr. Hayes had an "aversion to the Yankees" while he was at Webb's Academy, he fought for the Union during the Civil War. In combat, Hayes was a gallant and effective officer, sustained wounds, and rose to the rank of major general. At the end of the war, he returned to Ohio and became the nineteenth president of the United States from 1877 to 1881. His first lady, Lucy Webb Hayes, was the first president's wife to have graduated from college.[96]

Reflecting the conservatism of the school and its wealthy sponsors, Hayes reported that none of the students supported the abolitionist cause. He also confessed that he was learning much more than ever before and that the boys liked the school very much. Classes ran through most of the year, with the semesters separated by two vacation months in May and October. In 1838, the boys all scattered to the homes of friends and relatives on September 28. Bulloch's destination is unknown, but his travelling companions would have included Daniel Stuart Elliott. His stepbrother joined him at Webb's Academy as a member of the class of 1838.[97]

The two boys were probably looking forward to spending their October break with their sister Corinne and her husband Robert Hutchison in Saratoga Springs or Newport, Rhode Island. Since at least 1834, the Hutchisons were in the habit of spending a portion of their summer at these famous resort cities that catered to affluent patrons. Robert was on his way to Saratoga Springs in 1837 when James Stephens Bulloch contemplated sending his stepdaughter to join him there. Despite having spent most of the past two years in Connecticut, Bulloch's teenage son had obviously grown fond of Robert, Corinne and their first daughter. Affectionately known as Connie (or Conie), she was a beautiful child that Robert had named after her mother. The Hutchison's youngest daughter, Caroline Lucile, had just been baptized in May of 1837. Young James took a brief break from his studies and asked his father to pass along his love and kisses to the Hutchison family that summer.[98]

On Wednesday, June 13, 1838, the Hutchisons began their anticipated annual journey north. With one-year-old Caroline in their arms and three-year-old Connie firmly in hand, Robert, Corinne, and a servant nurse boarded the *Pulaski* in Savannah. The ship was a new side-wheel paddle steamer making its fourth trip to New York City. The steamship had a modern design, 206 feet long with a narrow 25-foot beam that sat low in the water. Reflecting the sensibilities of the times, the male and female sleeping arrangements were strictly segregated. The ladies' cabins were above the main deck where they could enjoy the fresh sea breezes. The gentlemen's cabins were separated from the ladies', one deck bellow. All was well that evening when the *Pulaski* called at Charleston, South Carolina, to take on additional passengers. They were underway at 6:00 the next morning expecting to spend a single night at sea. The ship was fully loaded with 129 passengers, including 57 women, 14 children, and a crew of about 37. Despite the crowded conditions, the cabins were spacious "containing every convenience" and the tranquil seas soon dispelled the travelers' cares.[99]

Captain David DuBois of the *Pulaski* confidently set his course for Baltimore, Maryland, the next stop before continuing on to New York City. The afternoon breeze was fresh and from the east. By 10:30 p.m., the night was clear and stars filled the sky from horizon to horizon. There was every promise of a fine night as most passengers settled into their beds. Just as the boatswain sounded six bells indicating 11:00, an ear-shattering noise jolted everyone awake. Witnesses said it sounded like the crack of a nearby thunderbolt. Immediately following this frightening blast came an even more ominous trembling and careening. The steamer's engines had stopped. The ocean swells began to pitch and roll the ship according to its whims. The crash of breaking china replaced the methodical slapping of paddle wheels upon the waves. The screams of the women and children only increased in their terror when the *Pulaski* quivered and rolled alarmingly to its port side. Then, every light went out.[100]

For a few interminable moments, there was only confusion, questions, and speculation. What had happened? Was it a collision; a grounding? It

took five minutes before the answer became obvious. The casualty assessment was far worse: "The boiler has burst, the boat is sinking, and we
shall be lost in five minutes!" The *Pulaski's* starboard boiler had exploded
and destroyed the promenade deck immediately above it. The blast killed
the Captain and everyone standing near him, and opened a large hole on
the starboard side. The ship was beyond recovery. Clambering to the upper
deck in the darkness, women and children crowded into one of the surviving life boats. The boat was so packed with panicked passengers that
the sailors could not operate the oars. Before their life boat could clear
the ship, the passengers' next conscious sensation was of drowning. The
steamer's keel was broken and its hull suddenly parted. Everyone was
thrown into the water. The engine and machinery that had been located
amidships dislodged from its mounts and slipped to the bottom of the
ocean. The separated bow and stern sections were left bobbing like over-
sized corks. Shocked passengers and crew found themselves struggling
and gasping in the cold, briny sea. Those strong or lucky enough to survive

**Explosion of the Steam Packet *Pulaski* in 1838. From S.A. Howland, *Steamboat
Disasters and Railroad Accidents in the United States*, 2d ed. (Worcester: Dorr,
Howland & Co., 1840), 46.**

the dunking, floated, swam, and crawled their way back aboard the remaining wreckage.[101]

The exhausted survivors who were able to pull themselves aboard the stern section, soon felt the waves begin to lap over their bodies. They had to climb higher and higher as the deck began to tilt at an almost perpendicular angle. "Quick as thought" they "were precipitated into the ocean" once again when the deck broke away and slid into the ocean. Parents struggled for their own survival as they attempted to maintain their tenuous hold on the hands and lives of their children and each other. The upper deck section, now released from the rest of the hull, was still buoyant enough to float. Although covered by six inches of water, it offered another chance of temporary refuge for the desperate passengers.[102]

Robert Hutchison was one of the lucky ones who gained this buoyant portion of the wreck. He had become separated from his wife and daughters after the ship broke in half and everyone was tossed into the sea. Thinking that he had lost them forever, the sparkling light from the quarter moon and stars offered him no solace. The illumination, however, did enable a man floating by on a smaller bit of flotsam to spot the almost two dozen persons on the floating deck.[103]

When the man came on board he was holding a beautiful three-year-old girl in his arms. The child recognized her father immediately and called, "Papa, papa!" Robert Hutchison replied, "Connie, Connie, my child!" He was overcome with emotion and could not contain his tears of happiness. The child that Robert thought was lost was found. Little Connie sensed the situation, and quickly adapted to her nightmarish circumstances. She did not ask for her mother Corinne, her nurse, or her sister Caroline. Seeing her father's apparent distress, she tried to divert his attention by pointing to the stars and saying, "Papa, papa, see the beautiful stars!"[104]

Her attempt to console Robert only increased his emotion. To keep his uncontrollable sobs of joy and despair from upsetting her, Robert asked Rebecca Lamar to hold Connie. The girl was shivering in the damp, cold sea breeze. She was wearing only her night slip and it was soaked. Miss Lamar was the sister of Hutchison's friend Gazaway B. Lamar. She took Connie in her lap and Robert covered them both with a camlet cloak made of silk and camel's hair that had floated onboard. Robert had also recovered his garment bag earlier and soon regained his composure by distributing the remainder of his relatively dry clothing for others to wear.[105]

Night turned to day and most of the survivors were hopeful of a timely rescue. They were only about 30 miles off the North Carolina coast and had sighted several ships in the distance. The survivors with Robert

Hutchison eagerly recovered a small boat and a basket. The basket contained two bottles of wine, some peppermint, and laudanum, the standard nineteenth century painkiller. Additional castaways joined them on their large piece of flotsam that they collectively converted into a raft with a makeshift sail. The persistent and reflected sunlight, however, began to blister the fair-skinned survivors; everyone suffered from thirst. The children and infirm among them were becoming exhausted. One man died that day. Dead bodies began to collect on the raft as their nightmare continued into the second day.[106]

Numerous sails came into view, but the survivors remained invisible to potential rescuers. The waves finally floated the dead off the raft, but the living had consumed the small supply of peppermint and one bottle of wine. One of the ladies slipped into a coma and died, never considering the possibility of removing her corset to improve circulation. They still had no water and no rain clouds were visible. In a small, plaintive voice, Connie asked her father, "Dear papa, when we get to New York won't you give me three cups of tea?" Robert replied, "Yes, my darling, as many as you want I will give you."[107]

The night brought a welcomed rainstorm that continued into the next morning, but it developed into a bone-chilling gale. When the wind and rain finally subsided, the survivors were even more exhausted from exposure to the wet and cold. The next crisis appeared in the form of a piece of floating wreckage that repeatedly bashed the raft and threatened to dislodge its occupants. One man became so alarmed that he jumped into their little boat and instigated a panicked chain reaction.[108]

At the time, Robert was holding his daughter tightly in his arms with the cloak wrapped around them. He instinctively ran after the man who quickly thought better of his actions and jumped back onto the makeshift raft. Rebecca Lamar described what happened next,

> Mr. Hutchinson then, in turning to retrace his steps, slipped upon the end of his cloak and tripped. In trying to recover himself, his hold was loosened, and the wind tore the cloak and child from his grasp, and bore them to the billows. He returned to his place and bowed his head, a broken-hearted man. The child was nearly lifeless. I noticed, as he passed me, the neck could not sustain the head, and the whole form seemed limp. ... Mr. Hutchinson, with his head down, [was] seemingly indifferent to life itself.[109]

Despite the shock and horror and losing his precious child a second time, Robert attempted to save those who remained alive, particularly the children. Miss Lamar was most appreciative that whenever she "called frantically for Mr. Hutchinson for assistance. He always came to my relief."[110]

Unfortunately for Rebecca, one of her nephews suffered the same fate as Robert's own daughter, but the other did survive thanks in part to Robert's efforts. Finally, on Tuesday morning, their fifth day adrift, a passing schooner, the *Henry Camerdon*, mercifully rescued them. Of over 160 passengers and crew on the *Pulaski*, only 59 survived, and 30 of those saved were on the *Henry Camerdon*. One of the fortunate few was Captain R.S. Hubbard a merchant captain from New York. He singled out Rebecca Lamar for her "firmness and self-possession—with her never failing effort to cheer and encourage them—and rally their despairing spirits. ... She was our preserving angel." She probably saved Robert Hutchison's life as well. She gave him meaningful, life-saving tasks that restored his own will to live.[111]

The consequences of this tragic incident were far-reaching for the Bulloch family. If Robert had died on the *Pulaski*, the Bulloch family's life would have taken a radically different course. In the immediate aftermath of his rescue, Robert became particularly close to his stepnephew, James Dunwoody Bulloch. Robert Hutchison provided the inspiration and support that James needed for his personal, professional and financial security. In turn, Hutchinson looked to his extended Bulloch family for comfort and understanding in his own personal time of need. He would repay their kind reception many times over and the feeling was mutual. Even after his death, the Bulloch ladies honored the memory of his wife and daughter. Mittie and Theodore Roosevelt named their youngest child Corinne. They called her "Conie."

2

The Bullochs of Roswell
and Navy Blue

After their prolonged stay in Connecticut, the Bulloch family returned to Savannah, only to find that they would be moving again. Mr. Bulloch had joined with Roswell King in a speculative real estate venture in upstate Georgia. King proposed building a resort town and a textile mill in a remote area about 230 miles northwest of Savannah that he had named Roswell. The site was at Vickery (Big) Creek, a tributary of the Chattahoochee River. It was twenty miles north of a new railroad terminus that would not incorporate into a city until 1847 upon completion of the railroad link to Savannah. That new city was Atlanta.

The Bullochs moved to Roswell from Savannah sometime in 1838. They selected their Roswell property at the highest point on the village bluff. The site was perfectly suited for a grand home with a view of the valley below and the smoky blue foothills to the north. While their new home, aptly named Bulloch Hall, was under construction, the Bullochs had several evolving options for temporary quarters. Roswell King and his son Barrington had built a large log cabin home called "The Castle." They added rooms and adjoining hallways for new settlers arriving from the coast that became known as the "Labyrinth." The Bullochs' also constructed a cottage for the family's use near the new home site. They later transformed the small home into slave quarters.[1]

For their primary dwelling while awaiting the completion of Bulloch Hall, they chose an abandoned Cherokee log farmhouse, about four miles east of the new home. It was situated on a 480 acre plot called Clifton farm. The federal government purchased the land from the Cherokee Nation and dislodged them from Georgia and Alabama. The government's intent was to sell or grant acreage to white settlers like King and Bulloch. In the aftermath of the sale, the Cherokees began their infamous trek to Oklahoma Territory called the Trail of Tears. Native Americans left behind everything they could not carry. On the Clifton acreage, James S. Bulloch raised cotton and, since his property was within Georgia's Dahlonega Gold Belt, he searched for gold. Henry Merrell's contemporary sketch titled "Digging Major Bulloch's Gold" shows two men panning for gold on the Bulloch property.[2]

The original settlers of Roswell envisioned an exclusive, healthy summer retreat. Roswell was closer and less expensive than the cooler, but distant cities of the North. James and Martha initially split their time between the coast and the rustic Georgia foothills of the Blue Ridge Mountains and left many of their belongings in Savannah. The initial living conditions in Roswell were primitive and the prospect of moving household goods by sailing sloops, ferry boats, and oxcarts over undeveloped roads was a daunting task. However, servants could accompany their masters to the foothills of Georgia without the risk of Northern abolitionists "wheedling them away." Mr. Bulloch continued to represent Savannah and Chatham County at the Union Party Convention in 1838. However, Martha Bulloch's physical condition had the greatest impact on the timing of the family's movements to Roswell. She not only celebrated her 39th birthday on August 15 of 1838, Martha delivered her eighth child, Charles Irvine Bulloch, in the late fall.[3]

By January of 1839, James Stephens was back in Savannah, but there was no doubt that the family intended to settle permanently in Roswell. They eventually moved their most valuable silver and several pieces of large furniture. These valuable, but unwieldy items included a mahogany dining table with extensions that could seat thirty-six people and a massive four-poster bed. Four of the children accompanied them to Roswell (Susan and Georgia Elliott, Mittie, and Anna Louise). Two of their slave couples also made the trip, including "Daddy" Luke Mounar and his wife "Maum" Charlotte. Luke was the butler and handyman whom Martha Bulloch had taught to read and write. Charlotte was the housekeeper and likely the mother of Nancy Jackson. The other slave couple performed the duties of coach-groomsman and cook.[4]

James and Martha may have been in Savannah through late April of 1839 in anticipation of the return of their two boys, James Dunwoody Bulloch (15) and Daniel Stuart Elliott (14). The stepbrothers had completed their studies in Middletown, CT, and fearlessly boarded the steamship *North Carolina* in New York City; just ten months after the *Pulaski* had exploded. Their return voyage took them to Wilmington, NC, and

Charleston, SC, before they arrived in Savannah on April 27. James had a career decision to make and several options to choose from. He could follow his family to Roswell, where he would face a highly speculative and uncertain future. The life as a planter and land speculator in rural Georgia did not appeal to the teenage boy. Perhaps he could leverage his family's influence in Savannah to pursue a banking or merchant apprenticeship. James also contemplated a trip to England and France with Robert Hutchison. There, they could visit his cousin William G. Bulloch who was completing his medical studies in Paris.[5]

His time at sea gave young James time to think clearly, for he reached a decision quickly. He decided to enter national military service. James Dunwoody Bulloch's decision to serve in the military was a natural one. Service to their state and nation was a well-established Bulloch family tradition. James' great-grandfather and grandfather had been army officers and his stepgrandfather was an acclaimed general. His father was a major in the Chatham Artillery and a member of the U.S. Military Academy's distinguished Board of Visitors. James' father had dutifully travelled to West Point during the Nancy Jackson trial to observe the examination of cadets. At West Point the elder Bulloch chaired a Committee on Internal Police and Discipline and inspected the cadets' hospital barracks, kitchens, pantries, and classrooms. His report noted a "wholesome supply of food," and a "highly commendable" stock of clothing and books. The rooms appropriated for Chemistry, Natural and Experimental Philosophy, and Mineralogy and Geology were however, "quite inadequate." The path to a career in the U.S. Army seemed wide open to any son of Major Bulloch.[6]

Like many children, young James decided to take a path that was similar to, but different than his father's. He opted to seek a commission as an officer in the U.S. Navy. In late June, a letter from the Secretary of the Navy James K. Paulding addressed to the aspiring sailor revealed the Navy's official response to his request. Secretary Paulding stated that as of June 21, 1839, James Dunwoody Bulloch was duly appointed an Acting Midshipman in the U.S. Navy, pending his acceptance. James penned his acceptance letter on his sixteenth birthday.[7]

His interest in the Navy could have originated with his exposure to the seafaring life as he grew up in Savannah. Maybe his voyages to and from New York had given him a taste for the salty air. Considering his close relationship with Robert Hutchison who had lost his wife and two young daughters at sea, a sailor's life appeared to be a remote possibility. Many of his family and friends would have discouraged such a hazardous career. As one family friend noted, "sea-sickness is a wise provision to prevent everybody going to sea. As it is, few go upon salt water unless they have business there." On closer examination, however, and in view of future events, the explosion of the SS *Pulaski* may have been the catalyst that prompted James' surprising choice.[8]

In January of 1839, Robert Hutchison had donated $150 toward a $1,100 "Testimonial of Gratitude" for Captain Eli Davis of the *Henry Camerdon* who had rescued the *Pulaski* shipwreck survivors. The castaways publicly hailed Captain Davis as an alert and compassionate hero, as compared to others who had callously passed them by. Robert Hutchison's contribution was the second largest, behind Mr. G.B. Lamar's generous donation of $500. Captain Davis used that money to purchase a house and lot in Philadelphia; he acquired a new schooner with the balance. In the midst of tragedy, James Dunwoody Bulloch saw the heroic. It was an ironic response to the catastrophe at sea.[9]

Despite his readiness to serve, the Navy moved with bureaucratic haste and did not issue Acting Midshipman Bulloch orders to report to the frigate USS *United States* until mid–September. This delay allowed James to spend time with his family in Roswell at their temporary quarters at Clifton farm. Although his stay in Roswell was a brief one, it made a lasting impression. Thirty years later, when he built a home of his own, he named it "Clifton." In Roswell, James just missed seeing the completion of Bulloch Hall as the family moved into the magnificent structure in the winter of 1839. It became one of Georgia's most famous neo-classical homes. Bulloch Hall survived the war and remains one of the South's finest examples of authentic temple-style Greek revival architecture.[10]

In 1923 a young journalist named Peggy Mitchell penned an article about Roswell's Barrington and Bulloch Halls, saying,

> Both dwellings are of colonial style of architecture, with white columns and wide porticoes. ... The tall white columns, glimpsed through the dark green of cedar foliage, the wide veranda encircling the house, the stately silence engendered by the century-old oaks, evoke memories of Nelson Page's "ole Virginia." The atmosphere of dignity, ease and courtesy that was the soul of the Old South breathes from this old mansion, as it stands at the end of a long walk bordered by old-fashioned flowers. ... Bulloch Hall ... stands on a sloping hill overlooking a beautiful little valley.[11]

Miss Mitchell observed that then as now, the "shoe-string" town of Roswell had known, "war and peace and romance, and remains a quiet old town, looking out at the world with dignity." Peggy Mitchell continued writing for the *Atlanta Journal* until May of 1926. Ten years later, under her given name of Margaret Mitchell, she published a Pulitzer Prize-

Bulloch Hall in Roswell, Georgia, as it appeared when the movie *Gone with the Wind* was released (Library of Congress).

winning novel that was made into an Academy-award winning movie. Although the characters and places described in *Gone with the Wind* were supposed to be fictional, it is clear that the reality of Roswell, Georgia, had a profound impact on the writer. The "atmosphere of dignity, ease and courtesy" that breathed from Bulloch Hall and its people, both living and dead, were resurrected in her romantic tale of the Old South.[12]

One of those idealized figures was James Dunwoody Bulloch. In a purposeful slip within *Gone with the Wind,* Margaret Mitchell identified "Admiral Bulloch" as the perfect example of an honest Confederate officer. This fictional character was a clear reference to James D. Bulloch. He always received a promotion to Admiral in the family's stories that its female members passed down to later generations. James' initial step toward becoming that romantic blockade-running secret agent occurred with his entry into the U.S. Navy on June 21, 1839. At 5 feet, 8 inches tall, the acting midshipman was a bit taller than the average nineteenth century adult male. Dark brown hair topped his lean frame. Even at the tender age of fifteen, he had a low, broad forehead. Whiskers would soon hide his small round chin and draw attention away from his large nose, small thin lips, and round face. His most notable feature, however, was a pair of dark, almost black eyes. They suggested the essence of the sensitively perceptive, intelligent, but secretive man he would become.[13]

Shortly after his enlistment, Midshipman Bulloch, transferred from the USS *United States* to the USS *Potomac* and set sail from Norfolk, Virginia, en route to "Brazil station" on May 13th. After spending a year literally learning the ropes on board the *Potomac,* he transferred to the new sloop-of-war USS *Decatur.* One of his commanding officers on the *Decatur* was Captain David Glasgow Farragut. Farragut would become the U.S. Navy's first admiral and its most celebrated naval hero during the American Civil War. Bulloch served aboard the *Decatur* until a few days before her departure for the United States in late 1842. Rather than return home with his ship, Midshipman Bulloch requested and received a transfer to the battleship-of-the-line USS *Delaware.* He remained with the *Delaware* through the remainder of her South American cruise and subsequent deployment to the Mediterranean in February 1843.[14]

The Bulloch family in Roswell closely followed their sailor's progress through influential friends. These included Georgia's former governor and current senator, Wilson Lumpkin and the Secretary of the Navy, J.K. Paulding. One of James' letters from Italy reached Bulloch Hall in September of 1843. As stepsister Susan Elliott, confessed, it had been "nearly four years since we parted and it seems a much longer time. I need not say we look forward with impatience to his return." Much had happened during Midshipman Bulloch's absence.[15]

The Roswell community was prospering. Jane and John Dunwoody (James S. Bulloch's former partner) had joined the Roswell community. They selected a lot adjacent to the Bullochs' and moved from their home in Sunbury in 1839. The residents of the Roswell Colony, as they soon called themselves, began to embrace their new home as something more than a convenient and less expensive summer retreat. The Colony had multiple and overlapping ties to New England, but retained a decidedly southern perspective on social and economic issues. Roswell King even laid out the village in the familiar style of a Connecticut town square. The residential section was to the west and the business section was to the east. Another essential element of their shared perspective was religion. The settlers were a homogeneous community of families who shared a Scottish heritage and a faith in God built around the Presbyterian Church. The church grounds were conveniently set aside just to the north of the square.[16]

The Bullochs, plus Martha's daughter Susan Elliott, the Dunwoodys (often spelled "Dunwody"), and their daughter Jane Marion, were charter members of the Presbyterian Church of Roswell. Seventeen of the 32 original members were slaves. One of the first official acts of the newly formed church was to baptize James and Martha's baby boy, Charles Irvine Bulloch, in October of 1839. The Reverend Dr. Nathaniel Alpheus Pratt was on hand to perform the sacrament for the Bullochs and one other baby boy. Rev. Pratt was family. He had married Roswell King's daughter Catherine Barrington nine years earlier. The reverend and his family permanently relocated from Darien, GA, to Roswell in May 1840. The church members had just completed a small sanctuary building reminiscent of their beloved Midway Church in Liberty County.[17]

The other important aspect of Roswell society was education. By 1839, the colonists had constructed a schoolhouse north of and adjacent to the church property. Although it was only a two room log cabin chinked and daubed with mud, it had the rather pretentious name of Roswell Academy. Like other more established academies in the South, Roswell's was co-educational and relied on male teachers who had graduated from Northern universities. One early educator was the Princeton graduate and Presbyterian minister, Rev. Aaron Hicks Hand. Rev. Hand's assignment to the Marietta/Rowell area ran from 1838 to 1841. Roswell's white children attended class daily, with the younger students in one room and the older children in the other. A mud chimney fired with pine knots provided heat in the winter. When a teacher decided to leave Roswell, classes had to be suspended until the settlers could hire a new one. Due to the shortage of educators and the remoteness of their location, the colonists even allowed a northern-educated woman to teach the younger boys and girls. It would be many years before women routinely took the place of men as teachers in the nation's public schools. Both Anna and Mittie Bulloch (aged 6 and 4 respectively in 1839) eventually attended classes at Roswell Academy.[18]

Other than church and school, communal activities were limited in Roswell. Weddings provided a happy exception. Everyone was invited and everyone attended, including the field slaves who stood outside watching from a respectful distance. The whole community contributed furnishings, made delicacies for the wedding supper, and decorated the cake. To accommodate everyone, the hosts extended their outside porches or "piazzas" using sheets and tent cloth. At night, lanterns brightly illuminated the sumptuously set tables and created an enchanted, glowing spectacle among the trees. James and Martha Bulloch hosted one of Roswell's first wedding parties for their niece, Jane Marion Dunwoody in the spring of 1840. The Bullochs' party set a high standard for Roswell's grand affairs and finery. The celebration lasted well into the night, with slaves dutifully standing by the saddled horses, waiting for the guests to leave by the light of a blazing fire.[19]

In Roswell, James and Martha assigned a young slave, known as a "little black shadow," to each of his children. Lavania, a pretty but slightly built girl, belonged to Mittie, and little Bess was Anna's mate. The slave girls served the dual role of playmate and servant, but slept on straw mats spread on the floor at the foot of their mistresses' bed. They also helped with the household chores and followed Mittie and Anna everywhere during the day. Lavania and Bess waited on the school steps with the other slave children while Mittie and Anna attended classes at the Academy. After class, Anna and Mittie would read aloud as the slave girls listened with rapt attention. In turn, the Bulloch girls visited the adjacent slave homes at night. The "nice little houses" were divided in two with a breezeway in between. The children were always welcomed there as they sat by the fireside and listened to the stories of the coachman Daddy Stephen and Daddy Luke, the butler and handyman. This happy imprint of an extended family that included household slaves made a lasting impression on the two young mistresses. The author Joel Chandler Harris captured their sentimental perspective of southern home life in his Uncle Remus stories. The two girls would one day pass these stories along to their own children, nieces, and nephews.[20]

In addition to tending to his wife and children, James Stephens Bulloch continued to mentor his deceased brother's son, Dr. William G. Bulloch. By 1839, Nephew William developed his plan to return to the United States after completing his medical studies in Paris. His Uncle James wrote a long encouraging letter that suggested places William should visit in the United Kingdom on his way home. He also shared information affecting the timing of his return to Georgia via Philadelphia where he would collect his younger sister Jane. Perhaps the most important part of his letter to William concerned gifts for James and Martha's two young daughters, Anna and Mittie, "The Ten dollars is for you to buy two as large and pretty wax dolls as you can get for the money, have the eyes to open and shut and have them put up in a box.... Should the money be more than enough, lay it out in ribbons." If William was unable to ship them out earlier that year, he would have carried the dolls with him when he returned to New York from Le Havre, France in November of 1839, just in time to delight the girls for Christmas in Roswell.[21]

On a more somber note, the first death in Roswell among the colonists came in the summer of 1841. Martha's youngest child, Charles Irvine Bulloch, died during an outbreak of scarlet fever. Charles was one of the two boys baptized in 1839 at the formation of the Roswell Presbyterian Church. He was only two years and nine months old. Charles was Martha's eighth child (the third by James S. Bulloch) and her third to die (all boys) while just a child. Charles Irvine's small headstone stood by itself on a tree-shaded knoll that became known as Founders' Cemetery east of town overlooking Vickery Creek, near the mill.[22]

That fall, Martha supplanted her grief with worry, for she was pregnant again at the age of 42. The isolated setting of Roswell could be a lonely one for Martha and the girls. Martha's niece from her marriage to Senator John Elliott, Jane Amarinthia Elliott Sever and her daughters Kate (Catherine Elliott, 14) and Jennie (Jane Elliott, 10) joined the Bullochs at Roswell for an extended visit during the winter and spring of 1841–1842. Jane's second husband, Charles Sever, had died a few years before and both she and Martha needed the company and support during that cold season. Jane and her daughters finally left Roswell in May of 1842 while Martha was eight months pregnant.[23]

Fortunately, Irvine Stephens proved to be a healthy baby when he was born in Roswell on June 25, 1842. The birth occurred two days after the nineteenth birthday of Irvine's half-brother, James Dunwoody Bulloch who was serving on Brazil Station in the USS *Decatur*. Irvine was Martha's ninth and last child. She had delivered her first baby 24 years earlier. In typical nineteenth century male fashion, her husband was absent as Martha prepared to deliver Irvine, their fourth child. Mr. Bulloch was at the state capitol in Milledgeville as the Cobb County representative to the Democratic State convention.[24]

James S. Bulloch also made modest attempts to replenish the household finances that the move from Savannah and the construction of Bulloch Hall had seriously depleted. James continued to work as an estate broker in Savannah for the sale of plantation property on the Savannah River. The family's primary income was through Bullochs' shares in the Roswell Manufacturing Company. The business panic of 1837 and lack of credit created a recessionary economy that lingered into the early 1840s. The secondary purpose of the Roswell Colony, its textile mill, became its signature industry. The mill supported many of the colonists during those hard economic times and even declared a 22 percent dividend in 1844.[25]

Letters alone would not have prepared Midshipman Bulloch for all the changes that had taken place during his four year absence. He and the entire crew of the USS *Delaware* were filled with impatient anticipation in mid–January of 1844 when their captain ordered a westerly heading out of Port Mahon on the Spanish Mediterranean island of Minorca. They were on their way to Norfolk, Virginia, and home. After an uneventful voyage across the Atlantic, they approached the Virginia coast and carefully navigated past Horseshoe shoals, Willoughby bank, and through Hampton Roads at high tide. The *Delaware* finally tied up at Norfolk's naval base, on March 4, 1844. The Navy placed the ship in reserve for an extensive overhaul. Eighteen days later the entire crew received 90 days shore leave. As soon as he was detached, Midshipman Bulloch made his way from Norfolk down to Wilmington, NC. There, he caught the fast steam packet SS *Gladiator* to Charleston where he arrived on March 27 before continuing on to Savannah and Roswell.[26]

As he approached the main entrance to Bulloch Hall from the east, Bulloch's carriage turned into a heart-shaped driveway, past coastal cedar and holly trees, and up to the steps accessing the front piazza. The wide porch stretched across the entire front of the building and welcomed James to a disproportionately small front door. After gingerly testing the silver front doorknob for absorbed heat from the afternoon sun, James walked into his family's new home. He saw a lofty center entrance hall flanked on the right by a butler's pantry and a formal parlor that opened into a large dining room. On the left were a matching parlor, the master bedroom, and a smaller room that served both as a nursery for little Irvine Stephens and a private sitting room for stepmother Martha. Large windows in every room helped circulate the summer breezes. Those same windows made it difficult to heat the home during the chilly early spring despite the eleven fireplaces that warmed every living space. At the top of the stairway was a smaller stairway that led to the backdoor for servant's use. The upstairs center hall accessed four large bedrooms where the weary sailor could settle in and enjoy his shore leave. His bedroom, like all the rest, had its own dressing room closet. A small sewing room separated the two front bedrooms. The third-floor attic was completely floored and open with a high ceiling. It was a wonderful place for storage, guest overflow in the cooler months, and year-round play for the children.[27]

As he adjusted to the steady decks of Bulloch Hall, brother Jimmie soon captivated Mittie and Anna with his exciting tales of life at sea. But all too soon, it was time for him to go. His only problem was that he had no idea where the Navy wanted him to go. In a letter dated June 18 mailed from the nearest post office in Lebanon, GA, Midshipman Bulloch reminded the Navy Department that his leave would expire in four days and he needed orders. He desired an assignment to a "receiving ship" or other service that would allow him to prepare for the Navy's officer school at Philadelphia. He wanted to study for the exam that would result in his promotion to "Passed Midshipman." The Navy finally responded on June 27, ordering him to the receiving ship USS *Pennsylvania* at Norfolk. Just missing Mittie's ninth birthday on July 8, brother Jimmie quickly made the difficult journey back to Norfolk, only stopping for a night in Charleston on July 10, before continuing on his way.[28]

By late August, Midshipman Bulloch was on his way to the Naval School at Philadelphia. The school's eight month curriculum was the precursor to the Naval Academy at Annapolis that opened in the fall of 1845. The Greek revival architecture of the Philadelphia Naval Asylum complex reminded Midshipman Bulloch of Bulloch Hall and made him feel very much at home. While in Philadelphia, James probably received a visit from his stepsister Susan Elliott and his cousin, Dr. William E. Dunwody. William graduated from New York University's Medical School on March 21, 1845. Susan accompanied the newly certified doctor back to Georgia via Wilmington and Charleston on the familiar SS *Gladiator* later that month.[29]

James did well at Philadelphia and graduated second in a class of 36. He received his warrant as a "Passed Midshipman" on July 2, 1845, but not before he once again visited the family in Roswell after classes completed in May. He had returned to the North by the time his orders to the USS *Erie* arrived. The *Erie* was a 32-year-old former sloop-of-war out of New York City that had served in the war of 1812 and was now merely an armed store ship. She was about to leave for Pacific Station, where tensions and the potential for conflict with either Mexico or Great Britain was high. The *Erie* departed New York's harbor in the early morning darkness of July 8, his sister Mittie's tenth birthday.[30]

After a long voyage interspersed with equally long port calls in South America, the *Erie* finally arrived on Pacific Station in November of 1845.

It was not until three months later however, that Midshipman Bulloch arrived in North America when the *Erie* called at Mazatlan, Mexico. Other members of the fleet were very anxious to see them, but not because they wanted to see old shipmates. The *Erie* carried letters from wives, sweethearts, and families. None were more recent than June 25, 1845, but the crew of the USS *Portsmouth* and the others ships of the fleet waited "with palpitating hearts anxious for them to get in and anchor."[31]

James D. Bulloch did not have to wait long for the start of his next adventure. On February 14, 1846, he got a very professionally satisfying Valentine's Day gift. He reported to the Sloop-of-war *Shark* as Acting Master under Lt. Neil M. Howison. No longer just another Passed Midshipman on a larger ship, James was the third in command of a warship behind the Captain and Lt. Woodhull S. Schenck. He had broad responsibilities for navigation, and daily operations, but his immediate duties were to prepare the *Shark* for a voyage to Honolulu and the Kingdom of Hawaii.[32]

The *Shark* finally departed Mazatlan at 4 p.m. on April 1. Acting Master and navigator James D. Bulloch set his course to the west, "weather delightful, breeze light, and variable." Arriving at Honolulu on April 23, the *Shark* brought welcomed newspapers from the U.S. They had New York papers up to February 5 and a New Orleans paper from February 21. The crew was soon busy refitting the ship, upgrading its armament, and replacing the copper that covered her outer hull as protection against incursions from tiny marine mammals that weakened the wood and reduced speed.[33]

While in the Kingdom of Hawaii, James also came in contact with Passed Midshipman Thomas H. Stevens and wife Anna. Tom was the Navy's storekeeper for the Islands. He had joined the Navy in 1836 from his hometown of Middletown, at the same time that James was a school boy in Connecticut. Tom and Anna arrived in Hawaii as newlyweds thirteen months earlier and now had a baby girl. They lived in a two story wooden home on the corner of Fort and Beretania streets, conveniently located only six blocks from the Honolulu Harbor Piers and seven blocks from Iolani Palace. The Stevenses shared their home with the congenial U.S. Consul Alexander G. Abell and his young wife, Sarah. The two engaging young couples maintained a lively open house and welcomed visiting Navy officers.[34]

In Roswell, the other Bulloch family members were busy planning sea adventures of their own. Martha and her two children by Senator Elliott, Susan and Georgia, travelled overland to Savannah and then to Charleston by steamship during the Christmas season of 1845. They were accompanied by Robert Hutchison and Cousin William G. Bulloch who had finally gained his medical doctorate. These travels were mere preludes to a voyage to Europe. Robert Hutchison was in the habit of spending his summers in Europe after the death of his wife Corinne. In 1846, he left for Liverpool on June 19. That year, James Stephens Bulloch also decided to visit Europe, but he did not sail with his friend Robert Hutchison. Instead of sailing with his wife Martha and their children Anna (11), Mittie (10), and Irvine (4), Mr. Bulloch departed New York for France with his two stepdaughters, Susan (25) and Georgia Elliott (23).[35]

One explanation for this curious timing and choice of traveling companions may have been Georgia's health. As a teenager, Georgia's poor health had been cause for concern within the family. She never slept alone for fear that her "paroxisms [sic] of suffocation ... might be fatal if she was not attended at the time. ... she has at times considerable pain in her chest and side." Always of a delicate constitution, Georgia would have appreciated the attentions of cousin, Dr. William G. Bulloch, who accompanied her, Martha, Susan, and Robert Hutchison to Charleston in December 1845. The next spring, the two young ladies and their stepfather boarded the sailing ship *Versailles* at Charleston's Union wharves. In the late morning hours of May 4, they sailed to Le Havre, France where William had recently completed his medical studies. Georgia may have hoped for medical treatment in Paris in addition to the expectation of cultural enlightenment. James and his two stepdaughters returned to New York from Le Havre, France on September 15, but did not continue their journey home for over a month, arriving at Charleston on October 29, 1846.[36]

While his father and stepsisters were in Europe, Midshipman Bulloch was in Pearl Harbor. On June 23, 1846, James' friends Tom and Anna Stevens wished him a happy 23rd birthday, *bon voyage*, and Godspeed when the *Shark* set sail after two months of refit in the islands. He realized that there was little chance that the young couple would cross his path anytime soon. Tom was due to return to the U.S. before the end of 1847 and James was on a special mission to protect U.S. interests against British incursions in Oregon Country and explore the Columbia River region. God must have had other plans, for they would meet again after similar, but unexpected mishaps.[37]

The *Shark* made the 2,500 mile journey to the coast of Oregon in 22 days, unaware that the U.S. and the United Kingdom had signed the Oregon Treaty on June 15. The agreement established the modern international boundary at 49° north and ceded Vancouver Island to the United

Kingdom. The *Shark* arrived at the intimidating mouth of the Columbia River mid-morning on July 18.[38]

The *Shark* narrowly managed to cross the bar with no damage, but soon grounded. The crew slowly "sounded and buoyed the channel from Cape Disappointment to Fort Vancouver," a distance of 100 miles. Upon reaching Vancouver thirty days later, American sailors from the *Shark* encountered Her Britannic Majesty's sloop *Modeste*. Somewhat to their surprise the American and Royal Navy sailors found a common bond in the remote territory. Equally unaware of the Oregon Treaty, the British officer's mess hosted excursions, balls, picnics, and races.[39]

The most anticipated of these lavish entertainments were theatrical performances. The directors prominently cast several local American women in female roles. The *Modeste*'s crew staged almost a dozen plays for Oregon citizens and the crew of the *Shark*. Most were by the successful eighteenth century British playwright and novelist Henry Fielding. In plays such as *Tom Thumb* and his novel *Tom Jones*, Fielding's clever dialogue and satirical plots often addressed political and gender issues. These issues included problems that arose when men and women reversed their traditional public and domestic roles and personalities. The *Modeste*'s popular theatrical performances in the Northwest frontier helped engender substantial international goodwill that continued after the *Shark* departed Fort Vancouver on August 23, 1846.[40]

Captain Howison was "under orders to come out of the river by the 1st day of September."[41] He was also in a hurry to join the fleet in the war against Mexico, "having heard overland of hostilities." Howison finally made it to an anchorage near the Columbia River Bar on September 8. On the afternoon of September 10, Howison "hauled on the wind" and out to sea. He had timed his exit poorly, for the tide, and waves caused him to lose the wind and control of his vessel. He let go an anchor, but it immediately snapped as if it had been a bit of packaging twine.[42]

The *Shark* struck violently on the bar and held fast. No amount of sail could release the vessel from the combined grip of the sand and force of the wind and tide. Nature or perhaps Father Neptune impressed this fact upon the crew as waves of green and white water, "immediately began to break over her broadside and told us too plainly that she should float over its surface no more." The crew had no hope of saving their ship, but the more important question was, "Can we save ourselves?"[43]

It was a survival situation that Midshipman Bulloch had only imagined in drills and the stories of his mentor and friend, Robert Hutchison. The prospect of rescuing helpless victims was likely one of the romantic reasons James had joined the Navy in the first place. Unfortunately, it seemed that he was the one who needed rescuing as every wave broke clear over the vessel. By 11:00 p.m., the waves abated as the tide shifted. This temporary lull allowed Howison to load all but twenty-four crew members aboard the three remaining boats.[44]

As the third most senior officer and navigator, Acting Master Bulloch was Captain Howison's choice to take charge of the three boats and get the crew safely ashore. The Captain, Lt. Schenck, Midshipman Davidson and twenty-one crewmen would have to remain onboard the wreck until Bulloch returned ... if they could survive that long. Remembering the fate of the *Pulaski* families who had lost their fathers and husbands, James volunteered to take the place of executive officer, Lieutenant Woodhull Smith Schenck who was a married man. He knew that the chances of returning to the wreck before everyone perished were slim. The loss of a husband and father often meant that the family had no support. However, both Schenck and Howison also knew that Midshipman Bulloch was the best man to lead the rescue.[45]

James and his three boats made it safely to shore on Clatsop Spit, south of the Columbia River bar entrance. The crew scavenged wood from the wreckage of the former sloop-of-war USS *Peacock* and built a fire to dry their clothes and thaw out from the numbing cold. But they had to go back. Hopefully, the fire would provide them a point of reference for a safe round trip. Relying on oars and strong backs, Bulloch and his most able seamen plunged back into the sea. Meanwhile, back on the *Shark*, the only parts not immersed were the bowsprit at the forward-most part of the schooner and the roofs of its two quarterdeck houses.[46]

Sunrise brought a new day and with it, the welcomed sight of Midshipman Bulloch. An hour later, "the wreck was completely untenable." Although the *Shark* was a total loss, all hands made it safely ashore. In his official report, Howison credited their survival to his crew's "cool exertions and orderly manner" in carrying out their duties.[47] In private letters to a concerned father, both the executive officer and captain of the *Shark* praised James' courage and ability. Executive Officer Schenck credited James for saving his life as well as all those who were with him on the wreck. Schenck's brother (Lt. James F. Schenck, later a Rear Admiral) cited the, "gallantry, perseverance and skill of your son, through whose exertions they [the 24 crewmembers of the *Shark*] were saved the next morning."[48]

Captain Neil Howison was even more effusive, saying without hesitation that, "there was no individual who did not feel assured to his heart's content, that if human energies could accomplish it, Mr. Bulloch would be in time for the rescue. And he was. An hour later or the least loss of time or mismanagement in his pull through darkness and breakers of five miles would have found us swept away."[49]

James and the rest of the *Shark's* crewmen finally rejoined the fleet at San Francisco in late January of 1847. Bulloch also returned to his former position as just another Passed Midshipman, first on the USS *Erie* and then on the *Warren*. It was an unhappy time for James. Unlike the captain who rescued Rebecca Lamar and Robert Hutchison, James only had the admiration of his peers. The Navy effectively demoted him in California, plus he had missed all of the fighting action in the war with Mexico. Now, he was on monotonous blockade and occupation duty along the coast of California.[50]

News of James' near disaster was late reaching the Bulloch family in Roswell. Susan, Georgia, and their stepfather had returned from their trip overseas. Mr. Bulloch had plunged back into Georgia State politics. In early March of 1847, James Stephens Bulloch chaired a committee in Marietta, GA, that drafted a resolution in support of the ongoing war against Mexico. Many anti-slavery advocates had opposed the war. In addition to a moral imperative, they feared that the addition of Texas and other territories as slave-holding states would tip the balance of political power toward the South. James Stephens Bulloch's argument was simple. "Though citizens may differ in opinion in relation to the propriety or the just causes of the war, yet, when the power with whom the people have reposed the authority to declare it has spoken, and the country is involved in it, no patriot can stand aloof and refuse his support." The resolution was a clear reflection of the sentiments of most Americans when their troops were in combat, and it reflected the family's feelings toward Midshipman Bulloch's own efforts.[51]

The discovery of gold at Sutter's Mill, California, in January 1848, shortly after the cessation of hostilities, helped mollify initial concerns about the wisdom of the war with Mexico. Gold fever also made it difficult to keep sailors from trying their hands at finding the precious metal. As one officer noted, "Sailors desert their ships as fast as they arrive on the coast, and several vessels have gone to sea with hardly enough hands to spread a sail. Two or three are now at anchor in San Francisco with no crew on board." The squadron commodore even limited shore leave for fear of desertions. Frustrated, Midshipman Bulloch considered resigning his commission.[52]

James' thoughts also returned to Roswell as he recalled his father's own mining venture on his property within Georgia's gold belt. Upon reflection, Bulloch decided not to resign, at least not until after he could get back to the East Coast and see what orders and opportunities might be available closer to home. Finally, in October 1848, while James was at Monterey, CA, he transferred from the *Warren* to the store ship USS *Lexington* that was headed for San Francisco to take in gold for the U.S. Treasury. More importantly, for Midshipman Bulloch, it was bound for New York. When the *Lexington* arrived at San Francisco Bay in early November 1848, it began loading provisions and a few official passengers for a long journey to New York. Included on the manifest were 232 troy ounces of California gold dust for the U.S. Treasury. Even more interesting were the passengers, including Thomas H. Stevens and his family, and most particularly Mrs. Anna Stevens.[53]

When they last met, Tom was the storekeeper in Honolulu where he and his bride Anna had arrived as newlyweds in March of 1845. When James left their company in June of 1846, the Stevens' household included Anna's brother, Henry Christie, who had accompanied them to Honolulu. The family also had welcomed a baby daughter, Ellen. She was born in the Kingdom of Hawaii, then known to Americans as the Sandwich Islands. Like James, Passed Midshipman Stevens had missed all the action in the war against Mexico. While Tom was with his wife on a tropical island paradise, James was stranded in the far Northwest, after the wreck of the *Shark*. When the time came for Stevens to depart Honolulu in December of 1847, the wartime action was over and James was languishing in Monterey Bay, having just transferred from the *Erie* to the *Warren*.[54]

For the Stevens' family, however, the action was just beginning. Not having a ship of his own or other official transport, Stevens had to book passage on a commercial sailing ship. On December 20, 1847, "Passed Midshipman Thomas Stevens, U.S. Navy, his lady and child, and his brother-in-law," two other female passengers, and crew of twenty set out from Honolulu on the Chilean sailing ship, the *Maria Helena*. They were bound for New Bedford, Connecticut on the 20-year-old former American whaling ship. After fourteen uneventful, but rainy, days at sea, they had settled into shipboard routine that left the passengers with little to do.[55]

In the early morning hours of January 4, 1848, the weather finally cleared, and there was a small excitement to break the monotony. Despite the lack of a moon to light their way, the crew had spotted a porpoise in the phosphorescent glow of the ship's bow wave alongside the ship. The *Maria Helena's* officers, crew, and passengers were all eager spectators and participants in the sport of harpooning of a porpoise. After they secured their prize safely on deck, the captain and passengers finally called it a night. It was about 2:00 a.m. before they went below and turned in for the night. The winds were light and variable easing the vessel along at a leisurely rate of about three knots. Using their sextant and chronometer, the captain and first mate calculated their position at about 40 miles east of Christmas Island (known as "Kiritimati" in Gilbertese). They were 1300 miles due south of Honolulu and 144 miles north of the equator.[56]

The first indication of danger appeared about an hour later when the helmsman thought he heard the sound of breakers. Through the dark, in a heart-stopping instant, he saw the foaming waves breaking over a shallow reef dead ahead. He turned the wheel hard to starboard and at the same time cried out, "Breakers ahead! Hard alee! Hard alee!"[57] His shout brought the second mate, the captain, Tom and Anna Stevens, and most everyone else rushing up to the deck. The order came too late. The ship struck with a shudder. The *Maria Helena's* chronometer must have been out of calibration, but now was not the time for recriminations. The captain had "a full consciousness of the danger and difficulty of his ship's position." Saving the ship was not an option; "from the moment she struck it was evident no human agency could save the ship. Every successive sea drove the ship with a surge further in-shore." Without prompt and professional action, they would all soon die.[58]

As the ship heeled dangerously to starboard, the captain advised Mrs. Stevens to go below, dress herself, and prepare to abandon ship with her child. The other lady on board, Miss Harriet B. Johnson of New Bedford, received the same instructions. Miss Johnson was accompanying the young daughter of Anthony Ten Eyck, the recently widowed U.S. commissioner to Hawaii. Below deck, "Mr. Ten Eyck's little daughter was sweetly sleeping beside her, entirely unconscious of the surrounding danger."[59] The ladies lost no time in gathering the two girls and a few possessions. In about an hour, they were aboard the ship's whaleboat with Tom Stevens, the ship's purser, and a few stout seamen at the oars. "During this time no expression of fear escaped from either of the ladies."[60]

Pulling out to seaward, the whaleboat held its position within sight of the ship. They were waiting for daylight to get their bearings and make a run for the shore. Onboard the *Maria Helena*, the crew cut away the masts to prevent even more damage to the salvageable portions of the wreck. Each of the three masts came down and went overboard with a tremendous crash that seemed amplified in the darkness. Within the whaleboat, each moment seemed an hour. The sights and sounds of their former sanctuary being dismembered only increased their anxiety and impatience for dawn. At about 6 a.m., they could see that the ship was only about 150 feet from the beach, in what is now appropriately named the Bay of Wrecks. The captain lowered a second small boat loaded with water, provisions and the luggage of the passengers.[61]

After determining the best point to venture through the surf, whaleboat prepared to head through the "seething breakers.... Soon a huge roller lifted the little boat far above the surrounding water, and she sped on like an arrow." They arrived at the beach, "without taking in a drop of water." With the deference due to ladies of the mid-nineteenth century, "the men immediately jumped into the water and hauled the boat close to the beach, when the ladies and children were carried on shore, without so much as wetting their feet."[62] The ladies and children spent the rest of the day seated on coral rocks holding a parasol and umbrella to shade the tropical sun. From this vantage point, they watched as the men went back and forth between the shore and ship, landing articles that might aid their survival as castaways. They also had time to consider what new dangers lay ahead. Other than a name and location, nobody had any idea about the nature of their new home.[63]

By the time everyone made it safely ashore, the castaways supposed that the island was, "inhabited by savages." While this thought was foremost on everyone's mind, it was the ladies who gave the thought expression. They had the luxury of not needing to appear manly. Six of the *Maria Helena's* crewmen had been shipwrecked two or three times before. The passengers, however, and particularly the women, had never been in this kind of survival situation. The women "did not hesitate to express, with deep concern, the distressing fears which occupied their thoughts, lest they, and all with them, were to fall into the hands of merciless cannibals." These "harassing doubts and gloomy forebodings" soon dissipated when they saw no signs of human occupation.[64]

As it became clear that they would not have to literally fight for their survival, the men recognized that their primary needs were shelter, food, and water. The material salvaged from the wreck provided bedding and sails to construct tents that were adequate shelters for the fair weather of a tropical island. In addition to the provisions from the ship, fish and fowl provided ample sustenance. On their first night ashore everyone gave thanks to God for their survival and ate a hearty meal. The exhausted men wrapped their blankets around them and slept under the stars. In the one hastily constructed shelter, "the ladies and children, and such of the passengers as could find room in the tent, sought repose from the fatigues and excitement of the day." Thus, even in a survival situation, the men and women sought to maintain their social equilibrium. The ladies had a home where they could hold domestic sway.[65]

The next day it became obvious that water was their greatest need. The few casks of water on hand could not sustain the twenty seven adults and two children for long. Although the island proved to be relatively large (about 150 square miles), it had no fresh water supply. Fortunately, the men soon discovered several casks of water left by another ship (the *Mozart*) that had wrecked less than a month before. This supply, combined with a makeshift water distiller, would ensure their survival for a few more weeks.[66]

Reminiscent of the ladies from the wreck of the *Pulaski*, Anna Stevens and Harriet Johnson provided faith, hope, and encouragement to the men. Although fully aware of the possibility of death from thirst or starvation,

> not a complaint, a murmur, or a repining word escaped the lips of the ladies, at that time, or any other, during their long and dreary three months' residence upon the island. Always cheerful and resigning themselves with a happy confidence, to that merciful Providence which had so signally preserved their lives, and those of the ship's company, they did much to keep up the spirits of the gentlemen, to encourage their labors for the comfort of all, and the labors of those engaged in active operations, designed for their ultimate rescue.[67]

As days turned into weeks, the survivors constructed improved living quarters. Large tents complete with hardwood frames and floors, made life more comfortable, especially for the passengers, captain and supercargo. The ladies' tent included, "a large table, benches, a china closet, book shelves, &c." Anna Stevens and Harriet Johnson typically stayed in their tent with the children during the day to avoid the heat and sun. They spent their time reading, discussing their chances for rescue, and taking care of their two young girls. The children's "cheerful, happy faces and prattle, served to beguile many an otherwise long and weary hour." After sunset, the ladies and gentlemen typically walked along the beach or sat on the rocks enjoying the cool of the evening sea breeze, and the pure sights and sounds of unspoiled nature.[68]

It was truly a paradise. There was plenty to eat and drink and everyone was fit and healthy. But they knew this blissful situation could not last. Under the captain's supervision, the men began work on the *Mozart's* salvaged longboat. They hoped to transform the boat into a schooner stout enough to sail the 1300 miles back to Hawaii. As the castaways attempted to haul the schooner across the breakers, they suffered their first casualty when one of the Chilean sailors drowned. Everyone mourned "the loss of the generous, kind-hearted and honest Juan." Finally, on February 8, the schooner cast off under the command of the first mate with five crewmen, aided by the sextant and chronometer from the *Maria Helena*. Anna and Tom Stevens were among those who cheered as they got underway. The couple added an extra prayer for a safe passage and timely rescue, for Anna was four months pregnant with her second child.[69]

The make-shift schooner reached Maui on February 28, and made Honolulu the next day. The U.S. commissioner, Anthony Ten Eyck, took personal charge of the rescue operation in hopes of saving his young daughter. He quickly gained the cooperation of local Hawaiians, who sent the schooner *Haalilio* the very next day. The French consul also dispatched a rescue ship (*Sarcelle*), with the *Maria Helena's* first mate and Mr. Ten Eyck onboard. The larger *Sarcelle* reached Christmas Island on March 16 and found that everyone was in good health; the *Haalilio* arrived the next day.[70]

However, a safe departure from the island proved to be more difficult for the castaways than their arrival. When the rescue ships were unable to penetrate the surf at the Bay of Wrecks, on March 21 the castaways began a difficult trek across desert wastes to the northern end of the island. The party consisted of the two ladies and their two children, four gentlemen, the captain, the two mates of the wrecked ship, the mate of the schooner, and twenty-two others. Four Hawaiians from the *Haalilio* were enlisted to tote Anna Stevens, who was now over five months pregnant. Anna's daughter Ellen added to the burden in her litter. Mr. Ten Eyck's little daughter was in the other litter, but Miss Johnson showed her mettle and elected to walk. It was March 25 before all the survivors finally got off Christmas Island. At Mr. Ten Eyck's request, the *Sarcelle* remained at anchorage until the next morning, "to enable the ladies to recover from their fatigue and prepare for the voyage."[71]

The *Sarcelle* returned to Hawaii on April 10 and the *Haalilio* arrived two days later; both received a joyous and thankful reception at Honolulu. Passed Midshipman Stevens resumed his naval duties at Honolulu, but his brother-in-law Henry Christie departed for San Francisco on June 10. Christie, probably with Tom's encouragement and support, was on the leading edge of the gold rush that followed the discovery at Sutter's Mill earlier that year while they were shipwrecked. Anna and Tom delayed their return to the East Coast until after the birth of their son on July 12, 1848.[72]

In San Francisco, Tom, Anna, and Ellen, plus the "boisterous heir" Thomas Holdup Stevens III, reunited with their fellow shipwreck survivor, James D. Bulloch. Since their parting in Honolulu seventeen months earlier, Tom and James had many experiences in common. The two Navy officers had missed the combat action of the Mexican War and they both had heroically survived a shipwreck and helped save everyone aboard their ship. The singular difference was that James (25) was single and Tom (29) was quite married to Anna (23). Their friendship would expand and deepen over the next twenty eight weeks as the Stevens family travelled as passengers onboard the USS *Lexington*. Measuring 127 feet long and 33 1/2 feet abeam, the small vessel guaranteed that they would be in intimate close quarters for the prolonged voyage to New York. It was a journey punctuated with port calls in Chile and Brazil. The effect of Mary Telfair's propinquity theory in male and female relations would once again be put to the test.[73]

After 75 days at sea, "a tedious but otherwise pleasant passage from San Francisco," the *Lexington* arrived in Valparaiso, Chile.[74] This South American port was the primary foreign base for U.S. warships sailing to and from Pacific Station. A contemporary traveler seeing Valparaiso for the first time admiringly reported that its harbor was "nestled like a beautiful fjord in high mountains, protected by a lighthouse on a high promontory. The city was bustling and modern, with an imposing promenade and substantial business houses." After a three week visit they set sail for Rio de Janeiro, Brazil where they arrived in mid–April.[75]

Perhaps feeling a bit of channel fever in their eagerness to get home, the *Lexington* only lingered in Rio de Janeiro for eight days, setting sail on April 21 for New York City. In their years of their absence from home, much had changed for the passengers and crew of the *Lexington*. One sailor who had joined the crew at San Francisco was looking forward to enjoying his new-found riches. He had accumulated $9,000 in gold dust after a "few months digging." Indeed, the *Lexington* was sailing against a tidal wave of fortune hunters and adventurers who were surging to the California gold fields.[76]

Although the Stevens were headed back to Erie, PA, for an assignment on the USS *Michigan*, James congratulated them on their "golden prospects in California." Tom and Anna Stevens had speculated in gold mining. Bulloch's advice about their investment was flavored with equal parts of financial and emotional envy,

> I hope you have placed your affairs in trusty hands. You know I always charged you with being negligent of your own interests. It will be a shame if you do not realize something handsome from your Pacific outlays. Perhaps it is well to be on the safe side, but you have doubtless estimated you expectations low at $20,000. ... You are like a fat Alderman greasy with good living, who cannot imagine that any one ever was hungry. Doubtless you have now no sympathy for me, but tell my sad tale to your sweet little wife, who is my dear little friend & whose woman's heart is ever open to a tale of woe.[77]

After a transit of over six months, the *Lexington* finally docked at New York City on June 10, 1849, just two weeks before James' 26th birthday. He completed his ship-board duties and detached from the *Lexington* two days later with 90 day leave papers in hand and most of three years' pay in his pocket. He was eager to get back home to Georgia and catch up on all the news, both happy and sad. However, something else was at work in the young man's life. James did not immediately head for home as he had done in the past. On June 13, he took a room at the Irving House, a New York City hotel known for catering to the rich and famous, such as vice president Millard Fillmore, Mexican War hero and explorer Colonel John C. Fremont, and the singer Jenny Lind.[78]

James then spent several days in Philadelphia in the company of Anna and Tom Stevens. Traveling with the happily married couple obviously had an effect on the 25-year-old Passed Midshipman Bulloch. Although not documented, he also would have visited and lodged with his stepsister Susan Elliott who had married a Philadelphia businessman, Hilborne West, the previous January. James reluctantly returned to New York City on June 21. The next morning he met with a "Miss Ellen," who was probably Anna Stevens' sister. Later that day, he finally took his leave of his new-found ladies of the North, and booked passage on the steamer *Cherokee* for Savannah via Charleston.[79]

After quietly celebrating his 26th birthday at sea, James arrived in Savannah on June 24. He then transferred to the U.S. Mail Steamer *Jasper* that arrived at Charleston, SC, two days later. "J.D. Bullock, U.S.N." [*sic*] then checked into the largest and finest hotel in town, the aptly named Charleston Hotel, prior to taking the train to Marietta via Augusta. Although Savannah also had a rail connection to Marietta, it was not as direct or as reliable as the line that originated in Charleston. From Marietta, James made the still-difficult, but familiar journey to Roswell on June 28.[80]

> In the afternoon I took a buggy for Roswell. Oh! How weary long the way seemed. Every mile of the twelve dragged itself out into a league. At last the old time honored mansions were in sight & then what a crowd of recollections both pleasing and painful come upon me. My mind passed in review many fond scenes of childhood cherished through long years, & sweet memory conjured up a thousand tender reminiscences. Those of the family circle whom time has spared are thank God in good health. Mother bears her weight of years most stoutly & with the meekness woman only knows, regards her cares & sorrows as the will of her maker.[81]

James' recent painful recollections included the memories of stepsister Georgia Amanda Elliott and the family's patriarch, James Stephens

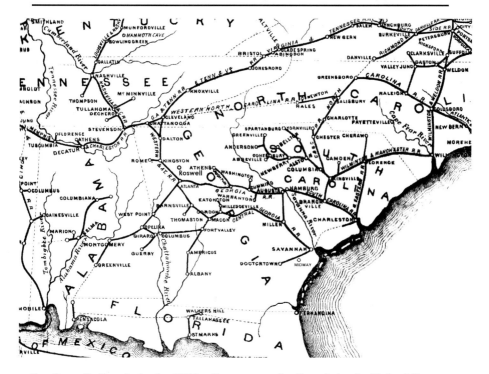

Southern Railroads in the 1850s. From map of railroads in the United States, *Sherwood & White's North American Railway Guide* **(Baltimore, MD, ca. 1857) (author's collection).**

Bulloch. After stepsister Georgia returned from Europe in the fall of 1846, she had continued her travels with her sister Susan. In 1848, they went by steamship from Savannah to Charleston in March and then on to New York City. Manifested as "Miss S.A. Elliott & Miss G.A. Elliott" the two young ladies returned to Charleston in mid–May with cousin Henry Macon Dunwoody (often spelled Dunwody). Henry had just graduated from Harvard Law School and the ladies were happy to escort him home. The sisters checked into the familiar Charleston Hotel before heading inland to Roswell.[82]

Georgia Amanda Elliott, Martha Bulloch's second daughter by Senator Elliott, came to her untimely end in Roswell when she died on September 29, 1848. She was only twenty-six and unmarried. In addition to her academic training, she was an accomplished musician who shared her knowledge with her stepsister Mittie. Georgia's final resting place was in Roswell's Founder's Cemetery near the grave of her half-brother Charles Bulloch. Following Georgia's death, her brother Daniel and a trusted

Roswell friend, Nicholas J. Bayard appraised Georgia's and her sister Susan's combined estate. The girls probably inherited the slaves through their father, Senator John Elliott, but, in keeping with eighteenth century norms, the girls had no land. The value of their slaves was $3,900 ($123,000 in 2015) and in addition to household servants, included two carpenters.[83]

The other painful memory for James was the death of his father. Major James Stephens Bulloch had died suddenly on Sunday, February 18, 1849, while teaching a Sunday school class at his beloved Roswell Presbyterian Church. His death made Martha a widow again. This time, there were four children still at home: Daniel (22), Anna (16), Mittie (14), and Irvine (7). Anna forever regretted that she neglected to give her father "his usual morning kiss, the first omitted in months," as she hurried off to church. The elder Bulloch left Bulloch Hall and his other real property to Martha.[84]

An appraisal of J.S. Bulloch's personal property conducted in early June only tallied up to $1755 ($57,000 in 2015). The inventory included three horses, a mule, twelve sheep, sixteen cattle, barnyard and household furnishings, and silver. It did not include Bulloch Hall and other property that Martha had previously acquired or inherited in her own name from her first husband and her father. The appraisal also did not include slaves, which probably equaled or exceeded the value of all the other items in his estate. The ubiquitous Robert Hutchinson served as administrator for the Bulloch estate.[85]

Fortunately, the family's affairs had also included happier episodes. On a Thursday evening in late January of 1849, Susan Ann Elliott (28) married Hilborne West (30) at Bulloch Hall. Although their first introduction may have been in Philadelphia, Susan and Hilborne began a serious relationship in Savannah in June of 1848. "Hill" as he was fondly known, did not return to his home in Philadelphia until early August, and by that time, he and Susan were engaged. Hill became a treasured brother-in-law and uncle to his extended family. A few years earlier, his sister Mary West had married Silas Weir Roosevelt, the older brother of Theodore Roosevelt, Sr. The couple named their first boy after Silas Weir's father, but they named their second son Hilborne.[86]

Due to the recent death of her sister Georgia less than four months earlier, Susan's marriage to Hill West was the most subdued in Bulloch Hall's history of lavish southern weddings. Although she was well past normal nineteenth century marrying age, Susan was still quite a catch. In addition to being a "beautiful" woman, she probably obtained full rights to the eight slaves that she and Georgia had jointly owned. She also had inherited some money from her father and stock in the Bank of Georgia.

After Robert Hutchison allocated Susan nine of her sister's eighteen shares, she had twenty three shares valued at $2,300 ($74,700 in 2015). Although Hilborne was intent on returning to Philadelphia, the newlyweds spent considerable time in Roswell over the next few years, assisting Martha with the management of Bulloch Hall.[87]

There is no record that James D. Bulloch received an inheritance from his father. Other than Bulloch Hall, its contents (including slaves), and a bit of land, there was very little remaining in the estate. Martha retained the property in her own name, including at least twelve slaves, but she had very little cash. A year later, she even had to borrow money from a Marietta store owner against the value of her home. Midshipman Bulloch may have been frustrated by the Navy's poor pay and glacial pace of promotion, but a career in the Navy seemed to be a better path than remaining in Roswell. His best option for increased pay within the Navy was duty with the U.S. Coast Survey. The Coast Survey was not as glamorous as service on a warship, but his midshipman's monthly pay would increase from $62.50 per month ($50 base, plus $12.50 sea pay) to $92.50 (additional $30 Survey Pay, equivalent to $3,000 in 2015). It was a financial boost of almost fifty percent. Not surprisingly, James promptly requested orders to the U.S. Coast Survey.[88]

The other happy event that James had missed while deployed to the Pacific Squadron was the wedding of his friend and mentor Robert Hutchison (46) to Mary Edmonia Caskie (26) of Richmond on October 3, 1848. Mary and Robert traveled to Savannah in mid–November of that year and would have been honored guests at the wedding of Hill West and Susan Elliott. Hutchison remained deeply involved with the Bulloch family as executor of Major Bulloch's estate. He was also an invaluable benefactor who had deep pockets, including Bank of Georgia stock valued at over $40,000 (over $1.3 million in 2015). That summer, Robert insured that Anna and Mittie were "never rigged out so well in their lives" with plenty of "dresses, bonnets, sashes, gloves, & pocket handkerchiefs."[89]

Although he had no significant financial gain from his family ties, Midshipman Bulloch rejoiced in his time with family and the respite from the rigors of his life at sea. When it came to Mittie and Anna, he demonstrated his keen powers of observation, writing that he was, "delighted with his two little sisters." He described the 16-year-old Anna as, "... a sensitive confiding little creature, all heart & soul, with large, soft slowly winking eyes & great long lashes. She does everything with gentleness, & has a way of nestling by her brother's side, which is truly touching." Mittie (14) was, "... black haired, bright eyed, and lively in her disposition with a ready tongue. She does everything by impulse & with an air of perfect self-confidence, but she is a warm hearted little darling."[90]

Having chosen the course of his professional life, James wrote the Navy Department from Roswell on August 3, requesting orders to the U.S. Coast Survey schooner *Morris*. The *Morris* was a former army transport that was modified for hydrographic work under the command of the engaging John Newland Maffitt. Maffitt was the son of a famous Methodist preacher and well known to be, "equally ready for a fight or a jollification, and whose preference for the latter would by no means interfere with his creditable conduct of the former." Although Maffitt was a popular commander, James' reason for selecting the *Morris* may have been related to geography. Maffitt and the *Morris* were operating off the coast of New England, near Long Island, NY. A posting in the North would provide a better chance of nurturing his "friendship" with Anna Christie Stevens in Erie, PA, or perhaps her sister, Ellen, in New York.[91]

While still on leave at Roswell, James wrote Anna Stevens a long letter. It was the type of letter that would be considered inappropriately familiar in modern times and perhaps for that era as well:

> My dear Mrs. Stevens,
>
> There is nothing more charming in the eyes of a young man than the possession of a female friend, one who unconnected with him by any ties of blood, has yet touched a sympathetic chord in his heart, & while gaining his affection & respect, has also won his confidence. ... I have felt the doors of my heart unfolding & the kindlier feelings of my nature spreading themselves around you, I have ever yielded to their inclination & have never checked but rather encouraged their development. .... I commence our correspondence with as much confidence & as little desire to conceal any of my own or my sexes [*sic*] weakness, as if I were addressing a sister. When we parted at the depot in Philadelphia, a feeling of real sadness came over me which increased to one of desolation when I kissed for the last time the dear lips of my precious sister. Amid a crowd of joyous passengers, I paced the steamer's deck unhindered & alone. T'was there I felt in full force the great affliction God had cast upon me, t'was then I realized the want of that sympathy you would so kindly have yielded me. .... be assured that you have & ever will retain the high respect & sincere friendship of,
>
> James D. Bulloch, late of the *Lexington*.[92]

James was clearly in love with love, and perhaps with Mrs. Stevens as well. The Navy had met his expectations for adventure and travel, but it removed him from frequent contact with the current and future ladies of his life. It also limited his opportunities for romance with acceptable candidates for matrimony. Fortunately for James, the Navy that had brought him together with Mrs. Stevens kept them apart as well.

In early August 1849, the Stevens family was settling into their new home at Erie, in western Pennsylvania. James was awaiting orders to the Atlantic coast. He returned to New York on the SS *Cherokee*, arriving from Savannah on August 12. James did not check into any of the New York hotels indicating that he had a quick connection for Saratoga Springs, NY. The resort city was still a favorite destination for southerners in general and Robert Hutchison in particular. Saratoga Springs was also a festive and convenient place for Midshipman Bulloch to wait for his orders while surrounded by society's most desirable young ladies. In August, the Navy Department finally directed him to join Captain Maffitt on the U.S. Coast Survey schooner *Morris* off Nantucket, Massachusetts. James sent his acknowledgement on September 1 from his new "home address" in New York state.[93]

By October, James had transferred with Lieutenant Commanding Maffitt to the schooner *Gallatin*. The *Gallatin* had been damaged while surveying the shallow coastal waters of New England and was on its way to Wilmington, Delaware for repairs. Over four months had passed since Passed Midshipman Bulloch had kissed the "dear lips" of Mrs. Anna Stevens. As evidenced by the other surviving letter addressed to both Tom and Anna Stevens, James continued to pine for female companionship and his tone was even more maudlin.[94]

> Already have twenty-five weary summers scorched me with their suns, & as many winters chilled me with their snows. Yet have I found no gentle female breast to 'beat in unison with mine,' but still [I] drag my weary way along in solitude & gloom. ... Doubtless you have now no sympathy for me, but tell my sad tale to your sweet little wife, who is my dear little friend & whose woman's heart is ever open to a tale of woe. She'll give me her pity & perhaps a helping hand to find a cure for melancholy, in the shape of a darling little wife as much like herself as possible.
>
> This simple allusion to Mrs. Stevens has made me quite oblivious of you, & I can scarcely refrain from continuing this letter to her, but as you charge me with being in your debt & I am anxious to cancel the obligation. You may have the benefit of the balance & I'll write her all by herself in a short time.[95]

After parting company with James, Tom Stevens had reported to the Great Lakes side-wheel steamer, USS *Michigan* based at Erie, Pennsylvania, where he and Anna had first met. During Tom's assignment to the *Michigan* (1849–1852), there was no apparent continuation of the "friendship" with Anna or Tom Stevens. The Stevens' and their children returned to San Francisco in 1852, where Tom assumed command of the *Ewing* with the U.S. Coast Survey. While the Stevens were in California, a young U.S.

Army officer and his wife purchased the brick home next door to their house on Green Street in San Francisco. This army officer became the infamous Civil War general known for his march to the sea and devastation of Georgia: William Tecumseh Sherman. Tom Stevens served the Union during the war and briefly commanded the famous ironclad, USS *Monitor*. He retired as an admiral. Anna raised nine children, including their first son, Thomas H. Stevens III, whom Bulloch had recalled so fondly. The "boisterous heir" followed in his father's footsteps, joined the Navy, and also retired as an Admiral.[96]

With no sweetheart of his own, James took comfort in the familial love he shared with his half-sisters, Anna and Mittie Bulloch. He wrote from the deck of the *Gallatin* that, "Last night I received a sweet letter from one of my little sisters, who are at boarding school at Columbia, S.C. She seems satisfied with her situation & gives a favorable report of every thing concerned. The studies are all well selected, but as in most of our schools, they are too much crowded."[97]

Like Martha's older daughters Susan and Georgia, Anna and Mittie attended a female academy that focused on academics in addition to the ornamental skills that refined ladies of the South were expected to attain. However, instead of sending them to a far-away and more expensive boarding school in the North, Martha chose the South Carolina Female Collegiate Institute in Barhamville. Generally known as Barhamville Female College, it was home to about 200 students each year. "The standard of the school was high and its tone was elegant, refined, and dignified. The best teachers from the North were employed, usually eight or ten constituting the faculty." Dr. Elias Marks founded the academy and the school prospered for over 50 years (1817–1869).[98]

One of the teachers on Dr. Marks' staff was Julia Warne Pierpont, a rare example of a woman who obtained employment outside the home. She was born in Connecticut and was one of Emma Willard's first students, and became the second wife of Dr. Marks in 1833. Miss Willard was the renowned educator who established the first female academy in the United States, fully two years before Catherine Beecher's school in Hartford. Mittie Bulloch was one of Julia's students. Mittie and Anna absorbed the school's nineteenth century philosophy about the proper focus of female education: "The torch of intellect is to be kindled on the altar of domestic affection."[99]

Barhamville offered a preparatory department with four years of study plus an optional postgraduate year. The core academic courses included algebra, geography, botany, history, mineralogy, writing/composition, rhetoric, chemistry, U.S. government, logic, astronomy, geology, natural & moral philosophy. Dr. Marks blended the concepts of Christian piety with the idea of separate male and female spheres. The ladies also learned domestic skills that had benevolent applications. The choices for these ornamental courses were many and varied. The curriculum included: dancing, music (piano, guitar, vocal), art (drawing, oil painting, watercolors), belles-letters (i.e., literature), embroidery, modern languages (French, Italian, Spanish), Latin, and German. The academy did not, however, offer Greek. This would have been a major deficiency for a male college-preparatory school. As exemplified by the schooling of their brothers James and Daniel in Connecticut, a proper nineteenth century collegiate education was defined by the study of the classics.[100]

The love of his scholarly sisters and his feelings for another man's wife was not what the 27-year-old sailor James D. Bulloch needed at this point in his life. Once again, the Bullochs' wealthy and gregarious friend and relative, Robert Hutchison, provided the necessary assistance. Robert's new wife had a very engaging sister named Elizabeth. She was also very available and willing to meet Midshipman Bulloch. Her first introduction to the Bullochs appears to have come just after Mary Caskie and Robert married in Richmond. On November 15, 1848, the newlyweds brought Elizabeth Caskie with them to Savannah when they returned from their honeymoon in New York. The 18-year-old Elizabeth would have to be patient however, because James Dunwoody Bulloch was still at sea. Lizzie, as she was fondly known, probably attended the wedding of Susan and Hill West at Bulloch Hall in January. This was the first of her many trips to Roswell and the beginning of a deep friendship that spread to all of Martha Bulloch's daughters, nieces, and one particular stepson.[101]

Lizzie Caskie split her time between Richmond and Savannah with her married sister Mary Hutchison. They were frequent house guests at the magnificent Bulloch Hall in Roswell. Unfortunately for James, she and Mary had returned to Richmond just prior to his arrival in June of 1849. The stars and their schedules were better aligned that winter when Bulloch's surveying schooner *Gallatin* shifted its base of operation to Charleston in early December. James' schedule, an understanding commander in Captain Maffitt, and his proximity to home, gave the eligible bachelor time to spend ashore, including Christmas in Roswell. It was not a coincidence that Lizzie happened to be visiting Bulloch Hall on her 19th birthday when the 26-year-old Passed Midshipman James Dunwoody Bulloch was home in February of 1850. During his brief visit, "Brother Jimmie" and the girls went on long carriage rides through the country and all were charmed by Lizzie's "gayety and vivacity of manner." James must have realized that she was the young lady that he had been longing for.[102]

With the approach of summer, however, it was time for visitors to leave the unhealthy heat of the Deep South. Lizzie was the first to depart. She returned to Richmond via Charleston in late April with her brother Edmund Caskie as an escort. Bulloch's survey schooner was still in the Charleston area and it is possible that the couple briefly met before Lizzie and Edmund continued on their way. Next to leave were Robert and Mary Hutchison. They made their annual trek to New York in May. Even the U.S. Coast Survey knew better than to remain on the coastal waters of South Carolina and Georgia during the summer months. The *Gallatin*, with Lt. Commanding Maffitt and James D. Bulloch still aboard, departed the Charleston area in early June to refit at Norfolk. By mid–July, the *Gallatin* had relocated to Nantucket Island, Mass. From this temporary base, the crew diligently surveyed the New England coast up to Boston until mid–November.[103]

When the *Gallatin* returned to Norfolk via New York for refit, James

The Roswell belles: Anna, left, and Mittie Bulloch (Anna, Theodore Roosevelt Collection, Houghton Library, Harvard University, TRC-PH-2 570.B87a; Mittie, Theodore Roosevelt Collection, Houghton Library, Harvard University, TRC-PH-1 570.R67m).

requested and received orders to detach from the Coast Survey and an additional ninety days leave, effective the first week of December. Fortuitously, he was close to Richmond, the family home of Robert Hutchison's wife, Mary and her sister Lizzie Caskie. Mary and Robert were in town for the birth of their daughter Nannie in late January of 1851. James Dunwoody Bulloch was also in Richmond, where he cradled the baby girl in his arms when she was "not more than a week-old."[104] Family friendships aside, the real purpose of James' presence in Richmond was to court the "exceedingly pretty" Miss Lizzie Caskie. The social season had arrived in Richmond with its seemingly endless series of receptions, balls, and outings. The fundamental purpose of these affairs was to find a suitable match that would lead to matrimony.[105]

Back in the "pleasant little town of Roswell," four teenage girls were preparing for similar events on a smaller scale.[106] The girls shared feelings of excitement and trepidation as sisters Anna (17) and Martha (Mittie) Bulloch (15) and their friends Julia Isabella Hand (18, daughter of Bayard and Elizabeth Barrington King Hand) and Florida Bayard (16, daughter of Nicholas and Sarah Glen Bayard) prepared for their own introductions. They were all "coming out" for presentation to society as young ladies during the winter and spring of 1850–1851.[107]

For all southern girls of refinement, "coming out" represented a distinct new stage in their lives. The timing for crossing this threshold varied, but it usually occurred after the young lady completed her formal schooling, between the ages of fifteen and eighteen. A key variable was the marital status of older sisters. A family might choose to withhold the introduction of a younger daughter if her older sister was not already safely engaged or married. The sibling consideration obviously did not deter Martha Bulloch from including Mittie, the youngest of the four Roswell debutantes, with her older sister Anna. Although all four young ladies enjoyed each other's company, they also were competing for the attentions of a very limited pool of appropriately eligible bachelors.[108]

A successful debut was an important milestone for every girl. The initial social festivity of the season was often an elegant ball. Each girl would wear a special dress made for the occasion. Typically, the dress was white to symbolize her purity and chastity. The family had an equal interest in her success and worked hard to present their daughters to men from the best social circles. Fathers and mothers spared no expense attending to her dress, jewelry, and other accessories. Those accessories might even include decorations and furnishings for the home. The intent was to magnify the family's status in ways designed to impress and entertain potential suitors. Each family expected their debutante to receive visitors and actively participate in all the dizzying rounds of social activities that might lead to an advantageous match.[109]

The young ladies worked to develop important personal skills that included clever conversation, dancing, and perhaps most importantly, flirting. Rather than spend time at home in study or assisting with house-

Ladies' "funnel" bonnets. From *Illustrated London News*, November 29, 1845 (author's collection).

hold chores, the debutantes devoted themselves to becoming "exquisitely beautiful and very fashionable." Anna and Mittie Bulloch were fully engaged in the "the gayeties of the fashionable world" as they assumed their new identities as "turned out" young ladies. Now that they had become southern belles of marriageable age, each would be referred to as Miss Bulloch and not by their first names.[110]

In the antebellum South, even the term "belle" had a precise meaning. Critics only bestowed the distinction as a "belle" upon those "turned out" young ladies who were not just available, but also highly sought after.[111] It was John McIntosh Kell, the former U.S. and Confederate Navy officer from Georgia, who affirmed Anna's and Mittie's status as true southern belles. He noted that the "sisters of Captain James D. Bulloch" were from a society "of culture and refinement" and pointedly described them as "great belles."[112]

It also appears that Anna was more than able to hold her own against competition from Mittie and her other friends. One report from Roswell, dated January 6, 1851, even suggested that Anna made the more favorable impression and that Mittie was left standing in her sister's reflected success:

> I am most gone with Anna B. [Bulloch]. She had gone and got a funnel bonnet like Susy's [Susan Elliott West's] and she looks out upon the wide prospective of admiring glances like one fully aware that approbations of the 'becoming thing' is only well merited, and she is not far from the right conclusion. It suits her to a fraction.... Mittie can come in for a small share of admiration on account of relationship.[113]

Anna was doing well in the fashion category of Roswell's social season, but the real winner would be the one who could attract a desirable suitor. An exciting opportunity arose in February when a 19-year-old young man from New York City came to call on the Bulloch sisters. He made the trip to Roswell at the invitation of Hill and Susan West. The newlyweds had recently returned to Roswell to help Martha with the management of Bulloch Hall. They were also managing the farm they had recently purchased from Mrs. Bulloch. While still in Philadelphia, Hill eagerly shared his feelings about Bulloch Hall's attractions. He, "adored the informal, fascinating plantation life, and loved the companionship of the two dainty, pretty girls ..., Martha [Mittie] and Anna Bulloch."[114]

Hill had met the gentleman through his sister, Mary West, who had married Silas Weir, the oldest of five Roosevelt sons. Hill was most impressed with Theodore, the youngest of the Roosevelt boys. Hill promptly invited Theodore to Roswell during the coming social season.

Young Mr. Roosevelt willingly obliged and that winter traveled from New York to Savannah, arriving on February 12, 1851. Although they knew Theodore was coming, nobody knew exactly when. As it was, he arrived at Bulloch Hall somewhat unexpectedly late on a Sunday evening. Not until the next day, Monday February 16, did the Bulloch ladies formally meet Hill's brother-in-law and the girls' new suitor.[115]

Anna and Mittie instantly "set their caps for him." Seeing their determination, a married family friend, George Hull Camp, knew that the poor lad was hopelessly outnumbered. George decided to have some fun with the two misses. With utmost sincerity, he told them that Theodore was already engaged to be married. This announcement "deranged all their plans and for a time they were inconsolable." Continuing his tease, Mr. Camp agreed to let Theodore "act as their escort on horse-back and visit the alley daily to arrange the pins and return the balls" for their popular indoor game of bowling.[116]

Theodore impressed everyone, male and female, but certainly not because of his good looks. One of the debutantes even described him as "very homely in feature of face." George Camp humorously excused himself from "answering the question if he was a handsome child on the modest ground of his resemblance to his father." Theodore was not handsome, but he had other qualities, "his figure was tall [six feet], slender, & graceful, & his manners were those of a polished gentleman." The ladies found his conversation captivating, helped in no small part by his penetrating, but sensitive blue eyes. George Camp observed that "the entire community are ready to acknowledge the extraordinary merits of the young gentleman." Without identifying which lady had captured Theodore's heart, he also opined that wedding negotiations with Reverend Pratt would soon be in order.[117]

Despite Mr. Camp's optimistic assessment, Roswell's social season did not culminate with any engagements or weddings. In fact, Theodore and the four debutantes remained decidedly unattached. All of the participants realized that the ultimate purpose of their "coming out" was matrimony. However, like most young ladies, the Roswell ladies wanted to prolong their reign as southern belles as long as they could. Excepting those young ladies who preferred solitude, intellectual, or Godly pursuits, southern women reveled in this brief interlude of perfection. It was a time of beautiful clothing, engaging people, interesting conversations, and events dedicated to their enjoyment. An adept belle who could sustain interest from a number of desirable suitors, but avoid commitment, might also increase her options. Within the paternalistic antebellum society, "coming out" was perhaps the only chance a lady would ever have to exercise true power over men. More importantly, it gave her a rare opportunity to shape her own destiny as she carefully attracted and selected a providential mate.[118]

While Roswell's social season was playing out to the enjoyment of his sisters, brother Jimmie redoubled his own romantic efforts. Throughout the late winter and early spring of 1851, his U.S. Coast Survey Schooner *Gallatin* operated between Cape Fear, NC, and Savannah, GA. Frequent port calls in Savannah and Charleston, allowed him ample time for shore leave and the pursuit of the lovely Miss Caskie. In mid–March, James left the *Gallatin* in Savannah and traveled by commercial steamer to Charleston on his way to Richmond. It was unusual for him to bypass an opportunity to visit his family in Roswell, but he had other things on his mind. Lizzie was in Richmond and susceptible to the competing attractions of that city's vibrant social season.[119]

Two other ladies commanded James' attention while he was in Richmond, Mary Hutchison and her baby Nannie. It had been seven weeks since Mary had given birth. She and the baby were about ready to rejoin Robert in Savannah. Rather than have her brother Edmund Caskie serve as Mary's escort, James happily agreed to make the journey with them. Most of his happiness however, was due to Lizzie. He and Miss Caskie were engaged. Now, all he had to do was obtain a Navy assignment that would permit him to plan a wedding date. To do that, he had to get back to his ship where he was expecting new orders. After bidding farewell to Lizzie, James headed for Charleston. First he traveled by rail to Wilmington, NC, with Mary, baby Nannie, "the fat rosy nurse Susan," and two servants. Wilmington's train station was just a few blocks from the docks where they boarded the U.S. Mail steamer *Gladiator*. The steamer safely arrived in Charleston where everyone, except the two slaves, spent the night at the Charleston Hotel.[120]

After finding separate quarters for the two female servants in Charleston, James also had to act as Robert Hutchison's agent on their behalf. In the antebellum south, slaves could not travel from one area to the next without permission from their owners. They had to carry the equivalent of a certified travel visa. For voyages at sea, the slave-owner or his agent also had to register slaves as cargo on the ship's manifest. James dutifully obtained the permits and listed the two female slaves as Patty (age: 50, height: 5' 0," complexion: black) and Florrie (age: 50, height 5' 4," complexion: yellow). After a good night's rest in Charleston, Bulloch and his entourage of five ladies again departed by steamship on April 21 and arrived at the Savannah piers later that same day.[121]

In early May James received orders to a surveying party under the overall command of Lieutenant Commanding Charles H. Blair. This assignment brought him to the surveying brig *Washington* as Acting Master. He had finally risen to the same temporary position he held five years previously on the USS *Shark*. The *Washington* operated out of Boston and conducted surveying operations along the familiar coast of Massachusetts and Rhode Island. After a brief refit at New York in June, the brig's crew continued to work the Martha's Vineyard and Nantucket areas. James had little opportunity for personal affairs during this busy summer and fall other than writing letters. Poor weather finally suspended their work in early November.[122]

Acting Master Bulloch navigated the *Washington* back the New York Navy Yard where she would spend the winter. James waited impatiently for the crew to secure the gangway to the pier. He had a wedding to attend in Richmond; his own.

3

Bonds Made and Broken

Not even the cold November rain of 1851 could dampen the spirits of Lizzie Caskie. Her fiancé, Acting Master James Dunwoody Bulloch, had joined her at the Caskie home in Richmond from his coast surveying ship in New York City. When he arrived, the Caskie family was experiencing a time of epic highs and lows. In late October, cousin John S. Caskie won his initial bid for election to U.S. House of Representatives as a pro–Union Democrat. On the opposite end of the spectrum, her sister Mary and Robert Hutchison's first child was seriously ill. The youngster had only recently celebrated her second birthday. Robert named her Mary Caskie Hutchison after her mother. On the evening of November 13, young Mary succumbed to convulsions at the Hutchison home in Savannah.[1]

The timing of Mary's death created a dilemma for James and Lizzie. Their wedding was set for November 19. Out of respect for Mary and Robert, it would have been better to postpone their nuptials until after the child's funeral. However, the demands of naval service made it difficult for James to plan additional time for personal matters. The adage and unstated policy was, "if the Navy had wanted you to have a wife, they would have issued you one." Understanding the circumstances, the Hutchisons temporarily interred their daughter in Savannah until they could give her a proper burial in the Caskie family cemetery at Richmond's Shockoe Hill that December.[2]

Trusting to God's benevolence, James and Lizzie pressed ahead with the wedding. Despite the sadness of young Mary's death, newspapers reported that the Caskie-Bulloch wedding "ceremony was a brilliant society event, both families being very prominent." The family pastor, Reverend Charles H. Read of the nearby United Presbyterian Church on Shockoe Hill, officiated. Their venue was the Caskie House at 1100 East Clay Street, just a block removed from the structure that came to be known as the Confederate White House. The Caskie House was a large two story building, fully sixty-three feet long, with a two-story portico in front and numerous outbuildings. It was an appropriately grand home for Lizzie's father, the tobacconist John Caskie, one of the wealthiest men in Virginia.[3]

The other important event of November 19 came in the form of official orders from the Navy Department. The Navy released the 28-year-old acting master from sea service and ordered to him shore duty at the U.S. Coast Survey Office at Washington, D.C. Fortunately, James did not have to report immediately. He and Lizzie would have time for a honeymoon. The newlyweds' choice of destinations would be unusual for later generations, but for the 28-year-old groom and the 20-year-old bride, it seemed quite appropriate. They headed south to see the Bulloch family in Georgia. Arriving in Savannah on November 30, they had time for a brief meeting with Robert and Mary Hutchison. They were able to spend almost a full month with the extended Bulloch family over the Christmas holiday. By December 30, they were back in Charleston and on their way to a new life together that would begin in the nation's capital city, much like Martha Bulloch had 32 years earlier.[4]

Even before arriving in Washington, James had been busy lobbying for a better position. The prospects of low pay and the long separations inherent in a Navy career were not attractive alternatives for the young couple. Their best short-term option was for James to seek a position on one of the commercial steamers carrying the U.S. Mail. Congress had recently mandated that the captains of these ships had to be U.S. Navy officers. Within the first few weeks of their arrival in Washington, James requested orders for the U.S. Mail Steamship *Georgia*. His letter noted that he was making this request with the knowledge and at the suggestion of Navy Lieutenant David Dixon Porter, the ship's captain. Even though Captain Porter knew of his excellent reputation, James most likely informed the captain of his interest and availability. Porter's endorsement helped ensure a speedy approval from the Navy Department. As a result, James remained anchored to a desk in Washington for less than three months.[5]

Although he was still in the Navy and under the command of Lieutenant David Dixon Porter, James' new position on the SS *Georgia* paid much better. Additionally, the couple was guaranteed to see each other more frequently as the ship made a regular circuit from New York to Havana, New Orleans, Panama, and back. Lizzie was a spirited and strong-willed young lady who was not shy about sharing her feelings concerning her husband's absence from her life. As first officer of a mail steamer, James at least temporarily avoided the two or three year deployment aboard a warship that was the norm for U.S. Navy sailors of the mid-nineteenth century. A more critical factor in his decision was Lizzie's health; she was not well. There had been early and ominous signs that the she did not have a robust constitution. During a winter visit to Roswell and Bulloch Hall before they were married, Lizzie was confined to her room due to an illness that lasted at least a week.[6]

Lizzie's sister, Mary Hutchison, was also very ill. Robert had moved her from Savannah in late May with the assistance of her cousin, Miss Mary Eliza Caskie. Mary needed to be with her parents in Richmond. Although the nature of Mrs. Hutchison's sickness is unknown, consumption, now known as tuberculosis, was a likely culprit. Mary died on a Saturday morning in early July of 1852. She took her final breath at the same grand Caskie House where James and Lizzie had been married just eight months before. Mary Hutchison was laid to rest in the nearby Shockoe Hill cemetery. Robert was now twice a widower and Lizzie Bulloch had lost her oldest sister. Their response to Mary's demise is not fully recorded, but one action they did take was highly unusual. Less than three weeks after Mary's death, the two went to Europe. Robert accompanied Lizzie (registered as "Mrs. E.C. Bulloch") and her close friend and cousin Mary Eliza Caskie to England on the SS *Atlantic*.[7]

The reason for their voyage is not clear, but Georgia and Susan Elliott had made a similar journey with their stepfather, James S. Bulloch, in 1846. They may have been seeking treatment for Lizzie's condition. She was suffering from symptoms of consumption/tuberculosis and may have contracted the disease from her sister Mary. Since Lizzie and James had been married for less than a year, it is unlikely that the primary purpose of her visit was a holiday tour of Europe apart from her husband. James' thoughts and whereabouts during his wife's trip are unrecorded. However, James had limited options in dealing with his wife's condition.

Acting Master Bulloch was first officer of the SS *Georgia*. Although it was a commercial steamer, he was an officer subject to orders of the Navy Department. However, Bulloch's U.S. Mail steamer *Georgia* was laid up in a New York shipyard from May through early August. His captain, David Dixon Porter, had taken temporary command of another U.S. Mail steamer, the *Crescent City*. Porter probably brought James along with him as his second in command, but it is also possible that James accompanied Lizzie during the first portion of her European trip. Unfortunately, James' service record does not indicate any leave during Lizzie's absence. Robert Hutchison, Lizzie, and cousin Mary Eliza finally returned to New York from Liverpool on October 18 in the SS *Arctic*. It is unlikely that James served on the *Atlantic* or *Arctic* even though they were U.S. Mail steamers. The two ships were owned by separate companies, operated under different contracts (than the SS *Georgia*), and James was not listed on either manifest.[8]

By the time Lizzie, Mary, and Robert returned to New York, the Secretary of the Navy had ordered Lt. Porter back to the *Georgia*. He was back in command when the *Georgia* got underway in early November, presumably with James continuing as his second in command. Based on family correspondence, James and Lizzie took an apartment in New York, but Lizzie also spent considerable time in Richmond while James was at sea. During these otherwise troubling times, James and Lizzie were not the only ones in the family who were active travelers.[9]

In the early spring of 1853, Mittie and Anna visited their stepsister Susan (usually referred to as Susy) and her husband Hill West in Philadelphia. Mittie just happened to be in town at the same time as her former suitor, Theodore Roosevelt. After parting company with the Bullochs in 1851, Theodore went on a grand tour of Europe and did not return to the United States until April of 1852. Now in his 21st year, Theodore embraced the spring of a new year with a rekindled interest in the raven-haired beauty from Roswell.[10]

When they last said goodbye in Georgia, Mittie had given Theodore a small gold thimble as a token of remembrance, probably thinking she would never see him again. Mittie was touched that Theodore had cherished the gift. From Philadelphia, she soon made the brief journey to New York City where she spent time with the Wests' in-laws, Silas Weir and Mary West Roosevelt. Mittie also visited with her own sister-in-law, Lizzie Bulloch, while brother Jimmie was at sea. The purpose of the visits to New York, however, had little to do with the in-laws. Mittie and Theodore were in love.[11]

Although she was only seventeen at the time, Mittie was no novice at handling men, especially potential suitors. She and her fellow Roswell debutantes had experienced three social seasons since their "coming out" of 1850. But when the youngest of those four young ladies conditionally accepted Theodore's proposal of marriage, Mittie was the first to be engaged. Most southern belles were reluctant to make an early commitment to any suitor. The transition from miss to matron marked a dramatic shift in roles and personal power. It was not a decision to be made in haste. A married woman not only lost most of her legal identity, she also lost control of her personal life. Mittie realized that she would have to submit to her husband in every respect.[12]

Antebellum engagements were usually lengthy ones. The most sought-after southern belles realized that the unbreakable bonds of matrimony were an inevitable outcome. Still, they resisted submission to its paternalistic bondage as long as possible. A long interval between proposal and marriage prolonged a woman's elevated status and control over her social life. An extended engagement also allowed a lady to gauge the character and commitment of her betrothed and explore her own feelings. Although she had no family fortune in her dowry, Mittie was clearly in the "belle" category of young ladies. It was also clear that she had no doubts about Theodore and no interest in putting him off. But first, Theodore had to receive mother

Martha (Mittie) Bulloch Roosevelt (Theodore Roosevelt Collection, Houghton Library, Harvard University TRC-PH-2 570.R67m).

Martha Bulloch's official blessing: in person.[13]

Theodore obligingly made a brief trip to Roswell in the early summer of 1853 to gain Martha's readily-given consent. After a few delays, the wedding date was set for that December in Roswell, just before Christmas. By nineteenth century standards, they had a whirlwind romance. Mittie was pleased that "Brother Jimmie's" service on the *Georgia* required him and Lizzie to live in New York City. They were close to Theodore, and Susy and Hill West were in nearby Philadelphia. This proximity helped the bonds of family love grow even stronger. Theodore visited the Bullochs frequently and developed an abiding friendship that extended to their close family members as well. Mittie was exceptionally pleased by Theodore's attachment to her "Brother Jimmie." Their relationship magnified Mittie's attraction to her future husband.[14]

Lizzie's health added a worrying undercurrent that affected the timing of the Bulloch-Roosevelt wedding. The ailing Lizzie stayed with Susy West in May of 1853 while James was at sea (May 5–25). Soon after the *Georgia* pulled into port, Theodore visited both James and Lizzie. He reported that, "Mrs. Bulloch has determined to accompany her husband on his next cruise; she seems much better and sends her best love." Lizzie took an unfortunate turn for the worse just three nights later. "Today I have been made quite melancholy by hearing that the same evening that I was there, after I left, Mrs. Bulloch had another hemorrhage. Mr. Bulloch does not seem to think it a severe one and still expects her I believe to go in the *Georgia* with him tomorrow. I intend ... this evening [June 5, 1853] ... [to] pay him a visit."[15] These regular updates on Lizzie Bulloch's condition allowed Mittie and her mother Martha to plan the wedding accordingly. They did not even consider inviting a large number of guests "from the first" due to "Lizzie Bulloch's precarious state of health."[16]

Lizzie did follow through with her plan to accompany her husband on his first cruise as ship's Master of the SS *Georgia*. Although they were celebrating his 30th birthday and his initial command at sea, the 24 day round trip to Havana and Panama was not a pleasant one. Upon their return, the Bullochs quickly boarded a steamship bound for Richmond. Perhaps her family would have better success nursing Lizzie back to health than they had the previous year with sister Mary. On July 9, five days after arriving in Richmond, Bulloch resigned his new position as captain of the *Georgia*. The steamer sailed under a new captain the very next day.[17]

Powerful personal feelings were driving James' professional decisions. When he resigned as captain of the *Georgia*, he also requested a one-year furlough from the Navy. He was one of many military officers who were seeking better-paying civilian employment in the post–Mexican War era. The over-manned peacetime Navy was happy to process his request quickly and granted his release on July 18. Five days later, James departed New York City as master of the fine commercial steamer *Black Warrior*. Once again, James had coordinated his moves in advance and requested official permission only after all the unofficial approvals were in place.[18]

Some might have thought it odd for a loving husband to accept a new position that regularly took him away from his ailing wife. However, Bulloch was not independently wealthy and his profession was the sea. They needed the additional pay James received as a civilian ship's Master. Another job benefit was health. The circuit of the *Black Warrior* from New York to Havana, Mobile, and back, was of shorter duration and an improvement to his previous route to and from Panama via Kingston, Jamaica.

Leaving Lizzie in Richmond after a 23 day break from his sailing routine, Captain Bulloch set off on his first voyage on the *Black Warrior*. Shortly after he returned on August 13, he called on Theodore Roosevelt in New York City. Other than being his future brother-in-law, the two men had become intimate friends. James had to cut the visit short when he received a telegram from the Caskies saying that Lizzie had another setback. James hoped for the best as he hurried to be with her. Most of the steamers, including the *Black Warrior*, had suspended their voyages to unhealthy tropical climates and entered the shipyard for routine maintenance and repairs. As a result, he was able to spend an extended time with the Caskies in Richmond.[19]

On October 1, when James returned from his second voyage as master of the *Black Warrior*, Lizzie's health was not his foremost concern for a change. Despite having taken the precaution of keeping his ship at anchor when he called at Mobile, the newspapers reported that "Capt. Bulloch was seized with what were considered unmistakable symptoms of fever." The New York Port Authority placed him in quarantine for patients with yellow fever. Theodore was the first to reach his side, for Mittie was still in Roswell preparing for their wedding. A few days later, Lizzie, once again accompanied by her cousin Mary Eliza Caskie, hurried from Richmond to help nurse James back to health.[20]

Unlike many in his family, James Dunwoody Bulloch was blessed with a robust constitution. He only had a mild case of the disease and promptly returned to duty. He cast off the *Black Warrior's* lines at noon on October 10, taking his ship to sea precisely on schedule. Lizzie's situation, however, was not improving and James had to consider his options for her care. As he had done on the *Georgia*, Captain Bulloch could take his wife to sea with him. However, as his own affliction demonstrated, it would not be safe until the sickly season had run its course. James understood the risk of exposing Lizzie's already-compromised immune system to the deadly fevers that mysteriously seemed to infest southern coastal areas. Despite yellow fever quarantines for both Mobile and Havana that lingered into the early fall, James decided to take desperate measures. Lizzie was rapidly declining and he simply had to do something.[21]

A Richmond newspaper story of 1905, drawn from faded memories and a family Bible, reported that the Bullochs lived in Mobile for a time. The article also said that Lizzie went to Havana for her health. It is most likely that Captain Bulloch welcomed his wife Lizzie aboard the *Black Warrior* in New York City on October 10, 1853, for a cruise to Havana and Mobile. His original plan may have been to attend Mittie's wedding at Bulloch Hall in Roswell on December 22. A daily steamboat service had just begun from Mobile to Montgomery, Alabama and there was a rail connection from there to nearby Marietta, making the difficult inland trip possible. There was also the hope that fresh sea air and more temperate winter climates might offer Lizzie some relief.[22]

In Roswell, plans were well underway for Mittie's marriage festivities. With the wedding set for late December, Theodore arrived at Charleston from New York City via Wilmington, NC, on December 15, 1853, aboard the steamer *Wilmington.* Traveling separately by rail were his parents, Cornelius V.S. and Margaret Roosevelt, and his brother, Cornelius Jr. Martha had private carriages ready to meet them at the Marietta railroad station for the final bumpy ride to Bulloch Hall. Mittie was eager to impress the Roosevelts and worried they would not appreciate the charm of rural Georgia. According to a local historian, Bulloch Hall was at its festive best, "decorated with holly berries, mistletoe, and pine boughs tied in bows of red satin ribbon. Garlands of ivy and Virginia creeper were draped along the balustrades, over windows and doors. Tall white tapers shone from polished silver candelabra on the tables, windows, and mantels."[23]

A Roswell family friend of the Bullochs reported that the "... wedding that has been so long talked of came off on the 22nd" of December. According to all who attended, "It was a grand affair."[24] Theodore's brother, Cornelius Roosevelt, Jr., Mittie's half brother Daniel Stuart Elliot, and neighbors Thomas E. King & Ralph Browne King acted as groomsmen. Mittie's four bridesmaids included her sister Anna, and her fellow Roswell coming-out debutante, Julia Hand. One of the bridesmaids provided Atlanta newspaper reporter Peggy (Margaret) Mitchell a firsthand account of the event. She remembered that they all wore "white muslin dresses made with full skirts and tight basque waists" and carried flowers with trailing clusters of evergreens.[25]

The bridesmaids preceded Mittie down the central staircase "of Bulloch Hall with the trailing clusters in our arms." "Mittie wore a white satin dress and a long veil that became her beautifully."[26] Mittie was a vision as she descended the stairs. As one of Mittie's fellow Roswell belles observed she was, "very pretty & bright. She was taller than her sister Anna, had black hair, dark grey eyes, fair rosy complexion, easy & graceful in her manners, lively in conversation, & very entertaining.... Always taste[ful] & and elegant in her dress, her features are long, [her] teeth, white."[27]

Mittie followed the procession as they turned to their left into drawing room that extended into the large dining room. She carried a small white prayer book that her dearest Thee had given her. "The ceremony took place in the dining room, and" the bridesmaids grouped themselves "just at the folding doors. Everything was beautiful." Mittie's cousin, Rev. James Bulloch Dunwody of South Carolina, attended the ceremony and

Bulloch Hall entry staircase (author's photograph).

recorded the marriage at his Presbyterian Church in McPhersonville, SC.[28]

> When the wedding was over, everybody crowded around congratulating the Roosevelts and kissing them and shaking hands.[29] A lavish supper followed. … The bride's cake was an enormous white tiered creation, frosted in delicate flowers, scrolls, and swirls of confection, decorated by Mittie and her friends at the 'cake icing' parties before the wedding. All of the guests, especially the Roosevelts, were impressed at having ice cream…. After dinner, Mittie and Theodore led the dancing to the music of [brother] Stewart Elliott's flute.[30]

The parties and celebrations continued through Christmas and into the next week. "The entertainment was splendid." The Roosevelts and other out-of-town guests finally departed Bulloch Hall and Roswell on Friday, December 30. Mittie was on her way to a new life in New York City. One important couple, however, had been conspicuously absent: James and Lizzie Bulloch.[31]

While most of the family was enjoying happy days in Roswell, Lizzie's condition continued to deteriorate. After briefly touching at Havana on December 15, James and his steamer, the *Black Warrior* arrived at Mobile two days later. He was not able to leave Lizzie to attend Mittie's wedding. During one of his week-long visits to Mobile, James probably moved Lizzie ashore. She was most likely accompanied by her cousin Mary Eliza Caskie and perhaps a servant, or a nurse who often travelled with her. It was with a heavy heart that James set sail from Mobile on Christmas Eve without his ailing wife. He returned to New York on New Year's Day, 1854.[32]

James Dunwoody Bulloch lived in family lore as a larger-than-life blockade running steamboat captain, but on January 8, 1854, he was quite ordinary. He had a desperate personal crisis that was beyond his power to control. It was with an added sense of urgency that he got the *Black Warrior* underway on its next scheduled run from New York to Mobile via Havana. His first voyage of the new year started badly when heavy weather off Cape Hatteras forced him into Charleston harbor for engine repairs. Three days later, he and the *Black Warrior* set sail for Havana, where he arrived at 7:00 p.m. on January 19.[33]

After impatiently depositing a troublesome 38-member Italian opera company in Havana, he departed for Mobile at noon on Saturday, January 21. Captain Bulloch finally anchored the *Black Warrior* in Mobile Bay at 10 P.M. on January 24. Tragically, while he was "waiting most anxiously for conveyance from his ship," he learned of his wife's death from a "kind considerate friend." Lizzie had succumbed to her illness in the late evening hours of the previous day at "his now desolate home" in Mobile.[34]

Bulloch telegraphed the sad news to Lizzie's family in Richmond, where they made arrangements for his deceased wife. Upon James' arrival at Havana, the *New York Times* correspondent reported, "We have regretted to learn of the death of the lady of Captain Bulloch [*sic*], of the *Black Warrior*, who died at Mobile. Her remains return by this steamer." From New York City, he escorted his young wife's remains for burial at the Caskie family plot in Shockoe Hill Cemetery, Richmond. The 22-year-old Elizabeth Caskie Bulloch was laid to rest on February 9, 1854, after less than two years and four months of marriage. The cause of her death was "consumption," the nineteenth century description of tuberculosis.[35]

Bulloch took comfort in the companionship and attentions of his family in New York, primarily his sister Mittie and her new husband Theodore (Thee) Roosevelt. Although never a permanent resident, Robert Hutchison was another frequent companion. In addition to being a father-figure and mentor, he was Bulloch's double brother-in-law through his deceased stepsister Corinne and his wife Lizzie's sister Mary. Robert maintained close relations with his Caskie in-laws and even sent Lizzie's surviving sister a riding horse as a present. A frequent traveler, he spent most of his time in Savannah, Richmond, New York, and Europe. When he was ready for a third attempt at matrimony, he found another bride in Richmond, Ellen Caskie, the first cousin of Lizzie Bulloch and Robert's deceased wife Mary.[36]

James Bulloch had his work as Captain of a merchant ship and the constant challenges of commanding men on stormy seas to occupy his mind. While he was still grief-stricken over the loss of his beloved Lizzie, James became entangled in a Cuban political imbroglio. The contretemps almost resulted in an 1854 prequel to Teddy Roosevelt's Spanish-American War of 1898. Fortunately, cooler heads prevailed and he continued as Master of the *Black Warrior* when the Spanish government in Havana agreed to release his ship and pay damages. A major change in Captain Bulloch's routine came in September of 1854. His shipping company switched his southern port of call from Mobile to New Orleans. The change would bring him into contact with the next significant lady of his life.

His new schedule usually gave him between four and seven days in New Orleans, depending on weather. He also had the varied challenges that came with commanding a large, ocean-going passenger and freight steamer in the 1850s. In addition to hurricanes and fog, offloading and onloading operations, Captain Bulloch had to discipline boisterous sailors who often fought or deserted. One of his chastised crewman took him to court as did a disgruntled fisherman who owned an improperly operated fishing boat. Both of these litigious sailors placed the blame for their misfortunes on Captain Bulloch and the *Black Warrior*. To their chagrin, each of these legal challenges resulted in dismissal and left the accusers responsible for all court costs.[37]

James was conspicuously very good at his job. He consistently set new records for speed and safety in moving people, goods, and hundreds of thousands of dollars in hard currency to and from New Orleans, Havana, and New York. He was solicitous to his passengers, sometimes stopping at plantations along the river to drop off individual planters and their families at their homes. Newspaper editors gushed that he was "an able commander" and an "urbane gentleman" who was "popular with our citizens and deserves it."[38]

It is perhaps no surprise that he was also a "general favorite of the ladies." He always paid particular attention to the occupants of the ladies cabin, gently tapping at the door to pass along important information and tending to their needs. In New Orleans, schedule permitting, he usually took a room at one of the country's largest and finest hotels, either the recently rebuilt St. Charles or the St. Louis Hotel. His affluent "cabin" passengers often joined him at these luxurious venues. Among them were some of the nation's most important families, such as the future U.S. Secretary of State, Hamilton Fish who travelled with his wife and daughter.[39]

In mid–December of 1854, three of James' closest female confidants arrived in New York. The primary purpose of their trip, however, was not to visit their lonely sailor. James was not even in town when they arrived. He had taken the *Black Warrior* to sea six days before their arrival on his scheduled route to New Orleans via Havana. Martha and daughter Anna Bulloch came to New York City from Charleston on December 15 in the SS *Nashville*, accompanied by Martha's daughter Susan and her husband Hilborne West. Hill and Susan were on their way back to Philadelphia, but Martha and Anna had important nursing duties to fulfill. Mittie was eight months pregnant. Her baby would be Martha's first grandchild and there was nothing that could keep her from her daughter's side.[40]

James returned from his voyage on January 2, just in time to distract his anxious brother-in-law from unnecessary worries. Mittie and Theodore's first child, Anna Eleanor Roosevelt, was born on January 7, 1855. Family members called her "Bamie" or "Bye" (a shortening of "Bambina") even as she grew into adulthood. For now, Bamie was the center of the family's attention. James' female relations soon realized that he too, needed their nurturing presence. His schedule would place him at sea aboard the *Black Warrior* on the one year anniversary of his wife Lizzie's passing.[41]

Two days after Bamie's birth, a young lady boldly marched down the wind-swept pier at the foot of Beach Street of New York City. She carefully crossed the gangway leading to the side-paddle-wheel steamer and into the warmth of the ladies salon. The 21-year-old Anna Louisa Bulloch had left her younger sister Mittie and child to mother Martha's care. Anna was the special guest of Master James D. Bulloch for the voyage of the *Black Warrior* from New York to Havana and New Orleans and return.[42]

Often thought of as the quieter and more sensitive of the two, Mittie's sea-going sister was more adventurous than most would suppose. Even with Brother Jimmie as her sponsor, Anna was among the few single women of her era who would risk the continuous excitement of a long round trip winter voyage. Ocean travel in the mid-nineteenth century was fraught with danger. As reported in the regular "Marine Disasters" newspaper columns, "tempestuous" storms, imperfect navigation, collisions, deadly disease, and horrific boiler explosions were common occurrences. The Bulloch family and friends had personal experience with maritime disasters through the sinking of the *Pulaski*, *Shark*, and *Maria Helena*.[43]

Additional shipwrecks would eventually impact the lives of Bulloch women, but not in the winter of 1855. Anna and Captain Bulloch arrived at the bustling port of New Orleans on January 18. That day, they obtained rooms at the luxurious St. Louis Hotel. Perhaps not coincidentally, James' good friend Captain Jesse Hart also took a room at the nearby St. Charles Hotel. Captain Hart and his wife had taken in an attractive and eligible young widow by the name of Mrs. Harriott Cross Foster. It was Captain Hart's opportunity to play match-maker to his friend James Bulloch. However, between his attention to his shipboard duties and his young sister, James had little time to mourn his wife's death, or consider a new love. Captain Hart's female houseguest would have to wait. James had to supervise the loading of the *Black Warrior* with its return passengers, bales of cotton, hides, sugar, candles, flour, and even 10 barrels of whiskey. He and Anna departed New Orleans in the *Black Warrior* precisely on schedule at 8 a.m. on January 25, only five days after arrival.[44]

By the time they returned to New York 8 days later, "Miss A. Bulloch" had weathered a North Atlantic gale, seen the exotic city of Havana, and experienced first class comfort in the largest and most cosmopolitan southern city of New Orleans. In New York, she continued to bask in the excitement of being with her big brother. On Tuesday evening, February 6th, friends of Captain Bulloch hosted a dinner in his honor at Delmonico's, New York's world-famous restaurant. They presented "the gallant captain with a splendid speaking trumpet, as a token of their regard for him as a man, and their appreciation of his abilities as a commander." Anna found it easy to admire an attentive brother who was so much admired by so many others.[45]

The other good news upon their return was that Mittie and her baby were doing well. It took Mittie over a month after the birth before she was finally able to walk across her room unassisted. Martha and Anna stayed with Mittie and Bamie through the early spring while Hill and Susan West remained in Philadelphia. Hill had left his Roswell farm under the supervision of long-time family friend George Hull Camp. Hill West was attempting to direct cultivation and planting in Roswell through correspondence. James' sailing schedule continued unabated as he made the monthly departure from New York on the ninth or tenth day of each month.[46]

With the spring thaw, Mittie was sufficiently recovered from the delivery to travel. However, to fully regain her health, her husband and mother both thought Mittie needed to leave the unhealthy city for the fresh air of Roswell. Hill and Susan decided to remain in Philadelphia as their dream of becoming Georgia planters began to fade into reality. This time, Theodore accompanied the ladies when they returned to Roswell in late April. Listed as, "Theodore Roosevelt, lady and infant, Mrs. [Martha] Bullock ... [and] Miss [Anna] Bullock [sic]" on the manifest, they sailed directly to Savannah on the SS *Augusta*.[47] Theodore remained only long enough to get Mittie settled before he returned to the family business in New York.

Mittie's stay in Roswell helped restore her health and it also made her realize how much she missed her husband. Soon after he left, she penned these words, "I feel as though I would never wish to leave your side again. You know how much I enjoy being with mother and Anna, but all the same I am only waiting until 'Thee' comes, for you can hardly imagine what a wanting feeling I have when you are gone."[48] The feeling was mutual, as Theodore confessed, "Indeed, bed does not offer me the same inducements as of yore and I rather regret when the time comes for me to retire alone."[49]

Although a poor substitute, "brother Jimmie" provided Theodore much-needed companionship. James even stayed with his brother-in-law while his *Black Warrior* was in port. Together, they visited with Theodore's family, dined, drank wine, talked, and laughed into the late hours of the night. Theodore realized that, "When brother Jimmie goes it will be still more desolate, in fact I don't know what I will do."[50] In Mittie's absence, the Bulloch-Roosevelt bonds of friendship had become permanently sealed, but the *Black Warrior* was ready to sail. On May 9, Theodore wrote Mittie that, "I bid good bye to Brother Jimmie this morning he said he would feel really homesick when he first went to sea this time, my house had seemed like a home to him. I will miss him very much too."[51]

Despite a schedule that kept him almost constantly at sea, James' love life took a more immediate turn for the better that summer. When he departed New Orleans on July 25, 1855, the *Black Warrior's* cargo included 496 bales of cotton, a load of wheat, tobacco, tallow, butter, and the widow Mrs. Harriott Cross Foster. Harriott and her husband, Joseph, had been living with Jesse and Mary Hart since 1850. The Harts had a sugar plantation upriver from New Orleans, near the village of Plaquemine. Captain Hart was a popular Mississippi riverboat captain who had invested his money wisely. Although Joseph Foster died suddenly a few years after he and Harriott had moved in with the Harts, Jesse and Mary continued to play host to his lovely widow.[52]

On August 3, James delivered the 26-year-old Harriott Cross Foster to New York City where she remained until the fall. Harriott waited for the *Black Warrior's* scheduled 2 p.m. departure for New Orleans on November 10, when James once again welcomed her aboard his ship. They were together for eight days and nights when the *Black Warrior* finally arrived at the levee shortly after noon. That same day, James checked into a hotel. This time he chose the St. Charles instead of the St. Louis. Jesse and Mary Hart's son, William, was there to welcome Harriott home. William Hart booked her into the same luxurious accommodations as Captain Bulloch before they returned to Plaquemine. These are the first recorded meetings in the sparse record of James and Harriott's courtship.[53]

As James' romance with Harriott began to gather steam, his professional life shifted to another steamer. In December, the "gallant and able" Bulloch transferred his command to the *Cahawba*, "the other fine vessel of the same line." When he changed ships, he brought John Rodgers, the ship's purser, with him from the *Black Warrior*. Rogers' wife accompanied him on the *Cahawba's* voyages to Havana and New Orleans.[54] James' observation of the couple's intimate companionship helped spur his "genial and affectionate disposition" into action. James made good use of the monthly visits to New Orleans as he energetically pursued Harriott.[55]

By the spring of 1856, the widow Harriott Cross Foster and widower James Dunwoody Bulloch were engaged to be married. In April, they arranged to meet in New Orleans at the St. Charles Hotel. However, in the antebellum South, even 27-year-old widows needed a chaperone. Mrs. Jesse Hart served as Harriott's escort. James, Harriott and Mrs. Hart used their time together for developing plans for their wedding at the Harts' plantation home.[56]

While one Bulloch prepared for a life-changing event, the remainder of his Roswell family made similar life-changing plans. While still in Roswell, Mittie hoped that Theodore and Brother Jimmie made "a mistake in thinking she [mother] is obliged to sell the house." She protested that Martha was not in debt, but Mittie worried that, "If she stays here, the repairs of this house would be much more than her furnishing the quarters."[57] By the time Mittie (listed as "Mrs. Rosevelt [*sic*] and infant") returned to New York City in late September, she became convinced that her mother should sell Bulloch Hall while she could.[58]

Back in Philadelphia, Hill and Susan West began to tie up loose ends.

One final piece of their Roswell property they had not sold was the slave William, a carpenter. Unfortunately, nobody in Roswell wanted to buy him. Hill could have found another buyer in Savannah, but Reverend Pratt owned William's wife. True to their benign paternalism, neither Hill West nor Rev. Pratt wanted to separate the couple. Roswell's slaves were still treated as property and had few individual rights. However, some slaves, both male and female, were able to influence important aspects of their lives by carefully manipulating their owners. Rev. Pratt eventually found a buyer for both William and his wife in Savannah, "where a good home awaited them." However, just when all seemed settled, William's wife "changed her mind and declined going. This embarrassed matters..." Finally, William convinced George Camp to buy him, "from proper motives and desires." George used $1,100 from his wife's account to purchase William from Hilborne West. Mr. Camp found that not only was William a good carpenter, he earned a dollar a day for his new master.[59]

For her part, Martha had to confront changing emotional and financial realities. Her only grandchild and two of her daughters were far-removed from Roswell. Even more importantly, the expenses of maintaining her cherished home had begun to overwhelm her meager resources. Martha had to down-size her household staff. Her motivation was a combination of altruism, practicality, and finances. She sold Anna's long-time servant Bess so that the slave could with be with her husband. Martha no longer needed as many servants and the sale of Bess, along with three others, helped balance her accounts. Just before Mittie's departure, Martha either sold her slave Henry and his family or used him as collateral to borrow between $2,500 and $2,700 (equivalent to $71,810–77,550 in 2015). By Christmas of 1855, Martha had rented Bulloch Hall and sold most of her furniture to her neighbor Tom King. Her trusted household slaves Daddy Luke Mounar and his wife Charlotte remained in place to help manage the home. In the late fall of 1855, Martha headed north with daughter Anna and son Irvine in tow, just as she had so many times in the past. This time, however, she had no plans to return.[60]

Although Martha relocated to Philadelphia, the nation's second largest city, one of her first communal acts was reminiscent of her arrival in tiny Roswell. She formed a new church. On April 3, 1856, she, along with "Hilborne West, M.D., Mrs. Susan E. West," and daughter Anna became charter members of the Tenth Presbyterian Church of Philadelphia, at the corner of Spruce and Seventeenth Streets. Their pastor, Rev. William P. Breed, and Hilborne West shared interests as managers for the Pennsylvania Colonization Society. The society was one of many that opposed slavery but saw immediate emancipation as unrealistic. The Society promoted and financed the return of freed slaves to American colonies in Africa and other tropical lands. The church's charter generously listed Hill as a medical doctor. Hill had decided to switch vocations and was a member of the Academy of Natural Sciences of Philadelphia in 1855, but he had not yet graduated from medical school. By the fall of 1856, Hill enrolled at the Jefferson Medical College in Philadelphia, where he graduated in 1858.[61]

The missing member of the family in the register of new church members was Martha's youngest child, the feisty Irvine Stephens Bulloch, a "big, well built" 15-year-old boy. Martha enrolled him in Dr. Faires' Classical Institute, one of the most exclusive and best college preparatory schools in Philadelphia. According to one of his classmates, Irvine was usually a well behaved student, but

> he [Irvine] sat behind a very offensive boy whom he felt it his duty to constantly chastise. This he did by giving him, from time to time, a loud smack in the face which could be heard throughout the school. ... Dr. Faires had a warm regard for Bulloch, who was a boy after his own heart, but he had told him repeatedly his assaults must stop. Catching him one day in the act, the Doctor became much enraged.... Seizing his heaviest cane, he ran across the room. Bulloch escaped to another aisle, the boys guarding his retreat as effectively as possible until he reached the door, when, raising his hand, he cried: "Dr. Faires, you cannot flog me and I do not want to fight with you. I know, of course, I will have to leave the school; so, good bye, fellows, I am awfully sorry to go."[62]

Rather than being expelled, Irvine completed his prep school work at Dr. Faires' Institute and entered the University of Pennsylvania in 1859 where he remained a student until the spring of 1861. For fun, or perhaps to help him channel his energy, Martha sent Irvine to New York in November of 1858 where he served as a deck hand for Theodore's brother, Robert B. Roosevelt. Robert was a successful lawyer and member of the New York Yacht Club. His yacht was the *Edda*, a "trim sloop yacht of fifteen tons, thirty feet long, painted white."[63] When Irvine was away at school in September of 1859, the *Edda* capsized in a squall. Tragically, the three female passengers drowned. As a result, Robert Roosevelt lost his enthusiasm for yachting, but Irvine did not. After he salvaged the *Edda*, Uncle Robert's wealthy friend and fellow Yacht Club member, Lawrence Waterbury, added Irvine to the crew of the *Julia*. She was "the queen of the yacht squadron" and had never been beaten in a race. Irvine remained a part-time deck hand on the *Julia* through the end of 1860.[64]

In addition to directing the activities of her youngest child, Martha continued to worry about all of her children. Her fully grown stepson James Dunwoody Bulloch was no exception. None of the Bulloch ladies had ever met Harriott, James' bride-to-be. As a result, they had considerable angst about his choice. In November, Martha expressed her concerns to Mittie in a letter written from her new home in Philadelphia. Martha's words also reveal a painful personal experience, perhaps stemming from her first marriage to Senator John Elliott, a man who was over twice her age. She told Mittie that, "I have been thinking a great deal of dear James. I hope he loves that lady. Of all things I think marriage without love must be the most uncomfortable."[65]

When James confidently captained the *Cahawba* out of New York harbor on January 12, 1857, he took a family member with him who could provide an unbiased opinion about the young widow. Brother-in-law Theodore Roosevelt was more than a passenger; he was the sole family member of the groom's wedding party. After briefly touching in Havana, they arrived in New Orleans on January 21. From there they rushed up river to Plaquemine, Louisiana and hired two carriages for an eight hour ride to Sunny Side plantation, the home of their hosts, Captain and Mrs. Jesse Hart. Sunny Side was "a residence of the raised cottage type, with a cypress upper story over a plastered-brick" lower level.[66] Despite the "execrable" roads that delayed their arrival until 10 p.m., they felt "fresh as larks" when they finally set foot inside the Hart's home on the east side of Bayou Grosse Tete. There, they "received a very hearty welcome and in about half an hour a haunch of venison a quantity of birds, hot coffee, wild duck, and fixing."[67]

Theodore dutifully described Harriott as having,

> light hair, blue eyes, and the ordinary peculiarities of a blond, but is dependent more on expression for her pleasant appearance than on anything else. Her figure is very tall but not awkward and she is what I think would be termed a fine looking woman by this casual observer. She calls me brother "Thee," and I think is one we will all learn to like exceedingly.[68]

Harriott's mother was the former Louise von Schaumberg from Louisiana and her father was Osborne Cross, a quartermaster supply officer in the U.S. Army. At the time of his daughter's wedding, Major Cross was in California and it appears that he and Mrs. Cross may have been separated by more than geography. Theodore made no mention of Mrs. Cross at the wedding and Major Cross does not appear in any of the family correspondence before or after the war.[69]

James and Harriott Cross Foster were married at the unusual hour of 1:00 a.m. on Friday, January 23. The reason for the late hour was supposedly "to have it over before the company arrived." However, it could not have been lost on James' conscience that January 23 was the third anniversary of his wife Lizzie's death. Deliberately placing that somber reminder behind them, the couple's ceremony "passed off delightfully." Theodore confessed that he "enjoyed everything to the full limit." He even helped prepare a salad for the wedding reception dinner that inadvertently mixed chicken and lobster. Surprisingly, the accidental concoction generated "twenty or thirty compliments upon my [Theodore's] dressing"[70]

The wedding party could not linger at Sunny Side. James had to hurry back to New Orleans to get the *Cahawba* underway on January 27. After the wedding, they headed back to New Orleans over the same muddy roads, stopping for dinner that included, "several bottles of first rate claret." Theodore was amazed at the drinking ability of the southerners, "Mittie, ... it beats anything you can conceive of."[71] A New Orleans newspaper editor congratulated his friend Captain Bulloch, "on his good fortune in securing to himself a mate of the voyage of life; and hope they may always experience favorable gales, clear skies, and pleasant havens." Theodore discretely made his way back to New York via another route, while Harriott traveled as an undocumented guest of the captain on the *Cahawba*.[72]

The Bullochs and Roosevelts all reunited in New York and entered into a pleasant routine of visits, dinners, carriage rides, and yacht races. As Theodore had predicted, "Sister Harriott" meshed well with her new family. Thanks, in part, to the frequent presence of Robert Hutchison, that new family circle extended to Bulloch's former in-laws, the Caskies of Richmond.[73]

It was not long before Harriott was expecting her first child. She returned to Louisiana in 1858 for the birth, possibly to be with her mother or Captain and Mrs. Jesse Hart. Once again, Harriott traveled as an undocumented passenger on her husband's ship. All was well on April 29 when she delivered James Dunwoody Bulloch, Junior. It was two days after her sailor husband had departed New Orleans on his return trip to New York. She and the baby were well enough to travel by late September. The proud papa then settled his family into "comfortable rooms in West 21st" Street in New York City. His stepmother Martha proudly noted that "little Jimmy is the largest child of his age that I have ever seen."[74]

In October, Martha and Anna Bulloch temporarily moved into Mittie and Theodore's New York brownstone at 33 East 20th Street. They had come in anticipation of the birth of Mittie's second child. When Mittie went into labor, her regular doctor was ill and could not attend to the delivery. Brother Jimmie was at sea, but Harriott helped Martha fetch her own doctor. Mittie was in great pain, and Martha reported that she "continued to get worse and worse until quarter to eight in the evening when the birth took place—She had a safe, but severe time." The Bulloch family's newest baby was a boy that Mittie named after his father. Theodore Roosevelt, Junior, became known to the family as Teedie, but the world would call him Teddy, the 26th president of the United States.[75]

The Roosevelts' brownstone home was close to the Bullochs' apartment and family contact was frequent. Those visits included the precocious 3-year-old Bamie Roosevelt. The arrival of a cousin and a younger brother delighted her. Bamie told her grandmother Martha Bulloch that, "she has two babies now, little Jimmie [Bulloch, Jr.] and her own little baby [Theodore Roosevelt, Jr.]."[76]

Other close family ties included Mr. and Mrs. James Caskie of Richmond. James was the brother of Lizzie and Mary, the deceased wives of Captain Bulloch and Robert Hutchison. The Caskies had invited Anna Bulloch to visit them in Richmond while she was in New York. Excited by the opportunity, she accepted. Shortly after the birth of the two baby boys, Anna returned to her sister Susan West's home in Philadelphia. From there, Robert Hutchison escorted Anna to Richmond for an extended visit that stretched into December. Miss Bulloch credited her older brother for the parties thrown in her honor and the attention everyone lavished upon her in Richmond, saying,

> How very popular brother Jimmie must have been here, so many of his old friends pay me attention for his sake. ... Mrs. Fitz Hugh Mayo ... chaperoned me to a large party entirely on brother Jimmie's account and dwelt in such enthusiastic tones on his fascinating manner ways and looks. ... Love to brother Jimmie and Hattie [Harriott] and do ask her how many teeth little Jimmie has. I have had to enter into the most minute detail in my description of him to old Mr. Caskie.[77]

One other important Bulloch lady joined the family while America was still a peaceful land. Harriott gave birth to their first daughter on January 17, 1860, once again while James was at sea. Harriott and James named her Jessie Hart Bulloch in honor of their wedding host, the sugar planter and riverboat captain Jesse Hart.[78]

James had taken command of a new-construction steamer named the *DeSoto* the previous August. Otherwise, he maintained his normal monthly sailing schedule. He was back at sea on Sunday, March 11, when stepmother Martha paid Harriott a visit. Harriott had not been well, so rather than attending church, Martha collected the five-year-old Bamie and together they went to see Harriott and her "little plump baby." Martha observed that Jessie was, "very good and sweet looking" and reported that, "James is devoted to it." Harriott quickly recovered from her illness despite trying to keep up with an infant and a rambunctious two-year-old. Martha noted that "Little Jimmie" was "as bad as ever with his mischief."[79]

Martha was back in New York City that winter to help Mittie with the birth of her third child, Elliott, who was born on February 28. Martha returned to Philadelphia where the June census recorded her, Anna, and Irvine as living with Dr. Hill and Susan West. Mittie, however, continued to suffer from post-partum health and depression issues. Her incapacity prompted Anna to become a full time and much-loved governess. Anna and Martha's financial situation also played a role in the decision, but Anna was clearly devoted to Mittie and her family. In an era that stigmatized single ladies of marrying age as "spinsters," Anna chose to shun matrimony at least until the Roosevelt children were older.

That summer, the Bullochs found a more permanent residence in Morristown, New Jersey. The resort city provided easy access to New York City, Philadelphia, and the areas of New Jersey that were popular with the elite families of New York. It became the Roosevelt clan's favorite summer retreat. Predictably, Martha spent much of her time there as well.[80]

Sadly, the idyllic days of peace and prosperity were not to last. The tipping point for the Bulloch family came on April 13, 1861. James was loading freight in New Orleans as Master of his latest steamship, the *Bienville*, when the news of Fort Sumter and the outbreak of civil war reached him. That same morning, he wrote the former Senator from Louisiana, Judah P. Benjamin, who was then the Attorney General of the Confederate States of America. James was prepared to go to war in the service of the Southern Confederacy.[81]

4

Ironclad Petticoats:
Confederate Belles at War

Harriott Bulloch was in the ninth month of her third pregnancy when her husband made his decision to fight for the South. Most of the Bulloch family was now north of the Mason-Dixon Line, as were their friends, property, and business interests. When James Bulloch returned to New York from New Orleans, he found a letter from the temporary Confederate capital at Montgomery, Alabama awaiting him. Judah P. Benjamin, the Confederate Attorney General had written to accept James' offer of service. He promptly resigned his command of the *Bienville*.[1]

James required only ten days to settle his personal and business affairs before departing by train and steamer for Montgomery. He had to insulate Theodore and Mittie Roosevelt and Hill and Susan West from knowing too much about his activities. The Lincoln government was in the process of suspending civil liberties in an effort to root out disloyal citizens. As a result, his primary trusted agents had to be his wife Harriott and stepmother Martha, who received title to his few possessions. His immediate family members, however, including the Roosevelts and Wests, were well aware of his basic plans.[2]

Only the presence of Theodore and Mittie and the rest of the Bulloch clan could ease the strain of this difficult separation. Harriott and the children would have to join him at a later date. But join him where and when? In his memoirs about his work in the secret service, James said little about family matters and never even mentioned the Roosevelts. However, he went to great lengths to make it appear that he knew nothing of his mission or final destination until after he arrived in Montgomery late on the evening of May 7. The truth of the matter was that two days before his arrival at the Southern capital, a Federal Customs agent at the Niagara Falls border crossing into Canada knew where he was going and what he would do when he got there. "Capt J.D. Bulloch" was headed for Liverpool, England. Upon arrival, he would purchase guns and warships for the Confederacy. If the federal government knew where he was going, so did Harriott. First, he had to get there and Harriott had a baby to deliver before she could travel.[3]

On his way to Montgomery, James spent a night in Philadelphia, where Martha, Anna, and Irvine Bulloch still lived with Hilborne and Susan (Susy) West. While James' natural characteristic was to be tight-lipped about his activities, the family was aware that his departure was permanent. He had to trust his pregnant wife, two children under the age of four, and all of his tangible assets to their care.

As the unity of the country disintegrated, Martha and Anna Bulloch were torn by conflicting bonds of family and finances. Their male family members had cast their lots with the Confederacy. James Dunwoody Bulloch was on his way to serve its navy. The youngest of the three, Irvine Stevens Bulloch, also went south in May, possibly in the company of his brother. Martha's only other son was Daniel Stuart Elliott.

Daniel was charming and handsome, well over 6 feet tall with engaging steel grey eyes. He was a talented musician, who had entertained at Mittie's wedding. He also had "a fine bass voice" and sang in the choir of Savannah's Independent Presbyterian Church with his wife, the former Lucinda Ireland Sorrel. The 32-year-old Lucy was a diminutive 5' 3" beauty with dark hair and eyes, a square chin, and fair complexion. Like Stuart, her singing voice "charmed her hearers," but there was little room in her heart for music in June of 1861. Stuart was a troubled soul who had a nasty habit of becoming involved in disputes that resulted in duels and at least two deaths.[4]

While the rest of the family migrated north, Daniel had remained in Georgia with his wife Lucy and their two children. By 1861, he was suffering from tuberculosis. Martha's instinct was to return home to Georgia, but the absence of male family members left her and Anna "without any available escort" to help them get there. Martha's need for a white male escort was more than conformity to southern cultural norms. She was more than capable of traveling alone, but there was a very real need for someone to protect her against physical and legal dangers from two countries at war.[5]

James' absence was a result of a call to service that came from the highest levels of the Confederate government. Irvine's was more impromptu and taken at his own initiative. In April of 1861, he had just begun the third term of his sophomore year at the University of Pennsylvania. By the end of May, Irvine was in Mobile. The next month he was in Savannah and then Roswell where he lobbied for a commission as an officer. Irvine's return to the South closely matched his brother's departure from New York. Although James gave no hint that Irvine accompanied him as he traveled south by rail and steamboat in early May of 1861, the timing is curiously coincidental.[6]

Irvine was in Savannah by the end of the month and had found a position in the Confederate Navy serving on the CSS *Savannah*, a former merchant steamer. Like his brother had been before him, Irvine was under the command of John Newland Maffitt. Maffitt happened to arrive in Montgomery on May 7, the same day as Irvine's brother James. At this point in the war, James could not take Irvine to Liverpool with him, but he probably had an unrecorded meeting with his former commander Maffitt. It would have been easy for James to persuade his former shipmate to include Irvine in Maffitt's crew and help him obtain a commission as a midshipman.[7]

Irvine covered his bases and applied for an officer's commission in the Confederate Army. On the last day of May, he garnered an influential endorsement from Colonel William J. Hardee. Col. Hardee, who would be promoted to Lieutenant General, commanded Fort Morgan and Fort Gaines protecting the entrance to Mobile Bay. In his endorsement, the colonel said that Irvine had "fine talents, [was] manly in his bearing, of robust constitution." Due to his youth and lack of experience, Hardee believed Irvine should enter service as a cadet.[8]

On May 13, 1861, while Irvine and James were busy traveling to their new assignments, the family suffered a tragic loss. Their close friend, relative, and benefactor, Robert Hutchison, died "very quietly" in Savannah.[9] Daniel Elliott's wife Lucy mourned Robert's loss saying, "indeed we have lost a friend, one I can never find again I am sure on Earth."[10] In anticipation of his demise, Robert was "in full possession of his mind" and signed his last will and testament on April 26.[11]

Other than Robert's two surviving daughters, Nannie and Ellen, the largest sum went to James Dunwoody Bulloch. James inherited Hutchison's books, wines, liquors, and household furniture. He also received the portraits of his grandfather Senator John Elliott and aunt/stepsister, Corinne Elliott, who had been Robert's first wife. The most significant portion of James' inheritance was $30,000 "in bonds of the City of Columbia." Other than James, Hutchison's primary beneficiaries were women. Martha received $5,000 and her daughters Susan, Anna, and Mittie received $1,000 each, as did Jane (Dunwody) Glen, Corinne Elliott Lawton, Corinne Louisa Quarterman, Nannie Caskie, and Mrs. Louisa Gilmer. Robert also left $5,000 to Martha's son Daniel Stuart Elliott. In an acknowledgement of Daniel's illness, Robert provided $1,000 each for Lucy and her two children in the event Daniel did not survive him. The Savannah Widows Society received $1,000 as did the Savannah Independent Presbyterian Church. Irvine received $1,000 as did four other male Bulloch relatives: Dr. William G., Joseph G. and Robert Hutchison Bulloch, and Robert's brother-in-law James K. Caskie.[12]

Robert left his "negro wench, Dinah, who has for many years been a faithful servant in my family," to Mrs. Louisa Porter of Savannah. True to his ethic of benign paternalism, Robert did not set Dinah free. Instead, he added $200, "to defray any expenses" associated with owning the slave. He then made this provision:

> Dinah shall receive out of my estate, a weekly allowance in money so long as the said Dinah may live of two dollars and fifty cents (2.50), and that the city, county and state taxes for which said Dinah may be liable, shall in addition be paid out of my estate. I hope that my dear friend Mrs. Porter may be induced to take Dinah into her own service; she will find her invaluable for fidelity, capacity and attachment.[13]

The remainder of Hutchison's estate went to his two surviving daughters, Nannie and Ellen. The 10-year-old Nannie was Robert's daughter by his second wife Mary Caskie (1833–1852). The 3-year-old Ellen was named after his third wife Ellen Caskie (1836–1858). Both girls had been living with their Caskie relatives in Richmond since Ellen's death, which had occurred one week after young Ellen's birth in March 1858. Robert named six male executors, including James D. Bulloch, Daniel Elliott, and Alexander Lawton. Both James and Lawton doubled as guardians for the girls along with Martha and Susan, Mr. and Mrs. James and Eliza Caskie, and their nephew James K. Caskie, Mrs. Porter, and Mrs. Gilmer.[14]

Robert's bequest was more than generous. Every $1,000 in 1861 was equivalent to about $28,200 in terms of 2015 purchasing power. Hutchison's largess, however, could only benefit those who could collect their inheritance. By joining the Confederate cause, James had not only abandoned a lucrative career, he left his substantial portion of the estate unclaimed.

By June 18, Irvine was in Savannah and had reported for duty with Captain Maffitt on the CSS *Savannah*. He took time to obtain a second endorsement for his army appointment from Brigadier General Alexander R. Lawton, who commanded Georgia's seacoast defenses. The general noted that Irvine was an "ardent and capable youth" who would make an excellent cadet. As one of the executors of Robert Hutchison's will, General Lawton also could advise Irvine on how to manage the inheritance of the Bulloch family members who were no longer in the South.[15]

The easiest way to transfer the funds to the Bulloch ladies in Philadelphia and New York would be to send a letter of credit via England or one of its colonies, such as the Bahamas or Bermuda. However, the Lincoln government had disrupted normal maritime commerce when it declared a blockade of southern ports in April of 1861. Although the Union fleet's initial blockade of Savannah proved to be ineffective, at this early stage of the war, merchants were not willing to risk challenging it. Irvine and James tried to have the bonds transferred to Martha, but Georgia's tax records for 1862 show that they were not successful. James' inheritance was still in place at Savannah in 1862. His share was valued at $30,000 in cash, plus $1,000 in household goods, and $2,500 in other property, for a total of $33,500. As difficult as it was to convert the city bonds into cash, James would have to take extraordinary measures to get possession of the household goods and other property.[16]

While he was in Savannah, Irvine also had time to visit his stepbrother Daniel Stuart Elliott, his wife Lucy, and their children. At this stage of Daniel's troubled life, friends and family called him "Stuart." In recent months, Stuart's health had taken a turn for the worse. The outbreak of the Civil War exacerbated Martha's worries about him and her own financial well-being. James and Irvine had gone off to war and she could no longer access her investments or her loved ones in the South. Fortunately, Martha's nephew William J. Bulloch of Savannah managed to send a dividend payment from her Georgia Central Railroad holdings through the lines. This unexpected infusion of cash, plus her Beaver Meadows (Pennsylvania) Railroad and Coal shares temporarily removed a "great cause of anxiety." Irvine's efforts to obtain Martha's cash from Robert Hutchison's estate also seemed promising. These positive developments, and the prospect of Stuart's move to Marietta to improve his health, lifted Martha's spirits.[17]

In Philadelphia, Susan and Anna were able to convince Martha to delay any decision about returning to Georgia, "until the fall." They argued that Stuart "may be benefited by the change up to Marietta and by that time some way may be [opened that is] more safe at least [and] not so expensive and long for one of her age." Susan and Hill West had provided Martha and Anna a home since 1855, but as a newly certified medical doctor, Hill's meager earnings could not sustain additional lodgers without assistance. With their finances back in order, Martha and Anna made arrangements to spend the summer at the beach resort city of Long Branch, New Jersey. They would stay at the luxurious Laird's Mansion House and they would not be alone. In fact, they were hoping for a proper escort in the person of Theodore Roosevelt, Sr.:

> Irvine is not here to take care of us. Hill says he will see that we get off safely for New York, if you could plan it so that you could meet us there and let us go from that place with you.[18]

Although Martha and Anna no longer had a mansion or servants of their own, their change in location or circumstances had no effect on their expectations about the respective roles of ladies and gentlemen. Gentlemen were supposed to shield their ladies from any unnecessary contact with the lower classes, including those inherently involved with public transportation. Anna, Martha, Mittie and her children all made it to Laird's resort without incident by mid–June. Although Mittie was six months pregnant with her fourth child, she found Long Branch to her liking. Theodore split his time between family and work in New York City. Part of his work was tending to the overseas travel arrangements for Harriott and her three children who resided in nearby Morristown, NJ.[19]

As the Bullochs and Roosevelts awaited developments in their comfortable summer quarters, Stuart Elliott followed through on his plans to relocate from Savannah. Shortly after his arrival at Marietta, Stuart impulsively decided to join his stepbrothers in military service with the Con-

Laird's mansion house resort, Long Branch, New Jersey. From *Frank Leslie's Illustrated Newspaper*, July 15, 1865.

federacy. Through a combination of self-deception and charm, he joined the army on July 4, 1861. Georgia's Governor, Joseph E. Brown, optimistically administered the oath at Camp McDonald, a training post on the Chattahoochee River, about six miles southeast of Marietta. The 36-year-old Stuart signed up as a private for the duration of the war.[20]

Irvine may have witnessed Stuart's swearing-in ceremony for he had been in nearby Roswell since June 21. Irvine turned 19 on June 25 and could have joined the army as a private along with Stuart. Irvine, however, was not destined to become a soldier. On August 24, 1861, Irvine Stevens Bulloch followed in his older brother's footsteps and received an appointment as an Acting Midshipman in the Confederate Navy. By the time of Irvine's commission, Private Stuart had transferred to a cavalry company of Phillip's Legion with the Georgia State Volunteers.[21]

James D. Bulloch was now a secret agent for the Confederate Navy, but he had to get out of the country before he could go to work. Rather than risk running the blockade, James decided that the safest route from Montgomery to Liverpool was via the inland route to Canada. On May 13, James boarded a train from Montgomery to Louisville and transferred to a river steamer. He arrived in Detroit by train two days later. From there, he crossed Lake Erie and arrived in Montreal via the Grand Trunk Railway on or about May 15. That day, a reporter from the Richmond *Dispatch* destroyed any secrecy that might have covered his mission. In a story filed from Montgomery, the reporter wrote that,

> A warrant for seven hundred thousand dollars has been recently drawn by the Navy Department for the use of J.D. Bullock [*sic*] ... for the probable cost of ten steam gun-boats for coast defenses, to be built or purchased as might be deemed most expedient. $400,000 of the amount was paid in bills of exchange on London, and the remainder by letters of credit on the Bank of Liverpool. Bulloch is in England, the agent of the Government in the matter.[22]

The story exposed James' secret mission before he even arrived in England, but at least he was out of the country. On May 17, James departed Montreal on the SS *North American*, bound for Liverpool via Quebec City. On the same day that he launched his eventful life as a not-so-secret foreign agent, his wife, Harriott, launched a new life of her own. Henry Dunwody Bulloch was born in New York City as his father made the twelve hour transit from Montreal to Quebec City. Once again, James was absent for the birth of his child. As the *North American's* bow plunged into the ocean swells, Bulloch had the confident hope that he and his fellow passengers would reach port safely. He prayed that his family and his new country would be equally fortunate.[23]

James had little time for personal matters when he arrived in Liverpool in early June of 1861. He had to establish his credentials and a large line of credit based solely on his personal credibility, which was considerable. Despite being hounded by agents hired by the Union government, James quickly signed contracts for two warships and got them under construction. They would become the famous Confederate cruisers, CSS *Florida* and *Alabama*. He also started moving supplies to the Confederacy, in conjunction with his Army counterpart, Caleb Huse, and the firm of Fraser, Trenholm. In mid–August, they dispatched the SS *Bermuda* to Savannah laden with 25,550 rifles and other valuable military supplies. It would be the first government-sponsored ship to test the blockade. In the midst of his wartime duties, James also made initial arrangements for his family to join him in Liverpool.[24]

Harriott had been raised in a military family and was accustomed to frequent relocations. She had landed on her feet after the death of her first husband in Louisiana. She was also wise enough in the ways of the world to travel on her own to New York and New Orleans. Now, she was the wife of a sailor who seemed to be gone every time she needed him most. Even with these experiences to bolster her confidence, she had never lived overseas or experienced the challenges of being the wife of a Navy man, much less of a government secret agent. Even with her obvious self-sufficiency, uprooting her entire household across an ocean in the midst of a war without her husband was a difficult task.

For her part, Harriott had to determine when to leave, what to take with her, and how to protect the property left behind. Unlike her counterparts in the South, she was not running away as a refugee. She was an immigrant, joining her husband overseas. Other refugee women of the South were forced to take charge of family affairs as they fled from bombarding Yankee fleets and invading armies. They had to improvise as they scavenged for transportation to uncertain destinations. Harriott was in charge of family affairs and her course was set for Liverpool. Her transportation options were limited, but they were clear cut. She would take a steamer from New York to Liverpool.[25]

Even though survival was not her chief worry, Harriott still had to contend with the culture shock of living in a foreign country. The language was familiar, but different. The people, manners, neighborhoods, shops, and schools were much different. Even worse, she was leaving her support circle of family and friends. She would have to find her own way to make a home and raise three children under the age of four.

The unseen hand of Mittie and her husband Theodore Roosevelt made Harriott's initial task a bit easier. They were the likely benefactors who provided the two maids and one manservant who accompanied Harriott and her three children to Liverpool. With Harriott in charge, her entourage set out from New York City in the SS *Persia* on August 28, 1861. Just over three months had elapsed since she gave birth to little Dunnie, and now she was headed for a new life in Liverpool.[26]

In Great Britain, James took a short break from his frenetic deal-making travels as a secret agent. He returned to Liverpool on September 4 where he eagerly greeted his wife and children two days later. After a four month separation, Harriott took comfort in the thought her family was finally reunited and far removed the bloody battlefields of America. She also brought her husband some fresh intelligence of her own. Traveling with her on the *Persia* was the new American Consul to Paris, John Bigelow, along with his wife, four children, and a servant. Bigelow later became the U.S. Minister to France and wrote an exposé of his machinations to thwart Bulloch's efforts on the Continent. Bigelow titled his book, *France and the Confederate Navy, 1862–1868: An International Episode.*[27]

James had found temporary quarters for his family at Mrs. Danley's boarding house (6 Oxford St.) in Liverpool. From her base of operations at the boarding house, Harriott managed the details of settling the family in a foreign country. She also graciously entertained her husband's fellow Confederate agents who frequently visited and dined with the family. All was not well, however. Soon after Harriott's arrival, James revealed his plan to run the blockade into the Confederacy. This unwelcomed, but predictable development meant that her husband would be risking his life in a war zone. During the first year of the war, the federal government threatened to execute Confederate privateers as stateless pirates. Although his ship, the SS *Fingal*, was primarily a blockade runner, it would indeed be carrying guns. James had every intention of mounting them and planned to blast his way into port if needed.[28]

Both Union and Confederate forces had been aware of Bulloch's intentions for several weeks. When the Confederate blockade runner *Bermuda* docked in Savannah, "under English colors" on September 18, its captain, Eugene Tessier, brought intelligence that, "Captain Bulloch and Mr. Edward C. Anderson will soon leave England, each in command of fully appointed steam vessels of war." Major Anderson was a former U.S. Navy officer and the former mayor of Savannah. He was in Liverpool as a major in the Confederate Army. His mission was to check up on Captain Caleb Huse, but he ended up assisting Huse and Bulloch with their military supply efforts. The intelligence carried on the *Bermuda* was only partially correct, but plans were clearly afoot for Bulloch and Anderson to return to Savannah.[29]

Back in New York City, Mittie delivered her own baby a month after Harriott's departure (September 27). Mittie named her second daughter Corinne, after her deceased stepsister and Robert Hutchison's first wife who had died on the *Pulaski*. Mittie's older sister Anna was there to assist with her growing brood of children. For most of the next four years, the 28-year-old Anna continued in her role as governess and teacher for the Roosevelt children. Her nursery included Anna's namesake Anna Eleanor (Bamie, 6), Theodore (Teedie, 35 months), Elliott (Ellie, 19 months), plus the infant Corinne, affectionately nicknamed "Conie." Martha Bulloch remained in Long Beach on the Jersey shore, where she awaited developments to see where she was needed most.

Martha advised her daughter Susan that, "We have not written to Harriott yet because we have heard that the House to which we direct is in bad repute here, consequently, our letters would not leave N. York." In fact, Harriott had not received any of their letters sent by U.S. mail. In August, U.S. President Abraham Lincoln had issued a proclamation that made all communications between the North and South unlawful. This action provided a semblance of legal cover for Union officials who already had been intercepting personal correspondence. Accordingly, Union postmasters kept an even closer watch on letters to or from suspected Confederates. This scrutiny forced the Bulloch ladies to seek alternative means of communication.[30]

Letters that James and Harriott sent from Liverpool to their female relations in the North suffered a similar fate, but from an entirely different source. One of Theodore Roosevelt, Sr.'s brothers, James Alfred Roosevelt, reported that he had seen letters from James D. Bulloch. According to the letters, the Confederate naval agent had asked "associates" to transfer his properties "to other parties so that it may not be confiscated by action of the United States Government." Mr. J.A. Roosevelt took this information to Hiram Barney, the U.S. customs official for New York. Mr. Roosevelt did not, however, reveal the names of Bulloch's associates, i.e., his brother Theodore and Martha Bulloch.[31]

Customs Officer Barney reported his discussions with James Roosevelt to U.S. Secretary of State Seward on July 10, 1861. Barney's report also included information derived from recent press clippings regarding Bulloch's efforts in England to purchase "ten warships ... at an expense about $750,000 for the use of the Southern Confederacy as a naval force." Barney rationalized Roosevelt's breach of family trust by observing that

Roosevelt was, "an ardent Union man and would feel bound to denounce a brother probably to save the Government, but he does not wish his name used if it can be avoided."[32]

The success of the *Bermuda's* run into Savannah further intensified Union government scrutiny of James' activities and everyone connected to him. Union spies had collected timely information about the *Bermuda*, including its cargo and probable destination, but they were unable to stop or intercept the shipment. As a result, James had frustrated and infuriated the Union Secretary of the Navy Gideon Welles and the entire U.S. diplomatic corps. Even though James only claimed a minor role in the *Bermuda's* success, U.S. officials saw the persistent handiwork of James Dunwoody Bulloch at work.[33]

James' role in the next blockade running adventure would take center stage, as he loaded his newest steamer, the *Fingal*, with an even larger cache of military supplies. Like the *Bermuda*, the *Fingal* would carry the British flag. This time, however, the British captain would only have nominal command of the steamer. James was the man in charge. The frustrated American Minister to the United Kingdom, Charles F. Adams, singled James out in a September dispatch to Secretary of State Seward, saying, "Mr. Bulloch appears to be the most efficient agent engaged in these operations."[34]

Union spies filed multiple reports about the *Fingal*. They even provided an accurate sketch of the ship and a full listing of its cargo, officers, and general destination. Despite the increased scrutiny, James successfully departed from Holyhead, Scotland on October 15. He was bound for Savannah via the island of Bermuda. After James departed on his dangerous mission, Harriott wrote her sister-in-law, Anna Bulloch, in New York with family news. Although she did not reveal her husband's destination, Harriott confided that he was gone and gave thanks that the children were well. Anna relayed the information to the rest of the family and added the good news that Harriott "likes Liverpool better than she did—She sees a great many southern friends there."[35]

One of Harriott's friends was stepsister Susan West's former doctor, J. Marion Semmes. Dr. Semmes was the brother of Commander Raphael Semmes of the Confederate Navy. Dr. Semmes, like Hilborne West, was a graduate of Jefferson Medical College. He also founded the Hospital for Women in New York City in the 1850s and became known as the father of modern gynecology." The identification of Dr. Semmes as Susan's doctor, suggests that the reason she and Hilborne never had children was a medical issue that the learned doctor could not resolve. By 1861, Dr. Semmes had become the attending physician to Empress Eugenie, the wife of the

French Emperor, Louis-Napoléon Bonaparte. Even though Dr. Semmes was based in Paris, near the imperial palace at Versailles, he evidently passed through Liverpool. Harriott mentioned that she had seen one of the doctor's books that had a special inscription on the fly leaf.[36]

By the fall of 1861, Harriott had recovered from her initial feelings of isolation and loneliness, and began to warm to her new life in England. She volunteered to forward any letters or packages that the Bulloch sisters might have for their family in the Confederacy. Of particular concern was the health of their stepbrother Daniel Stuart Elliott. Stuart was Martha Bulloch's youngest son by her first husband, Senator John Elliott. As his family had known for months, Stuart had the familiar and fatal symptoms of tuberculosis. By the end of September, the Confederate Army declared him unfit for duty due to "pulmonary disease causing repeated hemorrhages." He had been unable to perform his duties "for at least fifty days" out of the past two months. Before the doctors officially certified Stuart's medical discharge, his brother Irvine was at sea. Acting Midshipman Bulloch ran the blockade out of Charleston on the Confederate cruiser CSS *Nashville*.[37]

The *Nashville* arrived in Bermuda and was still in port when James D. Bulloch arrived as the *de facto* captain of the blockade runner *Fingal*. James and Irvine were able to catch up on family news when James dined aboard the *Nashville*. Ironically, James was headed west to the Confederacy and his brother Irvine was headed east for Southampton, England. James subsequently ran the *Fingal* into Savannah on November 12. He and Major Anderson delivered the largest shipment of Confederate military supplies during the entire war. Several months would pass before the Bulloch brothers would meet again in Liverpool.[38]

James quickly turned the *Fingal* over to Confederate officials in Savannah and hurried off to see the Secretary of the Navy, Stephen Mallory, in Richmond, Virginia. During his brief visit to the crowded Confederate capital, James probably stayed with his Caskie in-laws. He would have paid his respects at the graves of his first wife Lizzie as well as his brother-in-law and benefactor, Robert Hutchison. The visit also provided James an opportunity to visit his 10-year-old ward, Nannie Hutchison. Robert had appointed Bulloch as one of several guardians for his daughter by his second wife, Mary Caskie. James addressed one other bit of family business while he was in Richmond. That November, he asked the Navy Department to transfer his brother Irvine from the *Nashville* to the wardroom of the *Alabama*, his new cruiser being built in Liverpool.[39]

James soon returned to Savannah with the hope of running his armed blockade runner, the *Fingal*, back to England under the Confederate flag. The interlude in Savannah gave him the opportunity to visit his ailing stepbrother Stuart Elliott and his wife Lucy. James also took possession of his share of Robert Hutchison's estate from his home in Savannah. Unfortunately for Bulloch and the *Fingal*, the Union Navy had effectively occupied or blockaded all exits from the port. It was important for James to return to Liverpool and resume oversight of the two cruisers he had under construction. The blockade forced him and his small entourage of junior officers to travel overland to Wilmington, North Carolina. From there, they finally ran the blockade on the moonless night of February 5, 1862, as passengers on the *Annie Childs*. It is unknown whether James was able to carry all of his Hutchison inheritance with him from Savannah, but he was able to secure the dinner china and other household goods.[40]

When Martha Bulloch learned of her son Stuart's worsening illness, she could no longer be restrained. She was determined to return to Georgia. Martha had given up hope for a quick negotiated settlement of the Civil War that would have allowed her to return home in peace. The bloody Battle of Manassas/Bull Run on July 21st made it clear that the war would be a long and costly one. The danger to Southern coastal areas was also a certainty. In late August, a combined Union Navy and Army force easily occupied two Confederate Forts at Hatteras inlet in North Carolina. The fall of Port Royal in South Carolina on November 7, 1861, rattled the residents of Savannah and brought the war closer to home for the Bullochs. In response, wealthy Georgia families began to evacuate themselves and their portable property inland. Feeling stranded in the North, Martha desperately sought assistance to get through the battle lines that now separated the North and South.[41]

The best and perhaps the only avenue for that assistance was in the person of her son-in-law Theodore Roosevelt. Theodore was a robust 29 years of age at the outbreak of the war, but he did not serve in the military. Perhaps he chose to avoid active service out of deference to his wife's pro-southern feelings. Mittie could not bear the thought of her husband taking up arms against her three Confederate brothers, James, Irvine, and Stuart. However, as a member of the North's elite society, Theodore, along with all of his immediate male family members, had no expectation of military service.[42]

With the exception of a few political generals like Governor Nathaniel Banks of Massachusetts and Senator John Dix of New York, wealthy men of the North rarely served in the military. They easily avoided the initial calls for troops. When the nation needed even more men, Congress passed the Enrollment Act of 1863. This act might have placed wealthy able-bodied men at risk. However, an otherwise eligible male of means, like Theodore, could and did hire a substitute for about $1,000 (almost $20,000 in 2015). Despite its social inequity, the act was a successful piece of legislation. In less than a year, it added thousands of men to the army and over $12 million in exemption payments to the Union Treasury. Those who did the fighting cynically observed that it was a rich man's war, but a poor man's fight.[43]

Theodore had initially opposed the war factions, but when war became a reality, he was an ardent Unionist. Although he never enlisted, Theodore did fight for the women who were left at home when their sons and husbands went off to war. His social activism was the kind of selfless paternalism that the Bulloch ladies expected of their men, but never considered for themselves. Their domain was the home where they might encourage and support his noble efforts that were played out in public. Theodore and two wealthy friends were the driving force behind the Allotment Act of 1861. Theodore even temporarily relocated to Washington, D.C., in the fall of that year to lobby Congress and President Lincoln. His objective was to introduce and pass a bill that allowed soldiers to voluntarily, "allot a certain portion of their pay to their destitute families." As a first step, he met with President Lincoln's private secretary, John Hay, who arranged a successful private meeting that gained the president's endorsement.[44]

Most congressmen could not understand Roosevelt's moral rather than financial motivation for advocating the Allotment Act. Despite their misgivings, the Allotment Act became law on Christmas Eve of 1861. President Lincoln named Theodore and his two co-sponsors as the unpaid Allotment Commissioners from New York. Theodore was the most active of the three men. Their duties included convincing soldiers within New York army units to set aside money for direct monthly payments to their families. Theodore spent many days and nights traveling by train and horseback to meet face-to-face with soldiers in all kinds of weather. He was remarkably successful in joining men in their field camps and convincing them to sign up for the program. Although the allotment system was not fully operational until April, by mid–June 1862 the U.S. Treasury had distributed $470,376.30 to soldiers' families.[45]

Theodore's selfless work on behalf of families and his charming personality endeared him to the president's wife, Mary Todd Lincoln. Her friendship, however, was not always a positive attribute. The press loudly and routinely criticized Mrs. Lincoln for her extravagance and for the

Mary Todd Lincoln wearing inaugural gown (Library of Congress).

fawning characters who surrounded her. Theodore, however, was flattered by her attentions. Those attentions included an invitation to lavish, high-level White House events, a seat on the president and first lady's pew at church, afternoon carriage rides, and shopping excursions with Mrs. Lincoln. The more important and enduring friendship that Theodore developed during his time in Washington was with John Hay, Lincoln's private secretary.[46]

When Martha Bulloch turned to her son-in-law for assistance in going south, Theodore sought out his new friend, the president's 23-year-old private secretary. Just as he had introduced Theodore to the president, John Hay quickly arranged a meeting with Secretary of State William H. Seward. This arrangement did not take much effort on Hay's part. Seward was an astute politician who also happened to be the former Governor of New York. He was well aware of the Roosevelts' financial and political clout in New York City.[47]

Theodore, however, was not optimistic or encouraging about Martha's prospects to return to her home in Georgia. Unfortunately for Martha's plans, the Bulloch name had become notorious in the North. Union spies had reported Captain James Bulloch's shipment of arms and ammunition into Savannah on the *Bermuda*. James even had the temerity to personally command the *Fingal*, as it too eluded detention. The news quickly spread that James was on his way to the Confederacy with an even larger shipment of war material. On Valentine's Day, Theodore wrote Mittie about his plans, hopes, and fears for his mother-in-law's return to Georgia.[48]

> Hay is going with me to Seward's tonight who, on your mother's account I would prefer meeting first on a friendly footing.
>
> It seems very doubtful whether I can attain the pass in consequence of her connection with Captain Bulloch who is reported to have made a fortune by running in one cargo of contraband goods and to be now in Bermuda preparing to run in another.
>
> I have not given up all hope yet but will keep you informed of my prospects.[49]

Theodore was not fond of seeking out personal favors, but he was very good at it. After his meeting, he garnered Seward's approval for Martha and Anna to pass through the lines. The conditions were severe. They had to meet Theodore in Baltimore no later than the next Friday, March 7. From there he would escort Martha and Anna to Fort Monroe where they could board a flag-of-truce boat and cross into Confederate-held Norfolk. If they chose to leave, both women would have to swear an oath that they would never return.[50]

Martha was not alone in facing sudden decisions about where and with whom to live. Her former female neighbors and Georgia kin were confronting similar difficulties under harsher circumstances. The South's paternalistic social order did not function very well when the men were gone and could not make the ultimate decision. As a displaced southern widow,

Martha was the head of her household. She accepted Hilborne West's and Theodore's assistance, but those men had no control over her or her assets. Theodore advised against her departure, but it was Martha's decision.[51]

In the South, only the wealthy could run away from the invading Yankees. Very little of Martha's wealth remained, but she still owned Bulloch Hall and Roswell offered the prospect of a familiar sanctuary. Unlike most refugees who were resented by those in the communities where they landed, friends and family would welcome Martha and Anna back to Roswell. The village had always been something of a resort community. Families often resided in Roswell for only a portion of the year as the seasons and their moods dictated. Even though Martha had lived in the North for the past several years, Roswell was still home. There was little chance that the current residents of Roswell would treat her with the kind of disrespect that so many displaced aristocratic southern women experienced.[52]

Martha quickly reassessed her financial situation and how she might sustain herself if she left for Georgia. She considered exchanging her Beaver Meadows Coal & Railroad bonds for Jimmie Bulloch's Savannah City bonds. The Beaver Meadows income was not accessible in the South, just as there was no benefit from the Savannah bonds while she was still in the north. Another alternative was to sell the bonds or use them as collateral for a loan from Theodore. Martha had no other income and her projected dividends of $850 per year were insufficient for her and Anna to live on. Anna's concern was that her 63-year-old mother might not survive a long journey. Martha simply was not prepared to travel on trains crowded with human undesirables followed by extended stays in overtaxed accommodations, complete with fleas and bedbugs. In the end, Mittie's tears convinced Martha to stay. The thought of permanent separation from her daughters was more than she could bear.[53]

Meanwhile, the ships of Martha Bulloch's son Irvine and stepson James had literally passed each other in the night. Irvine and James Bulloch both reached their destinations in the Confederacy and England. At dawn on February 28, Irvine's CSS *Nashville* ran past the blockading fleet amid shot and shell and arrived at Beaufort, NC unharmed. Ten days later, James made it back to Liverpool via Dublin and Holyhead after leaving the *Annie Childs* in Queenstown, Ireland. Irvine left the *Nashville* in Beaufort and went to Norfolk. There, he spent five months on the captured schooner, the CSS *Plymouth*, and the new steam gunboat, CSS *Nansemond*. When the Union army forced the Confederates to evacuate Norfolk, Secretary Mallory finally approved James Bulloch's request to transfer his brother, Midshipman Irvine S. Bulloch, to England.[54]

In Georgia, Bulloch's *Fingal* remained bottled up at the Savannah River. At the time, it was arguably the finest ship in the Confederate Navy. However, she and her Mosquito Fleet cohorts in the Savannah Naval Squadron were too lightly armed to risk a direct confrontation with the Union blockading forces. It had become apparent that neither the Confederacy's Navy nor its Army fortresses could withstand the pounding of the Union Navy's big guns. In answer to the Union's superior number of ships and powerful guns, Confederate Secretary of the Navy Mallory advocated the construction of ironclads. He believed that a small number of these "invulnerable" warships could break the blockade and defeat the powerful, but wooden-hulled, ships of the United States Navy.

National interest in Mallory's innovative ironclad strategy gained momentum after the epic battle of the *Monitor* and *Merrimac* (CSS *Virginia*) in early March 1862. The *Monitor* kept the *Virginia* in check but not before the casemated ironclad ram had sunk two of the U.S. Navy's largest wooden warships at Hampton Roads, off Norfolk, VA. This success gave the Confederacy hope that their ingenuity and daring could thwart the overwhelming hordes of wooden-hulled Union blockaders. One of the more intriguing aspects of this enthusiasm for ironclads was the rapid formation of ladies' gunboat societies. Women of Norfolk, Richmond, Mobile, Charleston, New Orleans, inland cities on the Mississippi River, and Savannah all rallied to the cause.[55]

The gunboat societies offered southern women an opportunity to provide substantive aid to the war effort. Their purpose was to raise money and assist the Confederate Navy in building ironclads to protect their homes and communities. The women's efforts were not intended to just advance the interests of sons, husbands, and brothers, they were protecting themselves. The Confederate Army and Navy had taken most of their men away to distant battlefields. The men left behind were too few and too inadequate to the task of protecting women and children from the marauding Yankees. In their subtle way, the ladies' gunboat societies forced men to realize that they had left their dependent family members and homes defenseless. Since the Confederate government had not adequately provided for their protection, the ladies decided to do it themselves. The gunboat societies moved women from familiar domestic and nurturing roles into an extraordinarily different realm: active participation in building weapons of war.[56]

Rather than instigate a direct confrontation that might have alarmed the refined ladies and gentlemen of the South, the gunboat societies pledged that female participants would retain conventional roles. They

paid homage to paternalistic expectations by advocating that all participants adhere to appropriate feminine behavior. Their fund-raising activities relied on traditional feminine methods such as raffles, fairs, bazaars,
elaborate entertainments, and contributions from prominent citizens. The
societies selected respectable and influential men to act as the public face
of their initiatives. They also placed men in the important roles of treasurers and commissioners. The Societies' men assisted with fund-raising,
managing finances, and serving as intermediaries with Confederate construction and naval officials.[57]

In Georgia, numerous women's organizations supported the gunboat
society that officially became known as the Georgia Ladies Iron Clad Battery Association of Savannah. The idea for the ship, commonly called the
"Georgia Ladies' Gunboat," apparently originated with two sisters from
Macon. Mary Ann and Ella Ross set the initiative in motion on March 6,
1862 by suggesting a plan and naming agents to collect funds. About two
dozen Savannah women formed their own committee to translate these
general concepts into action. They appointed a three-member male steering committee and then selected five commissioners, and treasurers. This
small group of prominent men included Mr. G.B. Lamar who was both a
steering committee member and a commissioner. In just two days, the
ladies collected $3,600.[58]

Gazaway B. Lamar was a wealthy Savannah banker and cotton broker.
He had long-standing interests in ships and shipbuilding, including ownership of the ill-fated steamer *Pulaski*. Mr. Lamar had been on board the
steamship *Pulaski* when it exploded. He lost his wife and five of his six
children in the disaster, but was absolved of any blame. His sister Rebecca
was the person most responsible for saving James Bulloch's benefactor,
Robert Hutchison, after Robert had lost his own wife and two little girls.
After the *Pulaski* tragedy, the 63-year-old Lamar continued his interest
in shipbuilding and acquisition projects. In 1861, he had worked with
Charles Green and Andrew Low in their efforts to purchase, outfit, and
load a blockade runner in the United Kingdom. That ship turned out to
be the CSS *Fingal* that ran into Savannah under James Bulloch's command.[59]

Participation in the Savannah Ladies' Gunboat project rapidly spread
throughout the state. Newspapers enthusiastically printed "An Appeal to
the Women of Georgia" addressed to their "Dear Sisters." In a letter dated
March 10, Lizzie Hammond Willis cried out, "Sisters! Women of Georgia!
I make this appeal in no idle spirit. I believe the call to be imperative for
the protection of Georgia's interests, and I sincerely hope that every lady

and child within their limits will respond to the call as liberally as their circumstances will allow."[60]

Miss Willis' appeal was more than a romantic rant. The newspaper column below her letter included six other entries that listed individual contributions from 87 different women. The contributions ranged from as little as 50 cents to a maximum of $10 each. Miss Kate Ann McGinnis made a $1 donation and reported that, "I am a little girl seven years old. I enclose herein One Dollar as my mite for the Georgia Gunboat fund." Zeal for the project continued to spread. Georgia newspapers listed individual contributions in almost every issue. The articles served as both a public acknowledgement and a receipt for individual contributors. The reporting also helped spur competitive giving. Even servant slave girls and school children made contributions.[61]

Participants in the fundraising efforts included those ladies with connections to the Bulloch clan who remained in Georgia. Lucy Elliott's father, Francis Sorrel, was one of the five commissioners. Lucy was a silent partner in his efforts and probably influenced her father's selection as a commissioner. Lucy had to balance her work on behalf of the gunboat with her efforts to care for Stuart, who remained seriously ill with tuberculosis. Martha Bulloch's cousin, Mary Jones, was also hard at work collecting funds at her Montevideo plantation home in Liberty County, Georgia. By mid–March, Mary was "getting on well with her gunboat fund."[62] She completed her work on Saturday, April 5, and "handed the gunboat fund to Mr. Lamar in person."[63]

By July 15, the Ladies' Gunboat was almost ready for commissioning into active service. It had been just over three months since the two sisters from Macon had made the initial suggestion. The highly anticipated ironclad turned out to be little more than a "Floating Battery with propeller." The vessel was barely capable of self-propulsion. The limitations of Savannah's shipyards and machine shops and the lack of skilled workers dictated the limited result. Still, the Ladies' Gunboat was a remarkable achievement. The five commissioners and treasurers of the Ladies' Gunboat Association, including G.B. Lamar and Francis Sorrel, announced its completion in an open letter to "The Ladies of Georgia." After explaining their reasons for building what amounted to an armored barge with guns instead of a gunboat, the letter went on to say,

> The Floating Battery is now ready for any service that may be required, and it has been pronounced by military and naval men of intelligence as a complete success.
> To your patriotic and noble efforts LADIES OF GEORGIA, is the port of the

city of Savannah indebted for this powerful engine for its defence against the hateful foes who are committing depredations upon our defenceless [sic] coasts. ... We believe if the enemy should now attempt an attack by water, they will meet with such a reception from the powerful guns of "The Georgia Ladies' Iron-clad Battery" as will convince them that a country where the women are so decidedly intent upon resistance, cannot be conquered. ...

The Ladies, and other contributors to the Gunboat Fund, are respectfully invited to inspect the "Floating Battery" on Monday and Tuesday next, 14th and 15th instant, at the Exchange Dock.[64]

The ironclad battery was christened CSS *Georgia* and launched on July 19. Its completion, however, came too late to save Savannah's Fort Pulaski. The Union fleet had pounded the fort into rubble and forced the garrison to surrender on April 10. Fortunately for the Ladies' Gunboat, Fort Jackson below Savannah and Fort McAllister to the south on the Ogeechee River remained in Confederate hands and ironclad construction had continued. Commodore Tattnall assigned Lt. John Rutledge, four other officers, and about 40 men to assist with the *Georgia's* final outfit and to man its guns in the event of emergency. The opulent cabins of James Bulloch's *Fingal* provided berthing for Lt. Rutledge's officers. The ship's velvet upholstery and magnificent mirrors impressed everyone. *Georgia's* Assistant Surgeon Dr. Robert Reeve Gibbes gushed that the *Fingal* had, "the most elegant accommodations and apartments I have witnessed in any Ocean Steamer."

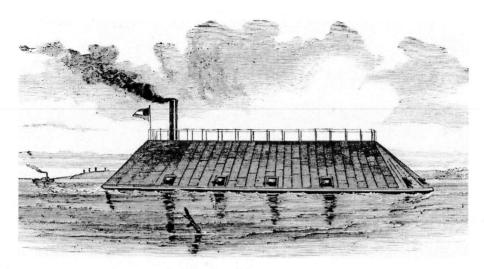

The ladies' ironclad CSS *Georgia*. From Paul F. Mottelay and Thomas Campbell-Copeland, eds., *Frank Leslie's Illustrations: The Soldier in Our Civil War*, vol. II (New York: Stanley Bradley Publishing Co., 1893), 313 (courtesy Naval Historical Center).

Lt. John Grimball confessed to his mother that he not been to Savannah in a month, "I rather like staying on ship board."[65]

In April, Gazaway B. Lamar offered to purchase the *Fingal* as a blockade runner, but Secretary Mallory decided that she could be put to better use. Later that month, the Confederacy lost New Orleans, and with it, the brothers Nelson and Asa Tift's unfinished ironclad, the CSS *Mississippi*. In early May, Mallory decided to offer the Tift Brothers another chance to complete an ironclad in Savannah. He soon awarded them a contract to transform the *Fingal* into an ironclad similar to the *Merrimac*/CSS *Virginia*.[66]

The Navy Department provided the bulk of the financing for the *Fingal's* conversion into an ironclad, but the Ladies' Gunboat account freed up additional funding for the *Fingal*. Like the CSS *Georgia*, the time from idea to launch and commissioning, was amazingly short. Renamed the CSS *Atlanta*, the *Fingal* was transformed into an ironclad. The Tift brothers launched the Confederate Navy's newest warship in the summer and commissioned it on November 22, 1862. More than just an immobile armored battery, the *Atlanta* was a full-fledged warship. Unfortunately, the additional weight of its armor and four guns increased the *Atlanta's* draft to 16 feet and reduced its speed and maneuverability. The shallow waters of the Savannah River allowed little room for error or tactical advantage for what might have been the South's most formidable river ironclad.[67]

While the ladies of Georgia were focusing on their ironclad initiatives, Irvine Bulloch successfully ran the blockade to the Bahamas in July as a passenger. In Nassau, he joined Commander Raphael Semmes, who was also on his way to England. Secretary Mallory had chosen Semmes to command James Bulloch's new cruiser, the CSS *Alabama*. Commander Semmes had been the captain of the Confederate Navy's first commerce-raiding cruiser, the CSS *Sumter*. He boldly ran that converted merchant ship out of New Orleans in June of 1861 and captured 18 Union ships before he was bottled up at Gibraltar in January of 1862. Semmes was ready for more action. The mutual achievements of Bulloch and Semmes forced Secretary Mallory to reconsider his promise to James that he would command one of his new warships. James had been so successful as a secret agent that his country could not afford to send him to sea. There simply was nobody else who had his ability to outwit Union spies and officials, overcome fiscal constraints, and deliver critical warships and supplies.[68]

Bulloch was a name that was often on the lips of Union spies, officials, and newspaper readers. For James, the unwelcome notoriety only made his covert activities more difficult to execute. Irvine, who was a mere midshipman, did not receive the same level of exposure, but newspapers did include his name among the list of officers on the *Nashville*. He also received some attention in an inaccurate article that included Irvine as one of the officers who allegedly hitched a ride to England on the HBMS *Bull Dog*, a British Royal Navy gunboat. In lieu of letters, these otherwise unwelcomed reports helped keep the Bulloch ladies loosely apprised of the activities and locations of their men. Irvine and James briefly reunited at Liverpool in early August 1862 as Irvine prepared to embark on his brother's fine cruiser, the CSS *Alabama*.[69]

Harriott notified Martha and her daughters of Irvine's arrival in Liverpool. Fully understanding a mother's concern about her youngest son, Harriott also addressed Irvine's mature frugality. In a letter to Susan West, Martha relayed Harriott's observations about Irvine while he was in Liverpool.

> she [Harriott] was very much pleased with him. She says he had, when he arrived there, every thing to make him comfortable and he had not drawn his pay for two months. He receives 55 dollars per month. He desired her to 'say to Mother he had never drawn the money which she desired him to; that it is still in Bank.'—From all this I infer he is no spend thrift.[70]

If the southern ideal had played out as expected, brave Confederate men would have protected their defenseless women and children from the rapacious Yankees. Stuart, Irvine, and Jimmie were the sons, brothers, and husbands that the Bulloch ladies had offered up to the altar of southern patriotism. The active service of their men led to physical suffering from exposure to enemy shells, the elements, and, most deadly of all, disease. For those honorable southern women who were left at home during the crisis, their chief duties were self-sacrifice and patient suffering. The reality of the Civil War, however, forced these supposedly defenseless women to fend for themselves. A war that was fought, at least in part, to preserve the safety and independence of the southern family, was achieving just the opposite.[71]

Martha and her daughters Susan, Mittie, and Anna all lived in the North before, during, and after the war. They also loved Northern men who supported the Union. In Harriott's case, she resided in neutral England, while her husband and in-laws served the South. Her father Colonel Osborne Cross continued his career as a senior Union quartermaster officer during the war. Harriott's brother, Edwin, died in battle wearing Yankee blue. One result of these mixed geographic and family alliances for the Bulloch ladies was a smaller dose of the bitter anti–Union vitriol that infected many of the women who had remained in the South.[72]

Confederate women of the leisure class typically did what they could, short of physical labor, to support their men on the front lines. They could not bear arms or show active courage on the battlefield, but they had ample opportunity to demonstrate passive courage at home. Southern women were unwilling to sit idle. They simply had to do something to contribute to the well-being of their men and the nation. Those activities usually leveraged domestic skills such as embroidering razor cases, knitting dozens of pairs of socks, and collecting and decorating soldiers' sewing kits.[73]

The Bulloch ladies residing in the North had severe obstacles to such overtly partisan support. The Lincoln government suspended writs of habeas corpus and often jailed individuals on mere suspicion of disloyal acts. Anything that could be construed as giving "aid or comfort to rebels" could have landed them in jail with no legal recourse. In the twentieth century, a fable arose that Mittie had defiantly displayed a Confederate flag at her New York City home when her husband Theodore was away. The story is pure fiction. Martha, Susan, Anna, and Mittie had to be careful about open expressions of their pro–Confederate proclivities.[74]

Mittie suppressed her pro-southern feelings in the presence of her Roosevelt in-laws. Her mother, Martha, simply retired to her room whenever she wanted to avoid Union officers or other unsavory house guests and topics. Mittie did not have that luxury. Partly out of loyalty to her husband and true to her southern sense of propriety, Mittie played the role of gracious hostess and devoted wife. Within the Northern version of nineteenth century paternalism, she had to avoid even subtle displays of southern sympathy. To do otherwise could have produced disastrous consequences that would have fallen most heavily on her husband. Despite these limitations, living in New York and Liverpool also offered unique opportunities to act on behalf of the South and their kinfolk.[75]

The Bulloch ladies in the North could rely on Harriott, who was safely situated in neutral Liverpool. She also happened to be married to the chief Confederate naval agent in charge of running supplies into the South. Harriott offered to relay letters and supplies to and from the Bulloch ladies in the North, Irvine, and other family members still in the South. Just before Irvine departed Portsmouth, England in the CSS *Nashville*, he had managed to post a letter to his mother that, not coincidentally, arrived in New York the same day as the one from Harriott. Harriott would prove to be a successful conduit for information and small packages throughout the war. Of all the Bulloch ladies, Stuart Elliott's wife, Lucy, and their two children in Georgia were the most isolated from the rest of the family.[76]

To frustrate scrutiny from Federal post office officials and her pro–Union Roosevelt in-laws, Mittie, Anna, and Martha, had to find creative ways of communicating with Lucy and Harriott. They usually relied on trusted friends as they traveled to and from Liverpool and other neutral ports in Canada, Bermuda, and Nassau. When sending these clandestine bundles, the ladies always waited until Theodore was out of town, as he often was while pursuing his Allotment Commission duties. Gathering the necessary supplies, the Bulloch ladies wrapped the parcels and placed them in a large basket. They then casually strolled to New York's Central Park "on a picnic" with the exuberant young Teddy (then called 'Teedie') and Bamie in tow. In the park, they met with a trusted courier who ensured the packages got to Harriott or one of James' blockade runners.[77]

Mittie's children Teedie and Bamie were full participants in the "hushed and thrilling excitement." They secretly packed and helped deliver boxes for their run past the Union blockading fleet. Inspired by family tales about the exploits of their Uncle Jimmie Bulloch, Teedie and Bamie relived these exhilarating experiences in a game of "running the blockade." Bamie played the role of the blockade runner while Teddy was always the Union Navy gunboat. She would dash across a bridge in Central Park and try to elude gunboat Teedie who chased Bamie and attempted to catch her before she reached a safe haven.[78]

Sadly, the packages to Lucy Elliott in Georgia soon included a black bombazine cloak. Bombazine was the traditional mid-nineteenth century silk and wool cloth used for mourning garments. Martha's son and Lucy's husband, Stuart died in August of 1862. Little is known about Lucy's personal struggles after Stuart's death in Marietta, but the Bulloch ladies continued to send packages to Lucy long after Stuart's death.[79]

Harriott dutifully shipped letters and trunks of "shoes for the children and boots for Lucy; also needles, sewing silk, writing paper," and other articles from Liverpool through the blockade into Charleston. Harriott's connection with her Bulloch in-laws was obviously more than mere attention to duty. When she delivered her fourth child on February 21, 1863, Harriott named him Stuart Elliott Bulloch, "after 'poor brother,' the prettiest baby she says she ever had." Later that year, Harriott forwarded a photograph of young Stuart to Martha who thought he looked very much like her son and his namesake.[80]

Lucy was not the only benefactor of Bulloch ladies' defiance in the very real game of running the blockade. Another early example of their success came in late December of 1862, when a package from Harriott arrived at Wilmington, NC on the blockade runner *Giraffe*. James K. Caskie, the brother of Bulloch's deceased wife Lizzie, wrote from Richmond that he had received the package of gloves, needles, thread, and

The blockade runner CSS *Giraffe*, renamed *Robert E. Lee* (Library of Congress).

other manufactured necessities. At the time, the Caskies were not able to confirm that Lucy Elliott's package had arrived.[81]

There was another, and even more secret partner in the Bulloch ladies' clandestine communications: Theodore's friend, Major General John Adams Dix, the Union general in command of Fort Monroe, Virginia. General Dix, like Secretary of State Seward, was a former governor of New York. He had also been a U.S. senator and secretary of the treasury. As of June 1862, he was in command of the Union forces opposite the Confederates at Norfolk.

In November, Martha provided this advice to her daughter Susan, "If you send a letter to Mr. Caskie, direct the inner envelope to Lucy and the outer to Gen. Dix, Commandant of Fortress Monroe." This seemingly innocent advice indicated that Lucy may have moved to Richmond to live with the Caskies. The letter also suggests intrigue. Major General John Adams Dix was one of several Union generals whose appointment hinged on his political prominence and ability to enlist soldiers to serve under him. Dix was also an ardent supporter of the Union and seemed to be an unlikely channel for passing information that might be considered disloyal.[82]

General Dix was well known to Theodore Roosevelt, Sr., who had met with him in February and again in October of 1862 at the general's headquarters in Fort Monroe. Among Dix's duties was management of official exchanges with Confederate forces across Hampton Roads at Norfolk via a flag of truce boat. By late 1862, Martha had abandoned her notion of going south, but she still needed to communicate with her family there, particularly the widowed Lucy Elliott. Theodore's meetings with General Dix as a New York Allotment Commissioner provided him opportunities to discuss family matters. After their last meeting in February, the Roosevelt and Dix families had become even closer. Harriott Bulloch's father, Colonel Osborne Cross, had married the widow of General Dix's brother in July![83]

The Cross-Dix wedding occurred less than 6 months after the death of Harriott's mother Louise. Colonel Cross' extended separations from his family during his career as an Army Quartermaster Corps officer had taken a toll. He was not even aware of his wife Louise's death until after he returned from California in March of 1862. Less than four months later, he married the widowed Mary Dix. She was a longtime acquaintance from their time together while assigned to Army posts in Louisiana.[84]

This new family connection also provided the Bulloch ladies new hope. Theodore could leverage his professional relationship and personal kinship with the General to find another path for their ostensibly innocent communications. General Dix apparently allowed these letters to pass back and forth through the lines as a personal courtesy to Roosevelt and their mutual rebel in-laws. This curious lapse in security was uncharacteristic of the man who had just presided over the commission that determined the fate of suspected spies such as Mrs. Rose O'Neal Greenhow. James Bulloch quickly realized the value of Martha's secret, double-envelope scheme. In January 1863, he advised the Confederate Secretary of the Navy Mallory to, "Send your letters to Mr. James K. Caskie, who has already forwarded you one from me." General Dix managed to keep his arrangement with the Bullochs and Roosevelts secret throughout his lifetime.[85]

James D. Bulloch's communications with the Navy Department discussed his two commerce-raiding cruisers, the CSS *Florida* and *Alabama*. He had returned to Liverpool to find the *Florida* ready to sail, but nothing had been done to outfit the ship as a man-of-war in his absence. James quickly had to resume his frenetic effort to get both ships underway before the Federal agents had them confiscated. In James' absence, Harriott continued to do her part. She located a suitable house for their growing family in the Liverpool suburb of Waterloo. The modest abode at 2 Marine Terrace provided a clear view of the wide Mersey River from its second floor.[86]

After the successful escape of the *Florida*, Union spies and informants became even more vigilant. They shadowed James wherever he went, but he knew who they were and how to give them the slip. When the *Alabama* was launched on May 15, 1862, those agents had fully alerted their Union masters of the cruiser's mission and capabilities. At the time, she was known as the "290." It was the 290th ship laid down at Laird's shipyard, but her official name was the *Enrica*. Bulloch selected the name simply to honor the woman who had christened the ship. He explained that the name *Enrica* was the "flexible and mellifluous" Spanish equivalent of Henrietta or Harriet.[87]

Bulloch never identified the lady who performed these duties, but within the reports of the Union spy Mathew Maguire and Bulloch's own account, there are clues about who she might have been. The flexibility of the name gave tribute to his wife, but it is clear that the lady who christened the ship was not Harriott. Maguire reported that Harriott and James Bulloch were indeed present at the christening, but Harriott did not perform the honors. One of Maguire's informants, a shipwright named Richard Broderick, said that "Captain Bulloch's wife was in one of the office windows, with other ladies. Her bonnet dropped from the window, he (Broderick) lifted it and passed it up to her." Harriott could not have broken a bottle of wine (or Champagne) on the ship's bow from the office windows that were perched above and away from the ceremonial christening.[88]

Bulloch himself provided a few hints that help narrow the candidates. In addition to her first name of Henrietta or Harriet, we can infer that the lady was a resident or citizen of Great Britain, old enough to christen a ship in 1862 and still alive and residing in the United Kingdom in 1883 when Bulloch published his account of the *Alabama*. It is also likely that she was a friend or acquaintance of Bulloch. She was probably connected to an influential person who was favorably disposed toward the Confederacy, but not directly connected to the government.[89]

There are several candidates that fit this description, including Irvine Bulloch's future wife and mother-in-law, both of whom were named "Harriet." Harriet Louisa Sears was 30 years of age at the time, but her daughter, Harriet Lelia, was only 11. Mrs. Sears' husband and father were U.S. Army officers. They all hailed from New York, and the Sears family had only recently returned to Liverpool (September 1861), making the Sears ladies unlikely namesakes.[90]

Another possibility was Harriet Pinckney Huse, the wife of Bulloch's army counterpart in Liverpool. James' endorsement had saved Captain Caleb Huse's job when his army superiors questioned the northern-born army officer's loyalty and effectiveness. In recognition of their friendship, Harriet and Caleb Huse honored James by naming a son after him. Mrs.

Huse eventually had a Confederate supply ship named in her honor, the *Harriet Pinckney*, but she was not the one who christened the *Enrica/ Alabama*. While James was anxiously preparing for the launch of his ship in mid–May of 1862, Mrs. Huse was equally busy preparing for the delivery of a baby. Her son, Norman Bulloch Huse, was born on June 2, 1862, in Auteuil, France.[91]

The mysterious lady who best fit the description of the *Enrica's* christening namesake was Harriet Low. Harriet was a British citizen who lived in nearby Leamington Spa with her sister Amy. Leamington was a haven for displaced Confederates and their families. The spa city was also at the junction of the Great Western and London & North Western Railways that provided ready access to both London and Liverpool. Harriet and Amy were the daughters of Andrew Low, a wealthy Savannah merchant who had Scottish roots and British citizenship. During Andrew's annual visit to his daughters in 1861, he and his partner Charles Green helped finance Bulloch's blockade running adventure on the *Fingal*. Mr. Low was arrested upon his return to the United States via Canada, but his daughters fortuitously had remained in England.[92]

Harriet Low, namesake of the CSS *Enrica/Alabama* (courtesy National Society of the Colonial Dames of America in the State of Georgia).

The 14-year-old Harriet Low was most likely the gracious lady who christened the ship that sent 53 Union ships to Davy Jones' locker. Andrew and his nephew John Low eventually joined Harriet and Amy in England. Harriet Low was precursor of the wealthy American heiresses who married cash-strapped British nobility after the war. Harriet eventually married the landowner, Major George Coke Robertson of the British Army, and she remained in England throughout her life. Although she died young, Harriet Low Robertson had become a respected benefactor in the local community by 1883. James Bulloch was careful to avoid any embarrassment by naming her as the *Enrica's* namesake.[93]

On the last day of July 1862, James orchestrated the brilliant, but hair's-breadth, escape of the *Alabama*. Dithering British officials had finally yielded to the relentless harping of Union consular officers and ordered the seizure of his cruiser. Just prior to the delivery of an order that would have prevented the sailing, James got the *Alabama* underway. He ordered a seemingly innocent, but timely all day sea-trial to test the ship's engines and performance. Privately, he instructed the trusted temporary captain of the *Alabama* (then still known as the *Enrica*) to prepare for a long voyage. To divert suspicion, he had the ship decorated with festive flags and pennants. Bulloch also invited distinguished ladies and gentlemen of Liverpool to join him on board for a pleasant day of sailing. The entertainment included "music and dancing, and an elegant luncheon." Harriott Bulloch was probably among those ladies.[94]

At the end of the day, Bulloch announced that he wanted to keep the *Enrica* out for an extra day. Just as he had planned, a steam tug named the *Hercules* was standing by to take the guests back to Liverpool. The *Enrica/Alabama* left Liverpool that day and never returned. Because of the hurried departure, James had to enlist additional crewmen to safely operate the vessel. Accordingly, he had the *Hercules* at the Liverpool piers early the next morning. The shipping master greeted him on the tug with forty potential crewmen, along with their wives and girlfriends. Bulloch described these ladies as being from "that class who generally affect a tender solicitude for Jack [sailor(s)] when he is outward-bound, and is likely to be provided with an advance-note."[95]

James was not prepared to allow females aboard his warship, but the shipping master feared, "it was a case of all or none." It seems that the women, "stood in various degrees of tender relationship to the men, and would not part with them unless they could first get a month's pay in advance or its equivalent." Commander Bulloch was in no position to parley, so he agreed to take the entire party on board the *Hercules* and out to the anchorage where he had secreted the *Enrica*. On the way, James formulated a plan to deal with the untenable situation.[96]

The harbor tug had no galley and it was about 4 p.m. before they came alongside the *Enrica*. The sailors and their

> fair friends were therefore hungry, and not in suitable frame of mind for business. The steward was ordered to prepare a substantial supper as quickly as possible, and when it was ready all hands were refreshed with a fair but safe allowance of grog, to add zest and cheerfulness to the meal.[97]

After allowing the men to smoke their after-dinner pipes, Bulloch eloquently encouraged them to join the crew of the *Enrica*. He promised a comfortable and well provisioned cruise to an unspecified port in the Western Hemisphere. He agreed to pay everyone one month's pay in advance and then described the scene,

> After a short consultation among themselves, all but two or three of the men agreed to go. Articles expressing the terms of the agreement had been prepared, and each man came down to the cabin in turn with his 'lady,' and signed, the latter receiving the stipulated advance in money, or a note for the equivalent.[98]

The women finally clambered back aboard the *Hercules* and departed the *Enrica* around midnight. The *Alabama/Enrica* was at last away, one day ahead of the Union warship sent to sink her.

A few days after the *Alabama's* escape, Captain Semmes met with Bulloch in Liverpool to plan his voyage of destruction. James had made arrangements to secretly rendezvous with the *Alabama* in the Azores, a Portuguese island colony off the coast of Africa. Both men decided to travel there and supervise the conversion of the *Enrica* into the warship CSS *Alabama*. Before their departure, Semmes was a guest at the Bulloch home in the suburb of Waterloo. Captain Semmes reported that, "I met his excellent wife, a charming southern woman, with whom hospitality was a part of her religious faith."[99]

During the war Harriott would play host to a constant stream of her husband's Confederates. One of the more charming of these was Seth Grosvenor Porter, one of Bulloch's former shipmates. His sister Laura was married to Cornelius V.S. Roosevelt, Jr., Theodore Roosevelt's older brother and former Roswell groomsman. Commander Bulloch recommended Mr. Porter to Secretary Mallory as a "man of courage and judgement." Porter departed Liverpool on the latest Confederate government-owned blockade runner, the *Giraffe*. Its commander was James' trusted friend James Duguid who also had taken James' first Confederate cruiser, the CSS *Florida*, to sea. Porter was headed for Bermuda, but when he learned that the Union fleet had illegally blockaded that island, he diverted to Nassau.[100]

In addition to his official duties, Porter carried Harriott's packages for the Caskies in Richmond and Lucy Elliott in Savannah. The *Giraffe* soon made its successful run into Wilmington with Harriott's packages, as Porter went his separate way up to Bermuda. He arrived there on Christmas Day, 1862. In Bermuda, Porter became the maritime shipping agent for James' army counterparts, including Major Norman Walker. Later, Porter commanded the blockade runners *Merrimac* and *Phantom* on behalf of the Confederate Army's Ordnance Department. As captain of the *Phantom*, Porter came in intimate contact with one of the most intriguing ladies who ever entered the Bulloch family's life. Her name was Rose O'Neal Greenhow, the famous (or infamous) "Rebel Rose."[101]

The widowed Rose Greenhow was a Washington socialite and celebrated Confederate spy. In the first year of the war, the Union detective Allan Pinkerton caught her in the act of passing encrypted messages to Confederate agents. Rose's capture came only after she had delivered critical information to Confederate General Beauregard before the first battle of Manassas, or "Bull Run" as the North called their humiliating defeat. Rose had recruited a number of refined young ladies as couriers. They all took advantage of the prerogatives of their gender to shield their treasonous activities.[102]

As Mary Chesnut observed in Richmond, just two weeks before the battle, "Women from Washington come riding into our camp, beautiful women. They bring letters in their back hair, or in their garments. 'They are spies'" Early in the war, Union officers were reluctant to violate the personal privacy or question the honor of women who dressed and acted like ladies, even ones of contemptuous deportment like Rose. After she was caught, the Yankees imprisoned her for over nine months without a trial. When the tribunal headed by General Dix exiled her to the South, she had to sign an oath to never return to the North. It was a promise she was happy to make and keep.[103]

Rose remained in Richmond through the summer of 1863. She was feted as a heroine, but she was short of money. President Jefferson Davis extended her his personal thanks and formulated a long-shot plan to leverage her flamboyant notoriety. He would send the indomitable Rose to Europe as his emissary in hope of gaining diplomatic recognition of the Confederate States. To do that, she would have to run the blockade out of Wilmington, North Carolina. That is where Rose's path converged with the Bullochs.[104]

In Wilmington, Seth Grosvenor Porter, a friend and relative of the Bullochs, had just completed loading his cargo of cotton on the appropriately named side-wheel steamer, the *Phantom*. On August 5, he was anchored just offshore and ready for sea, with two small exceptions. That day, Porter welcomed his only passengers aboard the fast blockade runner, Mrs. Greenhow and her daughter "Little Rose." The thoughtful captain escorted Rose to her stateroom where she observed that "everything good taste could suggest was provided for my comfort." This was Porter's initial cruise in the *Phantom* and he proved to be a wise choice as captain. His first command decision was to maneuver the ship very slowly down the Cape Fear River toward New Inlet. He was waiting for the high tide before making his dash into the open sea late that evening. Two other, more impetuous captains made ill-advised attempts to run out earlier, but ran aground.[105]

When the time was right, the *Phantom* lurched into motion, all ahead full, as the Union fleet caught sight of them. The blockading ships sent up flares that illuminated the night sky and indicated the blockade runner's heading. Guns fired wildly as the gunboats chased after the swift *Phantom*, all to no avail. For the next four days, the elusive blockade runner sped past successive gauntlets of Union warships until Porter arrived at his destination, the picturesque harbor of St. George's, Bermuda. Rose was impressed with the island's stone houses and white-washed roofs that captured rain in cisterns, the primary source of the island's fresh water. Captain Porter introduced Mrs. Greenhow to the island's large colony of Confederates who were equally impressed with her.[106]

Rose was intelligent, forceful, and very opinionated about the righteousness of the southern cause. She was not intimidated by weak-minded arguments of any man, regardless of his position or station, a rare trait in that male-dominated Victorian Society. Despite her forceful, outspoken, and independent personality, Rose had the habit of captivating everyone she met, both male and female. The most important southern female figure in Bermudan society was Georgiana Walker. She was the wife of the senior Confederate agent responsible for coordinating logistics with Major Caleb Huse and Commander Bulloch in England. Mrs. Greenhow liked and respected Mrs. Walker, who observed qualities in Rose that are not readily apparent in surviving photographs: "She [Rose] needs no cultivation of beauty, for Providence has blessed her with a high order of that. She is one of the most beautiful women I ever saw. She knows this & like a sensible woman, does not pretend to think the contrary."[107]

Mrs. Greenhow was finally able to continue her journey to Europe aboard the steamer named for Major Caleb Huse's wife. The *Harriet Pinck-*

ney sailed under the British flag, but it was Confederate-owned. In addition to her own daughter, Rose had another youngster under her care, the young nephew of James M. Seixas. Mr. Seixas was the Confederate War Department's agent at Wilmington who had helped secure Rose's passage on the *Phantom*. Along with four other passengers and a load of cotton for Major Huse in Liverpool, Rose and company sailed from Bermuda on August 29. The captain of the *Harriet Pinckney* decided to land at Falmouth on the English Channel rather than risk encountering the Union gunboats that patrolled the Irish Sea approaches to Liverpool.[108]

This change in destination forced Rose to travel by train another 240 miles from Falmouth to Liverpool, where she arrived late on the evening of September 14. The next morning she went to the offices of Fraser, Trenholm and "arranged my business." She secured financing for her personal expenses and activities on behalf of the Confederate government. She missed seeing Commander Bulloch who was in France. James was working to get the CSS *Florida* underway again from its refuge in Brest, France and urging his ironclad and cruiser construction efforts forward in Nantes and Bordeaux.

Rose remained in Europe for almost a year. During that time, she wrote a best-selling exposé of her adventures as a spy and prisoner in a miserable Yankee jail. Her book was titled, *My Imprisonment and the First Year of Abolition Rule at Washington*. Rose proved to be a passionate advocate, confident in the moral superiority of the southern cause. The interpersonal skills that she had honed during her time as a Washington socialite served her well in Europe. As her friend Georgiana Walker noted when visiting London in July of 1864, "She [Mrs. Greenhow] has certainly had the entrée to the very highest society. The Lords & Ladies & Duchesses are her constant visitors, & her invitations to dinner parties & balls are innumerable. She is to dine with Lady Palmerston [wife of the British Prime Minister] soon, & has gone thro' the rounds of most of the others."[109]

Her exciting story and ebullient personality thrilled an empathetic European audience and transformed her into the internationally renowned "Rebel Rose." She was the toast of England and France, garnering audiences with everyone from Lord Palmerston to Emperor Louis-Napoléon of France. She even met with Charles F. Adams, who was Abraham Lincoln's priggish minister to Great Britain and the son and grandson of U.S. presidents. Rose also met with Confederate Commissioners James Mason and John Slidell, Lord Derby, and the future Foreign Ministers Granville and Gladstone. Her traveling companion for some of these journeys through England and France was none other than James Dunwoody Bulloch.

Nineteenth century etiquette required gentlemen to escort a respectable lady when she traveled about the city and countryside. Commander Bulloch filled that role when he went to Paris in early February of 1864. He was working on complex contract negotiations for his ironclad warships in England and France at the time. For her part, Rose had met with Emperor Louis-Napoléon in late January of that year to urge official French recognition of the Confederate States. Forthright as always, she observed that, "when my opinions came in conflict with his preconceived opinions, he [Emperor Louis-Napoléon] admitted the force of my reason as only a great man could." Mason and Slidell anxiously waited at Rose's apartment for her report of the meeting with the emperor. They were disappointed to hear her accurate assessment that, "our only chance of recognition must now come from England."[110]

In Paris, she dined and socialized with Empress Eugenie and other dignitaries. She corresponded with Archduke Maximilian, the future Emperor of Mexico, but by February 6, she was ready to return to England. Commander James D. Bulloch escorted Rose to the train station. He ensured that she was comfortably situated in the "Ladies Only" salon on the train bound for Calais and the ferry to Dover. James did not follow Rose to England until mid-month, when he returned to Liverpool.[111]

Rose departed London for France on March 24. She was en route to see her daughter who was a student at the Sacré Coeur girl's school in Paris. This time, James accompanied Rose on both the train and ferry to France. The English Channel crossing was rough, with Mrs. Greenhow improbably claiming that everyone was sea sick except herself. James and Rose had several delays and shared cramped quarters, until they finally arrived at the luxurious Grand Hotel in Paris late that

Confederate spy Rose O'Neal and her daughter "Little Rose" Greenhow (Library of Congress).

evening. Unfortunately, the new, 80-room hotel near the Paris Opera House had no "place for our weary heads." At midnight, they finally located temporary accommodations at the nearby Amarante Hotel.[112]

In Paris, Rose spent time with her daughter and received a constant stream of visitors. Apparently, she did not see much of James until March 29, just before she was to leave for England. Mrs. Greenhow arrived at her apartment that night to put her young daughter to bed. There, she

> found Capt. Bulloch waiting for me. He is going off in the morning for which I am sorry, but he is one of the most active [and] intelligent of our agents. God speed him in his work. Altho' I have seen but little of him in Paris, I am very sorry he is going, for it is a pleasant thing to feel that a true friend is near and such he is to me.[113]

This is the last recorded meeting between the two. It was a private meeting in circumstances that, if publicized, would have given rise to speculation about the nature of their relationship. This was especially true in view of Rose's reputation for seduction and the couple's previous late-night traveling and sleeping arrangements. Mrs. Greenhow certainly had a way with men.[114]

The only other clue about their relationship was a letter from Confederate sympathizer John L. O'Sullivan to President Jefferson Davis in February of 1864. O'Sullivan's letter concerned an innocuous business meeting with Bulloch in Liverpool. At the end of the letter, however, he added an unusual comment without any explanatory context. He simply noted that Rose was, "quite a lioness in society, influential men are constantly seeking her, & she them." The comment had nothing to do with the rest of the letter and although not specified, O'Sullivan may have intended to suggest that there was a relationship between James and Rose.[115]

While she was in London, Rose did meet with her blockade running friend and Bulloch-Roosevelt brother-in-law, Captain Seth G. Porter, in early June. However, her attentions quickly turned to one of the officers from Commander Bulloch's cruiser, the CSS *Alabama*. The commerce raider had completed a destructive but exhausting cruise that ranged from the waters off Texas, to Brazil, South Africa, and Indo-China. In mid–June of 1864, the *Alabama* and Captain Semmes finally sailed into the English Channel. Semmes arrived at Cherbourg, France with hopes of refitting and perhaps turning over his command to another captain. When the USS *Kearsarge* arrived to blockade his exit, Semmes issued a challenge that amounted to a duel to the death between the apparently equally matched warships.

Unfortunately for the South, the *Alabama* lost the battle and slipped beneath the waves off the coast of France. The private British yacht, *Deerhound*, and a French pilot boat rescued most the crew. James travelled to Southampton with Confederate Commissioner Mason where they met Captain Semmes and other surviving members of the crew. One of the survivors with Semmes was James' brother Irvine. The news of the sinking preceded word about Irvine's survival. His mother and sisters in the U.S. had to suffer through days of anxiety to learn if Irvine had been one of the casualties. Martha had already lost one son during the war, but the loss of her youngest would have been especially cruel.

The victorious *Kearsarge* had plucked 54 of the Confederate sailors from the sea, and quickly paroled all but four of them. One of the prisoners was the wounded Joseph D. Wilson (1841–1880). Lieutenant Wilson was the *Alabama's* senior captured officer who officially surrendered his sword and the sunken ship to the *Kearsarge's* Captain, John Winslow. Eager for retribution and political leverage, the Union Navy was not inclined to grant Lieutenant Wilson a parole.

After recovering from his own injuries, Captain Semmes travelled to London with Commissioner Mason and the knowledge that Lt. Wilson was still a prisoner under house arrest. They needed the kind of assistance that only Rose Greenhow could provide. On July 11, the same day that Semmes and Mason approached her, Rose called on U.S. Minister Charles Adams and pleaded her case for Wilson's release. She argued that Captain Semmes had captured over 250 prisoners, including 19 U.S. military officers. He had released or paroled all of them unharmed. Two days later, the United States granted Lt. Wilson his parole.[116]

As was the case with most men who had intimate contact with Rose, there was some speculation that the 22-year-old Wilson and the 50-year-old Mrs. Greenhow had an intimate relationship. Mrs. Greenhow and Wilson did spend considerable time together and Rose continued to exude charms that belied her age. A month after negotiating his release, she and Lt. Wilson boarded the SS *Condor* in Greenock, Scotland for their return to the Confederacy. The *Condor* was the newest of Commander Bulloch's fleet of blockade runners. During the war, he personally purchased, leased, or managed 25 blockade runners on behalf of the Confederate government. The *Condor* was one of his finest acquisitions on behalf of the army.[117]

Getting underway on August 10, the *Condor* first stopped in Bermuda before heading to Halifax, Nova Scotia. They arrived there on September 6 and remained for 18 days. While in Halifax, they loaded coal and embarked the Confederate Commissioner to Nova Scotia, Judge John P. Holcombe. The primary reason for their delay was the moon, but romance played no part in the decision. The New Moon would not come into phase until September 30, so it was best to wait for the advantage of a dark night when they made their run back to Wilmington, North Carolina.[118]

By the early morning hours of October 1, the *Condor* was speeding toward the familiar New Inlet entrance of Cape Fear. Unfortunately for the *Condor* and particularly for Mrs. Greenhow, the Union gunboat *Niphon* discovered the fast blockade runner with its three distinctive funnels. The *Niphon* was about to open fire when she too came within range of Fort Fisher's protecting guns. The *Niphon* quickly withdrew under duress. But just as the *Condor's* crew and passengers breathed a collective sigh of relief, the hulking form of a large ship suddenly appeared directly ahead. Enveloped by darkness and frothy seas, the ship's pilot unwisely veered to starboard and the *Condor* shuddered to a sudden halt. Its hull was well and truly stuck. The *Condor's* startled pilot had discovered the uncharted wreck of a fellow blockade runner directly ahead. Just two nights earlier, the *Niphon* had chased the blockade runner *Night Hawk* onto Federal Shoals as she tried to run out of New Inlet. The *Condor* was hard aground on those same shoals less than 100 yards from the stranded *Night Hawk*.[119]

The ship that had seemed so safe and powerful earlier that day as it bounded through the ocean swells was a total loss. Its hull was broken in two. The blockade runner missed Bulloch's steady hand. Although the *Condor* was Commander Bulloch's ship, he was not its captain. His fine ship, its crew, and passengers were all immobilized in the shallow, roiling waters off Cape Fear. The *Condor's* most important passenger, Mrs. Rose Greenhow, considered James to be one her country's best men. Rose knew Bulloch as a friend, escort, protector, and perhaps something even more, but he was in Europe and she had to get ashore.

Rose was equally removed from the toasts and suitors of fashionable European salons. Cape Fear only offered crashing waves of cold saltwater to moisten her lips and fill her lungs. If she found hope in the thought that things could be worse, they soon were. The Union warship that had chased the *Condor* was preparing a boarding party that might capture them all. Rose did not fear death, but she could not, and would not, become a Yankee prisoner again. Commander Bulloch may have lost his fine steamer, but Rose had important dispatches to deliver. The Confederate commissioner to England had entrusted them to her care and she intended to deliver the letters personally to Secretary of State Judah Benjamin.[120]

Shouting above the roar of the wind and wave, Captain William Hewett, the *Condor's* distinguished 29-year-old British captain, pleaded with Rose to be patient. She should wait until daybreak when they could be rescued. Hewett was certain that if she left the ship that night, the surf, those huge breakers, would swamp their tiny life boat and everyone in it. She would be tossed into the raging sea and would surely die.[121]

Gaining her balance with difficulty on the pitching deck, she wiped away the briny spray and stated her mind. She was not intimidated by any man, even one like Hewett who had won the Victoria Cross for bravery in the face of the enemy. She was direct and undaunted. She would rather drown than rot and die in another Yankee prison. She had to get ashore. Now!!![122]

Hewett was on furlough from the Royal Navy, seeking adventure and profit. He did not, however, bargain for this kind of feminine determination; so he did as Rose demanded. Fearing shot and shell more than wind and wave, Rose and three of the Condor's bravest and most able seamen clambered aboard the small lifeboat. Soon after, the crew lowered them down the lea side of the stranded steamer. Mrs. Greenhow and her petticoats quickly disappeared into the darkness. With one last, futile scan of the dark and lifeless shoreline, Captain Hewett could only muse, "Dear lady, I pray those letters and your money belt were worth the risk."[123]

Rose was rightly confident in her ability to bend men to her will, but she had less influence on Father Neptune. At daybreak, lighters from shore rescued the crew of the Condor and most of its cargo just as Captain Hewitt had predicted. That morning, Thomas Taylor, the pursuer from the Night Hawk, made the gruesome discovery of Rose's lifeless body on the beach. All the men from the Condor survived, but Rose, weighed down by her clothes and gold, drowned. Taylor noted that she was "remarkably handsome"[124] and even "beautiful in death."[125]

Local officials auctioned off Rose's mementoes and other items from the ship that she had purchased for trade. As the Secretary of the Confederate Navy noted, the dispatches, "which are understood to have been in the hands of Mrs. Greenhow, were lost." All of the Confederacy honored her courage and mourned her loss, but Bulloch, the ever-discrete secret agent, made no mention of his fellow secret agent in any of his surviving writings. Ironically, the Confederates eventually floated and repaired the Night Hawk, the ostensible cause of the Condor's grounding.[126]

In assessing Mrs. Greenhow's life and death, the former Cape Fear pilot, James Sprunt observed, "She had lived past her beauty's prime, had drunk deep of fashion's and folly's stream of pleasure, had received the admiration and adulation of hundreds of her fellow-mortals, and had reached that point in life when those things no longer please, but pall on the senses. Her time had come."[127]

One other special Bulloch lady passed in 1864: family matriarch Martha Stewart Elliott Bulloch. After abandoning her attempt to "Go South" at the beginning of the war, Martha frequently stayed with her daughters Susan (Elliott) West in Philadelphia and Mittie (Bulloch) Roosevelt in New York. She also spent considerable time at the beach resort city of Long Branch, New Jersey. There, she stayed at the luxurious Laird's Mansion House and at the Roosevelt's nearby summer home. Martha spent the summer months of 1861 and 1862 in Long Branch and even extended her stay into the early fall.[128]

Martha had been the primary communications link between her Confederate sons and her southern daughters living in the North. Curiously, none of the many war-time family letters or photos that passed to and from James and Harriott Bulloch survived in the Roosevelt archives. This purge of family records could have been a post-war defensive reaction from overly cautious family members. Martha was an ardent and active supporter of the southern cause, contributing what she could to suffering southern prisoners as well as to her own stricken family members. Her overt sympathies could have harmed the Roosevelts in the government's post-war retribution against disloyal citizens. Martha did not, however, think of all Yankees as hateful or thieving as did so many of her contemporaries. She felt deeply for Hilborne West and Theodore Roosevelt, Sr., her two sons-in-law who had been so good to her and her daughters.[129]

Her son Irvine Bulloch was aware that his mother had been ill with a weak heart since July of 1864. He wrote Martha after the *Kearsarge* had sunk his Confederate cruiser, the *Alabama*. He was doing well and staying with his brother "Jim" and "Hattie" in Waterloo. Acting Master Irvine S. Bulloch had just received orders to report to the CSS *Shenandoah*, his brother's latest Confederate cruiser. Irvine would be at sea that day and he attempted to ease her worries about his safety,

> darling you need feel no anxiety on my account and sister Hattie will tell you in the course of a few weeks something of my whereabouts, so make yourself perfectly at ease blessed. Give my love to my dear little sisters kiss them all for me & kiss [sister] Mittie's little children, so Good bye dear, dear Mother, I'll write when ever able to send a letter.[130]

Irvine's letter, dated October 8, 1864, would be the last Martha would see from her youngest son. As the end drew near, Martha's eldest daughter, Susan, was at her bedside. One evening, without words, Martha extended her arm with her hand lying open on the pillow. In the morning, Susan asked what she was trying to do or say. Martha replied that she wished to pray, but felt too feeble to control her thoughts. She "held out her open hand to her Heavenly Father, well assured that he would know her meaning." Martha passed on October 30 at the age of 65 in Madison, New Jersey, a borough of Morristown.[131]

Morristown is where James and Harriott Bulloch had a home before leaving for Liverpool. It is possible they transferred that property to Martha. The Roosevelts also rented a summer home called Loantaka in this same community. This dual family connection to Morristown and Madison might explain Martha's presence in New Jersey rather than choosing to be at the home of one of her daughters as her health declined. With a tombstone simply labeled, "Martha Stewart Bulloch," the family buried her near, but not in, the Roosevelt family plot at Brooklyn's Green-Wood Cemetery.[132]

As one lady left the Bulloch circle, another soon arrived. The first hint of the new arrival came in mid–October 1864 when Harriott joined the ladies who presided at the "Great Southern Bazaar" in Liverpool. The purpose of the 5-day event was to raise money for the relief of southern prisoners who were wasting away and dying in Northern prisons. Opening on October 18 at St. George's Hall, the event generated numerous donations. The gifts and decorations were so sumptuous that they "dwarfed even the magnificent hall devoted to it [the Bazaar]." There were 12 stalls, one for each state of the Confederacy, plus Kentucky. Distinguished British and Confederate ladies presided at each stall. Harriott Bulloch, "the wife of Captain Bullock [sic], of the famous man-of-war" co-hosted the Georgia stall.[133]

Harriott had long been doing her part for the war effort in the domestic arena and was a vital communications cog for her husband and his family. The Great Southern Bazaar was her opportunity to make a more public contribution. For those who knew her situation, there was little surprise when visitors saw the contents of Harriott's stall. As the London Herald reported with a tinge of disappointment, "The 'Georgia' stall is very finely decorated externally, but the interior is devoted chiefly to baby linen." Harriott provided the inspiration for the contents, for she was five months pregnant with her fifth and last child. The baby girl arrived on February 14, 1865. She named her Martha Louise Bulloch after both her husband's stepmother and her own mother. The family called her Loulie.[134]

At some point during the war years, Harriott's younger sister, Annette Cross, came to live with her in Liverpool. Annette's arrival may have been related to the ill health of the Bullochs' second son, Henry (known as "Dunnie"). As Harriott reported in the fall of 1863, Dunnie had contracted rickets, a disease that bowed the arms and legs of children. By that winter, the "poor little fellow" was "encased in steel." The apparatus was a crude orthopedic device intended to straighten his limbs. It is more likely that Annette timed her arrival coincident with the birth of Martha Louise.[135]

Just as James' sister Anna Bulloch had done with the Roosevelts in New York, Annette earned her keep by acting as nursemaid to the growing and active Bulloch household at 3 Wellington Street, Waterloo. With no husband, an estranged father who was deployed to the western theater with the Union army, the 21-year-old Annette had few options to support herself. Employment for women outside the home remained limited. Even primary classroom teacher positions were generally reserved for men. Those women who did manage to find a teaching position still lived in poverty.[136]

The first reference to Annette's presence in Liverpool was at the wedding of Commander Bulloch's purser (accountant and clerk), Richard "Dick" Taylor. He and Fanny Willoughby Camp married on March 30, 1865, at the Sephton [*sic*] Parish Church outside of Liverpool. Taylor held the rank of Assistant Paymaster in the Confederate Navy, and Annette Cross was one of the official witnesses at the wedding. Just two days later, she and her sister Harriott entertained another young Confederate Navy officer, Lt. Douglas French Forrest.[137]

Lt. Forrest arrived at the Bulloch parlor where he anxiously awaited James' return. Harriott and Annette kept the young officer entertained until the harried secret agent finally arrived home late in the evening. Commander Bulloch had been attending to the widow of the Confederate shipping agent who had lost his life on his blockade runner *Lelia*. Perhaps inspired by her exposure to so many dashing naval officers, Annette would later marry the successful blockade running captain, Seth Grosvenor Porter.[138]

Annette's attraction to Confederate officers was common among discerning southern belles. During the Civil War, many women believed that only military men were worthy of their attentions. The South's public press encouraged this feeling. This preference was a natural extension of the southern ethos that held self-denial and service to others as central to a woman's mission. The ultimate demonstration of personal sacrifice was to support those who were risking their lives for the cause of the South. At the end of the war, these same women confronted another dilemma. The Union had an army infused with willing immigrants and a class of men who could not afford to hire substitutes. The most eligible bachelors of the North were still very much alive. In the South, three of every four white males between the ages of 18 and 50 served in the military. By the end of the war, able-bodied males comprised less than 5 percent of the white population. For young white women seeking husbands, the pickings were extremely thin and their economic prospects were equally poor.[139]

The plight of destitute southern women without husbands was not confined to the southern states. In his comprehensive role as an agent of the Confederate Navy, Commander Bulloch had a duty to care for the families of sailors who had deployed in his cruisers and blockade runners. In the United States, his brother-in-law Theodore Roosevelt, Sr., had labored to create a similar allotment system for the families of Union soldiers. In Liverpool, James not only performed this same duty for the Confederate Navy, he personally disbursed the funds and tended to individual needs. When Lt. Forrest first visited the Confederate office at 10 Rumford Place, he found Bulloch "besieged by wives & sweethearts of our tars with their allotment tickets." James diligently made these payments, even after the collapse of the Confederate States as a nation. His unselfish dedication to his sailors and their families was a testament to his character and helped insulate him and his family from some of the Union retribution visited upon others.[140]

As the American Civil War approached its inevitable conclusion, most of the Bullochs' friends and families who had been left behind in Georgia lost everything. More than simply demoralizing the white population, the Yankee Army's plundering path of destruction left southerners on the brink of starvation. Even those women who had been part of wealthy families could not simply welcome their men back home and return to the old ways. Very few families retained their wealth.[141]

The Bulloch ladies who had moved North prior to the war suffered none of these deprivations. They retained their dignity, their servants, and their belief in a benign, paternalistic society. They were still in charge at home and expected their men to tend to business in the public arena. Although the Bulloch ladies were not visible in a public sense, they maintained a general, but intelligent, awareness of their husband's business. They could and did calibrate the moral compasses of their men and helped guide them in their affairs beyond the threshold.

In Liverpool, Harriott Bulloch was caught somewhere in between the old and the new. Despite her distance from the battlefields, all had not been romance and happiness in her English household. In addition to the birth of three children, serious ailments, and the death of her mother, Harriott suffered the loss of a younger brother. Edwin (Edmund) had been "killed in battle" in the summer of 1863. Like her estranged father Osborne Cross, who eventually achieved the rank of brigadier general, Harriott's brother had worn Yankee blue. Now, she had to navigate a large family that now included her sister Annette, through the uncertain prospects of peace while living in a foreign land.[142]

5

Unreconstructed Confederates: Lifted on Angel's Wings

For most families, both Union and Confederate, the four long years of cursed war finally ended in May of 1865. The cost in lives was between 620,000 and 750,000 young Americans. Union armies had silenced the guns of the Confederacy and jailed Jefferson Davis along with most of his government. The Confederate Navy had lost all of James Bulloch's ironclads. The British government seized two of them and took them into their Royal Navy. The French government seized two others, with one of them eventually going to the Prussian Navy.[1]

Despite Bulloch's extraordinary success in getting the second French-built ironclad, the CSS *Stonewall*, under Confederate colors, the war was over by the time it reached Havana. The Union Navy had captured his former blockade runner *Fingal*, which had been converted into the ironclad CSS *Atlanta*, during its first engagement. The U.S. Navy rechristened the prize ship as the USS *Atlanta* and added it to the blockading fleet. The Confederates had scuttled the Ladies' Ironclad Gunboat, CSS *Georgia*, in the Savannah River at the approach of Sherman's army.[2]

The prolonged wartime anxiety of the Bulloch family in England was not a result of this litany of missed opportunities and Confederate failures. A full six months after the collapse of the South, Commander Bulloch's commerce raider *Shenandoah* still roamed the seas. It was a ship without a country. Even more important for the Bulloch ladies, Irvine Bulloch was one of its officers. If caught, Irvine could be tried and hanged as a pirate. The *Shenandoah* had sent 32 Union ships to the bottom of the ocean and most of those were New England whalers. Unaware that the war had ended, its Captain James I. Waddell had unwittingly sunk 21 of the ships on behalf of a nation that no longer existed. Not until the morning of

November 6, 1865, did the *Shenandoah* steam up the Mersey and lower the "Stainless Banner" of the Confederate States one last time.[3]

Peace was at hand, but the prospects of the Bulloch family in Liverpool were very much in doubt. President Johnson's amnesty proclamation did not include those Confederates who had been serving overseas. As the many admirers of James Bulloch had noted, he was scrupulously honest, "living in a very plain, simple style, though large sums of public money were passing through his hands." An unfortunate consequence of his honorable service was poverty. The Bullochs could only hope that competence and honesty would translate into a livelihood as a refugee in Liverpool.[4]

For the white women of the South among the merchant or planter classes, their impoverished circumstances sometimes forced them to leave home and earn wages. Many of these women felt betrayed. They had misplaced their trust in their government, their men, their servants, and their God. None of whom delivered them from the Yankees. The government, its armies and navies, and their own men were supposed to have protected them, but they did not. The servants that they had fed, housed, clothed, and nurtured abandoned them. Southern white women could not understand why their slaves would choose the uncertainty of freedom over a safe but hopeless life in bondage. Even God seemed to have turned against them. They either accepted their defeat as God's punishment for unknown sins or simply blamed God for allowing evil to triumph over good.[5]

Unlike their counterparts in the South, daily life for Bulloch ladies in the North continued much as it had before the war. The status of Harriott and her growing family circle in Liverpool was somewhere in between these extremes. For Harriott, nothing could be as it was before. If her family returned to the United States, her husband would be arrested. Confederates like James and Irvine Bulloch who had lived or operated in foreign countries were not eligible to sign a loyalty oath and receive amnesty. Despite the fall of the Confederate government and the uncertainty of life overseas, Harriott saw no reason to lose faith in her husband or her God. They were all alive and hopeful for a better future.[6]

Whatever hope the couple may have had, both Harriott and James were ill in early December 1865. Their sickness was probably a reaction to the tremendous strain they had been under. They had sufficiently recovered by December 9, to attend to the baptism of their children. They presented Jessie Hart, Henry Dunwoody, Stuart Elliott and Martha Louise Bulloch for baptism into the Church of England at the Parish of St. John Church in Waterloo. James, Jr., did not participate since he had already been baptized (christened) in the United States.[7]

James also attended to his family's financial security. He formed a partnership with his former Confederate clerk, Moses P. Robertson, and they began to work as cotton traders. James set up an office adjacent his old Fraser, Trenholm offices at 10 Rumford Place. After brother Irvine returned from his around-the-world cruise on the CSS *Shenandoah*, he also settled in Liverpool and began similar brokerage work.[8]

Back in New York, Anna Bulloch finally relinquished her nursemaid duties at the Roosevelt household. At 31 years of age, she was well past her debutante years, but still an attractive, intelligent woman. She was a bit shorter in stature than her younger sister Mittie, with light blue eyes and brown hair that framed a lovely oval face and a full, round chin. In personality, the two sisters were very dissimilar. Anna was the adventurous but introverted caregiver who rarely drew attention to herself.[9]

Southern ladies had typically defined themselves by their relationships to men, first as daughters and sisters, then as wives and mothers. Anna, no doubt, felt some pressure to avoid a life of spinsterhood, but she was confident enough to delay marriage and pursue other priorities. When she did decide to marry, not only did she choose a man who was seven years younger, she married very well. On June 5, 1866, Anna and the wealthy financier, James King Gracie, exchanged vows at the Presbyterian Church of the Transfiguration in Brooklyn. Theirs was a long and happy, but childless, marriage that drew another "Brother Jimmie" into the Bulloch-Roosevelt family.[10]

By ignoring antebellum social norms, Martha Bulloch's daughters had avoided another element of the social and economic upheaval experienced by their peers in the South. Young ladies in the South discovered that there were very few eligible men available after the war. They either had to lower their expectations and choose a mate quickly or risk having no choice at all. Thousands of widows and wives with broken or maimed husbands also had to assume unfamiliar roles as family provider and protector. Worse yet was the fear of starvation. All these privations led many southern women to harbor bitter feelings toward their Yankee conquerors. As one young lady from North Carolina explained, "I feel so hard, so pitiless. Gladly would I witness the death of each of those wretches.... God grant they may suffer in their houses, their firesides, their wives, and their children as they have made us suffer."[11]

Martha's three sons-in-law had all supported the Union during the war, yet none of them served in the military. Susan's husband Hilborne West became a much-loved uncle and pediatric physician. Despite his great potential, he was not ambitious and never achieved much in the way of financial or professional success. Theodore Roosevelt, Sr., was widely known and respected for his many charitable and public service achievements. Theodore had inherited most of his wealth and his capable brothers profitably managed the family's business affairs. Anna's husband, James King Gracie, was a successful investment banker and broker who came from a prominent family of politicians and bankers.[12]

The elevated social positions of the three brothers-in-law certainly played a role in their passive war-time roles. It would have been difficult for Susan, Mittie, or Anna to love a man who had fought against their brothers. Ironically, their husbands' lack of military service seemed to elevate the level of respect the Bulloch women and children had for the martial courage of James and Irvine Bulloch. For their part, the Bulloch sisters ably filled the traditional roles of wife and homemaker for their families. Anna and Mittie would become something more for their sister-in-law Lucy Elliot as well as James and Irvine Bulloch. The two sisters, and even Mittie's oldest daughter Bamie, assumed the role of benefactors for their entire extended family. These women were in positions to leverage the goodwill and vast resources derived from the fortunes of James Gracie and Theodore Roosevelt, Sr.

In England, James and Harriott continued to reside at No. 3 Wellington Street in Waterloo. James threw himself into his work as a cotton and commodity broker. By 1868, he had achieved a reasonable degree of prosperity. He and Harriott were confident enough in their future to begin construction on a new house in the Liverpool suburb of Waterloo. They named their new home "Clifton," recalling the name of the Bulloch family's farm when they first moved to Roswell, Georgia. Clifton was a "very comfortable 3 story brick, rough stone front, bay windows, handsome plate glass," home that also had a "drawing room, Library, and large Dining room, besides Kitchen, Pantry, and on first floor upstairs, nice closet room, bath rooms, etc."[13]

Financial considerations aside, the Bullochs' construction of a home in England made it clear that James and Harriott had decided against returning to the United States. They were putting down new roots, or perhaps they were just re-connecting with the Bullochs' Scottish ancestry in Great Britain.

The Liverpool Bullochs were not alone in their desire to recall happier times in the South during their youth. In 1868, Mittie and Theodore Roosevelt visited Roswell for the last time. It had been four years since the death of Martha Bulloch. Although the couple stayed with the Gouldings in Roswell, Mittie spent most of her time at Bulloch Hall. By then, the Jason Sylvester Wood family lived in the mansion. During her visit, Mrs. Wood gave Mittie one of the cut glass doorknobs from her mother's bedroom as a token remembrance of her beloved home. Hilborne West eventually sold Bulloch Hall to the Woods in 1872 in his role as executor of Martha's estate.[14]

Also in 1868, James and Irvine Bulloch remained among the group of former Confederates who were not eligible for reinstatement as U.S. citizens. To satisfy his longing to visit his sisters while avoiding arrest, Irvine made a covert trip to New York in hopes of briefly meeting with Mittie and Anna. Just prior to Anna's marriage to James Gracie, Irvine booked passage in a steamship's cramped steerage compartments under an assumed name. He carefully avoided compromising Theodore Roosevelt's position and only used private communications with his sisters. He set up a secret meeting in Central Park where he directed his sisters to meet him under the third tree to the left of the old Mall.[15]

Some observers mistakenly believed that the Bulloch brothers were never able to legally return to the United States and that James was ineligible for a pardon. To the contrary, President Andrew Johnson's "Christmas Amnesty" of December 25, 1868, provided pardons to all Confederates (except Jefferson Davis), who signed a loyalty oath. It was a pardon that James did not need and an oath he could not sign. On Saturday January 16, 1869, he submitted his papers for naturalization as a British citizen. His sponsors were four prominent citizens from the Liverpool area.[16]

Bulloch's memorial (application) for citizenship stated that he and his American-born wife had resided in nearby Waterloo for the past six years, except for "short temporary absences." He was careful to point out that two of his five children were British citizens from birth. He intended to "reside permanently in England and to carry on the business of a Merchant there." He had, "become greatly attached to this Country" and was "desirous to acquire the rights of a British Subject." It was one of the most rapidly processed applications in the history of the British Home Office. James D. Bulloch became a British citizen in less than a week.[17]

In these post-war years, die-hard southern women frequently blamed southern men for giving up too soon, or not trying hard enough. They berated any man who seemed too eager to accept defeat and submit to a loyalty oath, an act that was tantamount to surrendering their manhood. There is no indication that the Bulloch women held that view, but it is clear that they held James and Irvine in higher esteem because they did not submit or surrender. In fact, Anna, Mittie, and Mittie's children were the primary sources of the mistaken reports about James' and Irvine's status as unreconstructed Confederates.[18]

Liverpool offered the Bulloch family their best chance for a successful business and social life. Their only surviving parent was Harriott's absentee and remarried father, General Osborne Cross. Bulloch's brother Irvine and Harriott's sister Annette Cross were with them in Liverpool. They would soon be joined by Bulloch's ward, the 18-year-old Nannie Caskie Hutchison. James was one of her eight guardians that had included his now-deceased stepmother as well as stepsister Susan Elliott West. As part of his duties, James may have had active control over a portion of Nannie's financial assets until she reached the age of 21.[19]

It is uncertain how much of Robert Hutchison's estate actually made it into James' account. However, the Hutchison dinner china somehow survived the war, made its way across the Atlantic, and onto Harriott's dinner table. Several other of Hutchison's "old Savannah things" were in Liverpool including a "green dessert set, the same one we [Bulloch children] used to choose 'An apple or an orange my dear' from." James may have brought some of Hutchinson's household effects with him when he ran the blockade on the *Annie Childs* in 1862.[20]

The year 1869 would be a memorable one for the Bullochs: new citizenship, a new home, a new family member, and a joyous reunion with Mittie and Theodore Roosevelt and their four children. Eight long years had passed since Mittie had seen her brother Jimmie and Harriott Bulloch. Mittie and the children impatiently waited aboard ship "on the tip toe of fidgety anticipation" in the final moments before seeing her Liverpool kin. It was May 21 and after nine days at sea, the Roosevelts had arrived at the Mersey River on the steamship *Scotia*. Mittie's entire family made the trip including Theodore Sr., and all of their children: Anna ("Bamie," 14), Theodore Jr. ("Teedie," 10), Elliott ("Ellie," 9), and Corinne ("Conie," 7).[21]

Seeing that the *Scotia* was delayed by the low tide, James and Irvine hopped aboard a harbor tugboat and clambered aboard the ocean liner late that evening at its anchorage. "By the aid of lamps only half revealing the faces and excitement," the Roosevelt children were "wild with delight" when they finally saw their Uncles Jimmie and Irvine. The Bulloch brothers quickly collected the entire Roosevelt entourage from the vessel, and after a twenty minute ride on the tender, they finally arrived in Liverpool and settled into their rooms at the Adelphi Hotel.[22]

For ten days, the Roosevelts visited with Irvine, James, and Harriott Bulloch. Harriott was so overjoyed to see Mittie that she hugged and kissed her until she cried tears of happiness. When they recovered their composure, the two ladies went shopping in Liverpool's High Street for practical clothing during the Roosevelts' stay in England. Mittie also met and dined with Irvine Bulloch's fiancée Ella Sears. Mittie described Ella as the "freshest, dewiest pink rose bud, lovely eyes, dark, her picture is exactly like her, … soft white hands, blushing and affectionate."[23]

The young Bulloch and Roosevelt cousins played games together on the beach, in the yard, and in the park. They also went for a joy ride on a donkey. The ever-exuberant Teedie (Teddy) thought that donkeys were funny and tried to jump a fence on one, cutting his thigh in the process. Focusing their energies on more educational pursuits, the Bulloch and Roosevelt cousins explored the countryside with the adults. Brother Jimmie had written a Royal Navy friend, Admiral Hornby, and obtained cards of admission to "Knowsley," the palatial estate of the Derby family. Bulloch's admiral friend was the cousin and brother-in-law of the 13th Earl of Derby and was one of Britain's most capable seamen. Theodore Roosevelt, Sr., was able to attend "Derby Day" with Irvine Bulloch's future father-in-law, Henry B. Sears.[24]

While Theodore attended the spectacle now known as "Royal Ascot," the Bulloch brothers remained with Mittie and her family in Liverpool. Irvine's fiancée, Ella, entertained everyone with a fine mezzo soprano rendition of "The Wild Birds," accompanied by Harriott ("Hattie") on the piano. Everyone danced, "particularly Brother Jimmie and Hattie Sears," Ella's sister. At the dinner table, Mittie warmly recalled her childhood days and, "Uncle Robert's dinner China, I took great interest in all of the old Savannah things."[25]

The next day, Mittie's children, Theodore Jr., Elliott and Corinne, went to "dine with Hattie's children." Dunnie was a "lovely boy" with "beautiful hair and shaped head, brilliant complexion, but not a handsome mouth." Stuart had "light hair, large grey eyes, and rosy cheeks." Loulie (Martha Louise) was "chubby, solemn," had "lovely firm, peachy cheeks," and loved wearing lilac ribbons.[26]

The Roosevelt children were "invited by Jimmie's [James Bulloch, Jr.] teacher to take tea with her and see the boys play cricket. A day later, when it came time to tour Knowsley, baby [Loulie/Martha Louise] being sick, brother Jimmie could not accompany us." On May 27, while James stayed home with a sick baby, the three Roosevelt children visited Jimmie Jr.'s day and boarding school run by Madam de Zastro and Sons. There, they met one of Jefferson Davis' sons, probably the 12-year-old Jefferson Davis, Jr. Jeff and his 7-year-old brother William (Billy) had been resident students at Madam de Zastro's school since 1868. The Davis family had lived in England for several months between 1868 and 1870, but the boys remained in school when their parents returned to the United States. The school was near the Bulloch's home and the children of the two unreconstructed Confederates were regular playmates.[27]

Many scholars have accepted an additional, highly editorialized version of Teedie's meeting with the son of the former president of the Confederate States. These accounts cite the 1928 first edition of *Theodore Roosevelt's Diaries of Boyhood and Youth*. It seems that the editor of Roosevelt's diary could not describe the meeting between the future president of the United States and the son of Jefferson Davis without extending the Civil War to a Liverpool playground. The edited version of 11-year-old Teddy Roosevelt's diary cites his entry for that day as,

> We went to our cousins [*sic*] school at Waterloo. We had a nice time but met Jeff Davises [*sic*] son and some sharp words ensued. Papa came home from the Darbys [*sic*] where he has been for some days.[28]

However, Teedie's full, unaltered entry for Thursday May 27, 1869 was as follows:

> We went to Waterloo to our cousins [*sic*] school. I met Jeff Davises [*sic*] son there. Papa came home from the Darbey [*sic*] where he had been.[29]

Teddy's original diary made no mention of an altercation among the children and the "Darbey" was clearly the not the name of a friend. Teddy's reference was to the Ascot Derby (pronounced "Darh' bee"), a famous horse racing event that Papa Theodore Roosevelt attended with Mr. Sears, the father of Irvine Bulloch's fiancée.

The Roosevelts finally took their leave of the Bullochs and Liverpool on June 1 to continue their tour of Great Britain and Continental Europe. Theodore Roosevelt, Sr., briefly returned to Liverpool in late November, leaving his family in Italy. Theodore had to attend to his plate glass importing and manufacturing business. He took time to dine with Irvine, "Captain" Bulloch, and his partner Moses Robertson in Liverpool. The following day Theodore, Sr., delivered family letters to Harriott before tending to his business and rejoining the family in Italy. Theodore's separation from Mittie and the children belies the common perception of her inability to function independently. Mittie was quite capable and energetic in managing the household in her husband's absence, even in foreign lands.[30]

At this time in American history, wealthy Americans commonly indulged themselves in grand tours of Europe and the Mediterranean. Unlike American tourists of the twenty-first century, the duration of a typical tour was not merely a few weeks. The visit would continue for a year or more. The primary impetus for this particular trip certainly came from Mittie, for she had longed to see her two brothers and their families.

Her female counterparts in the post-war South had also assumed the traditionally masculine responsibility of planning for this type of adventure. Those ladies had hard experience in moving house in advance of invading armies when there were no males available for advice or assistance. Mittie had years of experience in moving house, but under much more benign circumstances as she moved back and forth between luxurious summer homes.[31]

The Roosevelts remained in Europe for almost a full year, moving north and south with the seasons through Holland, Switzerland, Italy, Austria, Prussia, Belgium, and France. They found that war had blurred some of the male and female distinctions between public and private arenas. For the Bulloch ladies particularly, their brothers' roles in the war had made faraway places events seem much closer and personally relevant. Mittie and the family finally returned to Liverpool the next spring for another reunion with the Liverpool Bullochs before leaving for New York. The only the exception was her eldest daughter Anna ("Bamie"), who remained in France.[32]

The remainder of the Roosevelt family, Mittie, Theodore and their children Teedie, Ellie, and Conie Roosevelt departed Liverpool on May 14. They traveled in the *Russia*, "a fine screw [steam] boat," the first of the Cunard line's transatlantic screw steamers. Their faces quickly faded out of sight as a misty rain fell on the Mersey. Fortunately for the future president, who suffered from chronic seasickness, the North Atlantic seas were mercifully calm, but not for long. When the *Russia* reached the North Atlantic, Teedie was disabled for a whole week. His illness was a reminder that Mittie had not accomplished all she and Theodore had hoped for during their time in Europe. They had been fabulously successful with the first goal: a joyous reunion with Mittie's brothers in Liverpool. The added hope that a change in climate would improve the asthmatic Teedie's health did not materialize. The third important goal had been set in motion, but she would have to wait to see if the results justified the risk.[33]

Theodore and Mittie had left their 15-year-old Bamie behind. They enrolled her as a student in Mademoiselle Marie Souvestre's finishing school in Fontainebleau, outside of Paris. Bamie's nearest family or even acquaintances were her Bulloch aunt and uncles in Liverpool. Always a mature, precocious child, Bamie had a facile, inquiring mind. Bamie's structured education had come to an end when her Aunt Anna Bulloch left the nursery to marry James Gracie. Both Mittie and her sister Anna had received a more formal education as they grew up in Roswell, and at Barhamville Academy in South Carolina.

Mittie's parents had always made education a priority for their children, including the girls. In fact, they sought out the best academies available for all of their children, and stepchildren. The pursuit of a quality education for older sisters and brothers (Susan, Georgia, James, and Daniel) was the reason Mittie had been born in Hartford, Connecticut. Even in the nineteenth century, education was a paramount factor in improving women's status. Unlike many of her peers, however, Bamie was not facing the prospect of having to pursue a career or even having to contemplate seeking wage-earning employment. She had such a fine intellect; it would have been a shame not to develop it as fully as possible.[34]

In the United States, the antebellum trend toward improving the equality of female education had continued. However, improvements in women's education were very slow and incremental. For example, Radcliffe College was not organized as an annex to Harvard until 1879. Even then, Harvard's all-male faculty instructed the Radcliffe women. During Bamie's teenage years, most U.S. female academies and colleges lacked scholastic rigor and continued to emphasize domestic and ornamental arts. The intent was to help young girls become informed conversationalists rather than competitors with men in business. Female academies promoted charm over knowledge. Given the limited choices in the United States, Theodore and Mittie chose Mlle. Souvestre's boarding school in France. Named *Les Ruches* (The Beehives), it was Europe's most prestigious academy for aristocratic young girls.[35]

Mlle. Marie Souvestre (Franklin D. Roosevelt Presidential Library, Hyde Park, New York, NPx 64–376).

Bamie would emerge from *Les Ruches* very well-schooled in world geo-politics, history, diplomacy, art, music, and literature. She was a particularly adept student and was one of Mlle. Souvestre's favored pupils. Bamie became an intelligent listener as well as an informed exponent on issues of import. Miss Roosevelt also gained poise in manner and dress, which helped not only her appearance, but her self-confidence, regardless of the setting or company.[36]

Bamie's presence in France gave her a literal front row seat to observe the machinations of European great power politics. On July 15, 1870, the French government declared war against Prussia in a conflict that soon engulfed all of Continental Europe. At first, Bamie only used her Uncle Jimmie's Rumford Street business address in Liverpool as a conduit to forward her mail. With the outbreak of war, James Bulloch was the relay hub for numerous telegrams and letters between France and New York. When France mobilized its army, Bamie Roosevelt found herself in the middle of a war zone. The French government even converted her school into a hospital. During those perilous times, Bamie's safe harbor was the Bulloch home in the Waterloo suburb of Liverpool. Just as her Uncle Jimmie had done so many times during the American Civil War, Bamie made her way to Le Havre by rail and then crossed the English Channel by ferry to Portsmouth. James' telegram to New York finally provided her parents the ironic, but welcome news, "Bamie is at Waterloo."[37]

Theodore Roosevelt Senior reflected the family's relief in a letter to Bamie that asked her to thank,

> Capt Bulloch for his last telegram. You are all safe now at all events and ... [I] feel more at ease with regard to you than I could have while you were in France. Then it will be so much pleasure for you to see them all in Liverpool. I recall my stay there with so much pleasure, your Aunt Hattie's motherly way of treating me a great deal better than I deserved. Ella, so sweet and pretty and affectionate if Irvine was not present to distract her attention. ...
> Your Uncle Jimmie and Irvine, I know, will take good care of you, but I am worried to have you indefinitely, almost I might say, forced upon them, although I know they are glad to receive you. Be just as sweet and good and as little trouble as possible, and if there is a shadow of doubt about your wearing your welcome out, come home the first good opportunity.[38]

Mittie expressed similar sentiments, "We are so glad you are safely in England and under Uncle Jimmie's care. Altho' of course perplexed & worried at the cause and well knowing how anxious the suspense must make you and the annoyance of your clothes being in Fontainebleau." Like her husband, Mittie was mindful that Bamie should not over-stay her welcome. She advised, "darling Bamie, I know the good hospitable heart of Aunt Hattie but after your have paid her a nice visit, I wish you to get your Uncle Jimmie or Irvine to get you a nice room in the same lodging house [used by] Uncle Irvine."[39]

As the Roosevelts awaited developments on the Continent, James Bulloch continued to send updates about their teenage daughter. The

Cambridge Road home he called "Clifton" already resonated with the voices of the five Bulloch children ages 5 to 12, plus 19-year-old Nannie Hutchison, a cook and 2 house keepers. Bamie added her energetic and intelligent voice to the mix along with that of her own maid who had accompanied her to Europe. On the French-German border, the Prussians waited with their army of over 300,000 men, biding their time. Sensing the inevitable, the French generals launched an unsuccessful preemptive attack in early August. About two weeks later, the Germans were in France and Louis-Napoléon faced defeat. With these developments, the Roosevelts hoped that the war would end quickly and that Bamie's sojourn in England would be more like a holiday than an evacuation. They remained thankful for the Bullochs' hospitality saying, "How kind & loving Aunt Hattie has been to you and dear brother Jimmie; what would we have done if they had not taken care of you?"[40]

Unfortunately, the war stretched through September and into October, and the Roosevelts resolved to bring Bamie back home to New York. On October 5, Theodore Roosevelt, Sr., once again boarded the Cunard line steamship, SS *Russia*, and rejoined his in-laws for another two weeks in Liverpool. There are no records of their activities in England during his stay, but changes were clearly afoot. When Theodore, Bamie, and her maid stepped ashore from the SS *Java* in New York City, James D. Bulloch was with them. He returned to the country of his birth for the first time since casting his lot with the Confederacy in 1861. This trip to the U.S. would be the first, but not the last, for the former secret agent and British citizen.[41]

James' motives for accompanying his brother-in-law and niece back to the United States combined business with pleasure. It would be an extended visit. After the Christmas holiday with the Roosevelts, he traveled to Mobile, Alabama. Mobile was the home of Raphael Semmes, the famous commander of James' commerce raider, the CSS *Alabama*. In addition to a probable reunion with his former comrade in arms, three cotton brokers from Manchester England checked into the same hotel as James. This rendezvous may not have been accidental. Just before he sailed to the U.S. with Theodore and Bamie, James was the traveling companion of former Confederate President Jefferson Davis as together they tried to drum up cotton brokerage business in Liverpool and Ireland.[42]

Davis had been in England on business and family matters. Wealthy friends and sympathizers were underwriting his wife Varina's stay in London as well as the Davis boys' schooling in Liverpool. Varina's sister Margaret also lived in Liverpool with her husband, Charles Stoess, head of the Bavarian consulate. Proximity and mutual needs allowed James to develop a post-war friendship with Jefferson and Varina Davis. The personal relationship between Mr. and Mrs. Davis had deteriorated in recent years. The prolonged strain of war, defeat, jail, impoverishment, and the constant threat of legal and physical retribution had taken its toll. The Davises had lived an ocean apart for almost a year and had little personal communication during that time. Adding to the tension was another, younger woman who had captured Jeff Davis' heart and the public's eye through scandalous newspaper accounts.[43]

In the midst of the Davis' personal drama, James checked into Mobile's Battle House hotel on December 29, 1870. The next day a "Mrs. V. Davis" checked into the nearby Campbell House hotel. Although Jefferson Davis remained in Memphis, Tennessee during the holiday period, James may have been working in conjunction with the cotton brokers, the former president, and his wife. Until she reverted back to a more traditional female role a few years later, Varina had been managing most of the Davis' meager household finances, just as she had during the war. Even though she had control of their personal accounts, it was unlikely that Varina would have conducted business with cotton brokers by herself. Whether her rationale was to avoid conflict or to shed an onerous burden, Varina eventually reverted to a more subservient role, like most of her southern contemporaries. As Jeff Davis began to reassert his paternalistic prerogatives, Varina stepped back from the more independent and public roles aligned with the women's rights movement of the North. The reason for her arrival in Mobile at the same time as James Bulloch also could have been purely for personal or social reasons.[44]

Jefferson Davis and James had not been close before or during the war. However, Davis was fully aware of James' character and his post-war financial circumstances. A decade later, with Varina's help, Davis wrote his history of the Civil war and made this observation:

> Captain James D. Bullock [*sic*], an officer of the old navy, of high ability as a seaman, and of an integrity which stood the test under which a less stern character might have given way, was our naval agent at Liverpool. In his office he disbursed millions, and, when there was no one to whom he could be required to render and account, paid out the last shilling in his hands, and confronted poverty without prospect of other reward than that which he might find in a clear conscience.[45]

By January, James had left Mobile and checked into another first class hotel in Baltimore, the Mount Vernon. Baltimore happened to be the home of another man who captained one of James D. Bulloch's cruisers. James I. Waddell of the CSS *Shenandoah* had returned to his home state of Maryland to live. He and his wife Anne had the opportunity to entertain the man who saved Waddell's life in 1865. James had seen to Waddell's care in Liverpool after the *Shenandoah's* voyage around the globe wrecked his health. Baltimore was also the new headquarters of Jefferson Davis' employer, the Carolina Life Insurance Company. Once again, James may have been acting in concert with Davis as they both tried to find their way in turbulent commercial seas.[46]

A letter from Theodore Roosevelt, Sr., caught up to James while he was in Baltimore. Theodore hoped that James could rejoin the family in New York on the following Tuesday, January 24, 1871. When they did meet, James allowed some of his business to take him back to his family's pre-war residence at Morristown and Madison, New Jersey. Mittie, Theodore, and their son Elliott accompanied James who drove "over to Madison to see the old place."[47]

Just as he was finalizing all his financial arrangements, James received devastating news from home. His youngest son "Dunnie" was dead. The illness had come on quickly. After exhibiting symptoms for only two days, Henry Dunwoody Bulloch, aged 9, died of *Scarlatina Anginosa* (scarlet fever). Medical science in the Victorian era had little understanding and fewer effective options to deal with scarlet fever. The disease proved to be fatal to the young boy whose immune system was already weakened by rickets. On February 21, Dr. Edward H. FitzHenry certified Dunnie's demise at Clifton, the Bulloch home in Waterloo. Shortly after James left New York, Theodore Sr., observed that, "Knowing his affectionate temperament you will realize how much the loss must affect him."[48]

As much as the loss of a son weighed on Bulloch's heart, it was Harriott's loving resiliency that fate had put to the test. Once again she had to face a life-altering experience without the benefit of her husband's presence. The additional stress of uncertain economic times only added to her anguish. The Bulloch household finances were treading on thin ice.

While he had been New York, Bulloch met with his newest brother-in-law, James King Gracie, who had married his sister Anna five years earlier. Gracie's banking connections extended from New York to Liverpool. James took advantage of the services and advice of the other "Brother Jimmie" while he promoted his own cotton brokerage business. The European market was having a negative effect on the world's economies and James' partnership with Moses Robertson was no exception. He was struggling, but he had the good fortune of having sisters who had married well-to-do Northerners. Equally fortunate, they all liked and respected James and were willing to help.[49]

The Bullochs had to improvise as they scrambled to sustain the family's moderately prosperous lifestyle in England. In addition to a grieving family of six, they had a cook and two housemaids to support. James had always traveled in first class cabins and stayed in first class hotels. Like his impoverished former Confederate countrymen, he and Harriott were reluctant to give up the trappings of a privileged lifestyle, especially when it came to travel arrangements and household servants.

Theodore Roosevelt, Sr., and James King Gracie continued to encourage James Bulloch's ventures, noting that, "I am glad he seems hopeful and has so good a thing." Irvine was struggling as well. His three sisters, Susan West, Mittie Roosevelt, and Anna Gracie, had all insisted on covering Irvine's unspecified debt of £1500 ($166,500 in 2015). Irvine also owed his brother-in-law Theodore another £400 that was probably related to his cotton brokerage business. Theodore suggested that Irvine pay what he could and then settle up the rest after he married Ella Sears, perhaps in the hope that her family would restore Irvine's fiscal solvency.[50]

Ella and Irvine's engagement was the one bit of good news that cheered the Bulloch family in an otherwise tragic year. During the war, Irvine had been engaged to a young lady from Richmond, but time and distance took its toll on that relationship. Irvine did not return from his around-the-world cruise on his brother's Confederate raider, the CSS *Shenandoah*, until November 1865. By that time, the 23-year-old Irvine did not have any likely candidates for matrimony.[51]

Ella had come to Liverpool in September of 1861 when she was just 12 years of age. Her father, Henry Beaufort Sears, was a former U.S. Army officer who had invented a diving bell. He had been working on a project to improve London's Victoria Docks since 1857 and then moved to Liverpool. Henry and Harriet Sears, Ella, and her younger sister Harriet Lilia (Hattie) all became fast friends with the Bullochs and the Roosevelts. After a long courtship, Ella and Irvine finally married in late September of 1871 at St. Bride's Parish Church. The church was just a few blocks away from their new home next door to Ella's parents at 77 Canning Street in Liverpool. Their marriage ceremony at the beautiful neoclassical Anglican Church must have brought back fond memories of happy times in the antebellum South.[52]

In the summer of 1872, Anna and her husband James King Gracie were finally able to visit the Bullochs in Liverpool. Little is known about their stay, but they remained in Liverpool for several days. Anna had not accompanied the rest of the Roosevelt clan during their trip to Liverpool three years earlier and she was making up for lost time. James Bulloch's relationship with his brother-in-law James Gracie became a close one over the next several years. Not to be outdone, Mittie Roosevelt's family followed Anna and James Gracie to Europe that fall.[53]

Mittie, Theodore, their four children, and a maid traveled to Europe for an extended stay that included two weeks in England. Again sailing on the SS *Russia*, a luxury steamer that catered to first class, or "cabin," passengers, the Roosevelts were once again bound for Liverpool. President Ulysses S. Grant had appointed Theodore Roosevelt, Sr., as the U.S. commissioner to the Vienna International Exposition commencing in the spring of 1873. Rather than just visit, Theodore decided to take his family on a grand tour of Europe, Egypt, and the eastern Mediterranean. The timing was ideal, since he and his brother James Alfred had decided to build new homes on adjoining West 57th Street lots in New York City. By remaining overseas for an entire year the family could avoid the disruption of construction and relocation from their brownstone on 20th Street. They could gain an education at the same time.[54]

When the family arrived in Liverpool in late October of 1872, the Bullochs were once again there to greet them, first Uncle Irvine and Aunt Ella and then Uncle "Jimmie" and Aunt "Hattie." They also met up with their cousins Cornelius and Hilborne Roosevelt who were with the Bullochs. Their mother, Mary West Roosevelt, the wife of Theodore's brother Silas Weir, soon gathered up her children and returned to the United States. It was only fitting that Mary was present at this meeting of the Bullochs and Roosevelts. She had been the original catalyst in bringing the two families together after her brother Hilborne West had married Mittie's stepsister Susan Elliot.[55]

The Roosevelts spent a week in Liverpool before moving on to London and continental Europe via London and Dover. While in Liverpool, the children played and got along well, particularly Teedie and young Jimmie, Jr. Although the local boys immediately identified young Theodore as a "Yankee and pestered me fearfully." The Roosevelts departed Liverpool with ample hugs, tears, and kisses.[56]

After touring Egypt and the Holy Land during the winter and tending to his duties in Vienna. Theodore, Sr., decided to return to New York in the spring to oversee the completion of the family's new home and help James Alfred with business affairs. Through the assistance of the American Consul, the Roosevelts placed their three younger children in German homes at Dresden. They hoped that Teedie, Elliott, and Corinne would learn the language and absorb the culture.[57]

Dresden was ideal since Lucy Elliott, the widowed wife of stepbrother

Stuart, was already there, living in reduced circumstances with her two children. Lucy had left Savannah the previous June. She spent a month in New York, where her two children, Maud and John, resumed their friendship with their Roosevelt cousins, as they had in previous summers. Lucy's primary intent however, was to enroll her children in an affordable German school. Mittie and Theodore may have even been the instigator of this plan with the intent of leaving their three youngest children in her care when they returned to Europe in the spring of 1873. Theodore, Sr., had sponsored Lucy's initial passport application and probably financed her travel and expenses for living abroad.[58]

Lucy was but one of many widowed white women in the South who were left to bear the greatest postwar burdens. The lack of a sufficient inheritance subjected Lucy to a lengthy period of relative impoverishment. She had two children to raise, feed, clothe, house, and educate. Like most southern women, Lucy had to assume the full responsibility for herself and her family. Fortunately, her stepsisters had married very well and were blessed with supportive husbands. Through her husband, Mittie (and perhaps the Caskies of Richmond) stepped in to rescue Lucy from a life spent merely trying to survive.[59]

With the support of Mittie and Theodore Roosevelt, Lucy, Maud, and John Elliott departed for the continent in July of 1871. Their ship, the SS *Vandalia*, landed in Portsmouth, suggesting that they first visited or stayed with James and Harriott. Lucy may have attended Irvine and Ella's wedding that September, but her eventual destination was Dresden. When Teddy, Elliott, and Corinne Roosevelt finally joined their Aunt Lucy in May of 1873, they played with their two Elliott cousins just as they had during happier times before the war in Madison, NJ. Together, the five cousins formed the "Dresden Literary American Club." They all met at Aunt Lucy Elliott's small Dresden apartment on Sunday afternoons. Under Lucy's watchful eye, they shared stories and poetry that they had written during the week.[60]

Theodore Roosevelt, Sr., returned to Liverpool in June on his way back to New York. The three youngest Roosevelt children were safely situated at Dresden and Mittie and Bamie were comfortably immersed in a spa at Carlsbad, Bohemia taking "the cures." Knowing that "Brother Jimmie" and Irvine were nearby provided an extra measure of family security. If Mittie needed any assistance while he was away, the Bulloch aunts and uncles were nearby and would rise to the occasion. Theodore Roosevelt, Sr., wrote to Mittie of his *bon voyage* party when he departed Liverpool on June 7, 1873, once again aboard the steamship *Russia*. While the women stayed home, James, Jimmie Jr., Irvine, Moses Robertson, and Irvine's father-in-law, Henry Sears, all came down to the pier to see Mr. Roosevelt off.[61]

Mittie's stay in Europe without her husband showed a remarkable strength of character that even her children often overlooked. Although the younger children were safely situated with responsible families and both Lucy Elliott and her Bulloch brothers were nearby, Mittie was essentially alone in a foreign land, but for the companionship of her eldest daughter. Instead of a strong, independent woman, her children saw her as an "exquisite 'objet d'art' [sic], to be carefully and lovingly cherished." Mittie's southern heritage probably nurtured this feeling as did her beauty,

> She was very beautiful, with black, fine hair—... fine of texture and with a glow that sometimes seemed to have a slightly russet shade, ... and her skin was the purest and most delicate white, more moonlight-white than cream-white, and in the cheeks there was a coral, rather than a rose, tint. She was considered to be one of the most beautiful women of the New York of her day.[62]

By September, Mittie and Bamie were in Paris purchasing furnishings for the new home and fully exhausting their line of credit. However, Theodore's inheritance from his father was over $1 million. This fortune, combined with a thriving plate glass business, meant that money was not a problem for Theodore and Mittie. They both had been buying household items throughout their travels, including Turkish rugs in Constantinople.[63]

As the Roosevelts' time in Europe was coming to an end, Irvine and Ella

Martha (Mittie) Bulloch Roosevelt, Dresden, ca. 1873 (courtesy National Park Service, Manhattan Historic Sites Archive).

joined Mittie and Bamie in Paris for a holiday. They then collected everyone for a return to Liverpool and the United States, stopping in London for "a little shopping." Never neglecting the children's education, everyone visited the British and the Kensington Museums (now known as the "Victoria and Albert") in London.[64]

Returning to Liverpool on October 8, Mittie Roosevelt and the three young children stayed with Ella and Irvine Bulloch. In recognition of her seniority among the children, Bamie joined Harriott and Nannie Hutchison at the Bulloch home in the suburb of Waterloo. During their visit, brother Jimmie Bulloch was absent on business, but that did not keep Mittie from having lunch with Harriott and Nannie. Mary West Roosevelt was also in Liverpool with the older members of her family and they all departed in the SS *Russia* on October 25, 1873. Perhaps inspired by all the comings and goings, Bulloch's ward, Nannie Hutchison, returned to the United States about two weeks later. Nannie sailed back to the United States, but luckily for James and Harriott, she did not sail out of their lives. She and her aunts would become the most important elements of the Bullochs' financial survival during the latter part of his life.[65]

The reason for James' absence from Liverpool during the Roosevelt visit was business, which was bad. In the spring of 1873, the fortunes of cotton brokerage firms like those of James and his brother Irvine suffered dramatic downturns. They were victims of a global depression that lasted through 1879 and longer in some regions. Irvine even considered returning to the United States permanently. In 1874, Ella and Irvine visited the Roosevelts' new home in New York City. While they were there, Theodore Roosevelt, Sr., arranged for Irvine to travel to Boston where he interviewed for a position in Memphis, Tennessee. Although he received the job offer, Irvine decided to decline. He returned to the United Kingdom with Ella and continued as a cotton broker and became one of the Liverpool Cotton Exchange's first arbitrators.[66]

Also in 1873, James and his clerk and partner of almost 10 years, Moses Robertson, decided to dissolve their partnership. Moses hoped to revive his fortunes in the United States where he returned with his wife and four children. Meanwhile, James turned his attention toward South America where he had spent many months as a young Navy midshipman. "Uncle Jimmie" had been in Pernambuco, Brazil in the fall of 1873 when Roosevelt Sr., visited Liverpool. His trips to Brazil involved the successful Brazilian entrepreneur, Baron de Mauá. The Baron had formed a steamship company with regular mail and passenger services between Brazil, the United States, and Europe. The Brazilian government elevated his title to

"Viscount" after the Baron sponsored the first successful submarine cable to reach Europe from South America in June of 1874.[67]

With her husband making multiple trips to Brazil, Harriott again had sole responsibility for managing the Bulloch household in Liverpool. In New York, the Bullochs' two brothers-in-law, James Gracie and Theodore, continued to help with the Bulloch finances. In 1873, they placed £200 (about $22,800 in 2015) in the Bullochs' account, with £125 of that amount for Harriott). In 1874, they added another $500. These payments were in addition to Mr. Roosevelt's successful role in cajoling a reluctant U.S. Navy officer to pay $400 that he owed to James.[68]

Theodore Roosevelt, Sr., also initiated a series of meetings and letters advocating payment for James' unpaid shares in the SS *Bienville*. At the outbreak of the Civil War, the U.S. Navy had purchased James' former command, the SS *Bienville*. The government paid all of the Northern owners for their respective shares, but none of the southerners, including James D. Bulloch who owned 10 of the 51 unpaid shares. Roosevelt's influence and personal appeals on James' behalf extended to the highest levels of the U.S. government including:

- William Maxwell Evarts (1818–1901), former U.S. Attorney General, member of the U.S. *Alabama* Claims commission, and future U.S. Secretary of State,
- J. Hubley Ashton (1806–1907), expert in international law, and former U.S. Assistant Attorney General,
- George M. Robeson (1829–1897), Secretary of the Navy,
- Hamilton Fish (1808–1893), U.S. Secretary of State, former Governor and Senator from New York.[69]

Also in the fall of 1874, Theodore, Sr., and his 14-year-old son Elliott (Ellie) accompanied Irvine and Ella Bulloch on their return to Europe. Papa Theodore Roosevelt was attending to his plate glass business interests. He hoped that Ellie might improve his health while he spent more time with his Bulloch cousins. When Theodore arrived in Liverpool, James was away. Harriott confided to her brother-in-law that her husband's lack of a permanent position made her "very anxious for her own sake and the children." Harriott was clearly under a great deal of stress as she wondered how her proud husband could support them without asking for help from his sisters.[70]

After James returned to Liverpool on November 14, Roosevelt reported to Mittie that Brother Jimmie seemed, "more his old natural self than he has been for years. I was so glad to tell him that I had secured his claim [for his *Bienville* shares], it helped raise his spirits. He recalled yesterday at dinner many of our old times together remembering the smallest details with evidently so much pleasure." Mr. Roosevelt would have been disappointed to know that it would be twenty-one years before the U.S. Treasury and Navy Departments, Congress, and court systems finally agreed to pay for Bulloch's claim. In 1895, thirty years after the end of the Civil War, Roosevelt's assistance finally yielded the much-needed sum of $8,510.62, worth about $251,700 in 2015.[71]

While in Paris, Theodore took the opportunity to visit Bulloch's former ward, Nannie Hutchinson. She probably was enrolled in a finishing school similar to Marie Souvestre's *Les Ruches* that Bamie Roosevelt had attended two years earlier. Other than his dislike for Nannie's female companion, little is known about their discussions. They certainly discussed James Bulloch, his family, and their financial situation. Theodore had to cut his visit short when his son Ellie suffered a severe asthma attack after a pillow fight with "Harriott's children." Aunt Ella helped nurse Ellie back to health, and Theodore Roosevelt, Sr., soon made a final trip across the ocean with his youngest son.[72]

Admiral Raphael Semmes, the captain of Bulloch's cruiser CSS *Alabama*, had observed that Commander Bulloch "has had the honor to come out of the war poor." In 1878, his words were never more true. James's reputation as an honest man was firmly intact, but his financial condition was not. By 1878, he had to sell his home in the Liverpool suburb of Waterloo. This was the same home that the Roosevelts had visited just prior to its completion in 1869 that he had affectionately named "Clifton." A lot had changed in nine years, but the most tragic was the untimely death of Mittie's husband, the brother-in-law, benefactor, and great friend of the Liverpool Bullochs. Theodore Roosevelt, Sr., died of colon cancer in February of 1878 at the age of 46.[73]

The family and most of New York City mourned Theodore's passing. The papers eulogized that, "It would be difficult to mention any good thing which has been attempted in the City during the past 20 years in which Mr. Roosevelt has not had part." Theodore's leadership included the State Board of Charities, the children's Orthopedic Hospital, the Metropolitan Art and Natural History Museums, Children's Aid Society, the Franklin Street Industrial School, and the Sanitary and Allotment Commission to name just a few of his noble enterprises.[74]

Theodore Roosevelt, Sr.'s interest in hospitals came at a time when American women were beginning to work in hospitals as nurses. During the Civil War, even southern women from the elite planter classes had taken positions as regular nurses in military hospitals. They had been encouraged by Florence Nightingale's heroic efforts during the Crimean War (1853–

1856). The first U.S. edition of Nightingale's book, *Notes on Nursing*, made a timely appearance in 1860 and helped legitimize the idea of female nursing. For the Bulloch ladies, only Lucy Elliott would have even considered the prospect of placing herself in such a public, unladylike situation. Mittie believed that it was her husband's duty to act as her public face and hands for charitable and humanitarian concerns, just as their father had for Martha. The press and parlor gossips were quick to paint those women who did stray from strict antebellum social norms as village courtesans, particularly if they had aided the other side.[75]

Theodore's death left Mittie a 43-year-old widow of independent means who had been very dependent upon her husband, both emotionally and in practical matters. Mittie was deeply devoted to her four children and her "gracious loveliness and deep devotion" always wrapped around them like a mantle. But as her daughter Corinne observed, "Owing to delicate health she was not able to enter into the active life of her husband and children." Bamie had always been the adult of the four children, spending her time with the grown-ups while the three younger children attended to childish things. Bamie had been continually at her father's side as he suffered and died from colon cancer.[76]

After Theodore Senior's death, Bamie stepped into the role as the *de facto* head of the Roosevelt household. Teddy was a 19-year-old student at Harvard and even he looked to his 23-year-old sister as a father-figure. She was "more like him [Theodore Roosevelt, Sr.] than any of the rest of the family."[77] Teddy needed her now and throughout the rest of his life, "for now that Father is gone you [Bamie] will have to advise me in many things."[78]

Although his father had the greatest impact on the young man, Teddy's boisterous temperament was much different. He and all the Roosevelt children absorbed equal parts of their mother's character. For all the many admirable qualities of Theodore Roosevelt, Sr., it was his wife, Mittie Bulloch, who instilled the pugnacious spirit and sense of martial duty that was evident in their son, the Rough Rider and future president. As Teddy's sister Corinne observed, "The fighting blood of James Dunwoody and Irvine Bulloch was the same blood infused through their sister [Mittie] into the veins of their young kinsman, the second Theodore Roosevelt, and showed in him the same glowing attributes."[79]

The Roosevelt children had immense respect and admiration for their father, but there was one aspect of his legacy that was lacking. Theodore Sr., had never placed his life on the line as a warrior in service to his county. Uncles Jimmie and Irvine Bulloch filled their romantic need for examples of heroic courage. The Roosevelt children mirrored their mother's love for her Brothers Jimmie and Irvine. Collectively, they fostered an admiring relationship that became stronger over the years. Teddy would later muse that,

> From my earliest recollection I have been fed on tales of the sea and of ships. My mother's brother was an admiral in the Confederate navy, and her deep interest in the Southern cause and her brother's calling led her to talk to me as a little shaver about ships, ships, ships, and fighting of ships, till they sank into the depths of my soul.[80]

Fired by these stories, Teddy and Bamie had invented the "running the blockade" game, but their interest in naval power and Navy officers was more than a childish infatuation. Bamie's attention to naval matters took longer to find expression, but Teddy's did not. He was convinced that the United States must a have a strong navy to assume its proper role as a great world power. His conviction would later find expression when he sought and achieved the position of Assistant Secretary of the Navy and in his policies as president. Teddy's concrete ideas about naval power began to take shape while he was at Harvard, shortly after his father's death. As he explained to a friend, "And when I first began to think, in any independent and consecutive order, for record at Harvard, I began to write a history of the Naval War of 1812. And when the professor thought I ought to be on mathematics and the languages, my mind was running to ships that were fighting each other."[81]

As he began to write the first of his many acclaimed works of history, Teddy was able to move on with his life without

Alice Hathaway Lee Roosevelt (Library of Congress).

a father. A significant milestone in that journey was his marriage to the beautiful Alice Hathaway Lee on his 22nd birthday in October of 1880. As a newlywed who had just completed his studies at Harvard, Teddy's manuscript on *The Naval War of 1812* languished. Happily, Uncle Jimmie Bulloch paid a visit to the Roosevelt home in the early spring of 1881. Teddy and his bride were there to greet him. After two days, Alice left for her home in Massachusetts, no doubt to give uncle and nephew more time together. That day, Teddy took the "dear old sea captain" on a carriage ride and spent several hours with him."[82]

James and Teddy also had time to coordinate their travel plans. The newlyweds were planning a belated four-month European vacation and Teddy obviously wanted to maximize his time with the Bullochs while they were in Liverpool. Accordingly, when Teddy and Alice departed New York on May 12, they stopped in Ireland and spent 10 days touring the Emerald Isle. They then headed to Liverpool where they met up with Teddy's aunts and uncles. James departed New York on May 21, and the "dear old sea captain" arrived just before the Roosevelts' departure for London on May 31.[83] In Liverpool, the couple stayed at the Bullochs' large home on 63 Upper Parliament St. They also visited with Uncle Irvine and

Young Theodore Roosevelt, right, admired and emulated his Uncle Jimmie Bulloch (Bulloch, from *Century Magazine*; 1882 photo of Roosevelt courtesy National Park Service, Manhattan Historic Sites Archive).

Aunt Ella at their smaller home on 19 Sefton Drive that Irvine had nostalgically named "Roswell." Teddy described their "lovely little house" as, "just too pretty for anything." Alice was especially taken with Ella and Irvine. Teddy then reported that Aunt Hattie was "as dear and motherly as ever." However, he was not at all pleased with the "everlasting slobbering" kisses of his younger cousins that his Aunt Hattie seemed to encourage.[84]

In September, Teddy and Alice returned to Liverpool, where they spent almost two weeks before departing for New York. Perhaps to avoid more unwelcome kisses from the Bulloch children, they stayed with Irvine and Ella. Cousin Jessie Bulloch joined them there as well. Alice and Ella took "a great fancy to one another," which was fortunate, since Teddy spent most of his time with his Uncle Jimmie.[85]

James provided the necessary encouragement and practical nautical savvy to get Teddy's manuscript moving again. As a result, G.P. Putnam's Sons published Roosevelt's book *The Naval War of 1812* in 1883. Although the book was dry and sometimes tedious, critics found the account comprehensive, accurate, and praiseworthy. Teddy Roosevelt went on to publish 37 other non-fiction books, but in his preface to his first, Roosevelt singled out his Uncle Jimmie Bulloch. He extended his, "sincerest thanks to Captain James D. Bulloch, formerly of the United States Navy ... without whose advice and sympathy this work would probably never have been written or even begun."[86]

Teddy reciprocated James' assistance by encouraging his uncle to begin work on a book of his own. It would be a story that only Commander James D. Bulloch could tell about Confederate shipbuilding efforts in Europe during the Civil War. Previous to his nephew's visit, the modest sailor was reluctant to publish, "a narrative which would appear to be so like a history of my own individual adventures and services."[87]

Almost 30 years earlier, Mittie had been delighted by the news that her husband and her brother Jimmie had stuck up a friendship in her absence. Her son knew she would be equally pleased to hear of the bond he had developed with his Uncle Jimmie. Teddy wrote his mother,

> As for me, I spend almost the entire time with the blessed old sea-captain, talking over naval history, and helping him arrange his papers, of which he has literally thousands, I have persuaded him to publish a work which only he possesses the materials to write, about the naval operations abroad during the last war, which were conducted and managed by him—including the cruise in the *Fingal*. I enjoy talking to the dear old fellow more than I can tell; he is such a modest high souled old fellow that I just love and respect him And I think he enjoys having some one to talk to who really enjoys listening. Of course, had I been old enough, I would have served on the North-

ern side; but I am none the less interested in his history on account of that, as I do not think partisanship should ever obscure the truth.[88]

Teddy had clearly changed his uncle's perspective. As a result, James decided to write a narrowly focused memoir, titled *The Secret Service of the Confederate States in Europe, or How the Confederate Cruisers were Equipped*. The book was practically devoid of references to his family or personal life, but unlike so many memoirs, it was accurate in its details regarding dates, places, people, and events. In his preface, Bulloch admitted that he wrote the book without expectation of profit. He wrote "from a sense of duty, and in compliance with the urgent request of many persons who took opposite sides in the Civil War, and who have thought that the future historian should be furnished with facts relating to the foreign-built navy of the Confederate States."[89]

Just prior to its publication in 1883, James revealed his conflicting emotions about putting his experiences in print, "It is always painful to be the historian of an effort, however great, which has ended in failure."[90]

The character and life of his Uncle Jimmie Bulloch helped inspire one of Teddy Roosevelt's most eloquent and famous speeches.

> It is not the critic who counts; not the man who points out how the strong man stumbles, or where the doer of deeds could have done them better. The credit belongs to the man who is actually in the arena, whose face is marred by dust and sweat and blood; who strives valiantly; who errs, who comes short again and again, because there is no effort without error and short-coming; but who does actually strive to do the deeds; who knows great enthusiasms, the great devotions; who spends himself in a worthy cause; who at the best knows in the end the triumph of high achievement, and who at the worst, if he fails, at least fails while daring greatly, so that his place shall never be with those cold and timid souls who neither know victory nor defeat.[91]

Teddy's imprint on his uncle's book continued when Harper & Company released the first U.S. edition in 1884. Teddy Roosevelt's ownership interest in the publishing firm certainly expedited its publication. Although it was a critical success and remains a valuable addition to any American Civil War library, James' income from the book was minimal. Unlike his prolific nephew, he never attempted another book and published no magazine articles. James' impact on his nieces and nephews, however, was undeniable. As Mittie's children grew into adulthood, they did not see their Uncle Jimmie Bulloch's failures. They learned instead to appreciate the goodness of the man and the love and respect he engendered from their parents, Mittie and Theodore, Sr.[92]

The satisfaction of having two acclaimed authors in the Bulloch/Roosevelt family was short-lived. On Valentine's Day of 1884 dual tragedies struck the Roosevelt household in New York City. First, Mittie Bulloch Roosevelt had come down with what was thought to be a cold. At 3 o'clock in the early morning hours of February 14, she succumbed to typhoid fever in the same first floor room where her husband had died six years earlier. That day, Teddy's wife Alice Lee was also critically ill. She was ensconced on the third floor of the Roosevelt home. She had just delivered her first child, also named Alice, two days before. At two o'clock in the afternoon the specter of death once again called at the home on 57th Street. The 22-year-old Alice Lee Roosevelt fell victim to Bright's disease (kidney failure), a complication of her pregnancy. Teddy

Alice Lee Roosevelt left, and Anna (Bamie) Roosevelt, ca. 1887 (courtesy National Park Service, Manhattan Historic Sites Archive).

Roosevelt's depth of anguish was profound. As he noted in his diary, "The light has gone out of my life."[93]

Bamie, of course, was the one who took responsibility for the new baby and for notifying family members of the situation. She had first sent an urgent telegram to Teddy beckoning him home. He was in Albany, New York, fulfilling his responsibilities as a State Congressman. Shortly after Mittie died, while Alice Lee's life hung in the balance, she sent a telegram to her Bulloch uncles in Liverpool. Uncle Jimmie Bulloch responded,

> The cable has never carried through the depths of the sea a sadder message than it has brought us today.
>
> I feel an overwhelming sentiment of grief, for which I can find no present consolation. ... but my heart and spirit are with you all this night.
>
> Irvine and I have only just returned from sending a brief expression of our feeling to you through the cable, and already you know that at this great distance, we are all moved by a common emotion. ... Oh! If I could only have

seen the dear hale face, before it was hid for all time. Perhaps it will not be long before I shall see it in the beautiful state. Who can tell? I send this to you dearest Bamie, but it is meant for all the dear children who are grieving this night. Our anxiety about dear Alice adds to our unhappiness, but we will doubtless learn how it fares with her. John xiv-18, With dearest love to all.

Your loving Uncle, James D. Bulloch.[94]

The cited verse from the King James Version of the Holy Bible reads, "I will not leave you comfortless: I will come to you." James hoped that a Divine comforter would come to the Roosevelt family, for both of the Bulloch brothers remained in England in 1884. James, more than anyone, understood his young nephew's loss. His own mother, Hettie, died at the age of 32 when he was only seven. Another sorrowful parallel was the death of his first wife, Lizzie Caskie. She had been born on February 15 and also died at the age of 22, after a marriage of less than three years.

Some dismissed Mittie as a beautiful but vapid and extravagant ornament for her husband. Granted, she was prone to seemingly petulant spells of sickness, and had an almost obsessive need for cleanliness of home and body. She certainly was beautiful and, thanks to her birth and marriage, she was also wealthy enough to afford extravagance. To those who measured value only by achievements wrought in the public arena, she was little more than a decorative wife. These unfair and inaccurate characterizations reflect historical and cultural bias. True to her southern roots, Mittie's domain was the home. Apart from the unconditional love she showered on her family, she encouraged and even expected her husband and other male family members to act out her values in public. Far from being unaffected by the emerging feminist activism in support of disabled veterans, destitute widows, and ragged, sickly orphans, Mittie believed that the initiative for reform rested with men, her men. To speak or act publicly in support of a worthy cause was simply not something a Bulloch lady could do and still call herself a lady. Just as southern officers had admired James D. Bulloch for his energy, "brains [and] dash," those who knew Mittie best saw those same splendid qualities in her and her offspring.[95]

In Liverpool, the shock of Mittie and Alice Lee's deaths only compounded the angst of the Bulloch household. In addition to his personal grief, James' financial situation had gotten even worse. In the autumn of 1884, James even sought Jefferson Davis' endorsement for the position of U.S. consul to Liverpool. James withdrew his request before Davis could act, but he and Harriott had to leave their large and comfortable home at 63 Upper Parliament Street. The Bullochs' new home was a more rural and modest two-story home at 30 Sydenham Avenue in Liverpool. By that time, James and Harriott's surviving male children were grown. The boys, James Jr. (26) and Stuart (21), had moved out on their own, but the two girls, Jessie Hart (24) and Martha Louise (19), still lived with their parents. Despite their reduced circumstances, Harriott retained the services of two domestic servants, including her faithful cook Agnes McCormick, who served the family for over 20 years.[96]

In 1886, James received another £225 from his former ward, Nannie Hutchison. He and Harriott had maintained an affectionate correspondence with Nannie and treated her like their own daughter. On the occasion of Nannie's 29th birthday, James affectionately thought back to 1851 when she was just a baby and he was still in the U.S. Navy. He recalled, "holding you in my arms when you could not have been more than a week old and very shortly afterwards, escorting you and your Mother, with the fat rosy nurse, Susan, from Richmond to Savannah." With this type of familial relationship it is not surprising that Nannie provided James with sufficient cash "to pay the bills which had so weighed upon me and that the cover note was at once used to clear them off."[97]

Despite these funds, James had to seek additional assistance from his sister Anna and her husband, James K. Gracie. It seems that the Bullochs no longer had the sheltering hand of Providence to sustain them. James confided to Nannie that, "I believe no trials are so hard to bear and so humiliating to a sensitive nature as those which compel one to accept if not to seek pecuniary aid." Brother-in-law Gracie had previously sent money to James and Harriott, but it was not enough. James worded his request in the best way possible to salve his wounded pride, "I felt inclined to tell Jimmie Gracie that the appeal to them was a spontaneous suggestion of your own [Nannie Hutchison's], and that I was conscious of having no right or purpose to press for further aide from him." James had fallen victim to the impoverished circumstances that had afflicted his fellow southerners twenty years earlier. James finally realized that he was utterly incapable of supporting his family without the help of his female relations.[98]

While the Bullochs struggled financially, Teddy Roosevelt rekindled a childhood romance with Edith Carow in 1886. Even after they were engaged, Teddy battled deep feelings that he was somehow guilty of being unfaithful to his deceased wife, Alice Lee. Although Edith was not a radiant beauty like Alice, the self-assured Miss Carow had piercing grey eyes and at 5 feet, 7 inches, was just two inches shorter than Teddy. Edith and Teddy planned to travel separately to Europe. He would rendezvous with his "secret" fiancée for a small wedding in London. When Teddy finally boarded the steamer in New York City, his travelling companion was sister Bamie. The ship's manifest listed them under the name of Mr. & Mrs. Merrifield, one of Teddy's Dakota ranching partners. Upon arrival in Liverpool on November 15 they gave up the ruse. Bamie stayed with the Bullochs in Liverpool, but Teddy pressed on to London where he married Edith on December 2 at St. George's Church in Hanover Square. After their nuptials, Teddy and Edith Roosevelt toured the European Continent for fifteen weeks and returned to New York in mid–March 1887. Teddy left no record to confirm whether he visited with the Bullochs in Liverpool.[99]

In the spring of 1887, Teddy's brother Elliott Roosevelt made plans for a similar trip to Europe with his beautiful bride Anna Hall. When Uncle James Bulloch had first learned of Elliott's engagement to the blue-eyed 18-year-old back in 1883, he took the opportunity to reveal a bit of his whimsical side. James composed a mock character reference, complete with an official lawyer's certification that lavished praise on the prospective bridegroom, Elliott, "nephew of the undersigned, a killer of tigers, and other savage beasts, and therefore presumably of a fierce and implacable temper, by those who knew him not, has at last fallen captive at the feet of a gentle maiden."[100]

Jessie Hart Bulloch Maxwell, March 1892 (courtesy Friends of the Archives of Dumfries and Galloway, Album 3, Page 59, Photo 5 [MH6_59_5]).

On May 19, 1887, Elliott and Anna Roosevelt's vacation took a tragic turn when their out-bound ocean liner, the SS *Britannic*, collided with the in-bound SS *Celtic*. The two White Star line steamers had collided in heavy fog about 350 miles east of New York harbor. Although over 20 of the *Celtic's* 450 passengers were lost, Elliott, Anna, their 2 ½-year-old daughter, Eleanor, and her nurse were all uninjured.[101]

The captain of the *Britannic* initially believed that his ship was sinking and ordered women and children to board the life boats. The Roosevelts, including little Eleanor and her father Elliott, her mother Anna Hall, Anna's sister, and a nurse were among those to abandon ship. Eleanor was "terrified at being dropped from the deck of the liner down into my father's arms in the big rowboat."[102] Some men "lost their heads" and began to force their way through the frightened crowd. Newspapers repeated one passenger's allegations that Elliott was one of those men. In Elliott's defense, the paper offered a qualified explanation, "Mr. Roosevelt, it seems, was told by the Captain to go in the boat, who felt that his duty was to look after his wife, child, and sister, who were with him."[103]

After the passengers had safely returned to port, the 2 ½-year-old Eleanor had no interest in boarding another ship. Her parents happily left her with their Aunt Annie and Uncle Jimmie Gracie. Elliott and Anna Hall then recommenced their grand tour of Europe as if nothing had happened. By late June, they were in London, unencumbered by a young child. They spent a day with Irvine and Ella Bulloch in Liverpool and briefly visited with their Uncle Jimmie and Aunt Hattie Bulloch before returning to London on June 27. The shipwreck and subsequent separation from her parents would leave permanent scars on the impressionable young Eleanor Roosevelt.[104]

Another Bulloch lady embarked on a transatlantic honeymoon in 1888. In the spring, Harriott and James' daughter Jessie finally departed the cramped family quarters at Sydenham Avenue. She married a successful Liverpool merchant with the unlikely name of Maxwell Hyslop Maxwell. Theirs was a long (49 years) and, although they never had any children, a very happy marriage.[105]

For their honeymoon trip, Jessie and Max decided to visit the United States. Older brother James Bulloch, Jr., joined them and together they made an April voyage to New York. James, Jr., was combining business with pleasure. He had been a District Manager for the New York Life Insurance Company in Liverpool, but had accepted a position with a large tobacco brokerage house in Lynchburg, Virginia.[106]

In May and June, all three of the visitors from Liverpool stayed with the Roosevelts as well as their Aunt Anna and Uncle Jimmie Gracie at Oyster Bay on Long Island, New York. Teddy found Max to be conceited, very commonplace, and not even half the vigorous chap he thought himself to be. Teddy characterized his Cousin Jessie as "silly."[107] She had become hysterical when she got lost walking from the boat house and up to Aunt Anna's home. In short, they were perfect for each other. Teddy emphatically approved of the marriage, telling Bamie, "oh Lord, how glad I am he married Jessie!"[108] They were a "dear good couple." Teddy also retained his boyhood fondness for cousin Jimmie. He was "much more easy to get along with, and seems a pleasant, manly fellow—a thorough Englishman."[109]

James Dunwoody Bulloch, Jr., at the age of 30, had enjoyed a successful professional and business life back in Liverpool. He had begun his career as a cotton broker before taking the position with the New York Life Insurance office in Liverpool. There, Jimmie also continued the family's military tradition as a member of a local Liverpool militia troop who soon gave him an officer's commission. Jimmie, Jr., was an accomplished athlete and a star member of several silver cup-winning cricket and football (soccer) clubs. The Gentlemen's Committee of Liverpool's Infant Orphan Asylum accepted him as a member in 1883, and three years later, he was its president.[110]

Cousin Jimmie's pleasant interlude with the Roosevelts, however, would be his last. He departed Oyster Bay and New York for Lynchburg, Virginia to attend to his new career with a large tobacco brokerage house. While he was there, Jimmie became violently ill during the last week of August. He died seven days later. His sister Jessie or his Aunt Anna Bulloch Gracie telegraphed the heart-rending news across the ocean to his parents. Back in Liverpool, the Bullochs could only mourn the loss of another son, their eldest and brightest hope. At least James and Harriott could support each other, for this time they were together when they learned of his death. To honor Jimmie Junior's memory, the Liverpool Orphan Asylum initiated an annual "Bulloch Memorial Prize" shortly after Jessie's husband Max Maxwell became treasurer of the organization. The prize recognized the "best boy of all those leaving the Institution during that year, provided that he was admitted under the age of seven years."[111]

Mittie's children came to recognize their Uncle Jimmie's need for emotional as well as financial support as he grew older. Prior to his son's death, he had expressed hurt feelings when Mittie's children failed to answer several of his letters. However, coincident with the visit of Jessie, Max, and Jimmie, Jr., he received a "most affectionate letter" from Corinne, the youngest of the Roosevelt children. He was "very sorry that I should have been led to say anything to you about the seeming neglect of my nieces and nephews—dear precious Mittie's children."[112]

The financial plight of their elderly Aunt and Uncle Bulloch and their sorrowful loss resonated with Bamie in a more substantive way. In 1888, Bamie sent her Uncle Jimmie another $1800. Teddy learned of Bamie's largess through his wife Edith and promptly sent Bamie $100 as an installment for his share of Bamie's gift. Teddy had recently suffered financial setbacks of his own, particularly his cattle ranching investments in the Dakota Bad Lands. He confessed that "I am not well enough off to halve it with you now; but I will give you $100 a year until I do halve it."[113] Less than a month later, Teddy also asked his good friend, Senator Henry Cabot Lodge of Massachusetts, to investigate the eligibility of his "dear old uncle" for a Mexican War veteran's pension, "It is literally everything to him." There is no indication that James ever received a pension for his service with the naval battalion during the Mexican War.[114]

After a succession of careers as a U.S. Navy officer, commercial ship captain, Confederate secret agent, and British merchant, James Bulloch was no longer able to support himself or his family. Circumstances forced him to swallow his pride and accept the help of his female relations. That help came from his sisters, their husbands and children, his female ward, and finally, his own daughter. This role reversal had the females playing the part of family provider. Their prolonged and loving protection allowed James, Harriott, and Martha Louise to continue the relatively comfortable lifestyle that the Bulloch family had expected and enjoyed for generations.

6

New Women Out of the Nineteenth Century

As James and Harriott Bulloch entered their elderly years, they became more aware of the spiritual aspects of life. Reflections of God's blessings and the afterlife were common in James' later letters, especially those to his former ward, Nannie Hutchison. Standing 5 feet, 5 inches tall with grey eyes, Nannie was 34 years of age when she married. The groom was 46-year-old John Tempest Dawson of Halifax, Canada. Nannie only consented to the marriage after she consulted with James. As an American citizen, she was concerned about the legality of her marriage to a Canadian in the United Kingdom. With James' advice and blessing, the couple married on June 30, 1885, at Elham, in the southeastern English County of Kent. Nannie and John then settled in nearby Eastbourne on the English Channel. James and Harriott were especially fond of Nannie and acted more like surrogate parents than aunt and uncle.[1]

Like many of the Bulloch ladies, Nannie did not succumb to the postwar matrimonial mania. She was secure enough emotionally and financially that she did not have the type of anxiety that often led to hasty, ill-considered matches in hope of finding affection, stability, and security The fondness that "Uncle Jimmie" and "Aunt Hattie" felt for the couple burst into full flower when Nannie gave birth to Olga Tempest in March of 1889. Since James' and Harriott's daughters never had children and Stuart was still a bachelor, Nannie's baby gave them an opportunity to assume the cherished role of grandparents. Aunt Hattie, soon to be known as "Gramm," was present at Olga's birth while "Uncle Jimmie" remained in Liverpool.[2] It did not take James long, however, to make the almost 300 mile trip to see "wee Olga." After he returned to Liverpool on May 9, he imagined that he could still feel Olga's, "light weight nestling in my arms."[3]

Bulloch also was fond of Nannie's husband John, who by 1891 was a retired businessman of independent means with four household servants and a nursemaid. Two years later, he and Nannie had a boy, Francis Gilmer Tempest. Once again, "Aunt Hattie" attended the birth.[4] John seemed to be equally fond of his poor Bulloch relations, since he had no apparent objections to the "generous provisions" Nannie made for the Bullochs' personal expenses.[5]

The Dawson household remained a happy one during James and Hattie's lifetime. However, John Dawson began to develop symptoms of paranoia, believing that someone was trying to destroy his reputation. In 1909 he confessed in a note, "I cannot go on living; the life is too terrible. Friend after friend has dropped me. ... I am taking my wife with me to save her from it all. If I have not the courage, God help her and my two poor children."[6]

Something other than courage drove John Dawson to his act of madness. He and Nannie had taken a room at the opulent Morley's Hotel on Trafalgar Square in London. At about 2 p.m. on Wednesday, February 24, 1909, they entered the adjacent National Portrait Gallery and went to the Arctic room in the east wing. They "appeared to be absorbed in the pictures" that honored the doomed sailor and Arctic explorer, John Franklin. The couple passed "from one to the other as if criticising them." They began to quarrel, and in front of two "tailoresses" on a half-holiday, Dawson shot his wife in the back of the head and then turned the gun on himself. He died instantly; Nannie lost a great deal of blood on the parquet floors, but did not die until about two hours later at nearby Charing Cross Hospital.[7]

Newspapers throughout the United Kingdom and United states carried lurid details of the tragic event under the headline, "Man Shoots His Wife and Commits Suicide." The Medico-Psychological Association of Great Britain and Ireland published a synopsis of the case in their *Journal of Mental Science.* Nannie's tragic story continued to echo into the twenty-first century as books, online histories, and newspaper articles continued to ponder the rationale and impact of the very public murder-suicide. The National Portrait Gallery remained open, but closed off the bloody room and later converted the area into an office space and covered the blood-stained floor with carpet.[8]

Although fate spared the Bullochs the agony of living through this heartache, James found himself more and more in the role of a nurturing comforter. Among the important figures to benefit from his reassuring words were Jefferson and Varina Davis. James' last letter to the former president was in July of 1889. He wrote in response to a letter from Davis that his brother-in-law Charles Stoess had handed to James. Jefferson hoped that James could supply information that would refute published allegations from former Confederate General Pierre Beauregard. During the Civil War, the general had achieved an early victory at Manassas (Bull Run) with the assistance of Rose Greenhow. Soon afterwards, however, Beauregard had a hostile relationship with the meddling Davis. The general wrote several post-war books and articles that blamed Davis for the South's defeat.[9]

In his response to Davis' request, Bulloch flatly refuted Beauregard's claim. The facts did not support the allegation that President Davis missed an opportunity to break the Union blockade when he refused an offer of warships from the United Kingdom early in the war. Bulloch used terms like "a senseless waste of money ... impossible" and "the impracticability of such an undertaking."[10]

Bulloch's letter may have provided some small comfort to the 81-year-old Davis, but its effects were short-lived. On December 6, 1889, the first and only president of the Confederate States of America died. The embittered General Beauregard could only observe that, "We have always been enemies. I cannot pretend I am sorry he is gone."[11]

The sensitive and thoughtful Bulloch, however, penned an eloquent letter to Varina Davis the following day:

> This morning's papers have given to the British public intelligence of an event which has doubtlessly aroused a thrill of emotion throughout the Southern States of the American Union, and has already been the theme of much comment on this side of the Atlantic.
> The first thought that arises in the mind and hearts of the small colony of Southerners in this land of refuge, is one of sympathy with you and the children of him who was the chief figure in the Great war of Secession, and the Chief victim of its failure.
> Politicians at the North have said many malicious things of him, and unhappily, some of his own people in the south have helped to harass his declining years by petulant complaints. ...
> At some future day an impartial historian will tell the story of those troubling years, 1861 to '65, and Mr. Davis' name will then be found grouped with those who have made great sacrifices for conscience sake, and have devoted every faculty earnestly, faithfully, unselfishly, to their country's service.
> This conviction must be your hope, though its fruition may be long delayed, and it should be your consolation also.
> All the members of my family join in warmest expression of sympathy with you.
> Believe me, Very sincerely yours,
> James D. Bulloch[12]

Just as her husband was the Confederacy's only president, Varina Davis was the first and only Confederate first lady. When the new republic was fighting for its survival and recognition as an independent nation, Varina had been under great pressure. She had to follow the idealized role prescribed for southern matrons. Despite her mixed personal feelings, it was important for her to project an image of domestic loyalty to both her husband and to the nation. Like other ladies of the south, she believed that in return for assuming a domestic role, the males in her life would provide security and protection. As the ultimate symbol of Confederate failure, her husband could do neither. After the war, Varina referred to herself as an unprotected mother who had to raise four children with little or no support from her husband. Still, she loved Jefferson and always had done what she thought a wife should do. At the end of Jeff Davis' life she was at his side, trying to nurse him back to health.[13]

Like most of the Bulloch ladies, Varina had been educated in the north (New York and Philadelphia), was well-read, and intelligent. When Jefferson Davis died, she no longer felt bound by the duties of her marriage to the leader of a lost cause. To the consternation of many southerners, she moved to New York City. There, she began writing a regular column for Joseph Pulitzer's *New York World*. Although the paper was an exemplar of yellow journalism, the editors assumed a balanced approach to women's issues. It celebrated traditional women's roles as wives and mothers and opposed universal suffrage, but supported equal pay for equal work. Varina's newspaper job became her main source of income.[14]

When Varina died on October 16, 1906, twentieth-century America had begun to move beyond the bitterness of the war. Newspapers throughout the nation eulogized her positive qualities. Even President Teddy Roosevelt was among those who telegraphed his condolences and sent a wreath. It would take another 72 years before President Jimmy Carter signed a Joint Resolution that restored Varina's husband's civil rights as a citizen of the United States.[15]

The Liverpool Bullochs' next opportunity to comfort Americans in grief came just over two years later. Their handsome nephew, Elliott Roosevelt, had become an irresponsible alcoholic. His literal downfall began after he tumbled from a trapeze and became addicted to painkillers. Elliott fled to Europe in 1890 with his wife Anna Hall and their children, Eleanor and Elliott Junior. Elliott had his mother's engaging blue eyes and dark hair, but little of Mittie's poise under pressure, or his brother's ability to constructively focus his energy. Elliott cycled through recovery and relapse as he checked himself into and out of European treatment centers. To add to his troubles, he had impregnated a servant girl in New York who named Elliott as the father of her child. By February of 1891, Bamie responded to his wife's appeal for help. Bamie joined Anna Hall and the children in Vienna, Austria, where Anna was pregnant with their third child.[16]

After Bamie arrived in Vienna, Elliott checked himself out of his Austrian sanitarium and deposited everyone in Paris. There, he once again relapsed into abusive alcoholism. He also commenced an affair with an American mistress, as Anna gave birth to Gracie Hall in early June. No longer able to influence Elliot and unable to protect Anna, Bamie shepherded her and the children onto a steamship at Le Havre, France, in August of 1891. After they returned to New York, Teddy applied for a writ of lunacy that would allow him to take over Elliott's affairs. Teddy later settled on less scandalous alternatives, as news of his brother's excesses found their way into the New York newspaper headlines. At this point in time, family letters are silent about the Liverpool Bullochs' participation or even awareness of the attempted salvation of Elliott's disintegrating family. However, as later events and letters reveal, they were clearly aware of their nephew's promiscuity and loss of self-control.[17]

Teddy sailed from New York City to Europe on January 9, 1892, determined to force Elliott to relinquish control of his assets and commit himself to an alcoholic sanitarium in the United States. He spent a week with Elliott in Paris where Teddy refined his undocumented plan to escort his younger brother back to New York via Liverpool. In July and August of 1891, his Uncle Irvine Bulloch had visited his Roosevelt family in the United States. During this time, Teddy undoubtedly explained Elliott's situation to his uncle. He also discussed his combined efforts with Bamie to salvage the situation and solicited his aunts' and uncles' assistance in the coming year. Teddy set that plan in motion after he deposited Elliott with the Bullochs in Liverpool for safe-keeping in late January 1892. Teddy then boarded the SS *Lahn* in Southampton and returned to New York City on February 7, after a ten day voyage.[18]

Accompanied by his 68-year-old Uncle James Dunwoody Bulloch, Elliott followed Teddy to New York five days later. Registered as "E. Roosevelt" and "J.D. Bullock," they departed from Liverpool on the White Star liner SS *Teutonic* and arrived in New York City on February 11. After safely enrolling Elliott at the Kelley Institute for the treatment of addiction, James spent time with his niece, Corinne and her family. At 5 feet, 5 inches tall with brown hair, sensitive blue eyes, and fair skin reminiscent of her mother's, Corinne had grown into an intelligent and attractive woman. Ten years earlier, she had married the 29-year-old Douglas Robinson, Jr., when she was 20 years of age. In his brief stay in New York, James enjoyed time with her 8-year-old son Teddy Douglas, as well as his sister and brother-in-law Anna and James Gracie. James returned to Harriott and Liverpool on the SS *Britannic* about a month later.[19]

These traumatic events had a significant impact on the entire extended family, but most particularly on Elliott's 7-year-old daughter, Anna Eleanor. Unfortunately, the upheavals in her life were only beginning. Although she had never been close to her mother, Eleanor thought she was "one of the most beautiful women I have ever seen."[20] Even a contemporary *New York Times* reporter saw Anna Hall Roosevelt as "one of the most beautiful and popular women in New York society." Her beauty would be frozen in memory, for on December 7, 1892, Eleanor's 29-year-old mother Anna Hall Roosevelt died of diphtheria. Elliott was still "exiled" to Virginia working for his brother-in-law Douglas Robinson, and was not present when Anna Hall died in New York.[21]

Eleanor adored her father and was only vaguely aware of his indiscretions. Despite his shortcomings as a husband, Elliott had lovingly impressed upon his daughter Eleanor that she was a "miracle from heaven." He called her his "Little Nell" after the character in Dickens' *The Old Curiosity Shop.* Eleanor's mother was more aloof and referred to the little girl as "Granny" due to her old fashioned ways and, perhaps, because she was "less attractive" than her glamorous mother. After Anna Hall's death, Eleanor had assumed that she would rejoin her father. The realization that she would not devastated her. Instead, she and her two siblings lived with their maternal grandmother. In less than two years, Eleanor would lose her brother to scarlet fever, and worst of all, she lost her father. In 1894, Elliott died of complications from a drunken-binge-induced carriage wreck, but the true cause of death was his own, uncontrollable internal demons.[22]

His uncle, James King Gracie,

Mittie and Theodore's youngest daughter, Corinne Roosevelt (Library of Congress).

took charge of Elliott's funeral arrangements and his burial in the family plot at the Green-Wood cemetery of Brooklyn. Uncle Jimmie Gracie was all too well versed in these matters. His wife, 46-year-old Anna Bulloch, had died in June of 1893 from complications after a routine operation. All of the European Bulloch family sent Mr. Gracie "very sweet & touching letters" that offered their heart-felt condolences, including "Irvine & Ella," "Bro. Jim," "Hatty" [Harriott], and "Loulie" [Martha Louise] Bulloch, and "Jessie" and "Max" Maxwell.[23]

During his nine years of marriage to Anna, James King Gracie developed strong feelings for the Liverpool Bullochs. When he and his niece Corinne Roosevelt Robinson traveled to Green-Wood cemetery, they took extra care to put flowers on Mittie's grave on behalf of both Irvine and James Bulloch. In addition to his financial support to the Bullochs during his lifetime, James Gracie was equally generous in death. When he died in November of 1903, the Gracie estate's value was over $500,000 ($14.11 million in 2015). Of that amount, he remembered James and Harriott's spinster daughter Martha and Irvine's wife Ella with bequests of $10,000 each. James Gracie also allocated $30,000 to his nephew President Theodore Roosevelt. His grand-niece, Eleanor Roosevelt, split $15,000 with her sister Gracie Hall Roosevelt, and Bamie received $30,000. Even Maud Elliott, the daughter of Daniel Stuart and Lucy Elliott received $2,900.[24]

When Elliott died on August 14, 1894, Bamie was across the ocean in London. The telegram about Elliott reached her Uncle Jimmie and Bamie at about the same time. In a letter to Corinne, James observed that Bamie "would feel the shock with especial acuteness because of her separation from all of you and the consciousness that she could take no part in the solemn and touching committal of his body to its final resting place." On her way back to New York, Bamie stopped

(Anna) Eleanor, left, and her father, Elliott Roosevelt, April 30, 1889 (courtesy Franklin D. Roosevelt Presidential Library, Hyde Park, NY, NPx 80–46).

in Liverpool for a few days and stayed with her cousin Jessie Bulloch Maxwell, before boarding the *Teutonic* on September 5, 1894.[25]

Bamie had been in London since mid–December of 1893 at the behest of her Hyde Park cousin, James "Rosy" Roosevelt. She was the godmother of his two children with Helen Astor, the daughter of one of America's wealthiest men. Rosy was the half-brother of Franklin Delano Roosevelt, and had been appointed first secretary of the U.S. embassy in London. Shortly after Rosy arrived in London, his wife Helen's health began to deteriorate and cousin Rosy asked Bamie to join them in London. He hoped Bamie would care for his two children, aged 12 and 14 and act as hostess for diplomatic events. When Helen died suddenly, Bamie accelerated her departure and arrived in England on December 16. She quickly took charge of Rosy's household and endeared herself to the children. Despite being a 39-year-old spinster with no husband to escort her to the royal court, Bamie obtained a rare audience with Queen Victoria at the insistence of the American ambassador. She quickly became the American Embassy's primary hostess for all social events at the Court of St. James.[26]

Bamie's lively intelligence and her genuine interest in people and ideas caused even the stodgiest characters of London society to see the beautiful person behind those electric blue eyes. She had overcome a curved and slightly deformed spine through the love of her parents, the respect of her siblings and peers, and sheer force of will. These qualities were not lost on the U.S. Embassy's naval attaché, William Sheffield Cowles. When Bamie returned to London after Christmas of 1895, her friendship with the 48-year-old Navy officer developed into a romance. Her announcement that she intended to marry Lieutenant Commander Cowles surprised and even "dumbfounded" Teddy and the rest of the family in the United States. Teddy was, however, delighted to learn that Cowles was "an officer in our Navy."[27]

Will Cowles had been at the embassy since November of 1892. In his 45-year Navy career, he would command a warship in the Spanish-American War, become Commander-in-Chief of the Asiatic Fleet, and rise to the rank of Rear Admiral. Brother-in-law Teddy helped advance Cowles' career after he became Assistant Secretary of the Navy. Teddy's influence led to Cowles' appointment as President McKinley's Naval Aide and other command assignments. Cowles was not particularly handsome and tended toward portliness. However, in his full dress blues, he still turned heads at embassy affairs. He also appreciated a strong-willed woman with an independent mind. Although the depth of feeling Bamie had for her equally middle-aged husband might be questioned, he was dear to her heart. He closely matched her romantic ideal of a dashing and honorable

Eleanor Roosevelt wearing her wedding dress in New York City, March 17, 1905. (courtesy Franklin D. Roosevelt Presidential Library, Hyde Park, New York, NPx 58–31).

naval officer that her mother had described so vividly when she was a child. She felt a natural attraction to Will Cowles that echoed her mother's admiration of her heroic brothers Jimmie and Irvine Bulloch.[28]

The wedding at St. Andrews, Westminster, was a grand affair that garnered headlines in newspapers throughout the United States and Great Britain. "The church was crowded with a brilliant assemblage of English and American Guests." The guests included the American ambassador and his wife, lords and ladies, admirals, generals, princes, countesses, and other persons of note. Family members from the United States included sister Corinne and her husband Douglas Robinson and brother-in-law James King Gracie. Teddy was unable to attend. Cousin Rosy Roosevelt had the honor of leading Bamie to the altar and hosting the grand reception. Although there is no record of the Liverpool Bullochs' presence, the papers listed Jessie Bulloch Maxwell's brother- and sister-in-law, Mr. and Mrs. Walter H. Maxwell among the prominent dignitaries. Unless there were health issues for the elderly Bulloch aunts and uncles, they would have been among the several hundred anonymous guests who delivered presents to the happy couple.[29]

Contemporary admirers usually described Bamie with terms such as witty, smart, reassuring, hospitable, serious, poised, mature, wise, or energetic, but never as pretty. Her spinal "deformity" created a slightly hunched appearance that she tried to overcome by maintaining an erect posture.[30] Nonetheless, at 40-years-of-age, Bamie was still a beautiful bride.

> Her robe was of ivory satin duchesse, trimmed with lace and orange blossoms, with a long square-cut train. She wore a tulle veil, edged with costly Brussels lace, and a wreath of small orange flowers fastened with superb diamond ornaments.[31]

Bamie's affectionate nickname for her stout husband was "Mr. Bearo." They remained happily married for over 27 years. The Bullochs and Roosevelts welcomed Commander Will Cowles into their family circle. Uncle Jimmie Bulloch visited the newlyweds in London after they completed their honeymoon tour of Europe. James' thoughts about the role of women had slowly evolved over the years as the women in his life progressively assumed larger roles. The Bulloch women were the primary mangers of household and family business affairs during the prolonged absences or demise of their husbands, fathers, and sons during and after the war. In speaking at length with his niece Bamie, James found it unusual but not objectionable for her to have and express well-informed and insightful opinions. In an earlier generation, geo-political, economic and similar issues were exclusive male domains, of no concern to the women-folk. As

Teddy humorously reported to his sister, "Uncle Jimmie has written me how greatly he enjoyed his visit, and I was greatly amused at one sentence in which he said he 'was surprised and pleased to notice the intelligent interest Bamie took in her husband's pursuits'!!"[32]

Teddy Roosevelt had a modern outlook on the emerging and rightful role of women in society. Inspired by the strength of the women in his own life, Teddy's senior dissertation at Harvard had been entitled, "Practicability of Giving Men and Women Equal Rights." Young Theodore believed and advocated that justice demanded equality under that law, whether or not the parties were equal in other respects. Teddy's niece Eleanor would later embrace her uncle's ideas of equality for women and take them to higher levels. Of the male figures in her young life, her Uncle Ted was the conduit for Eleanor to absorb the influence of her Bulloch uncles. Her Auntie Bye provided the female version of those same qualities as a dignified lady.[33]

The Civil War had exposed the absurdity of considering women as the "weaker sex" who were incapable of physical or mental exertion. There were no logical reasons why they could not or should not become writers, clerks, doctors, and lawyers. Still, many women preferred security over independence. There was great danger for women if they were suddenly expected to compete directly with men. Women would be physically and economically vulnerable in a harshly competitive social order. Social conservatives feared that a rapid breakdown of traditional sexual roles would ultimately destroy the home, weaken moral values, and claim many female victims in the process.[34]

When Eleanor's mother died, Bamie lived just two blocks away and she continued to mentor and nurture her young niece as she had for her own siblings and their children. Teddy Roosevelt was a Civil Service Commissioner in Washington, D.C., at the time, and did not move back to New York City until 1895 when he became police commissioner. President Theodore Roosevelt stood in for Eleanor's father as "Uncle Ted" when she married a distant cousin named Franklin Delano Roosevelt in 1905. Eleanor's Harvard-educated husband would seek and obtain positions as the Assistant Secretary of the Navy and Governor of New York. Franklin was quite openly following in the footsteps of Eleanor's uncle on his path to the presidency. Although neither Roosevelt ever served in the Navy, they shared mutual beliefs about the importance of naval forces as an instrument of power and global influence. Then as now, strong women favored gentlemen who were bold and confident leaders. The Bulloch women found that men with an added pinch of sea salt had added flavor.

In addition to other factors, it is natural that Eleanor, like her Auntie Bye, would be drawn to such a man.[35]

While Eleanor mentioned her great-uncle James D. Bulloch in the published tribute to her father, her Bulloch uncles are absent in her autobiography. Those published recollections omitted several important events from Eleanor's early life, including her first abortive voyage to Europe with her parents in 1887. The shipwreck and subsequent separation of over four months from her parents had a great impact on Eleanor's later life. She suffered from a fear of heights and water that also evoked feelings of abandonment.[36]

Of the shaping personalities in her life, Eleanor's namesake known as Aunt Bye provided the example of a commanding presence who equaled or exceeded that of most men of learning and influence. Even when he was president, Teddy Roosevelt seldom made an important decision without first consulting his sister Bamie. Her home in Washington was popularly known as "the Little White House." Even Teddy's daughter Alice Longworth observed that, "There is always someone in every family who keeps it together. In ours, it was Auntie Bye."[37] For Eleanor, her namesake aunt had the greatest impact on her adolescent and teenage years, both directly and indirectly. As noted in her autobiography, Auntie Bye was, "an inspiration and one of the wisest counselors I ever knew."[38]

Alice Longworth also believed that, "If Auntie Bye had been a man, she would have been president."[39] Alice's intent was to describe her aunt's incredible intellectual prowess, personal charisma, and wisdom. She was not expressing Bamie's frustrated ambitions, for the idea of a woman rising to the position of president, remained an impossibility throughout the twentieth century. Like most southern white women, Bamie seldom questioned the racial, class, and sexual dogmas of her society. Even though Teddy Roosevelt's Bull Moose Party was the first to endorse women's suffrage, women like Bamie silently opposed the suffragettes. She believed that intelligent women like herself could manage, direct, and influence people and events behind the scenes, without multiplying the "stupid" vote.[40]

As a teenager, shortly before she married Franklin, Eleanor came to appreciate the Navy and sailors like her great-uncles James and Irvine Bulloch through her Aunt Bamie and her husband, Admiral Cowles. After spending time with the two of them, Eleanor realized that,

> "men who are our officers in the Army and Navy, while they receive little financial compensation, are enormously proud to serve their country. They and their wives have a position which is their right by virtue of their service

regardless of birth or of income. Quite a new idea to a provincial little miss from New York!"[41]

Inspired by Bamie's example and at her insistence, Eleanor traveled to Europe in 1899 where she enrolled in Marie Souvestre's boarding school for girls. After the Franco-German war that had so abruptly intruded on Bamie's schooling in 1870, Mlle. Souvestre relocated her school to England, near Wimbledon. The voyage to England was Eleanor's first trip across the ocean since her shipwreck disaster of 1887. She remained in her stateroom the entire cruise.[42]

There is no direct evidence that Eleanor met with her Bulloch relations while she was a student in England, but for a young Roosevelt lady an ocean away from home, family ties remained important. Eleanor's awareness of her great uncle and his family in England was apparent. When Eleanor and Franklin traveled to England on their honeymoon, they first stopped in Liverpool to see Ella Bulloch and the other surviving Bulloch family members. In a compilation of her father's letters in 1832, Eleanor described her Bulloch uncles this way:

> Irvine was grandmother's own younger brother. Irvine was the man who fired the last shot on the *Alabama*.
> Captain James Dunwoodie [sic] Bulloch—famous blockade runner in the Southern Navy in the Civil War. Active in the Secret Service and responsible for the bringing of the *Alabama* to Liverpool. Half-brother of my grandmother.[43]

Perhaps even more revealing is the letter from James D. Bulloch that Eleanor included in the tribute to her father that she published in 1932. She used the period between Franklin's election as president in 1932 and his inauguration in 1833 to selectively compile and edit Elliott's correspondence. The letters ranged from the 1880s until his untimely death in 1894. James Bulloch had sent the letter to his nephew shortly after Elliott became engaged to Anna Hall in 1880. Her great uncle's eloquent description of Elliott conformed to the wistful image Eleanor had of the man he could have been.

> Elliott Roosevelt is a proper young man and has always been dutiful as a son, tender as a brother, affectionate as a nephew, true and loyal as a friend, and I feel therefore well assured that he will be all these combined to the "Sweet Charmer" who has taught him that the capabilities of love in the heart of a man are not wholly fulfilled until he has found an object who, though coming from without the circle of his own family, may yet be brought within it, and who may possess herself of his *whole* heart and yet leave his affection towards others *undiminished*.[44]

As for James and Harriott Bulloch, they continued to live in their unpretentious but comfortable home at 30 Sydenham Avenue in the Liverpool suburb of Waterloo. Through the first half of the 1890s, they maintained two domestic servants, including their longtime cook, Agnes McCormick. Their 26-year-old daughter Martha Louise remained at home and tended to her now-elderly parents. She also earned a modest income as a music teacher. Music was a skill she inherited from her father who had taken singing lessons as a child and played the violin as an adult.[45]

The number of people carrying the Bulloch surname inherited from James Stephens Bulloch grew smaller as the century neared its end. On July 3, 1897, 68-year-old Harriott Cross Bulloch, the blonde southern belle from Louisiana, died of peritonitis resulting from a malignant abdominal condition. Harriott had mended James Dunwoody Bulloch's heart after the death of his first wife. She was the mother of five children, the first three born while her sailor husband was at sea and the last two while he was at war. She had managed households on two continents, uprooting herself and three small children from home and family across the Atlantic Ocean during the Civil War. Unlike most mid-nineteenth Century American women, she was accustomed to independent decision-making. Prior to the war, James spent more time at sea than at home. During the war, he not only worked long hours, but was away for weeks and months at a time. He ran the blockade into and out of the Confederate States and traveled throughout Europe acquiring ships and supplies. He spent those four long years tending to the needs of others while she

Martha Louise (Lulie) Bulloch on a swing, September 7, 1894 (courtesy Friends of the Archives of Dumfries and Galloway, Scotland, Album 5, Page 13, Photo 1 [MH1_13_ 1]).

managed household affairs. After the war, James often took extended trips to North and South America as he pursued his business interests.[46]

In addition to Harriott raising five of her own children, she was also a surrogate mother to Nannie Hutchison, whose tragic death mercifully occurred long after the Bullochs' passing. Harriott provided a home for her own sister as well as a constant stream of her husband's extended family and coterie of business and military associates. During the war, Harriott suffered the loss of her mother and a brother who fought for the Union. After the war, she endured the unique parental pain of losing two of her children. First, her 9-year-old "Dunnie" died of scarlet fever while her husband was away. Harriott's oldest boy, Jimmie Jr., died suddenly after he relocated to the United States as a young adult. Stuart Elliott Bulloch, her sole remaining son, departed England in late June of 1892 on the SS *Rome*. He was bound to a new life in Australia. As James commented at the time, Harriott helped Stuart prepare "for his long voyage and has been rather depressed since." She never saw Stuart again.[47]

Teddy Roosevelt, who had recently become Assistant Secretary of the Navy, wrote Bamie a note agreeing to "go in" with his sister on an "arrangement for dear old Uncle Jimmie." The date was shortly after Harriott's funeral and although he did not specify the nature of the "arrangement," it was probably financial. Bamie and her husband Will Cowles had returned to the United States at the conclusion of his tour as naval attaché in April of 1897. They were well-aware of the Bullochs' personal and financial health.[48]

A year later, the youngest of the Bulloch siblings, 56-year-old Irvine, died from a cerebral hemorrhage. By this time, James and his "spinster" daughter Martha Louise had moved in with Jessie and her husband Max Maxwell. They all attended Irvine's funeral, along with Irvine's widow Ella, her sister, and mother. John Low, James' former Confederate shipmate, British citizen, and long-time friend and neighbor also attended.[49]

John Low and the other surviving family members were present at another Bulloch funeral three years later. On January 7, 1901, James Dunwoody Bulloch succumbed to age and disease at Jessie and Max Maxwell's home in Liverpool. The 77-year-old's death certificate nostalgically registered his occupation as "Naval Representative of the late Confederate States of America (retired)." Among the many who came to pay their respects were five clergymen, and teachers from the St. Thomas Day School, as well as representatives of the Liverpool Nautical College, and the Orphan Boys' Asylum. Their attendance was a testament to the time and effort James had devoted to young people in his post-war years.[50]

Jessie and Max lived a long but childless life together, spending their later years at one of England's finest hotels, the splendid Adelphi in Liverpool. When the 75-year-old Max Maxwell died in 1937, he left almost £19,000 ($1,572,000 in 2015) to his widow Jessie, who died four years later. Jessie left effects valued at over £13,500 to her brother-in-law, Walter Hyslop Maxwell. James and Harriott's son, Stuart Elliott Bulloch served in the Australian Army during World War I. He listed his age as 40 rather than 52, to avoid rejection for being too old. For unknown reasons, Stuart decided to change his name after 1919 by dropping Bulloch, and adopting his middle name instead. After the war, he married a young war widow and had a son, James Stuart Elliott, who served honorably and even heroically in World War II.[51]

Although most accounts indicate that James D. Bulloch died penniless, he did leave his youngest daughter Martha his personal effects valued at just over £200 ($28,480 in 2015). Martha Louise Bulloch never married and remained in Liverpool all her life, residing with Jessie and Max as they moved from home to hotel. She inherited $10,000 upon the death of her Aunt Anna Bulloch's husband James King Gracie in December of 1903. She may have received additional funds when Nannie Hutchison Dawson died at the hand of her husband in 1909. In any event, she invested wisely. When Martha, the last of James and Harriott Bulloch's children, died on March 7, 1947, she left an estate valued at over £21,100 ($916,600 in 2015). She also resided at the Adelphi Hotel and like her sister Jessie, left her estate to Max's younger brother, Walter Hyslop Maxwell.[52]

Their father, James D. Bulloch, had great achievements as a secret agent and naval officer. He left an indelible imprint on subsequent military tactics, strategy, and technology. Their Uncle Irvine had been the family's man of action, spending more time at sea on warships than any other Confederate Navy officer. The family's most notable legacies, however, were reflected in the women who were left behind.

The Bulloch ladies, particularly Mittie and her sister Anna, were the unofficial preservers of the memories of their Confederate brothers. Like thousands of other southern ladies, they carefully passed on the tales of their loved ones' adventures and achievements to their children and grandchildren. The family's universal respect for the person, if not their cause, emerges in all of Mittie's children's written recollections of James and Irvine Bulloch.[53]

Because they had moved North, most of the Bulloch ladies had a protective buffer from the devastation of the American Civil War. The war convulsed southern society and its effects rippled through every aspect of each southerner's life. The physical destruction of the South's infra-structure and the abolition of chattel slavery undermined the wealth and political power of the planter elite. It also transformed the interrelated social hierarchies. White men found themselves at the apex of a patri-archal social pyramid that no longer existed. Southern males had been defeated and impoverished. They had utterly failed as providers and pro-tectors, but their women had not failed at all. In fact, by necessity, they had disproven the notion that women were by nature dependent and help-less.[54]

The Bulloch women were able to sustain their antebellum life styles through fortunate, but deliberate family connections and marriages. These Bulloch ladies adapted and gracefully moved through society, while retain-ing many of their old ideals within a new social context. Their poor south-ern relations like brothers James and Irvine Bulloch, and sister-in-law Lucy Elliott, became beneficiaries of the Bulloch ladies' more robust cir-cumstances.

In many ways, it was the men who changed most after the Civil War. In 1912 for example, Theodore Roosevelt's Bull Moose Party, became the first political party to endorse women's suffrage. When the required num-ber of states ratified the Nineteenth Amendment for women's suffrage in 1920, most of those 36 states had not yet granted women the right to vote. The force of the arguments that women had sufficient intellect, social awareness, patriotism, strength of body and character, and every other relevant attribute of citizenship were just too strong to refute.[55]

Nineteenth century women in positions of social and economic power like the Bullochs did not seek or desire remarkable changes in their public roles. Despite their lack of public advocacy for social change, the Bulloch and Roosevelt women were major contributors to a subtle shift in American cultural norms. The demise of the family's male providers and protectors during the latter part of the nineteenth century occurred while the affluence and influence of the family's female members increased. Strong-willed Bulloch women thought and lived independently and became the benefactors for their friends and families. As the post–Civil War generation grew into maturity, the pace of change increased. Necessity gave way to industrial age practicality and to justice under the law.

The Bulloch ladies were flexible as they adapted to their changed cir-cumstances both in Europe and in the North. They did not, however, aban-don their long-standing respect for traditional feminine values. They had no compelling reason to shed all of the old and suddenly become something entirely new. They blended some of the new with a lot of the old, particularly their southern ideals about what it meant to be a lady. They continued to succeed in their traditional roles as nurturing women who managed the affairs of home and family. Even as the surname of the Bullochs of Roswell faded into history, the Bulloch women subtly assumed more masculine roles as advocates, providers, and protectors.[56]

Appendix:
The Bulloch
Women and Men

Astor, Helen Schermerhorn (1855–1893). Wife of James Roosevelt ("Rosy") Roosevelt, Jr. (1854–1927); Anna Eleanor (Bamie) Roosevelt Cowles was godmother to her two children, Helen and James ("Tadd") Roosevelt, III; her brother, Colonel John Jacob "Jack" Astor IV (1864–1912) died on the RMS *Titanic*.

Bayard, Florida (1834-1917). One of two other teenage girls "coming out" with Anna and Mittie Bulloch in 1850-1851. Married John J. Seay, a steamboat captain, in 1875.

Beecher, Catharine Esther (1800–1878). Founder of the Hartford Female Seminary attended by the Bulloch stepsisters Corinne and Georgia Elliott.

Bulloch, Anna Louisa. See: Gracie, Anna Louisa Bulloch (1833–1893).

Bulloch, Elizabeth (Lizzie) Euphemia Caskie (1831–1854). James D. Bulloch's first wife.

Bulloch, Ella Clitz Sears (1849–1911). Wife of Irvine S. Bulloch; befriended Elliott and Anna Hall Roosevelt and their daughter Eleanor.

Bulloch, Harriott M. Cross Foster (1829–1897). James D. Bulloch's second wife and mother of James Jr., Jessie, Henry, Martha, and Stuart.

Bulloch, Hester (Hettie) Amarin- thia Elliott (1797–1831). Daughter of John and Esther Dunwody Elliott; wife of James Stephens Bulloch, mother of James. D. Bulloch.

Bulloch, Irvine Stephens (1842–1898). Youngest child of Martha Stewart and James Stephens Bulloch; married Ella Clitz Sears (1871); Confederate Navy Lieutenant.

Bulloch, James Dunwoody (1823–1901). Son of James S. and Hettie Elliott Bulloch; married Lizzie Caskie (1851) and Harriott Cross (1854); half-brother of Anna, Mittie, and Irvine Bulloch; U.S. Navy (1839–1854); Confederate Navy secret agent in Europe.

Bulloch, Jessie Hart. See: Maxwell, Jessie Hart Bulloch (1860–1941).

Bulloch, Martha Louise (Loulie) (1865–1947). James D. and Harriott's youngest daughter; never married, lived with parents and sister Jessie and Max Maxwell.

Bulloch, Martha Stewart Elliott (1799–1864). Stepmother of James D. Bulloch and Corinne Elliott Hutchison; mother of John Whitehead (1818–1820), Susan Ann, Georgia Amanda, Charles Williams (1824–1827), and Daniel Stuart Elliott; mother of Anna, Martha (Mittie), Charles Irvine (1838–1841), and Irvine Stephens Bulloch.

197

Caskie, Mary Edmonia, see: Hutchison, Mary Edmonia Caskie (1822–1852).

Caskie, Mary Eliza, (1829-1894). Cousin of Lizzie Caskie Bulloch and sister of Robert Hutchison's third wife, Ellen. Accompanied Lizzie and Robert to Europe (1852).

Caskie, Nannie Euphemia, (1824-1857). Sister of Lizzie Caskie Bulloch; married Samuel J. Harrison (1845).

Cowles, Anna Eleanor ("Bamie") Roosevelt (1855–1931). Theodore Jr.'s older sister and mentor to her namesake niece, Eleanor; married U.S. naval attaché in London (1895).

Cowles, Rear Admiral William Sheffield (1846–1923). Bamie's Roosevelt's husband, former U.S. naval attaché to Great Britain.

Cross, Annette, See: Porter, Annette Cross (1844–).

Cross, Mary Beam Johnson Dix (1810–1879). Second wife of Harriott Bulloch's father Osborne; widow of LtCol Roger Sherman Dix (brother of MajGen John Adams Dix).

Cross, Osborne, (1804–1876). Union army brigadier general; father of Harriott Foster Bulloch; married J. Louise Duval von Schaumberg (1832) and Mary Beam Dix (1862).

Davis, Varina Banks Howell (1826–1906). Wife and first lady of President Jefferson Davis, C.S.A.

Dawson, John Tempest (1838-1909). Husband of Nannie Hutchison; shot wife and self at London's National Gallery.

Dawson, Nannie (Nancy) E. Hutchison (1851-1909). Daughter of Robert Hutchison and Mary Edmonia Caskie; ward of the Bulloch and Caskie families; wife of John Tempest Dawson; murder-suicide victim in London's National Portrait Gallery.

Dawson, Olga Tempest (1889-1955). Daughter of Nannie Hutchison and John Tempest Dawson; surrogate grand-daughter for James D. and Harriott Bulloch in Liverpool.

Dunwody, Jane Marion (1821-1885). Daughter of John and Jane Irvine Bulloch Dunwoody; married Rev. Stanhope W. Erwin (1840), Dr. William E. Glen (1851), and Adam L. Alexander (1865).

Elliott, Charles William (1824–1827). Son of Senator John and Martha Stewart Elliott.

Elliott, Daniel Stuart (Stewart) (1826–1862). Son of Martha Stewart Elliott Bulloch and Senator John Elliott; married Lucy Sorrell; died of tuberculosis during the Civil War.

Elliott, Esther Dean Dunwody (1775–1815). First wife of John Elliott, mother of Hester Amarinthia who was James S. Bulloch's first wife and the mother of James D. Bulloch.

Elliott, Georgia Amanda (1822–1848). Daughter of Martha Stewart Elliott Bulloch and Senator John Elliott; attended school in Connecticut with sister Georgia.

Elliott, Jane Elizabeth (1809–1829). Daughter of John Elliott and Esther Dunwody Elliott; married Bulloch family friend John Law (1828).

Elliott, Lucinda (Lucy) Ireland Sorrel (1829–1903). Widow of Daniel Stuart Elliott; moved to Dresden, Germany (1871–1873) and supervised Mittie Roosevelt's children.

Empress Eugenie (Eugénie de Montijo) (1826–1920). Empress consort and wife of the French Emperor, Louis-Napoléon Bonaparte.

Gracie, Anna Louisa Bulloch (1833–1893). Daughter of Martha Steward and James Stephens Bulloch, Mittie's older sister; married James King Gracie (1866).

Gracie, James King (1840–1903). Married Anna Bulloch in 1866; New York financier who provided financial support to the Bulloch family in Liverpool.

Greenhow, Rose O'Neal (1817–1864). Confederate spy known as 'The Rebel Rose" who befriended James D. Bulloch and Seth G. Porter; drowned while running the blockade.

Hand, Julia Isabella (1833–1911). One of two other teenage girls "coming out" with Anna and Mittie Bulloch (1850–1851); married Henry M. Anderson (1854).

Huse, Harriet Pinckney (1832–1911). Wife of Major Caleb Huse (CSA), mother of Norman Bulloch Huse; namesake of Confederate supply ship, *Harriet Pinckney*.

Hutchison, Corinne Louisa Elliott (1814–1838). Daughter of Senator John Elliott with his first wife Esther; married Robert Hutchison, drowned in the wreck of the *Pulaski*.

Hutchison, Mary Edmonia Caskie (1822–1852). Second wife of Robert Hutchison, mother of Nannie, older sister of James D. Bulloch's first wife Elizabeth (Lizzie).

Hutchison, Nannie (Nancy) E. See: Dawson, Nannie (Nancy) E. Caskie (1851–1909).

Hutchison, Robert (1802–1861). Husband of Corinne Elliott and James D. Bulloch's first wife's sister Mary Caskie; lost wife Corinne and two daughters in *Pulaski* explosion.

Jackson, Nancy (Nannie) (1813–1906). Bulloch nursemaid slave for Mittie and Anna, brought to Connecticut and freed by court action (1837).

Low, Harriet (1847–1891). Possible namesake of the *Enrica/Alabama*, daughter of Andrew Low, lived in England with sister Amy, married British Army Major George Coke Robertson.

Low, Juliette Magill Kinzie Gordon (1860–1927). Daughter-in-law of Bulloch family-friend Andrew Low of Savannah; founded Girls Scouts of America.

Maxwell, Jessie Hart Bulloch (1860–1941). Eldest daughter of James and Harriott Bulloch; married Maxwell Hyslop Maxwell.

Mitchell, Margaret ("Peggy") M. (1900–1959). Author of *Gone with the Wind*; wrote feature article about Bulloch Hall, Mittie and Theodore Roosevelt's wedding (1923).

Porter, Annette Cross (1844–). Harriott Cross Bulloch's younger sister; married blockade-runner captain Seth Grosvenor Porter (ca. 1866).

Porter, Seth Grosvenor (1835–1910). Blockade runner captain; brother of Laura (wife of Cornelius V.S. Roosevelt, Jr.); married Harriott Cross Bulloch's sister Annette Cross.

Robertson, Harriet Low. See: Low, Harriet (1847–1891).

Robinson, Corinne (Conie) Roosevelt (1861–1933). Mittie and Theodore's youngest child; named after Corinne Elliott Hutchison; married Douglas Robinson, Jr.

Roosevelt, Alice Hathaway Lee (1861–1884). Teddy Roosevelt's first wife; died on the same day and in the same home as mother-in-law Mittie Bulloch Roosevelt (February 14).

Roosevelt, Anna Eleanor. See: Cowles, Anna Eleanor ("Bamie") Roosevelt (1855–1931).

Roosevelt, Anna Eleanor (1884–1962). Daughter of Elliott and Anna Hall Roosevelt, namesake of her Aunt Anna (Bamie); First Lady as wife of Franklin Delano Roosevelt.

Roosevelt, Anna Rebecca Hall (1863–1892). Elliott Roosevelt's wife and mother of first lady Eleanor Roosevelt.

Roosevelt, Corinne (Conie). See: Robinson, Corinne (Conie) Roosevelt (1861–1933).

Roosevelt, Edith Kermit Carow (1861–1948). Second wife and First Lady of President Theodore Roosevelt.

Roosevelt, Gracie Hall (1891–1941). Daughter of Elliott and sister of Eleanor Roosevelt; became an alcoholic.

Roosevelt, Laura H. Porter (1833–1900). Wife of Cornelius Van Schaack Roosevelt, Jr. (1827–1887); sister of Harriott Bulloch's brother-in-law, Seth Grosvenor Porter.

Roosevelt, Martha (Mittie) Bulloch (1835–1884). Mother of Anna (Bamie), Elliott (Ellie), Corinne (Conie), and

President Theodore Roosevelt; Eleanor Roosevelt's aunt.

Roosevelt, Silas Weir. (1823–1870). Eldest brother of Theodore, Sr.; married Mary West, the sister of Mittie and Anna's brother-in-law Hilborne West.

Roosevelt, Theodore (Teedie/ Teddy) Jr. (1858–1919). Son of Theodore and Martha (Mittie); married Alice Hathaway Lee (1880) and Edith Kermit Carow (1886); uncle of Eleanor Roosevelt; 26th president of the United States (1901–1909).

Roosevelt, Theodore (Thee) Sr. (1831–1878). Husband of Mittie Bulloch, father of Anna (Bamie), Theodore (Teddy) Jr., Elliott (Ellie) and Corinne (Conie) Roosevelt.

Sears, Harriet ("Hattie") Lelia (1851–1912). Sister of Irvine S. Bulloch's wife Ella.

Sears, Harriet Louisa Clitz (1832–1909). American-born mother of namesake daughter Harriet ("Hattie") and Irvine's wife Ella; wife of Henry Beaufort Sears (1824–1880).

Souvestre, Marie (1830–1905). Feminist founder and head school mistress of Les Ruches in France and Allenswood in England; mentor to Bamie and Eleanor Roosevelt.

Sever, Catherine "Kate" Elliott (1827–1899). Grandniece of Martha Stewart Elliott Bulloch; visited Bulloch Hall with her mother and sister (1839–1840).

Sever, Jane Amarinthia Elliott (1805–1871). Niece of Sen. John Elliott's brother; wife of Charles Sever (1795–1834); visited Bulloch Hall with her two daughters (1839–1840).

Sever, Jane "Jennie" Elliott (1831–1874). Visited Bulloch Hall with mother Jane and sister Kate (1839–1840); married Alexander M. Harrison (1829–1881).

Stevens, Anna Maria Christie (1824–ca. 1885). Shipwrecked with husband Thomas H. Stevens, Jr. (1844) and daughter while pregnant; friend of James D. Bulloch.

Stevens, Thomas Holdup, Jr. (1819–1896). Friend of James D. Bulloch; Navy store keeper in Hawaii (1845–1848); commanded USS *Monitor*, promoted to Rear Admiral.

Stewart, General Daniel (1761–1829). Martha Stewart Bulloch's father who served in the Revolutionary and Indian Wars.

Stewart, Martha Pender (1763–1784). First wife of Martha Stewart Elliott Bulloch's father General Daniel Stewart.

Stewart, Sarah Salley Hines (1776–1829). Third wife of Martha Stewart Bulloch's father General Daniel Stewart.

Stewart, Susannah Oswald (1770–1807). Martha Stewart Elliott Bulloch's mother and second wife of her father General Daniel Stewart.

Stoess, Margaret Howell Graham de Wechmar (1842–1930). Sister of Varina Davis; married Charles Stoess, the Bavarian consul to Liverpool (1869).

Stowe, Harriet Beecher (1811–1896). Teacher at Hartford Female Seminary; friend of Bulloch family pastor Rev. Charles C. Jones; author of *Uncle Tom's Cabin* (1852).

Walker, Georgiana Freeman Gholson (1833–1904). Wife of C.S.A. Major Norman S. Walker (1831–1913) in Bermuda; moved to England (1864–1878); friend of Confederate spy Rose Greenhow; kept private journal (published 1963).

West, Hilborne (Hill) T. (1818–1907). Brother of Mary (Mrs. Silas Weir Roosevelt); married Susan Elliott at Bulloch Hall; businessman and medical doctor in Philadelphia.

West, Susan (Susy) Ann Elliott (1820–1895). Daughter of Martha Stewart and John Elliott; married Hilborne West at Bulloch Hall (1849).

Chapter Notes

Abbreviations: ABG—Anna (Bulloch) Gracie; ARC—Anna ("Bamie") Roosevelt Cowles; DANFS—Dictionary of American Naval Fighting Ships; ER—Eleanor Roosevelt (daughter of Anna Lee and Elliott Roosevelt, wife of FDR); GHS—Georgia Historical Society, Savannah; GPO—Government Printing Office; JDB—James D. (Dunwoody) Bulloch; MBR—Martha or Mittie (Bulloch) Roosevelt; MSB—Martha (Stewart, Elliott) Bulloch; MOC—Eleanor S. Brockenbrough Library, Museum of the Confederacy; NARA—National Archives and Records Administration; NYT—*New York Times*; ORA—Official Records of the Army in *The War of the Rebellion: A Compilation of the Official Records of the Union and Confederate Armies*; ORN—Official Records of the Navy in *The War of the Rebellion: A Compilation of the Official Records of the Union and Confederate Armies*; RG—Record Group; SEW—Susan (Elliott) West; SHC—Southern Historical Collection, Manuscripts Department, Wilson Library, University of North Carolina at Chapel Hill; TR—Theodore Roosevelt, Jr.; TR Sr.—Theodore Roosevelt, Sr.; TRC—Theodore Roosevelt Collection, Houghton Library, Harvard University, Cambridge, MA

Introduction

1. Walter E. Wilson and Gary L. McKay, *James D. Bulloch: Secret Agent and Mastermind of the Confederate Navy* (Jefferson, NC: McFarland, 2012), 297; Sanford to Seward, 4 Jul 1861, Despatches, Belgium, vol. 5 and Dispatch 14, Morse to Seward dated Jul 19, 1861, within a covering Dispatch, Aug 23, 1861, quoted in Hariet Chappell Owsley, "Henry Shelton Sanford and Federal Surveillance Abroad, 1861–1865," *The Mississippi Valley Historical* Review 48, no. 2 (Sep 1961), 214.

2. Theodore Roosevelt, *Theodore Roosevelt, An Autobiography* (New York: Charles Scribner's Sons, 1920), 15.

3. Margaret Mitchell, *Gone with the Wind* (1936, reprint; New York: Simon and Schuster, 2007), 424.

4. George C. Rable, *Civil Wars, Women and the Crisis of Southern Nationalism* (Urbana: University of Illinois Press, 1991), 5–6.

5. Rable, *Civil Wars, Women*, ix.

6. J. David Hacker, "A Census-Based Count of the Civil War Dead," *Civil War History* 57, no. 4 (Dec 2011), 307–348.

7. Lilian Rixey, *Bamie: Theodore Roosevelt's Remarkable Sister* (New York: David McKay Co., 1963), v; Rable, *Civil Wars, Women*, x; Betty B. Caroli, *The Roosevelt Women* (New York: Basic Books, 1999), 121–122; Sylvia J. Morris, *Edith Kermit Roosevelt, Portrait of a First Lady* (New York: Coward, McCann, and Geoghegan, 1980), 98.

8. Catherine Clinton, *The Other Civil War: American Women in the Nineteenth Century* (New York: Hill and Wang, 1984), 79; Rable, *Civil Wars, Women*, 287.

9. Clinton, *The Other Civil War*, 39; Rable, *Civil Wars, Women*, x, 8.

10. Clinton, *The Other Civil War*, ix; Drew Gilpin Faust, *Mothers of Invention: Women of the Slaveholding South in the American Civil War* (New York: Vintage Books, 1997), 4.

11. Rable, *Civil Wars, Women*, 288.

Chapter 1

1. Wilson and McKay, *James D. Bulloch*, 9; Philip Morgan, *African American Life in the Georgia Lowcountry: The Atlantic World and the Gullah Geechee* (Athens: University of Georgia Press, 2011), 131–132; Elizabeth Austin Ford, "The Bullochs of Georgia," *The Georgia Review* vol. 6, no. 3 (Fall 1952), 326; Lucian Lamar Knight, *Georgia's Landmarks, Memorials, and Legends*, vol. II (Atlanta: Byrd Printing, Co., 1914), 837. Note: Colonel Elliott's son and Hettie's father was the third American "John" in the Elliott line.

2. Morgan, *African American Life in the Georgia Lowcountry*, 131–132; Ford, "The Bullochs of Georgia," 326; Knight, *Georgia's Landmarks*, 837.

3. Clarece Martin, *A Glimpse of the Past, The History of Bulloch Hall and Roswell Georgia* (1973; reprint, Roswell: Lake Publications, 1987), 3–4; Joseph Gaston Baillie Bulloch, *A History and Genealogy of the Families of Bellinger and De Veaux and Allied Families* (Savannah: The Morning News Print, 1895), 105–106. Archibald's parents were James Bulloch (1701–1780) and Jean Stobo (1710–1750).

4. Martin, *History of Bulloch Hall*, 6.

5. New Georgia Encyclopedia, www. newgeorgiaencyclopedia.org, "Daniel Stewart (1761-1829)"; Martin, *History of Bulloch Hall*, 6; Pride of Liberty, "Sunbury, by Kate Jones Martin," www.prideofliberty.com; Marriage Records, 1828–1978, The Georgia Archives, Morrow.

6. John B. Mallard, "Liberty County, Georgia, an Address Delivered at Hinesville, July 4, 1876," *Georgia Historical Quarterly*, vol. II, no. 1 (Mar 1918), 12–13; *Atlanta Constitution*, Nov 1, 1885; Liberty County Historical Society, www.liberty-history.org; Charles Edgeworth Jones, *Education in Georgia* (Washington: U.S. GPO, 1889), 19–20.

7. William Harden, "William McWhir, an Irish Friend of Washington," *Georgia Historical Quarterly*, vol. I, no. 3 (Sep 1917), 217; Pride of Liberty, "Reverend William McWhir and the Sunbury Academy," www.prideofliberty.com.

8. *Savannah Republican*, Jan 03, 1818; *Atlanta Constitution*, Nov 1, 1885; Connie Huddleston, "A Social and Economic History of the James Stephens Bulloch Family

of Bulloch Hall, Roswell, Georgia," 10; Erskine Clarke, *Dwelling Place: A Plantation Epic* (New Haven, CT: Yale University Press, 2005), 23.

9. *Charleston Carolina Gazette*, Jul 11, 1818.

10. *Atlanta Constitution*, Mar 29, 1902.

11. Ibid.; Caroli, *The Roosevelt Women*, 26–27, citing ARC memoirs, TRC, 4.

12. Biographical Directory of the U.S. Congress, s.v., "Elliott, John" http://biogui-ide.congress.gov/scripts/biodisplay.pl?ind ex=E000124; *Atlanta Constitution*, Mar 29, 1902; Joseph G. B. Bulloch, *A Biographical Sketch of the Hon. Archibald Bulloch, President of Georgia, 1776–77* (Privately published, 1900), 11–13.

13. Clinton, *The Other Civil War*, 38, 39, 41.

14. *New York Commercial Advertiser*, Feb 21, 1820.

15. *The Georgian*, Savannah, Apr 22 and Jun 17 and 22, 1824; Find a Grave, www.findagrave.com, s.v. "Stuart Elliott"; www.Ancestry.com, *Georgia, Select Births and Christenings, 1754-1960*.

16. *Savannah Republican*, Mar 24, 1820.

17. *Milledgeville Reflector*, Jun 16, 1818; *Savannah Republican*, Jul 6, 1819, Mar 11 and 24, 1820.

18. *The Georgian*, Savannah, Nov 26, 1821, Nov 5, 1822, and Jun 25, 1830.

19. *The Georgian*, Savannah, Feb 12, 1822, Jan 1, 1825; Frank O. Braynard, *S.S. Savannah, the Elegant Steam Ship* (Athens: University of Georgia Press, 1963), 4–5, 31, 71; Wilson and McKay, *James D. Bulloch*, 8. Nicholas was an ancestor of both Roosevelt presidents and First Lady Eleanor Roosevelt.

20. City of Savannah, "A List of Mayors and Aldermen of the City of Savannah, Georgia, 1790—2012," http://www.savannahga.gov/DocumentCenter/View/1971, citing Thomas Gamble, Jr., *A History of the City Government of Savannah, Ga., from 1790 to 1901* (Savannah: City Council, 1900); *The Georgian*, Savannah, Apr 5, 1822, May 13, 1822, Mar 3 and 9, 1824, Apr 13, 1829, Jun 17, 1829; *Savannah Republican*, Dec 11, 1823. James Stephens Bulloch made an unsuccessful bid for city Alderman in 1830; see: *The Georgian*, Savannah, Sep 7, 1830.

21. Clinton, *The Other Civil War*, 59; Rable, *Civil Wars, Women*, 8.

22. *The Georgian*, Savannah, Apr 18, 1822, Mar 18, 1825, May 29, 1826, Apr 22, 1828, Feb 20, 1829, Dec 9, 1829.

23. *Darien Gazette*, "Death Notice," Sep 22, 1821 (courtesy Bulloch Hall); John Elliott to James Smith, Oct 6, 1821, MS 1065, Box 1, Folder 3, Reverend John Jones family papers, Hargrett Rare Book and Manuscript Library, University of Georgia Libraries.

24. Given names in the Bulloch family reflecting female lineage include Irvine Stephens Bulloch, Daniel Stewart Elliott, Elliott Roosevelt (father of Eleanor Roosevelt), and Archibald Bulloch Roosevelt (son of Teddy Roosevelt).

25. Clarke, *Dwelling Place*, 75-76; *Charleston Courier*, Jan 5 and Aug 25, 1827; *The Georgian*, Savannah, Aug 11, 1827.

26. Charles J. Johnson, Jr., *Mary Telfair: The Life and Legacy of a Nineteenth-Century Woman* (Savannah: Frederic C. Beil, 2002), 94.

27. Rable, *Civil Wars, Women*, 24; Brent Holcomb, "Senator John Elliott," www.quarterman.org/who/senelliott.html; probate file for John Elliott, Probate Court, Liberty County Courthouse (Hinesville, GA, 1827–1834), 11. Note: Despite the apparent sale of Laurel View, Martha and James retained an interest in the crops of both Laurel View and Cedar Hill at least through 1837.

28. *The Georgian*, Savannah, Mar 3, 1828, Mar 9 and Nov 12, 1929.

29. *The Georgian*, Savannah, Jun 6, 1829, Jan 23, 1832; Martha House Gunning, *Historical & Genealogical Collections of the Martha Stewart Bulloch Chapter, Volume 592* (Roswell, GA: Martha Stewart Bulloch Chapter, NSDAR, 2001), 115, as cited in Huddleston, "A Social and Economic History," 12.

30. *The Georgian*, Savannah, Oct 22, 1829; *Macon Weekly Telegraph*, Jul 4, 1832; Rable, *Civil Wars, Women*, 24.

31. *The Georgian*, Savannah, Jun 30, 1829; *New York Evening Post*, Jul 7, 1829.

32. *The Georgian*, Savannah, Oct 28 and Nov 02, 1829; Johnson, *Mary Telfair*, 145-148, 410.

33. Rable, *Civil Wars, Women*, 18-19, 275; *Concord* (NH) *Observer*, Oct 11, 1819. Senator Elliott had been an honorary vice president of the American Education

Society, a national organization headquartered in Boston that provided financial assistance to pious young men seeking an education.

34. *The Georgian*, Savannah, May 4, 1830 and May 17, 1831.

35. *The Georgian*, Savannah, Sep 7 and Oct 2, 1830; Athens (GA) *Southern Banner*, Apr 5, 1834; Clarke, *Dwelling Place*, 101.

36. *The Georgian*, Savannah, Feb 26, 1831 (courtesy Connie Huddleston and Bulloch Hall).

37. *Macon Weekly Telegraph*, Mar 5, 1831.

38. *The Georgian*, Savannah, July 12, 1831.

39. *The Georgian*, Savannah, Apr 5, 1832; Mary Telfair, *Mary Telfair to Mary Few: Selected Letters, 1802-1844* (Athens: University of Georgia Press, 2011), 106–107; Johnson, *Mary Telfair*, 93–94.

40. Telfair, *Mary Telfair to Mary Few*, 106-107; Psalms, King James Version, 139: 14.

41. Maria Edgeworth, *Tales of a Fashionable Life*, Chapter IV, The Absentee (1823; reprint, Boston, Samuel H. Parker, 1826), 285.

42. Mary Telfair, *Mary Telfair to Mary Few*, 107.

43. JDB to Anna Christie Stevens, Jul 11, 1849, James Dunwody Bulloch Papers (#3318-z), SHC.

44. *The Georgian*, Savannah, Dec 3, 1831, Jan 23, Apr 5, May 30, Sep 27, Nov 27, Dec 15, 1832. Note: J.S. Bulloch was trustee for Ann M. Gray and her son Franklin V. Gray (21).

45. *The Georgian*, Savannah, Dec 15, 1832.

46. *The Georgian*, Savannah, Sep 6, 1827; James Patterson, *The Old School Presbyterian Church on Slavery* (New Wilmington: Vincent, Ferguson and Co., 1857), 18.

47. William A. Hotchkiss (comp.), *A Codification of the Statute Law of Georgia* (Augusta: Charles E. Grenville, 1848), 770, 824-836; Chatham County Ordinary Office, Register of Free Persons of Color, 1780—1865. J.S. Bulloch was guardian for: Edward (1829) and Joseph (1829-1830) Beard, Liberty Co. ship carpenters; William Stewart 1831; Sam Boyd (1831—1832), Priscilla Boyd 31, wash woman,

Savannah, 1831—1846; Young Caesar (1828-1840, died aged 68), laborer in Chatham Co.

48. *Georgia Tax Digests, 140 volumes* (1821-1827), Georgia Archives, Morrow.

49. *The Georgian*, Savannah, Mar 10, 1822.

50. Patterson, *The Old School Presbyterian Church on Slavery*, 1, 8: Alexander Gross, James B. Scouller, et al., *A History of the Methodist Church, South: The United Presbyterian Church; The Cumberland Presbyterian Church and the Presbyterian Church, South, in the United States* (New York: The Christian Literature Co., 1894), 29-32; Roger C. Richards, *History of Southern Baptists* (Bloomington, IN: CrossBooks, 2012), 87, 91, 94-101.

51. Gross, *A History of the Methodist Church, South*, 29-32.

52. *New York Commercial Advertiser* and *New York Evening Post*, Jun 5, 1835; *Charleston Courier*, Jun 4, 1835; Johnson, *Mary Telfair*, 211, 213.

53. MSB to John Jones, Dec 15, 1836, MS 1065. Box 1 Folder 3, Reverend John Jones family papers, Hargrett Rare Book and Manuscript Library; Elihu Geer (comp.), *Geer's Hartford City Directory and Hartford Illustrated* (Hartford: Elihu Geer, 1882) with reprint of 1842 edition. The block numbers along Hartford Main Street have been renumbered; the 100 block is now the 800 block.

54. Clarke, *Dwelling Place*, 69, 83-84.

55. Clinton, *The Other Civil War*, 45; Joan D. Hedrick, *Harriet Beecher Stowe: A Life* (New York: Oxford University Press, 1994), 31-32, 50-51.

56. Catharine E. Beecher, *A Treatise on Domestic Economy* (Boston: T.H. Webb & Co., 1842), 27-29, 32-33.

57. Beecher, *Treatise on Domestic Economy*, 27-29, 32-33. Catharine Beecher founded the Western Female Institute in Cincinnati (1832) and then went on to help found a number of other institutions in the Midwest that provided women access to higher education.

58. Paul Finkelman, *An Imperfect Union: Slavery, Federalism, and Comity* (1981; reprint, Union, NJ: Lawbook Exchange, 2000), 127; James Mars, *Life of James Mars, A Slave Born And Sold In Connecticut*, 6th ed. (Hartford: Case, Lockwood & Co., 1868), 33-34; *The Liberator*, Jul 7, 1837.

59. Finkelman, *An Imperfect Union*, 127; David E. Swift, *Black Prophets of Justice: Activist Clergy Before the Civil War* (Baton Rouge: LSU Press, 1989), 215-217; Mars, *Life of James Mars*, 33-34 (quoted material); *The Liberator*, Jul 7, 1837.

60. *The Liberator*, Jul 7, 1837.

61. Ibid.

62. Ibid.

63. Peter George Mode, *Source Book and Bibliographical Guide for American Church History* (Menasha WI: George Banta Publishing Company, 1921), 573-574; Patterson, *The Old School Presbyterian Church on Slavery*, 8.

64. *The Liberator*, Jul 7, 1837.

65. Ibid.

66. Mars, *Life of James Mars*, 34.

67. Ibid. (quoted material); Ancestry.com, U.S. Census, 1880, s.v., "Nancy Jackson."

68. Mars, *Life of James Mars*, 33-35; *The Liberator*, Jul 7, 1837 (quoted material).

69. Finkelman, *An Imperfect Union*, 127-130.

70. L.J. Critchfield, *Reports of Cases Argued and Determined in the Supreme Court of Ohio*, vol. 6 (Cincinnati: Robert Clarke & Co., 1874), 699; MSB to John Jones, Dec 15, 1836, MS 1065. Box 1 Folder 3, Reverend John Jones family papers, Hargrett Rare Book and Manuscript Library.

71. *The Times*, Hartford, CT, Jun 17, 1837.

72. Ibid.

73. Mars, *Life of James Mars*, 35.

74. Hedrick, *Harriet Beecher Stowe*, 31-32, 50-51; Clarke, *Dwelling Place*, 298.

75. Roswell C. Smith, *Smith's Quarto Geography* (New York: Cady & Burgess, 1848-1850), 14.

76. Sydney E. Morse, *System of Geography for the Use of Schools* (New York: Harper & Brothers, 1844-1850), 67.

77. Finkelman, *An Imperfect Union*, 127-130.

78. Mars, *Life of James Mars*, 33-35.

79. *The Times*, Hartford, CT, Jun 24, 1837.

80. Ibid., Jun 17, 1837.

81. *The Liberator*, Jul 7, 1837.

82. Ibid., Aug 4, 1837 (quoted material); Clarke, *Dwelling Place*, 101-105; Hedrick, *Harriet Beecher Stowe*, 50-51.

83. *Charleston Courier,* Aug 22, 1837.
84. *Richmond Inquirer,* Aug 29, 1837.
85. J.S. Bulloch and M. Bulloch to R. Hutchison and C. Hutchison, Jul 7, 1837, Robert Hutchison papers, GHS, Ms. 2226, Box 1, Folder 1; Catherine Elliott Sever (with introduction by Monroe F. Cockrell), "A Memory of the South," *After Sundown* VIII (Dec 1957) (quoted material).
86. Ancestry.com, U.S. Census, 1850, 1870, 1880, s.v., "Nancy Jackson"; Nannie (Nancy) Jackson to President Theodore Roosevelt, Sep 30, 1901 (courtesy Kit Collier), and Sep 6, 1902, Theodore Roosevelt Papers, Manuscripts Division, Library of Congress.
87. Nannie (Nancy) Jackson to President Theodore Roosevelt, Sep 30, 1901 (courtesy Kit Collier), and Sep 6, 1902, Theodore Roosevelt Papers, Manuscripts Division, Library of Congress.
88. Nannie (Nancy) Jackson to President Theodore Roosevelt, Sep 30, 1901 (courtesy Kit Collier), and Sep 6, 1902, Theodore Roosevelt Papers, Manuscripts Division, Library of Congress; *NYT,* Oct 15, 1906; New York *Sun,* Oct 28, 1906.
89. James D. Bulloch, *Secret Service of the Confederate States in Europe,* vol. 2 (New York: G. P. Putnam's Sons, 1884), 312, 310, 308 (quoted material). Martha's adult children by John Elliott and their spouses did own slaves.
90. J.S. Bulloch and M. Bulloch to R. Hutchison and C. Hutchison, Jul 7, 1837, Robert Hutchison papers, GHS, Ms. 2226, Box 1, Folder 1. Note: Daniel and his sisters Susan and Georgia Elliott were technically James Dunwoody Bulloch's uncle and aunts, but the relationships were more like siblings.
91. Ibid. Jane and William Dunwoody may have been in Philadelphia attending school along with their older and similarly named cousins, Jane and William Bulloch.
92. J.G.B. Bulloch, *A History of the Glen Family of South Carolina and Georgia* (Washington, D.C.: J.G.B. Bulloch, 1923), 71–72 (quoted material); Richard Henry Greene (ed.), et al., "William Gaston Bulloch," *The New York Genealogical and Biographical Record,* vol. 44, Jan 1913, 232; J.S. Bulloch and M. Bulloch to R. Hutchison and C. Hutchison, Jul 7, 1837, Robert Hutchison papers, GHS, Ms. 2226, Box 1, Folder 1 (quoted material).

93. Isaac Webb, *Catalogue of the Pupils of Isaac Webb, Esq., Private Boarding School* (Middletown, CT, 1839), 3–5, 7.
94. Ibid., 6 (quoted material); Rutherford Birchard Hayes, *Diary and Letters of Rutherford Birchard* Hayes: vol. 1, 1834–1860 (Columbus: Ohio State Archæological and Historical Society, 1922), 15–26. Note: Webb died suddenly in 1842, and the school soon closed; the DeKoven family owned Maple Grove until 1889 when Wesleyan University converted it into its first women's dormitory, named Webb Hall, but better known as Quail's Roost, a reference to its female residents. After Wesleyan stopped accepting female students in 1909, the university converted it to a bookstore and post office until it burned in 1929.
95. *The Georgian,* Savannah, May 9, 1827, May 16, 1829, May 17, 1831, Jan 18, 1832; *Macon Weekly Telegraph,* May 23, 1829, Feb 13, 1834; Webb, *Catalogue of the Pupils of Isaac Webb,* 3–5, 7. Note: Eli Whitney, III, son of the famous man who had invented the cotton gin at Mulberry Grove, near Savannah, was a member of the class of 1834. William Law was also the brother of James S. Bulloch's brother-in-law, Dr. John Stevens Law.
96. Webb, *Catalogue of the Pupils of Isaac Webb,* 4; Hayes, *Diary and Letters of Rutherford Birchard Hayes,* 16 (quoted material). One of Hayes' key accomplishments as president was to begin dismantling the Reconstruction burdens imposed on the defeated Southern states.
97. Hayes, *Diary and Letters of Rutherford Birchard Hayes,* 16; Webb, *Catalogue of the Pupils of Isaac Webb,* 4–6.
98. *Charleston Courier,* May 12, 1840; J.S. Bulloch and M. Bulloch to R. Hutchison and C. Hutchison, 7 July 1837, Robert Hutchison papers, GHS, Ms. 2226, Box 1, Folder 1; Ancestry.com, *Georgia, Select Births and Christenings, 1754–1960,* s.v., "Caroline Lucile Hutchison." Corinne Elliott Hutchison was Daniel's half-sister and James' step-sister.
99. *Charleston Courier,* Jul 2, 1838, and May 12, 1840; *Southern Patriot,* Charleston, SC, Jun 14, 1838; Mrs. Hugh McLeod (Miss Rebecca Lamar), "The Loss of the Steamer *Pulaski*," *Georgia Historical Quarterly* 3, no. 2 (Jun 1919), 67 (quoted material); David Slick, *Graveyard of the*

Atlantic: Shipwrecks of the North Carolina Coast (Chapel Hill: University of North Carolina Press, 1952), 28.

100. McLeod, "The Loss of the Steamer *Pulaski*," 63-95; *Charleston Courier*, May 12, 1840.

101. *Charleston Courier*, May 12, 1840; McLeod, "The Loss of the Steamer *Pulaski*," 63-95 (69 quoted material).

102. McLeod, "The Loss of the Steamer *Pulaski*," 63-95 (72 quoted material).

103. Ibid. *Charleston Courier*, May 12, 1840.

104. Ibid. (73 quoted material).

105. Ibid.

106. Ibid.

107. Ibid., 77-85 (78–79, quoted material).

108. Ibid., 79-85.

109. Ibid., 85, 86 (quoted material). Note: Miss Lamar refers to Hutchison's daughter as both Connie and Corinne.

110. Ibid., 88.

111. *Charleston Courier*, Jul 2, 1838 (quoted material); Slick, *Graveyard of the Atlantic*, 40.

Chapter 2

1. Henry Merrell, James L. Skinner, ed., *Autobiography of Henry Merrell* (Athens: University of Georgia Press, 1991), 130, 141, 179; Martin, *History of Bulloch Hall*, 11.

2. David Williams, *The Georgia Gold Rush: Twenty-Niners, Cherokees, and Gold Fever* (Columbia: University of South Carolina, 1993), 4, 12, 110, 115; Merrell, *Autobiography*, 177.

3. Martin, *History of Bulloch Hall*, 9; Huddleston, "A Social and Economic History."

4. J.S. Bulloch (Savannah) to W.G. Bulloch (Paris), Jan 24, 1839, in Bulloch, *A History of the Glen Family*, 71-72; Sever, "A Memory of the South"; Martin, *History of Bulloch Hall*, 9.

5. *Charleston Courier*, Apr 27, 1839.

6. *The Liberator*, Aug 4, 1837; James S. Bulloch, "Report of Committee on Internal Police and Discipline. June 16, 1837," *Army and Navy Chronicle*, vol. V, no. 1 (Jul 6, 1837), 4–5 (quoted material).

7. U.S. State Department General Records, National Archives. Record Group 59, Microfilm Publication M1372, 694 rolls, Passport Applications, 1795–1925, s.v. "A. Hutchison" and "J.S. Bulloch"; J.S. Bulloch to W.G. Bulloch (Paris), Jan 24, 1839, Bulloch, *A History of the Glen Family*, 71-72; NARA, RG 45 Naval Records Collection and Library, Bulloch to Paulding, Jun 25, 1839, entry 147.

8. Merrell, *Autobiography*, 137.

9. *Philadelphia Public Ledger*, Jan 22, 1839.

10. Michael D. Hitt, *Bulloch Hall* (Roswell, GA: Self-published, 1995), 2; Martin, *History of Bulloch Hall*, 13; Wilson and McKay, *James. D. Bulloch*, 10. Note: Willis Ball was the master builder for Bulloch Hall and several other notable homes in the historic town of Roswell. Contrary to many popular descriptions, Bulloch Hall was never a plantation home.

11. *Atlantic Journal Magazine*, June 10, 1923.

12. Ibid.

13. U.S. State Department General Records, National Archives. Record Group 59, Microfilm Publication M1372, 694 rolls, Passport Applications, 1795–1925, s.v. "A. Hutchison" and "J.S. Bulloch"; Mitchell, *Gone With the Wind*, 892 (quoted material); Roosevelt, *Theodore Roosevelt, An Autobiography*, 15.

14.. New York *Evening Post*, May 15, 1840; JDB Service Record, Jan 26, 1934, Washington, D.C., U.S. Naval Historical Center, *DANFS Online*. s.v. "Potomac," *http://www.hazegray.org/danfs/frigates/p otomac.htm*, and s.v. "Decatur," *http://www.history.navy.mil/danfs/d2 /decatur-i.htm*; RADM Ernest McNeill Eller, ed., *Dictionary of American Naval Fighting Ships*, vol. VII (Washington: GPO for the U.S. Navy Department, Naval History Division, 1981), 413–414; J. Thomas Scharf, *History of the Confederate States Navy* (1887; reprint, New York: Gramercy, 1996), 783–784; Bulloch, *Secret Service*, I: 91–92; Wilson and McKay, *Bulloch*, 11-12.

15. Susan A. Elliott to Kate (Catherine Elliott Sever), Sep 26, 1843, TRC, courtesy Bulloch Hall; William Lumpkin to James K. Paulding, Mar 28, 1840, University of Virginia Brock Collection Misc. Reel 5071.

16. Merrell, *Autobiography*, 130, 141, 150, 168–169.

17. Sever, "A Memory of the South"; Alfred Nevin, ed., *Encyclopædia of the Presbyterian Church in the United States*

of America (Philadelphia: Presbyterian Encyclopædia Publishing Company, 1884), 300; Martin, *History of Bulloch Hall*, 16. The other baby boy was John Bayard Hand (1839–1877), son of Rev. Aaron H. and Elizabeth Coit Boswell Hand of Connecticut.

18. Sever, "A Memory of the South"; Martin, *History of Bulloch Hall*, 10, 11, 16; Nevin, *Encyclopædia of the Presbyterian Church*, 300. Rev. Hand was the brother-in-law of Eliza Barrington King Hand; his wife, Elizabeth Coit Boswell Hand, was also a founding member of the Roswell church and their son John Bayard Hand was the other child baptized with Charles Irvine Bulloch.

19. Merrell, *Autobiography*, 184–185; Sever, "A Memory of the South"; *The Charlotte* [NC] *Journal*, Marriage Notices, April 23, 1840. Jane Marion Dunwoody married Rev. Stanhope W. Erwin on Apr 19, 1840; he died on Aug 18 that same year.

20. Sever, "A Memory of the South"; Martin, *History of Bulloch Hall*, 10, 11; Theodore Roosevelt to J.R. Nutting, Jun 4, 1901, The RAAB Collection; Julia Collier Harris, *The Life and Letters of Joel Chandler Harris* (Boston: AMS Press, 1918), 508–517.

21. Bulloch, *A History of the Glen Family*, 71–72 (quoted material); Greene, "William Gaston Bulloch," The New York Genealogical and Biographical Record, vol. 44, Jan 1913, 232; *Charleston Courier*, Nov 09, 1839.

22. Roswell Historical Society, Inc., "Roswell's Historic Founder's Cemetery," www.roswellgov.com/DocumentCenter/Home/View/2026; Sever, "A Memory of the South."

23. Anna (Dana Sever) and John (Elliott Sever) to Catherine Elliott Sever, Dec 6 and 12, 1841, Kingston (MA) Public Library, Vertical Files OC2 – Sever Family; New York *Evening Post*, Jun 01, 1842. Jane and her daughters visited Roswell Nov 1841 to May 1842, traveling by train, the Brig *Sterling*, and carriage from Kingston, MA.

24. *Macon Weekly Telegraph*, Jun 21, 1842. The convention convened on June 20, 1842, and selected Howell Cobb and William H. Stiles as candidates for Congress. Both were successful in their bids. Howell Cobb served for five terms,

became speaker of the House, was governor of Georgia (1851–1853), secretary of the Treasury under President Buchanan (1857–1860), and a Confederate major general. William H. Stiles served in the U.S. House of Representatives for one term, became chargé d'affaires to Austria (1845–1849), and served as a Confederate colonel.

25. *Charleston Courier*, Nov 12, 1842; Merrell, *Autobiography*, 130, 141; U.S. Congress, House, *A Biographical Congressional Directory, 1774 to 1903*, 57th Congress, 2d Session, Ex. Doc. 458 (Washington: GPO, 1903), 461, 821. J.S. Bulloch was the agent for the estate sale of the Hugh Rose Rice Plantation on the Savannah River in Nov 1841.

26. U.S. Navy Order log, JDB Service Record; Wilson and McKay, *Bulloch*, 40; Charleston *Southern Patriot*, Mar 27, 1844; *Charleston Courier*, Mar 28, 1844.

27. Hitt, *Bulloch Hall*, 2; Martin, *History of Bulloch Hall*, 15.

28. JDB Service Record; Charleston *Southern Patriot*, Jul 11, 1844.

29. JDB Service Record; University of New York Medical Dept., *Annual Announcement of Lectures* (New York: Joseph H. Jennings, 1848), 15; New York *Herald*, Mar 21, 1845; *Charleston Courier*, Mar 31, 1845.

30. Eliza Barrington King Hand to Tamar Platt Hand, Oct 29, 1844, Connecticut State Library, State Archives, Record Group 69, Manuscript Collections, Aaron Hand Family Letters, Ser. 1, Aaron Hand Family Letters, Box 1 Folder 15, Letters from Georgia, 1841–1846; New York *Commercial Advertiser*, May 27, 1845; New York *Herald*, May 30, 1845; *Daily Union*, Washington, D.C., Jul 3, 1845; Scharf, *History of the Confederate States Navy*, 783–784; JDB Service Record; U.S. Navy, *Register 1848*, 68; *Brooklyn Daily Eagle*, Jul 8, 1845; *Daily National Intelligencer*, Washington, D.C., 12 Jul 1845; *Charleston Courier*, 14 Jul 1845.

31. Henry Bulls Watson, *The Journals of Marine Second Lieutenant Henry Bulls Watson, 1845–1848, Occasional Papers*, ed. Charles R. Smith (Washington, D.C.: History and Museums Division Headquarters, U.S. Marine Corps, GPO, 1990) 77.

32. Watson, *Journals*, 79–80, 94–95;

George H. Himes, "Letters by Burr Osborn," *The Quarterly of the Oregon Historical Society* 14, no. 4 (Dec 1913): 363; *The Friend*, Honolulu, May 1, 1846. In addition to Howison, Schenck, and Bulloch, the officers included Wm. S. Hollins (purser); Edward Hudson (assistant surgeon), John M. Maury (captain's clerk), and S. McLanahan (passed midshipman), George T. Simes, and Hunter Davidson (midshipmen).

33. Watson, *Journals*, 94 (quoted material), 95; U.S. Congress, "Report of Lieut. Neil M. Howison, United States Navy," 30th Congress, 1st Sess, Misc House Doc. no. 29, Oregon, 1; *The Friend*, Honolulu, May 1, 1846.

34. Richard A. Greer, "A.G. Abell's Hawaiian Interlude," *The Hawaiian Journal of History*, vol. 29 (1995): 59.

35. Charleston *Southern Patriot*, Dec 17, 1845, May 4 and Oct 30, 1846; *Charleston Courier*, Dec 18, 1845; New York *Spectator*, Jun 27, 1846 and Sep 19, 1846; New York *Evening Post*, Sep 16, 1846; Letter from James S. Bulloch to Hon. James Buchanan, Secretary of State, Apr 18, 1846, NARA, Passport Applications, 1795-1905, Roll 018, 01 Apr 1846—30 Sep 1846.

36. J.S. Bulloch and M. Bulloch to R. Hutchison and C. Hutchison, Jul 7, 1837, Robert Hutchison papers, GHS, Ms. 2226, Box 1, Folder 1 (quoted material); Charleston *Southern Patriot*, and Apr 24, May 4, and Oct 30, 1846.

37. *The Friend*, Honolulu, Apr 01, 1845; U.S. Congress, "Report of Lieut. Neil M. Howison," 1.

38. U.S. Congress, "Report of Lieut. Neil M. Howison," 1.

39. Gregory P. Shine, "'A Gallant Little Schooner': The U.S. Schooner Shark and the Oregon Country, 1846," *Oregon Historical Quarterly* 109, no. 4 (Winter 2008): 548, 553; Himes, "Letters by Burr Osborn," 361.

40. Shine, "A Gallant Little Schooner," 548; Jill Campbell, *Natural Masques: Gender and Identity in Fielding's Plays and Novels* (Stanford: Stanford University Press, 1995), 8, 19-23, 209; Wilson and McKay, *Bulloch*, 12-13.

41. U.S. Congress, "Report of Lieut. Neil M. Howison," 5.

42. Ibid., 7 (quoted material); Himes,

"Letters by Burr Osborn," 357, 363; Shine, "A Gallant Little Schooner." 553, 555, 557.

43. Shine, "A Gallant Little Schooner," 553-554; U.S. Congress, "Report of Lieut. Neil M. Howison," 5-6; *Oregon Spectator*, Oct 01, 1846.

44. Shine, 554; Himes, "Letters by Burr Osborn," 356-357.

45. Himes, "Letters by Burr Osborn," 357; Jas. Findlay Schenck to J.S. Bulloch, 25 Nov 1848, JDB Collection, 1847–1954, MS0283, Mariners' Museum Library, Newport News, VA; *Oregon Spectator*, Oct 01, 1846.

46. Shine, "A Gallant Little Schooner," 554; U.S. Congress, "Report of Lieut. Neil M. Howison," 5-6; Himes, "Letters by Burr Osborn," 357; Schenck to Bulloch, Nov. 25 1848, JDB Collection, MS0283, Mariners' Museum Library; *Oregon Spectator*, Oct 01, 1846 (quoted material).

47. *Oregon Spectator*, Oct 1, 1846.

48. Schenck to Bulloch, Nov 25, 1848, JDB Collection, MS0283, Mariners' Museum Library.

49. Howison to Bulloch, Aug 5, 1847, JDB Collection, MS0283, Mariners' Museum Library.

50. U.S. Congress, "Report of Lieut. Neil M. Howison," 3, 10; Howison to Bulloch, Aug 5, 1848, JDB Collection, MS0283, Mariners' Museum Library; Wilson and McKay, *Bulloch*, 13-14; *Niles Weekly Register*, vol. 75, "Navy," (Philadelphia: Jan 24,1849): 50.

51. Washington, D.C., *Daily Union*, Mar 15, 1847.

52. *Pittsburgh Gazette*, Dec 12, 1848 (quoted material); Schenck to Bulloch, Nov. 25 1847, JDB Collection, MS0283, Mariners' Museum Library.

53. Merrell, *Autobiography*, 177; *Californian*, San Francisco, Nov 11, 1848; *Niles Weekly Register*, vol. 75 (Philadelphia: Jan 24, 1849): 50, 178; Thomas Oliver Larkin, *The Larkin Papers* VIII, 1848-1861, edited by George P. Hammond (Berkeley: University of California Press, 1962), 31; New York *Weekly Herald*, Jun 16, 1849.

54. *The Friend*, Honolulu, Apr 1, 1845, and May 1, 1848; New Orleans *Times-Picayune*, Mar 18, 1848; U.S. Census, 1850 and 1860, NARA publications M432 and M653, RG: 29 NARA, Washington, D.C.

55. *The Friend*, Honolulu, May 1, 1848 (quoted material); T.H. Stevens, "The

Wreck of the Maria Helena," in, *Adventures at Sea* (New York: Harper Brothers, 1908), 186; *Whaleman's Shipping List and Merchants Transcript*, New Bedford MA, Aug 8, 1848; New York *Spectator*, Aug 7, 1848.

56. New York *Spectator*, May 1, 1848.

57. T.H. Stevens, "The Wreck of the Maria Helena," 187.

58. *The Friend*, Honolulu, May 1, 1848 (quoted material); *New York Commercial Advertiser*, Aug 5, 1848; New York *Spectator*, Aug 7, 1848; *Whaleman's Shipping List and Merchants Transcript*, New Bedford MA, Aug 08, 1848.

59. *The Friend*, Honolulu, May 1, 1848.

60 Stevens, "The Wreck of the Maria Helena," 188.

61. *The Friend*, Honolulu, May 1, 1848.

62. Stevens, "The Wreck of the Maria Helena," 191.

63. *The Friend*, Honolulu, May 1, 1848.

64. Ibid.

65. Ibid.

66. *The Friend*, Honolulu, May 1, 1848; Stevens, "The Wreck of the Maria Helena," 193.

67. *The Friend*, Honolulu, May 1, 1848.

68. Ibid.

69. *The Friend*, Honolulu, Jun 1, 1848; Stevens, "The Wreck of the Maria Helena," 193; *Whaleman's Shipping List and Merchants Transcript*, New Bedford MA, Aug 8, 1848; New York *Spectator*, Aug 7, 1848; New York *Commercial Advertiser*, Aug 5, 1848.

70. *The Friend*, Honolulu, Jun 1, 1848; *Whaleman's Shipping List and Merchants Transcript*, New Bedford MA, Aug 8, 1848; New York *Spectator*, Aug 7, 1848; New York *Commercial Advertiser*, Aug 5, 1848.

71. *The Friend*, Honolulu, Jun 1, 1848 (quoted material); *Whaleman's Shipping List and Merchants Transcript*, New Bedford MA, Aug 8, 1848; New York *Spectator*, Aug 7, 1848; New York *Commercial Advertiser*, Aug 5, 1848.

72. *The Friend*, Honolulu, Jun 1 and Jul 1, 1848; *New York Commercial Advertiser*, Aug 5, 1848; New York *Spectator*, Aug 7, 1848; *Whaleman's Shipping List and Merchants Transcript*, New Bedford, MA, Aug 8, 1848; *Army and Navy Register* 56, no. 1786, Washington, D.C., Oct 10, 1914. Thomas Holdup Stevens III followed in

his father's (and grandfather's) footsteps and like his father, achieved the rank of admiral. He returned to his birthplace on August 12, 1898, and participated in the ceremony to accept Hawaii as a U.S. Territory.

73. JDB to Anna Christie Stevens, Jul 11, 1849, JDB Papers (#3318-z), SHC (quoted material); *Californian*, San Francisco, Nov 11, 1848; *The Brooklyn Daily Eagle*, 11 Jun 1849; *Enquirer*, Richmond, VA, Jun 12, 1849; U.S. Naval Historical Center, *DANFS Online*, s.v. "Lexington," http://www.history.navy.mil/danfs/l/lexington.htm.

74. *Indiana State Sentinel*, Apr 21, 1849.

75. U.S. Congress, House of Representatives, *Message from the President of the United States*, 31st Congress, 1st Session. Ex. Doc. no. 17 (Washington, D.C.: GPO, 1850), 872; New York *Weekly Herald*, Jun 16, 1849; Elizabeth Fleming. Rhodes, *On The Fringe Of Fame: The Career of Richard Bland Lee II in the South and West, 1797–1875* (Pasadena, CA: Castle, 1990), accessed at Washington and Lee University, *http://leearchive.wlu.edu/papers/books /fringe/08.html* (quoted material); *Niles Weekly Register*, Philadelphia, Mar 21, 1849.

76. New York *Weekly Herald*, Jun 16, 1849; *The Brooklyn Daily Eagle*, 11 June 1849 (quoted material).

77. JDB to Thomas Holdup and Mrs. Anna Christie Stevens, Oct 30, 1849, JDB Papers (#3318-z), SHC.

78. JDB Service Record; New York *Commercial Advertiser*, Jun 13, 1849; *Brooklyn Daily Eagle*, Apr 2 and Jun 25, 1849, and Aug 15 and Sep 4, 1850. Capt. (Jas. Findlay) Schenck, the brother of Bulloch's shipmate on the *Shark*, also checked into the Irving House on Jun 13, 1849.

79. JDB to Anna Christie Stevens, Jul 11, 1849, JDB Papers (#3318-z), SHC; *Savannah Republican*, Jun 25, 1849.

80. *Savannah Republican*, Jun 25, 1849; *Charleston Courier*, 27 Jun 1849.

81. JDB to Anna Christie Stevens, Jul 11, 1849, JDB Papers (#3318-z), SHC.

82. Charleston *Southern Patriot*, May 16, 1848; *Charleston Courier*, May 17, 1848; Harvard Law School. *Catalogue of the Students in the Law School* (Cambridge: Welch, Bigelow, & Co., 1859), 36, 117.

83. Martin, *History of Bulloch Hall*, 18; Huddleston, "A Social and Economic History," 19; Rable, *Civil Wars, Women*, 24.

84. Wilson and McKay, *Bulloch*, 15; Florida Bayard Seay to Charles Jones Pratt, 1901, in Connie M. Cox and Darlene M. Walsh, eds., *Providence: Selected Correspondence of George Hull Camp* (Macon, GA: Indigo, 2008), 555 (quoted material).

85. Huddleston, "A Social and Economic History," 19-20.

86. *Charleston Courier*, Mar 16 and Jun 13, 1848; *Savannah Republican*, Feb 3, 1849; Martin, *History of Bulloch Hall*, 19; New York *Evening Post*, Aug 08, 1848.

87. *Savannah Republican*, Feb 3 and Apr 12, 1849, and May 21, 1850; Corinne Roosevelt Robinson, *My Brother, Theodore Roosevelt* (New York: Charles Scribner's Sons, 1921), 12 (quoted material); Martin, *A Glimpse of the Past*, 19; Huddleston, "A Social and Economic History," 20, 23.

88. Martin, *History of Bulloch Hall*, 18; Huddleston, "A Social and Economic History," 23; Ancestry.com, *Georgia, Property Tax Digests, 1793-1892*; Wilson and McKay, *Bulloch*, 303 fn63; Major Archibald Howell, an owner of the Lebanon Flour Mills and a family friend, generously "bought" Bulloch Hall for $3,350 on Feb 7, 1850; Martha eventually repaid the debt and continued to live in the home.

89. *Savannah Republican*, May 21, 1850; New York *Spectator*, Nov 16, 1848; *Charleston Courier*, May 10, 1849; Ruth Ann Atwood Dunwody to Jane Margaret Atwood, Apr 12, 1848, in Cox and Walsh, *Providence: Selected Correspondence*, 99 (quoted material).

90. JDB to Mrs. Anna Christie Stevens, July 11, 1849, JDB Papers (#3318-z), SHC.

91. Chester *Chronicle*, Sep 12, 1863 (quoted material courtesy of Richard Harris).

92. JDB to Anna Christie Stevens, Jul 11, 1849, JDB Papers (#3318-z), SHC.

93. *Savannah Republican*, Aug 09, 1849; New York *Evening Post*, Aug 13, 1849; Official Navy Order log; JDB Service Record; Wilson and McKay, *Bulloch*, 16.

94. Official Navy Order log; JDB Service Record; Wilson and McKay, *Bulloch*, 16.

95. JDB to Thomas Holdup and Mrs. Anna Christie Stevens, Oct 30, 1849, JDB Papers (#3318-z), SHC.

96. William Tecumseh Sherman, *Memoirs of Gen. W.T. Sherman*, edited by James Gillespie Blaine (New York: C. L. Webster & Company, 1891), 135. The *Michigan* was later renamed the *Wolverine*; its prow is on display at the Erie Maritime Museum (see: www.flagshipniagara.org). In 1854, a junior engraver named James Abbott McNeil Whistler used Tom's sketch of "Anacapa Island in Santa Barbara Channel" to create his one and only chart for the U.S. Coast Survey. Whistler added two flocks of seagulls to the engraving to make the map more interesting. Whistler did not respond well to authority or structure; as a result, the USCS terminated him after two months. Whistler, however, learned enough about etching techniques with the USCS that he became one of the greatest artists of his era. See: U.S. Coast Survey Map, "Anacapa Island in Santa Barbara Channel," 1854.

97. JDB to Thomas Holdup and Mrs. Anna Christie Stevens, Oct 30, 1849, JDB Papers (#3318-z), SHC.

98. Candace Bailey, *Music and the Southern Belle: From Accomplished Lady to Confederate Composer* (Carbondale: Southern Illinois University Press, 2010), 82 (quoted material); *Columbia (SC) State*, Mar 15, 1903; E.J. Watson (Comm.), *Handbook of South Carolina: Resources, Institutions and Industries of the State*, 2nd ed. (Columbia: State Dept. of Agriculture, Commerce, and Immigration, 1908), 196 (quoted material).

99. Candace Bailey, *Music and the Southern Belle*, 82 (quoted material); *Columbia (SC) State*, Mar 15, 1903; Watson, *Handbook of South Carolina*, 196.

100. Watson, *Handbook of South Carolina*, 196; Mary Kelley, *Learning to Stand and Speak: Women, Education, and Public Life in America's Republic* (Chapel Hill: University of North Carolina Press, 2006) 72; Christie Anne Farnham, *The Education of the Southern Belle: Higher Education and Student Socialization in the Antebellum South* (New York: New York University Press, 1994), 66-67, 108-109.

101. New York *Spectator*, Nov 16, 1848; *Savannah Republican*, Feb 3, 1849.

102. *Charleston Courier*, 10 May and Dec 17, 1849, and Jan 10, 1850; *Baltimore*

Sun, Dec 15, 1849; George Camp to Jane Atwood, Feb 21, 1850, in Cox and Walsh, *Providence: Selected Correspondence*, 152–153 (quoted material).

103. *Charleston Courier*, May 01 and 20, 1850; New York *Commercial Advertiser*, May 21 and Jun 13, 1850; Boston *Daily Atlas*, Aug 24, 1850; New York *Evening Post*, Aug 24 and 30, 1850; New York *Spectator*, Sep 23, 1850; *Baltimore American and Commercial Daily Advertiser*, Nov 27, 1850.

104. *Baltimore American and Commercial Daily Advertiser*, Nov 27, 1850; JDB Service Record; JDB to Nannie Hutchison Dawson, Jan 24, 1880, Box 3 Folder 23, Hutchison-Dawson Papers, MS 2226, GHS (quoted material).

105. Jacquelin A. Caskie, *The Caskie Family of Virginia* (Charlottesville: Conway, 1928), 52 and *Richmond Times-Dispatch*, Oct 23, 1905 (quoted material).

106. John McIntosh Kell, *Recollections of a Naval Life: Including the Cruises of the Confederate States Steamers Sumter and Alabama* (Washington: Neale, 1900), 43.

107. Jane Marion Dunwody Erwin to Jane Atwood Camp, May 29, 1850, in Cox and Walsh, *Providence: Selected Correspondence*, 173.

108. Anya Jabour, *Scarlett's Sisters: Young Women in the Old South* (Chapel Hill: University of North Carolina Press, 2007), 117; Jane Marion Dunwody Erwin to Jane Atwood Camp, May 29, 1850, in Cox and Walsh, *Providence: Selected Correspondence*, 173.

109. Jabour, *Scarlett's Sisters*, 117–122.

110. Ibid., 120 and 117.

111. Ibid., 117.

112. Kell, *Recollections of a Naval Life*, 43.

113. George Hull Camp to his wife Jane Atwood Camp, Jan 6, 1851, in Cox and Walsh, *Providence: Selected Correspondence*, 187-188.

114. Hermann Hagedorn, *The Boys' Life of Theodore Roosevelt* (New York: Harper and Brothers, 1918), 8; Historical Society of Pennsylvania, Historic Pennsylvania Church and Town Records; Reel: 231; Silas Weir Roosevelt to Mary West in Robinson, *My Brother*, 12-13 (quoted material).

115. *Savannah Republican*, Feb 13 1851; David McCullough, *Mornings on Horse-back* (New York: Simon and Schuster, 1981), 48; George Hull Camp to Jane Margaret Atwood, Feb 20, 1851 in Cox and Walsh, *Providence: Selected Correspondence*, 209.

116. George Hull Camp to Jane Margaret Atwood, Feb 20, 1851, in Cox and Walsh, *Providence: Selected Correspondence*, 209.

117. George Hull Camp to Jane Margaret Atwood, Feb 20, 1851, and Florida Bayard Seay to Charles Jones Pratt, 1901, in Cox and Walsh, *Providence: Selected Correspondence*, 209 and 555 (quoted material); NARA, Passport Applications, RG: 59, M1372, Roll: 36, May 13, 1851, s.v. "Theodore Roosevelt"; Martin, *History of Bulloch Hall*, 19.

118. Jabour, *Scarlett's Sisters*, 117, 118, 122, 124, 128, 133.

119. U.S. Congress, Senate, *Annual Report of the Superintendent of the Coast Survey*, 32d Congress, 1st Session, Senate Ex. Doc. no. 3, 41–42, 115, 118; *Charleston Courier*, 10, 20, and Mar 1851; *Savannah Republican*, 11 Mar 1851; Mary Caskie Hutchison to Robert Hutchison, Mar 28, 1851. Hutchison-Dawson Papers, GHS.

120. *Charleston Courier*, Apr 21, 1851; JDB to Nannie Hutchison Dawson, Jan 24, 1880, Box 3 Folder 23, Hutchison-Dawson Papers, MS 2226, GHS (quoted material).

121. NARA, SE Region (Atlanta), Morrow, GA, *Coastwise Slave Manifests, 1801 – 1860*, RG: 36, *Records of the U.S. Customs Service*; ARC Identifier: 1151775; *Charleston Courier*, Apr 21, 1851; *Savannah Republican*, Apr 22, 1851.

122. JDB Service Record; *Boston Evening Transcript*, May 23, 1851; *Alexandria (VA) Gazette*, June 11, 1851; U.S. Congress, Senate, *Annual Report of the Superintendent of the Coast Survey*, 32d Congress, 1st Session, Senate Ex. Doc. no. 3, 41–42, 115, 118; *NYT*, Nov 6, 1851; Emma Martin Maffitt, *The Life and Services of John Newland Maffitt* (New York: Neale, 1906), 78–79; U.S. Navy, *Register 1852*, 66–67, 116; *Daily Union*, Washington, D.C., Oct 25, 1851.

Chapter 3

1. Andrew R. Dodge, *Biographical Directory of the United States Congress, 1774-2005* (Washington, D.C.: GPO, 2005), 797; Caskie, *The Caskie Family*,

52–54; *Savannah Republican*, Nov 18, 1851; Ancestry.com, *Savannah, Georgia Vital Records, 1803–1966*. John S. Caskie went on to represent Richmond and the surrounding counties in Congress for four terms.

2. Find A Grave, *www.findagrave.com*, s.v. "Mary Caskie Hutchison," Shockoe Hill Cemetery; Ancestry.com, *Savannah, Georgia Vital Records, 1803–1966*.

3. Richmond *Times Dispatch*, Oct 23, 1905 (quoted material); Mary Wingfield Scott, *Houses of Old Richmond* (Richmond: Valentine Museum, 1941), 128–131.

4. JDB Service Record, *Savannah Republican*, Dec 1 and 30, 1851; *NYT* Dec 10, 1851.

5. JDB Service Record, *Savannah Republican*, Dec 1 and 30, 1851; Rene De La Pedraja, *A Historical Dictionary of the U.S. Merchant Marine and Shipping Industry: Since the Introduction of Steam* (Westport, CT: Greenwood, 1994), 672.

6. JDB Service Record; *NYT*, 25 Mar 1852; Richmond *Times-Dispatch*, Oct 23, 1905; Camp to Atwood, Feb 7 and 18, 1850, in Cox and Walsh, *Providence: Selected Correspondence*, 147, 155.

7. NARA, U.S. Customs Service, RG 36 *Passenger Lists, New York*, 1852, Roll: *120*; SS *Arctic*; New York *Evening Post*, Jul 24 and Oct 18, 1852; *Charleston Courier*, Oct 21, 1852.

8. *New York Tribune*, Aug 26, 1852; *NYT*, Oct 29, 1852; NARA, U.S. Customs Service, RG 36 *Passenger Lists, New York*, 1852, Roll: *120*; SS *Arctic*; New York *Evening Post*, Oct 18, 1852; *Charleston Courier*, Oct 21, 1852.

9. *New York Tribune*, Aug 26, 1852; *NYT*, Oct 29, 1852; NARA, U.S. Customs Service, RG 36 *Passenger Lists, New York*, 1852, Roll: *120*; SS *Arctic*; New York *Evening Post*, Oct 18, 1852; *Charleston Courier*, Oct 21, 1852.

10. Robinson, *My Brother*, 12–13; McCullough, *Mornings on Horseback*, 48; New York *Weekly Herald*, 24 Apr 1852; *Charleston Courier*, Apr 23, 1852; Martin, *History of Bulloch Hall*, 19.

11. Robinson, *My Brother*, 12–13; McCullough, *Mornings on Horseback*, 48; TR Sr. to MBR, Jun 5, 1853, bMS Am 1785.2(100), TRC; Martin, *History of Bulloch Hall*, 19.

12. Martin, *History of Bulloch Hall*, 19;

Jabour, *Scarlett's Sisters*, 116, 125, 137–138. Mittie was the only one of the four debutantes who married while still a teenager (18). The others first married at ages that ranged from 21 (Julia Hand), to 32 (Anna), and 41 (Flo Bayard).

13. Jabour, *Scarlett's Sisters*, 161–164.

14. MBR to TR Sr., July 26 (quoted material), 1853, bMS Am 1785.7(34), TR Sr. to MBR, May 31, 1853, bMS Am 1785.2 (100), TRC.

15. TR Sr. to MBR, Jul 26, 1853, bMS Am 1785.2(38), TRC and Robinson, *My Brother*, 14–15 (quoted material); Jane Atwood Camp to Elisabeth Hitchcock Camp, Jan 4, 1854, in Cox and Walsh, *Providence: Selected Correspondence*, 294–295. Coughing up blood is a classical symptom of tuberculosis (consumption).

16. MBR to TR Sr., Jun 9, 1853, and Oct 17, 1853, bMS Am 1785.7(34), TRC.

17. *NYT*, May 6 and 26, 1853; TR Sr., to MBR, May 31 and Jun 5, 1853, bMS Am 1785.2(38), TRC; *NYT*, Jun 30, 1853.

18. JDB Service Record; *NYT*, Jul 6, 1853.

19. TR Sr. to MBR, Aug 18, 1853, Transcripts, early family correspondence, bMS Am 1785.7(38), TRC.

20. *NYT* Sep 27 and Oct 7, 1853; New Orleans *Times-Picayune*, Sep 28, 1853; TR Sr. to MBR, Aug 18 and Oct 3–5, 1853, bMS Am 1785.7(38), TRC.

21. *NYT*, 11 Oct 1853; TR Sr. to MBR, Oct 10, 1853, bMS Am 1785.7(38), TRC.

22. Richmond *Times Dispatch*, Oct 23, 1905; *NYT*, Dec 21 and 29, 1853; New Orleans *Times-Picayune*, Dec 17, 1853.

23. Ruth Ann Atwood Dunwody to Jane Atwood Camp, Nov [10], 1853 and Thomas Edward King to Walter Bicker Camp, Nov 22, 1853, in Cox and Walsh, *Providence: Selected Correspondence*, 292 and 293; *Charleston Courier*, Dec 15, 1853; Martin, *History of Bulloch Hall*, 21 (quoted material); Jane Atwood Camp to Elisabeth Hitchcock Camp, Jan 4, 1854, in Cox and Walsh, *Providence: Selected Correspondence*, 295.

24. Jane Atwood Camp to Elisabeth Hitchcock Camp, Jan 4, 1854, in Cox and Walsh, *Providence: Selected Correspondence*, 295.

25. Florida Bayard Seay to Charles Jones Pratt, 1901, in Cox and Walsh, *Prov-*

idence: *Selected Correspondence*, 56; Peggy (Margaret) Mitchell, "Bridesmaid of 87 Recalls Mittie Roosevelt's Wedding," *Atlantic Journal Magazine*, Jun 10, 1923 (quoted material); Martin, *History of Bulloch Hall*, 21. Mary Cooper Stiles, and Evelyn King were the other two bridesmaids. Former Roswell debutante Florida Bayard, also attended and wrote a brief account of the event.

26. Mitchell, *Atlantic Journal Magazine*, Jun 10, 1923.

27. Florida Bayard Seay to Charles Jones Pratt, 1901, in Cox and Walsh, *Providence: Selected Correspondence*, 555 (quoted material); Martin, *History of Bulloch Hall*, 21.

28. Martin, *History of Bulloch Hall*, 21; Mitchell, *Atlantic Journal Magazine*, Jun 10, 1923 (quoted material); *Atlanta Constitution*, Oct 27, 1901; Leleh (Lillie) Dunwoody Waddell, "Reminiscences of the Dunwody-Bulloch Families" (Staunton, VA: typed manuscript, Oct 1905), courtesy Bulloch Hall; Florida Bayard Seay to Charles Jones Pratt, 1901, in Cox and Walsh, *Providence: Selected Correspondence*, 556. Rev. Dunwody recorded the marriage on Dec 18, the date he probably left for Roswell; other secondary sources claim that Roswell's Rev. Nathaniel Pratt (who was the uncle of Rev. Dunwody's wife Laleah) performed the ceremony.

29. Mitchell, *Atlantic Journal Magazine*, Jun 10, 1923.

30. Martin, *History of Bulloch Hall*, 24.

31. Jane Atwood Camp to Elisabeth Hitchcock Camp, Jan 4, 1854, in Cox and Walsh, *Providence: Selected Correspondence*, 295 (quoted material); Martin, *History of Bulloch Hall*, 24; Mitchell, *Atlantic Journal Magazine*, Jun 10, 1923; Florida Bayard Seay to Charles Jones Pratt, 1901, in Cox and Walsh, *Providence: Selected Correspondence*, 556.

32. *NYT*, Oct 7, Dec 3, 9, 17, 24, and 29, 1853, Jan 3, 1854; *New York Tribune* Dec 29, 1853, Jan 2, 1854. Although the passenger list did not include Lizzie, she would have been an undocumented crew member as the wife of the Captain.

33. *NYT*, Jan 10, 18 and 19, 1854; New Orleans *Times-Picayune*, Jan 20 and 27, 1854.

34. New Orleans *Times-Picayune*, Jan 25, 26, 28 (quoted material) and 31, 1854.

Note: the *NYT* of Feb 7, 1854 erroneously reported that the *Black Warrior* arrived at Mobile on Jan 20, 1854.

35. *NYT* Feb 8, 1854; Robert Jones, "Photographs of headstone and burial card," email to authors, Feb 6, 2009.

36. Caskie, *The Caskie Family*, 36, 44; TR Sr. to MBR, May 31, 1853, bMS Am 1785.2 (100), TRC

37. New Orleans *Times-Picayune*, May 16, 1856, Apr 15 and Sep 25 1858.

38. New Orleans *Times-Picayune*, Jun 22 and Sep 21, 1856 and Oct 7, 1859.

39. New Orleans *Times-Picayune*, Mar 20 and 21, 1855 and Apr 5, 1860 (quoted material); Octavia Walton Le Vert, *Souvenirs of Travel* I (New York: S.H. Goetzel & Co., 1857), 287.

40. New York *Evening Post*, Dec 11, 1854; *NYT*, Dec 16, 1854.

41. *NYT*, Jan 3, 1855; ancestry.com; Mittie's third child, Elliot Roosevelt, named his first child Anna Eleanor, after his older sister Bamie. Known as Eleanor, she became the nation's first lady after she married a distant (fifth) cousin named Franklin Delano Roosevelt.

42. New Orleans *Times-Picayune*, Jul 7, 1850, and Jan 18, 19, 24, and 25, 1855.

43. On Jan 9, 1855, the day of the *Black Warrior's* departure, the *New York Times* headlined two "Marine Disasters."

44. New Orleans *Times-Picayune*, Jul 7, 1850, and Jan 18, 19, 24, and 25.

45. *NYT*, Feb 3, 1855; New Orleans *T-Pic*, Feb 16, 1855, citing the New York *Mirror*; Hilborne West to George Hull Camp, Feb 14, 1855, in Cox and Walsh, *Providence: Selected Correspondence*, 396.

46. Hilborne West to George Hull Camp, Feb 14, 1855, in Cox and Walsh, *Providence: Selected Correspondence*, 395–396.

47. *NYT*, Apr 23, 1855.

48. MBR to TR Sr., May 2, 1855 in Robinson, *My Brother*, 15–16, and bMS Am 1785.7(34), TRC.

49. TR Sr. to MBR, May 1, 1855, bMS Am 1785.2(100), TRC and McCullough, *Mornings on Horseback*, 52.

50. TR Sr. to MBR. May 1, 1855, bMS Am 1785.2(100), TRC and McCullough, *Mornings on Horseback*, 52; TR Sr. to MBR, May 6, 1855 (quoted material).

51. TR Sr. to MBR, May 8–9, 1855, bMS Am 1785.2(100), TRC.

52. New Orleans *Times-Picayune*, Jul 7,

1850, and Jan 18, 19, 24, and 25, 1855; NARA, Census RG: 29, 1850, West Baton Rouge, LA, Roll: M432_229, page 224B, Image 452.

53. New Orleans *Times-Picayune*, Nov 19, 20, 1855; NARA, Census RG: 29, 1850, West Baton Rouge, LA, Roll: M432_229, page 224B, Image 452; *NYT*, Aug 2, Nov 12, 1855.

54. New Orleans *Times-Picayune*; *NYT*, Dec 20, 1855 (quoted material), Jan 6, 1856, May 23 and Dec 26, 1857.

55. New Orleans *Times-Picayune*, Dec 20, 1855 (first quote), Jan 6, 1856, May 23 and Dec 26, 1857; MSB to MBR, Nov 21, [1856], bMS Am 1875.2(17), TRC (second quote).

56. New Orleans *Times-Picayune*, Apr 6, 7, and 19, 1856.

57. MBR to TR Sr., May 18, 1855, bMS Am 1785.7(34), TRC.

58. *NYT*, Oct 1, 1855.

59. Hilborne West to Trustees for Jane Atwood Camp, Feb 7, 1856, and George Hull Camp to Talcott Hale Camp, Apr 1, 1856 (quoted material), in Cox and Walsh, *Providence: Selected Correspondence*, 426.

60. MBR to TR Sr., Jul 28, 1855, bMS Am 1785.7(34), TRC; McCullough, *Mornings on Horseback*, 53; Thomas Edward King to George Hull Camp, Sep 5, 1855, and George Hull Camp to Elisabeth Hitchcock Camp, Dec 25, 1855, in Cox and Walsh, *Providence: Selected Correspondence*, 412, 419–420; Martin, *History of Bulloch Hall*, 22, 37. The city of Roswell acquired Bulloch Hall in October 1977 through the Heritage Trust Program and a Georgia Department of Natural Resources matching grant. The Roswell mayor and city council appoint a Historic Preservation Commission that maintains the home as a vibrant cultural center for the community and state.

61. Rev. William P. Breed, *West Spruce Street Presbyterian Church of Philadelphia: 1856–1881* (Philadelphia: Sherman & Co., 1881), 14–16 (quoted material); Philadelphia *Public Ledger*, Oct 15, 1856; George M. Gould (ed.), *The Jefferson Medical College of Philadelphia: A History, 1826–1904* II (New York: Lewis, 1904), 111; Philadelphia College of Physicians, *Transactions*, 3d Ser. vol. 9 (Philadelphia: Dornan, 1887), cccv; MSB to MBR, Nov 21, [1856], bMS Am 1875.2(17), TRC.

62. Edward J. Nolan, ed., *Proceedings of the Academy of Natural Sciences of Philadelphia* 62 (Philadelphia: Academy of Natural Sciences, 1910), 258 fn1.

63. Pennsylvania University, *Biographical Catalogue of the Matriculates of the College, 1749–1893* (Philadelphia: Society of the Alumni, 1894), 235; Irvine S. Bulloch to Hon. L.P. Walker, Roswell, GA, Jun 21, 1861 with enclosures dated May 31 and Jun 18, 1862, NARA, RG: 109 M346, Confederate Civilian Files, Roll: 0118, Irvine S. Bulloch; *New York Herald*, Sep 2, 1859 (quoted material).

64. *New York Herald*, Jul 17, 1860. Mr. Waterbury's 12-year-old daughter, her governess, and his sister were the three ladies who drowned on the *Edda*.

65. New Orleans *Times-Picayune*, Dec 20, 1855; MSB to MBR, Nov 21, [1856], bMS Am 1875.2(17), TRC (quoted material).

66. J.G.B. Bulloch, *Archibald Bulloch*, 17; Louisiana Writer's Project, comp., *Louisiana: A Guide to the State* (1941; reprint, St. Clair Shores, MI: Somerset, 1973), 572 (quoted material).

67. TR Sr. to MBR, Jan 25, 1857, bMS Am 1785.7(38), TRC (quoted material). TR Sr. erroneously dated his letter 1856 instead of 1857; New Orleans *Times-Picayune*, Jan 21 and 28, 1857.

68. TR Sr. to MBR, Jan 25, 1857, bMS Am 1785.7(38), TRC.

69. Wilson and McKay, *James D. Bulloch*, 26–27, 105–106; Raymond W. Settle, *The March of the Mounted Riflemen* (1940; reprint, Lincoln: University of Nebraska, 1989), 20. General Cross died in New York City at the Roosevelt Hospital on Jul 15, 1876.

70. TR Sr. to MBR, Jan 25, [1857], bMS Am 1785.7(38), TRC (quoted material).

71. Ibid.

72. New Orleans *Times-Picayune*, Jan 21 and Jan 28 (quoted material), 1857; *NYT*, Jan 27, Feb 2, 4 and 5, 1857.

73. TR Sr. to MBR, May 31, 1857, bMS Am 1785.7(38), TRC.

74. *NYT*, Oct 5, 1858; TR Sr. to MBR, May 31, 1857, bMS Am 1785.7(38) and MSB to Susan (Elliott) West, Oct 4 and 15 (quoted material), 1858, bMS Am 1785.2 (19), TRC.

75. Edmund Morris, *The Rise of Theodore Roosevelt* (New York: Coward,

McCann, and Geoghegan, 1979), 32; MSB to Susan (Elliott) West, Oct 28, 1858, bMS Am 1785.2(19), TRC (quoted material). The original Brownstone structure at this address has been rebuilt and the address is now 28 E. 20th St. (See: National Park Service, Theodore Roosevelt Birthplace, *www.nps.gov/history/history/online_books /presidents*).

76. MSB to SEW, Oct 15 and Nov 1, 1858, bMS Am 1785.2(19).

77. MSB to Susan (Elliott) West, Oct 15, 1858, bMS Am 1785.2(19), and Anna L. Bulloch to TR Sr. [no date, about Dec 10, 1858], bMS Am 1834(2), TRC (quoted material).

78. Record Office Liverpool, England, "Register of Baptisms in the Parish of St. John Waterloo, in the Court of Lancaster" (London: Shaw & Sons, 1865), 1; *NYT*, Jan 20, 1860.

79. MSB to SEW, Mar 12, 1860, bMS Am 1785.2(19), TRC (quoted material).

80. TR Sr. to MBR, May 31, 1857, bMS Am 1785.7(38) and MSB to SEW, Oct 15, 1858, bMS Am 1785.2(19), TRC; U.S. Interior Department, Census Office, Eighth Census, 1860, Morris Township, Morris County, NJ, series M653, roll: 703, p. 68, s.v. "Capt J. D. Bullock"; *NYT*, Oct 5, 1858.

81. Bulloch, *Secret Service*, I, 38; Wilson and McKay, *James D. Bulloch*, 34-35.

Chapter 4

1. *NYT*, Apr 23, 1961; Bulloch, *Secret Service*, I, 36, 38.

2. MSB to SEW, bMS Am 1875.7(4), Oct 9, 1861, TRC.

3. U.S. War Dept., *The War of the Rebellion: A Compilation of the Official Records of the Union and Confederate Armies,"* ser. 3, vol. 1 (Washington: GPO, 1899), 445–447. On Jun 10, Secretary of State Seward forwarded Hollis White's report to U.S. Consul Morse of Liverpool, who acknowledged receipt on Jul 19.

4. Certificate of Disability for Discharge for Stuart Elliott, Oct 30 – Nov 2, 1861, and Muster Rolls Aug 1 – Oct 31, 1861, NARA, RG: 109 M266, Compiled service records of Confederate Soldiers, Georgia, Roll: 0594, Phillip's Legion, Stewart Elliott; Lucy Ireland (Sorrel) Elliott to MSB, Jun 17, 1861, MC-1, TRC, courtesy Bulloch Hall; William Harden,

Recollections of a Long and Satisfactory Life (1934; reprint, New York: Negro Universities Press, 1968), 73 (quoted material): NARA M1372 Passport Application Roll 0174 Lucy Ireland Elliott, filed July 10, 1871; *Macon Weekly Telegraph*, Feb 24, 1857. Daniel Elliott killed Thomas S. Daniell in a duel on Feb 16, 1857.

5. Anna (Bulloch) Gracie to TR Sr., Jun 1, 1861, bMS Am 1834.1(278) (quoted material); Rable, *Civil Wars, Women*, 268; Catherine Clinton, *Tara Revisited, Women, War, and the Plantation Legend* (New York: Abbeyville, 1995), 44.

6. Pennsylvania University, *Biographical Catalogue of the Matriculates*, 235; Irvine S. Bulloch to Hon. L.P. Walker, Roswell, GA, Jun 21, 1861 with enclosures dated May 31 and Jun 18, 1862, NARA, RG: 109 M346, Confederate Civilian Files, Roll: 0118, Irvine S. Bulloch; Wilson and McKay, *James D. Bulloch*, 37–39.

7. Maffitt, *John Newland Maffitt*, 220, 222. In his 1866 application for a ship's Master Certificate, Irvine listed his service on the *Savannah* as Mar-Oct 1861; see: Ancestry.com, Master's Certificates. Jan 31, 1866, Greenwich, London, UK: National Maritime Museum, s.v. "Irvine S. Bulloch."

8. Irvine S. Bulloch to Hon. L.P. Walker, Roswell, GA, Jun 21, 1861, with enclosures dated May 31 and Jun 18, 1862, NARA, RG: 109, M346, Confederate Civilian Files, Roll: 0118, Irvine S. Bulloch (quoted material).

9. Charles C. Jones to Rev. and Mrs. C.C. Jones, May 21, 1861, in Robert Manson Myers, *The Children of Pride, A True Story of Georgia and the Civil War* (1972; reprint, New Haven: Yale University Press, 1984), 62–64.

10. Lucy Ireland (Sorrel) Elliott to MSB, Jun 17, 1861, MC-1, TRC, courtesy Bulloch Hall.

11. Charles C. Jones to Rev. and Mrs. C.C. Jones, May 21, 1861, in Myers, *The Children of Pride*, 64 (quoted material); Last Will and Testament of Robert Hutchison, Apr 26, 1861, GHS.

12. Lucy Ireland (Sorrel) Elliott to MSB, Jun 17, 1861, MC-1, TRC, courtesy Bulloch Hall (quoted material); Last Will and Testament of Robert Hutchison, Apr 26, 1861, GHS. Established in 1822, the Savannah Widows Society remains the

oldest foundation in Georgia still in existence.

13. Lucy Ireland (Sorrel) Elliott to MSB, Jun 17, 1861, MC-1, TRC, courtesy Bulloch Hall; Last Will and Testament of Robert Hutchison, Apr 26, 1861, GHS (quoted material).

14. NARA, M6531860 U.S. census, s.v. "James K. Caskie" and "James Caskie"; Lucy Ireland (Sorrel) Elliott to MSB, Jun 17, 1861, MC-1, TRC, courtesy Bulloch Hall; Last Will and Testament of Robert Hutchison, Apr 26, 1861, GHS; Find A Grave, www.findagrave.com, s.v., "Robert Hutchison" and "Ellen Laura Hutchison." Robert Hutchison's remains were eventually reinterred in the Caskie family plot at Shockoe Hill Cemetery in Richmond.

15. Irvine S. Bulloch to Hon. L.P. Walker, Roswell, GA, Jun 21, 1861, with enclosures dated May 31 and Jun 18, 1862, NARA, RG: 109, M346, Confederate Civilian Files, Roll: 0118, s.v. "Irvine S. Bulloch" (quoted material).

16. Georgia Archives, Tax Digest, 1862, Chatham, s.v. "James D. Bulloch"; MSB to SEW, Oct 9, 1861, bMS Am 1875.7(4), TRC.

17. ABG to TR Sr., Jun 1, 1861, bMS Am 1834.1(278), TRC (quoted material); Wilson and McKay, James D. Bulloch, 37–38. The Beaver Meadows Railroad and Coal Co. had 26 miles of rail and coal mining operations 75 to 100 miles northwest of Philadelphia, PA.

18. ABG to TR Sr., Jun 1, 1861, bMS Am 1834.1(278), TRC (quoted material); Rable, Civil Wars, Women, 268.

19. ABG to TR Sr., Jun 15, 1861, bMS Am 1834.1(278), TRC; MSB, to SEW, Jul 20, 1861, bMS Am 1785.8(447), TRC; MBR, to ABG. May 22–26, 1869, TRC, bMS Am 1785.8(455), TRC.

20. ABG to TR Sr., Jun 1, 1861, bMS Am 1834.1(278), TRC; Lucy Ireland (Sorrel) Elliott to MSB, Jun 17, 1861, MC-1, TRC, courtesy Bulloch Hall; Certificate of Disability for Discharge for Stuart Elliott, Oct 30—Nov 2, 1861 (quoted material) and Muster Rolls Aug 1 – Oct 31, 1861, NARA, RG: 109, M266, Compiled service records of Confederate Soldiers, Georgia, Roll: 0594, Phillip's Legion, s.v. "Stewart Elliott."

21. Irvine S. Bulloch to Hon. L.P. Walker, Roswell, GA, Jun 21, 1861 with enclosures dated May 31 and Jun 18, 1862, NARA, RG: 109, M346, Confederate Civilian Files, Roll: 0118, Irvine S. Bulloch. Irvine was in Richmond when he received his commission; he reported to Flag Officer Tattnall on September 4 before officially reporting to Captain Maffitt's wardroom on the CSS Savannah. See: NARA, RG: 45, M1091, CSN Subject Files, Roll: 0019, Acceptances.

22. ORN II: 2, 83; Bulloch, Secret Service, vol. I, no. 48; Newbern Weekly Progress, May 28, 1861 (quoted material).

23. Bulloch, Secret Service, I, 48; Record Office Liverpool, "Register of Baptisms in the Parish of St. John Waterloo," 1; Wilson and McKay, James D. Bulloch, 38.

24. Charles C. Jones, Jr., to Mary Jones, Sep 18, 1861, in Myers, Children of Pride, 115; Wilson and McKay, James D. Bulloch, 48–49; Bulloch, Secret Service, I: 71; U.S. Naval Historical Center, DANFS Online, s.v. "Bermuda" http://www.history.navy.mil/ danfs/b5 /bermuda.

25. Rable, Civil Wars, Women, 181.

26. NYT, Aug 29, 1861.

27. Edward C. Anderson, Confederate Foreign Agent: The European Diary of Major Edward C. Anderson, ed. William S. Hoole (Tuscaloosa, AL: Confederate, 1976), 54; NYT Aug 29, 1861; John Bigelow, France and the Confederate Navy, 1862–1868: An International Episode (New York: Harper & Brothers, 1888).

28. Wilson and McKay, James D. Bulloch, 52; Anderson, Confederate Foreign Agent, 71–72; James North Diary, Oct 7, 1861, James Heyward North Papers (862-z) and James Dunwody [sic] Bulloch Papers (3318-z), Southern Historical Collection, Wilson Library, University of North Carolina, Chapel Hill.

29. Charles C. Jones, Jr., to Mary Jones, Sep 18, 1861, in Myers, Children of Pride, 115 (quoted material); Wilson and McKay, James D. Bulloch, 48–49; Bulloch, Secret Service, I: 71; U.S. Naval Historical Center, DANFS Online, s.v. "Bermuda" http://www.history.navy.mil/ danfs/b5 /bermuda.

30. MSB to SEW, Nov 15, 1862 and Apr 8, 1863, bMS Am 1875.2(19), TRC. Proclamation 86: Prohibiting Commercial Trade with States in Rebellion, Aug 16, 1861.

31. ORA, ser. 2, vol. 2, 18 (quoted material); Wilson and McKay, James D. Bulloch, 47.

32. ORA, ser. 2, vol. 2, 18 (quoted material).

33. Bulloch, *Secret Service*, I: 71; ORN, ser. I, vol. 6, 331; TR Sr. to MBR, Feb 14, 1862, bMS Am 1785.7(38), TRC.

34. Bulloch, *Secret Service*, I: 71; ORN, ser. I, vol. 6, 331 (quoted material).

35. Bulloch, *Secret Service*, I: 71, 116; Anderson, *Confederate Foreign Agent*, 81; MSB to Susy (Susan Elliott) West, Nov 16, 1861, bMS Am 1785.7(4), TRC (quoted material).

36. MSB to SEW, Nov 16, 1861, bMS Am 1785.7(4), TRC; *NYT*, Jun 4, 1855 (quoted material); *Charleston Courier*, Aug 7, 1857. Some historians criticize Dr. Semmes' (often misspelled as "Sims") early treatment of slaves as unethical; others refute those opinions as culturally biased and contrary to contemporary documentation. See: Sarah Spettel and Mark Donald White, "The Portrayal of J. Marion Sims' Controversial Surgical Legacy," *The Journal of Urology*, vol. 185 (Jun 2011), 2424–2427, and L. L. Wall, "The Medical Ethics of Dr. J. Marion Sims: A Fresh Look at the Historical Record," *Journal of Medical Ethics*, 32 no. 6 (Jun 2006); 346–350.

37. MSB to SEW, Nov 16, 1861, bMS Am 1875.7(4), TRC; Certificate of Disability for Discharge for Stuart Elliott, Oct 30 – Nov 2, 1861 (quoted material) and Muster Rolls Aug 1 – Oct 31, 1861, NARA, RG: 109, M266, Compiled service records of Confederate Soldiers, Georgia, Roll: 0594, Phillip's Legion, s.v. "Stewart Elliott"; Robert B. Pegram, "The Cruise of the CSS *Nashville*: The Report of Lieutenant Robert B. Pegram, CSN," *The Virginia Magazine of History and Biography* 66, no. 3 (Jul 1958), 345–346.

38. Thomas R. Neblett, "Major Edward C. Anderson and the C.S.S. Fingal," *The Georgia Historical Quarterly* 52, no. 2 (Jun 1968), 146–147; RADM Ernest McNeill Eller, ed., *Civil War Naval Chronology, 1861–1865* (Washington: GPO for the U.S. Navy Department, Naval History Division, 1971), I-37.

39. New Orleans *Times-Picayune*, Oct 17, 1862; Wilson and McKay, *James D. Bulloch*, 55–58; ORN II: 2, 105–106.

40. Bulloch, *Secret Service*, I, 151; Wilson and McKay, *James D. Bulloch*, 65–66; MBR to ABG, May 22–26, 1869, TRC, bMS Am 1785.8(455), TRC.

41. Wilson and McKay, *James D. Bulloch*, 48, 62; Eller, *Civil War Naval Chronology*, I-23 and I-31-32. Forts Hatteras and Clark fell on Aug 29, 1861.

42. McCullough, *Mornings on Horseback*, 56–58; David S. Heidler and Jeanne T. Heidler, *Encyclopedia of the American Civil War: A Political, Social, and Military History* (2000; reprint, New York: W.W. Norton, 2002), 487–488.

43. McCullough, *Mornings on Horseback*, 56–58; Heidler and Heidler, *Encyclopedia of the American Civil War*, 487–488.

44. McCullough, *Mornings on Horseback*, 58–60; Robinson, *My Brother*, 21–22 (quoted material); Edward K. Spann, *Gotham at War: New York City, 1860–1865* (Wilmington, DE: Scholarly Resources, 2002), 59. William E. Dodge, Jr., and Theodore B. Bronson were the other two commissioners.

45. *Brooklyn Daily Eagle*, Dec 31, 1861; *NYT*, Jan 10 and Nov 18, 1862; McCullough, *Mornings on Horseback*, 60–61; Robinson, *My Brother*, 22–23, 29–32. $470,376.30 = $11.61 million in 2015.

46. Robinson, *My Brother*, 25–28; McCullough, *Mornings on Horseback*, 60. Hay became Theodore Roosevelt, Sr.'s lifelong friend; he was successful in private and public life, including stints as secretary of state for Presidents McKinley and Theodore Roosevelt, Jr.

47. Wilson and McKay, *James D. Bulloch*, 38.

48. TR Sr. to MBR, Feb 14, 1862, bMS Am 1785.7(38), TRC.

49. Ibid.

50. TR Sr. to MBR, Mar 1–2, 1862, bMS Am 1785.7(38), TRC; McCullough, *Mornings on Horseback*, 62.

51. Faust, *Mothers of Invention*, 34–35; McCullough, *Mornings on Horseback*, 62.

52. Faust, *Mothers of Invention*, 42–43.

53. MSB, to SEW, Oct 9 and Nov 7, 1861, bMS Am 1785.7(4), TRC; TR Sr. to MBR, Mar 1–2, 1862, bMS Am 1785.7(38), TRC; ABG to TR Sr., Jun 1, 1861, bMS Am 1834.1(278); McCullough, *Mornings on Horseback*, 62; Faust, *Mothers of Invention*, 42–43. $850 = $20,980 in 2015.

54. *Richmond Whig*, Mar 4, 1862; Bulloch, *Secret Service*, I: 150–151, 382; Ancestry.com, Master's Certificates. Jan 31, 1866, Greenwich, London, UK: National Maritime Museum, s.v. "Irvine S. Bulloch";

NARA, RG: 45, M1091, CSN, Personnel lists; U.S. Navy Department, *Naval War Records, Office Memoranda No. 8, Officers in the Confederate States Navy, 1861–65* (Washington: GPO 1898), 21.

55. Judith E. Harper, *Women During the Civil War: An Encyclopedia* (New York: Routledge, 2004), 180–181; Faust, *Mothers of Invention*, 28–29; Cara Vandergriff, "'Petticoat Gunboats': The Wartime Expansion of Confederate Women's Discursive Opportunities Through Ladies' Gunboat Societies," Master's Thesis, University of Tennessee, 2013, 1–5.

56. Faust, *Mothers of Invention*, 28–29; Vandergriff, "Petticoat Gunboats," 3–4.

57. Harper, *Women During the Civil War*, 180–181; Faust, *Mothers of Invention*, 28–29.

58. Vandergriff, "Petticoat Gunboats," 66; *Daily Constitutionalist*, Macon, GA, Mar 9, 1862; *Macon Telegraph*, Mar 15 and Jul 10, 1862; *Columbus Daily Enquirer*, Jul 18, 1862; Maurice Melton, *The Best Station of Them All: The Savannah Squadron, 1861–1865* (Tuscaloosa: University of Alabama Press, 2012), 119. $3,600 = $88,880 in 2015.

59. Wilson and McKay, *James D. Bulloch*, 290; Erik Calonius, *The Wanderer: The Last American Slave Ship and the Conspiracy That Set Its Sails* (2006; reprint, New York: St. Martin's, 2008), 13–26; Charles Green to Maj. Benjamin W. Thompson, Jun 16, 1861, and Charles Green to G.B. Lamar, Aug 2, 1861, NARA, RG: 109, M346 Confederate Civilian Files Roll: 0563, G.B. Lamar.

60. *Daily Constitutionalist*, Augusta, GA, Mar 20, 1862.

61. *Daily Constitutionalist*, Augusta, GA, Mar 18 and 20, May 13, 1862; *Macon Telegraph*, May 5, 1862; Vandergriff, "Petticoat Gunboats," 61.

62. *Macon Telegraph*, Jul 10, 1862; Rev. Charles C. Jones to Lt. Charles C. Jones, Jr., Mar 24, 1861 (quoted material).

63. Lt. Charles C. Jones, Jr., to Rev. and Mrs. C.C. Jones, Apr 7, 1861, in Myers, *The Children of Pride*, 217–219 and 222–223.

64. *Macon Telegraph*, Jul 10, 1862.

65. Melton, *The Best Station of Them All*, 121.

66. Ibid., 126, 130.

67. Eller, *Dictionary of American Naval Fighting Ships*, vol. VII, 490, 501; U.S. Naval Historical Center, *DANFS Online*. "Atlanta," http://www.history.navy.mil/danfs/a13/atlanta-i.htm.

68. Wilson and McKay, *James D. Bulloch*, 88, 103.

69. *Richmond Whig*, Mar 4, 1862; New Orleans *Times-Picayune*, Oct 17, 1862. HBMS (Her Britannic Majesty's Ship).

70. MSB to SEW, Oct 1862, bMS Am 1785.2(19), TRC.

71. Rable, *Civil Wars, Women*, 155.

72. Ibid.

73. Faust, *Mothers of Invention*, 22–23; Rable, *Civil Wars, Women*, 143.

74. Blanche Wiesen Cook, *Eleanor Roosevelt*, vol. 1, *1884–1933* (New York: Viking, 1992), 29; 5 U.S. 137 (1803); U.S. Presidential Proclamation 93 Suspending the Writ of Habeas Corpus (1862) (quoted material), American Presidency Project, http://www.presidency.ucsb.edu/ws/?pid=69782; McCullough, *Mornings on Horseback*, 56.

75. MSB to SEW, Oct 1862, bMS Am 1785.2(19), TRC.

76. 5 U.S. 137 (1803); U.S. Presidential Proclamation 93 (1862), http://www.presidency.ucsb.edu/ws/?pid=69782; MSB to SEW, Feb 26 and Oct, 1862, bMS Am 1785.2(19), TRC.

77. MSB, to SEW, Dec 5, 1862, bMS Am 1785.2(19), TRC.

78. Rixey, *Bamie*, 12.

79. MSB to SEW, Dec 2, 1862, Apr 3 and 8, 1863, bMS Am 1785.2(19), TRC.

80. MSB to SEW, Dec 5, 1862, (first quote) and Apr 8, 1863 (second quote), bMS Am 1785.2(19), and MSB to SEW, Dec 31, 1863, bMS Am 1875.7(4), TRC; birth certificate; Liverpool Record Office, "Register of Baptisms in the Parish of St. John Waterloo," 1.

81. Stephen R. Wise, *Lifeline of the Confederacy* (Columbia: University of South Carolina Press, 1988), 233; MSB, to SEW, Jan 30, 1863, bMS Am 1785.2(19), TRC.

82. Robinson, *My Brother*, 20, 30–31; MSB to SEW, Nov 10, 1862, bMS Am 1785.2(19), TRC (quoted material).

83. Robinson, *My Brother*, 20, 30–31; Settle, *The March of the Mounted Riflemen*, 18; *NYT*, Mar 17, 1862; MSB to SEW, Feb 26, 1862, bMS Am 1785.2(19), TRC; Wilson and McKay, *James D. Bulloch*, 106.

Lt. Col. Roger Sherman Dix was a hero of the Mexican War, but died of cholera in the United States in 1849; he was the second husband of Mary, who outlived all three of her army officer husbands.

84. Robinson, *My Brother*, 20, 30–31; Settle, *The March of the Mounted Riflemen*, 18; *NYT*, Mar 17, 1862.

85. MSB to SEW, Feb 26, 1862. bMS Am 1785.2(19), TRC; Robinson, *My Brother*, 30–31; Ann Blackman, *Wild Rose: Rose O'Neale Greenhow, Civil War Spy* (Westminster, MD: Random House, 2005), 217–228; ORN Ser. II vol. 2, p. 345–346 (quoted material); Bulloch, *Secret Service* I, 394–395; Morgan Dix, *Memoirs of John Adams Dix* I (New York: Harper & Brothers, 1883), 167, 210, 246.

86. ORN, ser. II, vol. 2, 165–166.

87. Andrew Bowcock, CSS *Alabama: Anatomy of a Raider* (London: Chatham, 2002), 41; Bulloch, *Secret Service*, I: 227–229.

88. Spy report, 1861–1863, JDB Collection, MS0283, Mariners' Museum Library.

89. Bulloch, *Secret Service*, I: 227–229; Wilson and McKay, *James D. Bulloch*, 76.

90. *NYT*, Aug 25, 1861.

91. Anderson, *Confederate Foreign Agent*, 31; Wilson and McKay, *James D. Bulloch*, 298. Another son, Harry McLaren Pinckney Huse, would become a U.S. Navy vice admiral, Medal of Honor winner, and have a namesake ship, the USS *Huse* (DE-145).

92. Caroline Couper Lovell, *The Light of Other Days* (Macon, GA: Mercer University Press, 1995), 177; Old Etonian Association, *The Eton Register, Part II, 1853–1859* (Eton: Privately Printed, Spottiswoode, 1905), 32; Wilson and McKay, *James D. Bulloch*, 51–53, 56, 76, 290, 309, 311.

93. Wilson and McKay, *James D. Bulloch*, 295; National Society of The Colonial Dames of America in the State of Georgia, "The Andrew Low House," *http://nscdaga.org/about-us/*. Andrew Low, II, left an estate valued at $3 million ($5.7 billion in 2015). Harriet died of cancer in 1891 at the age of 43. Among her many civic contributions was the restoration of All Saints Church at Stanton on the Wolds. Andrew Low's daughter-in-law, Juliette Gordon Low, was the founder of the Girl Scouts of America.

94. Wilson and McKay, *James D. Bulloch*, 80–83; Kell, *Recollections of a Naval Life*, 184 (quoted material).

95. Bulloch, *Secret Service*, I: 238–240.

96. Ibid., I: 240.

97. Ibid.

98. Ibid., I: 241.

99. Wilson and McKay, *James D. Bulloch*, 69, 77–90, 144; Raphael Semmes, *Memoirs of Service Afloat, during the War Between the States* (Baltimore: Kelly Piet & Co., 1869), 413 (quoted material).

100. ORN II: 2, 232–233 (quoted material); Bourne to Lafitte, Dec 15, 1862, in Frank E. Vandiver, *Confederate Blockade Running through Bermuda, 1861–1865* (Austin: University of Texas Press, 1947), 31–32; ORN I: 1, 588; Wilson and McKay, *James D. Bulloch*, 73–74.

101. ORA I: 2, 227, 233–234. The *Giraffe* was renamed the *Robert E. Lee.*

102. Blackman, *Wild Rose*, 6, 182–185; Clinton, *The Other Civil War*, 84.

103. Blackman, *Wild Rose*, 239; Mary Boykin Miller Chesnut, *A Diary from Dixie* (1949; reprint, Cambridge: Harvard University Press, 1994), 76–77 (quoted material).

104. Blackman, *Wild Rose*, 250, 255–259.

105. Gorgas to Seddon, Aug 3, 1863, NARA, RG: 109, M346, Confederate Civilian Files, Roll: 0812, s.v. "Grosvenor Porter"; Rose O'Neal Greenhow, *European Diary*, http://www.onealwebsite.com/RebelRose/, 1–3.

106. Greenhow, *European Diary*, 5–6.

107. Blackman, *Wild Rose*, 246; Georgiana Gholson Walker, *The Private Journal of Georgiana Gholson Walker, 1862–1865*, ed. Dwight Franklin Henderson (Confederate, 1963), 53 (quoted material).

108. Greenhow, *European Diary*, 25–27; Stansbury to Seixas, Aug 28, 1863, in Vandiver, *Confederate Blockade Running through Bermuda*, 90.

109. Walker, *Private Journal*, 104.

110. Greenhow, *European Diary*, 48, 50; Wilson and McKay, *James D. Bulloch*, 157–160.

111. Greenhow, *European Diary*, 50–53.

112. Ibid., 64.

113. Ibid., 65–66.

114. Ibid.; Blackman. *Wild Rose*, 246.

115. Jefferson Davis, *The Papers of Jefferson Davis: October 1863–August 1864*, vol. 10, ed. Lynda Lasswell Crist (Baton Rouge: Louisiana State University, 1999), 246. O'Sullivan, who coined the term "Manifest Destiny," was U.S. minister to Portugal 1854–1854, and (along with Huse and Henry Hotze) attended the London wedding of the colorful Confederate spy Belle Boyd to former Union Navy Lt. Samuel Hardinge on Aug 25, 1864.

116. Wilson and McKay, *James D. Bulloch*, 166; Greenhow, *European Diary*, 112–114.

117. Wilson and McKay, *James D. Bulloch*, 297, 322 fn23.

118. ORN II: 2, 818; ORN I: 10, 438, 484: ORN II: 3, 1239–1240.

119. ORN I: 10, 492—501; Thomas E. Taylor, *Running the Blockade* (London: John Murray, 1896), 124–125; Wise, *Lifeline of the Confederacy*, 109,196-198.

120. ORN II: 2, 767-768.

121. Taylor, *Running the Blockade*, 128.

122. Ibid., 59, 91; *Illustrated London News*, Jul 13, 1861.

123. Taylor, *Running the Blockade*, 59, 91; James Sprunt, *Chronicles of the Cape Fear River, 1660-1916* (1916; reprint Wilmington: Broadfoot, 1992), 452, 489-490.

124. Taylor, *Running the Blockade*, 125-128.

125. Sprunt, *Chronicles of the Cape Fear River*, 490.

126. Taylor, *Running the Blockade*, 126; Sprunt, *Chronicles of the Cape Fear River*, 490; Mallory to JDB, Nov 17, 1864, ORN II: 2, 767-768 (quoted material).

127. Sprunt, *Chronicles of the Cape Fear River*, 489.

128. MSB to SEW, Jul 20, 1861, bMS Am 1875.8(447), Oct 9, 1861 and Jul 12, 1862, bMS Am 1875.7(4), TRC.

129. Rable, *Civil Wars, Women*, 229.

130. JDB to Irvine, Oct 4, 1864, MOC, Bulloch, Irvine Stephen, Papers; Irvine to MBR, Oct 8, 1864, bMS Am 1834.1(249), TRC (quoted material).

131. Breed, *West Spruce Street Presbyterian Church of Philadelphia*, 44; Irvine Bulloch to MSB via MBR, Oct 8, 1864, bMS Am 1834.1(249), TRC.

132. MBR to ARC, Mar 3, 1871, bMS Am 1834.1(194), and Theodore Roosevelt, Jr. to ARC, Oct 26, 1896, bMS Am 1834

(529), TRC; Robinson, *My Brother*, 34; Wilson and McKay, *James D. Bulloch*, 28; Anna and her husband, James King Gracie, were buried in the same lot; Mittie and Theodore and many other members of the family were buried a short walk away (Lot: 15305, Section: 162); see: *www.greenwood.com*.

133. *Wilmington Journal*, Nov 10, 1864. Virginia, North Carolina, South Carolina, Georgia, Florida, Kentucky, Tennessee, Alabama, Mississippi, Louisiana, Texas, and Arkansas were represented.

134. Faust, *Mothers of Invention*, 22–23; *Wilmington Journal*, Nov 10, 1864; Lancashire County, England, records, West Derby; Birth Certificate, s.v. "Martha Louisa Bulloch."

135. MSB to SEW, Oct 28 and Dec 31, 1863, bMS Am 1875.7(4), and MBR to ABG, 22 May 1869, bMS Am 1785.8(455), and May 26, 1869, Transcripts, early family correspondence, TRC.

136. Lancashire County, England, records, West Derby; Birth Certificate, s.v. "Martha Louisa Bulloch"; Rable, *Civil Wars, Women*, 278.

137. Lancashire County, England, records, West Derby; Birth Certificate, s.v. "Martha Louisa Bulloch"; Douglas F. Forrest, *Odyssey in Gray: A Diary of Confederate Service, 1863–1865*, ed. William N. Still, Jr. (Richmond: Virginia State Library, 1979), 294; *Lancashire Anglican Parish Registers*. Preston, England: Lancashire Archives, Pr 2882/10, 18, s.v. "Richard Taylor."

138. Forrest, *Odyssey in Gray*, 294; Settle, *The March of the Mounted Riflemen*, 18.

139. Faust, *Mothers of Invention*, 17, 30–31.

140. Forrest, *Odyssey in Gray*, 294.

141. Rable, *Civil Wars, Women*, 177.

142. MSB to SEW, Dec 31, 1863, bMS Am 1875.7(4), TRC.

Chapter 5

1. Hacker, "A Census-Based Count of the Civil War Dead," 307-348; Wilson and McKay, *James D. Bulloch*, 295

2. Wilson and McKay, *James D. Bulloch*, 295; Eller, *Dictionary of American Naval Fighting Ships*, vol. VII, 490, 501; U.S. Naval Historical Center, *DANFS*

Online. "Atlanta," http://www.history.navy. mil/danfs/a13/atlanta-i.htm.

3. Gary McKay, *The Sea King: The Life of James Iredell Waddell* (Edinburgh: Birlinn, 2009), 176–219; Tom Chaffin, *Sea of Gray: The Around-the-World Odyssey of the Confederate Raider Shenandoah* (New York: Hill and Wang, 2006), 374–376.

4. Semmes, *Memoirs of Service Afloat*, 413.

5. Faust, *Mothers of Invention*, 80; Rable, *Civil Wars, Women*, 223

6. Wilson and McKay, *James D. Bulloch*, 210.

7. Wilson and McKay, *James D. Bulloch*, 211; William Fitzhugh Carter to Robert R. Carter, Dec 6, 1865. Colonial Williamsburg Foundation Library, Shirley Plantation Collection, Container 18 Folder 7; Liverpool Record Office, Register of Baptisms, 1.

8. Wilson and McKay, *James D. Bulloch*, 210, 224.

9. Florida Bayard Seay to Charles Jones Pratt, 1901, in Cox and Walsh, *Providence: Selected Correspondence*, 555; Robinson, *My Brother*, 17.

10. Faust, *Mothers of Invention*, 139–140; New York Society Library, "New York City Marriage and Death Notices: 1857–1868," *http://www.nysoclib.org/king/king3. html*; *NYT*, Jun 6, 1866.

11. Faust, *Mothers of Invention*, 139–140; Rable, *Civil Wars, Women*, 163, 179 (quoted material).

12. Robinson, *My Brother*, 13; Wilson and McKay, *James D. Bulloch*, 38, 213, 289.

13. MBR to ABG, 22 May 1869, bMS Am 1785.8(455) and Transcripts, early family correspondence to Sep 1869 from Liverpool, TRC.

14. Charleston (SC) *Evening Post*, Oct 20, 1900; Martin, *History of Bulloch Hall*, 36.

15. Robinson, *My Brother*, 36–38.

16. U.K. National Archives, Home Office, Naturalisation Application, Jan 16, 1869, Certificate 6059, s.v. "James Dunwody Bulloch" (sic).

17. Ibid.; Wilson and McKay, *James D. Bulloch*, 222–224.

18. Rable, *Civil Wars, Women*, 227; Roosevelt, *Theodore Roosevelt: An Autobiography*, 15–16, 18; Robinson, *My Brother*, 36–37.

19. Summary and biographical note, Robert Hutchison Papers, 1815–1897, GHS.

20. Last Will and Testament of Robert Hutchison, Apr 26, 1861, GHS; MBR to ABG, May 22, 1869, bMS Am 1785.8(455) and Transcripts, early family correspondence to Sep 1869 from Liverpool, TRC (quoted material).

21. *NYT*, May 13, 1869; *Anglo-American Times* May 29, 1869; MBR to ABG, May 22, 1869, bMS Am 1785.8(455) and Transcripts, early family correspondence to Sep 1869 from Liverpool, TRC (quoted material). James D. Bulloch's stepsister Susan Elliott West with husband Hilborne (Dr. H.T. and Mrs. West) and three other West family members may have been traveling to Liverpool just three days behind them on the steamship *Helvetia*. See: *NYT*, May 16, 1869.

22. MBR to ABG, May 22, 26, and June 2, 1869, bMS Am 1785.8(455), and Transcripts, early family correspondence to Sep 1869 from Liverpool, TRC.

23. MBR to ABG, May 22, 1869, TRC, bMS Am 1785.8(455), and Transcripts, early family correspondence to Sep 1869 from Liverpool, TRC.

24. Ibid.; Theodore Roosevelt Diaries and Notebooks, 1858-1919, MS Am 1454.55(2), TRC, 70–72.

25. MBR to ABG, May 22, 1869, bMS Am 1785.8(455), and Transcripts, early family correspondence to Sep 1869 from Liverpool, June 2, 1869, TRC.

26. Ibid.

27. Ibid.; TR Sr. to Anna Bulloch Gracie, 30 May 1869; bMS Am 1785.7(36), TRC; Jefferson Davis to A. Dudley Mann, Nov 4, 1868, in Davis, *The Papers of Jefferson Davis*, vol. 12, xlvi, 9, 324–326, 492–493. Micheline de Zastro and Sons day and boarding school was at 9 Waterloo Road.

28. Theodore Roosevelt, *Theodore Roosevelt's Diaries of Boyhood and Youth* (New York: Charles Scribner's Sons, 1928), 16.

29. Theodore Roosevelt Diaries and Notebooks, 1858-1919, MS Am 1454.55 (2), 71, TRC. There are numerous variations between the published boyhood diary and the actual manuscript, e.g., on May 23 there is no mention of Irvine and his engagement to Ms. Sears that was cited in the published account.

30. TR Sr. to ARC, Nov 22, 1869, bMS Am 1834.1(201), TRC; Morris, *The Rise of Theodore Roosevelt*, 55–56; Wilson and McKay, *James D. Bulloch*, 230; McCullough, *Mornings on Horseback*, 67.

31. Robinson, *My Brother*, 42; Rable, *Civil Wars, Women*, 182.

32. Roosevelt, *Theodore Roosevelt's Diaries*, 31–216; Rable, *Civil Wars, Women*, 266.

33. Morris, *The Rise of Theodore Roosevelt*, 56–57; Rixey, *Bamie*, 13; Theodore Roosevelt Diaries and Notebooks, 1858 1919, MS Am 1454.55 (6), 156–157 (quoted material), TRC; *NYT*, May 26, 1970; Wilson and McKay, *James D. Bulloch*, 231.

34. Rixey, *Bamie*, 13–17; McCullough, *Mornings on Horseback*, 89; Clinton, *The Other Civil War*, 121, 129.

35. Rable, *Civil Wars, Women*, 276, 277; McCullough, *Mornings on Horseback*, 89; Cook, *Eleanor Roosevelt*, vol. 1, 30. Harvard's first female professor appeared in 1919; 29 years later, Harvard had its first tenured female professor.

36. Rixey, *Bamie*, 13–17.

37. Michael Howard, *The Franco-Prussian War* (1961; reprint, London: Routledge, 2001), 55–60; TR Sr. to JDB, No date, approx Aug 22, 1870, TR Sr. Letter Book, Feb 1869—Jun 1873, *96M–46(1), 164 and TR Sr. to ARC, Aug 15, 1870, bMS Am 1834.1(201), and MBR to ARC, Sep 4, 1870, bMS Am 1834.1(194), TRC. Curiously, Bamie's biographer, Lilian Rixey, mentions nothing of her escape from France and interlude with the Bullochs.

38. TR Sr. to ARC, Aug 25, 1870, bMS Am 1834.1(201), TRC.

39. MBR to ARC, Sep 4, 1870, bMS Am 1834.1(194), TRC.

40. Ibid. (quoted material); Geoffrey Wawro, *The Austro-Prussian War: Austria's War with Prussia and Italy in 1866* (New York: Cambridge University, 1997), 87–90, 169–185.

41. *NYT*, Nov 10, 1870; NARA, RG :36, U.S. Customs Service, 1870, Arrival: New York, Roll: M237_336, Line: 32, List number: 1039; TR Sr. to JDB, approximately Oct 3, 1870, TR Sr., letter book, Feb 1869–Jun 1873, *96M–46(1), 188, TRC. Wilson and McKay, *James D. Bulloch*, 233. TR Sr. had planned to travel on the SS *Russia* but chose the *Scotia* instead.

42. *Mobile Register*, Dec 29 and 30, 1870; Jefferson Davis to Varina Howell Davis, Sep 18, 1870, in Davis, *The Papers of Jefferson Davis*: vol. 12, xlvi, 9, 324–326 and 492–493; JDB to Davis, Oct 26, 1871, MOC, Jefferson Davis Family Collection, Box 6.

43. Davis, *The Papers of Jefferson Davis*: vol. 12, xlvi, li, 9, 324–326, 492–493; JDB to Davis, Oct 26, 1871, MOC, Jefferson Davis Family Collection, Box 6; Wilson and McKay, *James D. Bulloch*, 234; Joan E. Cashin, *First Lady of the Confederacy, Varina Davis's Civil War* (Cambridge, MA: Belknap Press, 2006), 185, 192, 195-198, 200; London Metropolitan Archives, Saint Peter, Belsize Park, Register of Marriages, P81/PET, Item 003. Rev. Francis W. Tremlett, the unofficial chaplain of the European Confederates, officiated at the ceremony in April of 1870.

44. *Mobile Register*, Dec 29 and 30 (quoted material), 1870; Davis, *The Papers of Jefferson Davis*: vol. 12, xlvi, li, 9, 324–326, 492–493; JDB to Davis, Oct 26, 1871, MOC, Jefferson Davis Family Collection, Box 6; Cashin, *First Lady of the Confederacy*, 171, 183, 195, 209; Rable, *Civil Wars, Women*, 17.

45. Jefferson Davis, *The Rise and Fall of the Confederate Government*, vol. II (New York: D. Appleton and Co., 1881), 248.

46. McKay, *Sea King*, 233–235; TR Sr. to JDB, Jan 21, 1871, TR Sr., letter book, Feb 1869–Jun 1873, *96M–46(1), 279.5; Cashin, *First Lady of the Confederacy*, 191.

47. TR Sr. to JDB, Jan 21, 1871, TR Sr., letter book, Feb 1869–Jun 1873, *96M–46(1), 279.5, and MBR to ARC, Mar 3, 1871 (quoted material), bMS Am 1834.1(194), TRC; Cashin, *First Lady of the Confederacy*, 191.

48. TR Sr. to Capt. D.M. Fairfax, Mar 18, 1871 TR Sr., letter book Feb 1869–Jun 1873, *96M–46(1), 324, TRC; Lancashire County, England, records, West Derby; Waterloo, Death Certificate, s.v., "Henry Dunwoody Bulloch."

49. MBR to ARC, Mar 3, 1871, BMS Am 1834.1(194), TRC; Wilson and McKay, *James D. Bulloch*, 234. JDB could have made an undocumented return to Liverpool sometime between November 1970 and January 1871.

50. U.K. National Archives, Census

Returns of England and Wales, 1871, Kew, Surrey, Public Record Office, 1871 Class: RG10, Piece: 3838, Folio: 78, Page: 4, GSU roll: 841922; TR Sr. to James K. Gracie, Jun 22, 1875, and TR Sr. to Irvine S. Bulloch, Sep 4, 1871, TR Sr. letter books, Jun 1874– Feb 1876 and Feb 1869–Jun 1873, *96M 46(1), 507 and 426, TRC. £400 = $44,400 in 2015.

51. MSB to SEW, Apr 3, 1863, bMS Am 1785.2(19), TRC.

52. *NYT*, Aug 25, 1861; New York *Tribune*, Nov 14, 1856, Jun 26, 1857; United States Military Academy Association of Graduates, *Tenth Annual Reunion of the Association of the Graduates of the United States Military Academy, at West Point, New York. June 12, 1879* (New York: D. Van Nostrand, 1879), 96; George W. Cullum, *Biographical Register of the Officers and Graduates of the U.S. Military Academy from 1802 to 1867* (1879; reprint, Bedford, MA: Applewood, 2009), 149; A. Green and Company, *Directory for Liverpool and Birkenhead, 1870* (London: A. Green and Co., 1870), 137. Henry B. Sears graduated no. 14 of 59 in the USMA class of 1846 that included George B. McClellan (#2), Thomas J. (Stonewall) Jackson (#17), and George E. Pickett (#59).

53. *NYT*, Jun 30, 1872; Robinson, *My Brother*, 53; TR Sr., to James K. Gracie, Feb 19, 1874, TR Sr. letter book, Jun 1873–Jun 1874, *96M–46(1), 350, TRC; Wilson and McKay, *James D. Bulloch*, 243.

54. *NYT*, Oct 16–17, 1872; *Anglo-American Times*, 2 Nov 1872, 17; H.W. Brands, *TR, the Last Romantic* (New York: Basic, 1997), 32; McCullough, *Mornings on Horseback*, 127.

55. Theodore Roosevelt Diaries and Notebooks, 1858–1919, MS Am 1454.55(8), 2–3, TRC.

56. Ibid., 4–8, TRC; Brands, *TR*, 93; Wilson and McKay, *James D. Bulloch*, 241.

57. Robinson, *My Brother*, 71.

58. Ibid.; *NYT*, Jun 14, 1871; NARA, M1372, Passport Application, Roll 0174, Jul 10, 1871, s.v. "Lucy Ireland Elliott."

59. Clinton, *The Other Civil War*, 89; Faust, *Mothers of Invention*, 6; Rable, *Civil Wars, Women*, 240

60. New York *Commercial Advertiser*, Jul 18, 1871; Robinson, *My Brother*, 71.

61. TR Sr. to MBR, Jun 7 and 8, 1873, bMS Am 1785.2(100), TRC; Morris, *The*

Rise of Theodore Roosevelt, 73; Robinson, *My Brother*, 78.

62. Robinson, *My Brother*, 18.

63. MBR to TR Sr., Oct 11, 1873, bMS Am 1834.1(194), TRC; Rixey, *Bamie*, 22.

64. Ibid.

65. MBR to ARC, Oct 11, 1873, bMS Am 1834.1(194), and MBR to TR Sr., Oct 11, 1873, bMS Am 1875.7(34), TRC; *NYT*, Nov 6, 1873; Passenger Lists, Ancestry.com, SS *Russia*, 1873, Arrival: New York, Microfilm roll: M237_384, Line: 9, List number: 1198 and (SS *Cuba*), M237_385; Line: 9, List number: 1250.

66. London *Sun and Central Press*, Mar 26, 1873; Lawrence James, *The Rise and Fall of the British Empire* (1994; reprint, London: Abacus, 2004), 200–202; *NYT*, Jul 29 and Oct 8, 1874; *Anglo-American Times*, Oct 24, 1874; Irvine S. Bulloch to Ellerton L. Dorr and Col, Sep 2, 1874, TR Sr., letter book, Jun 1874–Feb 1876, *96M–46(1), 105-106, TRC; *NYT*, Jul 25, 1898.

67. TR Sr. to ARC, Oct 18, 1873, bMS Am 1834.1(201), TRC; *NYT*, Nov 6, 1873; Bulloch, *Secret Service*, I: 63; Anyda Marchant, *Viscount Mauá and the Empire of Brazil* (Berkeley: University of California Press, 1965), 112, 226-228; Wilson and McKay, *James D. Bulloch*, 243.

68. TR Sr. to Hewitt, and Ashton, Aug 18, 1873, and to James K. Gracie, Feb 19, 1874, *96M–46(1), TR Sr., letter book, Jun 1873–Jun 1874, 79, 350; TR Sr. to Capt. D.M. Fairfax, Mar 18, Jun 14, Jul 6, Oct 6, and Nov 4, 1871 and to JDB, Jul 6, Jul 22, and Nov 10, TR Sr., letter book Feb 1869–Jun 1873, *96M–46(1), 324, 402, 407, 413, 450, 471-472, 476, TRC.

69. TR Sr. to Hewitt, and Ashton, Aug 18 and 20, 1873, and Gracie, Feb 19, 1874, *96M–46(1), TR Sr., letter book, Jun 1873–Jun 1874, 79, 350, TRC; U.S. Treasury Dept., *Decisions of the Comptroller of the Treasury, Containing Decisions of Robert B. Bowler, Comptroller, and Edw. A. Bowers, Assistant Comptroller*, vol. II (Washington: GPO, 1896), 86.

70. TR Sr. to MBR, Nov 9 and 14, 1874 (quoted material), bMS Am 1785.2(100), TRC; U.S. Treasury Dept., *Decisions of the Comptroller*, 84-89.

71. TR Sr. to Ashton, Aug 20, 1873, to Fish, Nov 1, 1873, and to Robeson Aug 21, 1874, *96M–46(1), TR Sr., letter books,

Jun 1873–Jun 1874 and Jun 1874 – Feb 1876, 87, 189-190, and 88-89 and TR Sr. to MBR, Nov 27, 1874 (quoted material), bMS Am 1785.2(100), TRC; U.S. Treasury Dept., *Decisions of the Comptroller*, 84-89.

72. *NYT*, Dec 18, 1874, July 8, 9, and 18 Aug, 1877; TR Sr. to JDB, Jul 7, 1877, TR Sr. letter book, 668, TRC.

73. Semmes, *Memoirs of Service Afloat*, 413 (quoted material).

74. *NYT*, Feb 11, 12 (quoted material), 13, 1878.

75. Faust, *Mothers of Invention*, 92; Clinton, *The Other Civil War, American*, 81.

76. Robinson, *My Brother*, 18 (quoted material).

77. Anna Roosevelt Cowles, comp., *Letters from Theodore Roosevelt to Anna Roosevelt Cowles, 1870–1918* (New York: Charles Scribner's Sons, 1924), 27 (letter dated Mar 3, 1878).

78. Ibid., 28 (letter dated Mar 17, 1878).

79. Robinson, *My Brother*, 17.

80. Ferdinand Cowle Iglehart, *Theodore Roosevelt, the Man as I Knew Him* (New York: Christian Herald, 1919), 121-122.

81. Iglehart, *Theodore Roosevelt*, 122.

82. Entries for Mar 25, 28, and 29, 1881, *Personal Diary of Theodore Roosevelt, 1881*, TR Papers, Manuscripts Div., LoC.

83. *NYT*, May 12 and 21, 1881; Entry for May 29, *Personal Diary of Theodore Roosevelt, 1881*, TR Papers, Manuscripts Div., LoC (quoted material).

84. TR to MBR, Jun 5, 1881, MS Am 1541.9(109), TRC.

85. Entries for Sep 10, 14, and 22, 1881, *Personal Diary of Theodore Roosevelt, 1881*, TR Papers, Manuscript Div., LoC; TR to ARC, 14 Sep 1881, MS Am 1834, TRC; Cowles, *Letters from TR to ARC*, 50.

86. Theodore Roosevelt, *The Naval War of 1812*, vol. 1, 3d ed. (New York: G.P. Putnam's Sons, 1900), 6-7 (quoted material).

87. JDB to Jefferson Davis, Jul 22, 1881, in Jefferson Davis, Rowland Dunbar, ed., *Jefferson Davis, Constitutionalist: His Letters, Papers, and Speeches* 9 (Jackson, MS: Mississippi Dept. of Archives and History, 1923), 1-4 (quoted material).

88. MBR to TR, Sr., May 11, 1855, bMS Am 1785.2, TRC; TR to MBR, Sep 14, 1881, bMS Am 1834(963–1010), TRC (quoted material), also in Cowles, *Letters from TR to ARC*, 50.

89. Bulloch, *Secret Service*, I: iii–iv (quoted material).

90. JDB to Gilmer, May 4, 1883, MOC, Confederate Navy Collection: Bulloch, James D. (quoted material).

91. TR speech excerpt, Apr 23, 1910, Sorbonne, Paris, France, "Citizenship in a Republic."

92. Robinson, *My Brother*, 17.

93. McCullough, *Mornings on Horseback*, 282-283; Morris, *The Rise of Theodore Roosevelt*, 240-241.

94. Wilson and McKay, *James D. Bulloch*, 254; JDB to Anna Bulloch Cowles, Feb 14, 1884, bMS Am 1834, TRC.

95. Rable, *Civil Wars, Women*, 285-286; John M. Brooke, *Ironclads and Big Guns of the Confederacy, the Journal and letters of John M. Brooke*, ed. George M. Brooke, Jr. (Columbia: University of South Carolina, 2002), 162; Anderson, *Confederate Foreign Agent*, 104; McCullough, *Mornings on Horseback*, 64–68, 365.

96. JDB to Jefferson Davis, Nov 25, 1884 and Jan 9, 1885, MOC, Jefferson Davis Family Collection, Box 6; U.K. National Archives, Census Returns of England and Wales, 1881 and 1891, Lancashire, Liverpool, RG:11 and RG: 12, piece 3626 and 2941, folio 56 and 5, p. 9 and 3, s.v. "James D. Bulloch."

97. JDB to Nannie Hutchison Dawson, Jan 24, 1880 (quoted material) and Jun 26, 1886, MS 2226, Box 3 Folder 23 and 25, Hutchison-Dawson Papers, GHS.

98. JDB to Dawson, Jun 26, 1886, Hutchison-Dawson papers, MS 2226, Box 3, folder 25, GHS; Rable, *Civil Wars, Women*, 154.

99. Wilson and McKay, *James D. Bulloch*, 258; Morris, *Edith Kermit Roosevelt*, 99; NARA, RG: 36, U.S. Customs Records, M237, Roll: 513, 1887, New York, Line: 23, page 19; Harriott Bulloch to Nannie Caskie Dawson, Jun 29, 1887, Hutchison-Dawson Papers, MS 2226, GHS.

100. NARA, Passport Applications, Ser: M1372; Roll: 240, s.v. "Anna B. Hall"; Elliott Roosevelt, Eleanor Roosevelt (ed.), *Hunting Big Game in the Eighties, the Letters of Elliott Roosevelt Sportsman* (New York: Charles Scribner's Sons, 1933), 147-148 (quoted material).

101. Joseph P. Lash, *Eleanor and Franklin* (New York: W.W. Norton, 1971), 29-30; Cook, *Eleanor Roosevelt*, vol. 1,

48–49; The New York *Sun*, Oct 23, 1887; *NYT*, Oct 24, 1887; Harriott Bulloch to Nannie Caskie Dawson, Jun 29, 1887, Hutchison-Dawson Papers, MS 2226, GHS. Box 3, Folder 26; JDB to Elliott Roosevelt, Jul 19, 1883, in Roosevelt, *Hunting Big Game in the Eighties*), 147–148.

102. Roosevelt, *Hunting Big Game in the Eighties*, 158.

103. *NYT*, May 22, 23, and 29 (quoted material), 1887; Cook, *Eleanor Roosevelt*, vol. 1, 48.

104. Joseph P. Lash, *Eleanor and Franklin* (New York: W.W. Norton, 1971), 29–30; Cook, *Eleanor Roosevelt*, vol. 1, 48–49; The New York *Sun*, Oct 23, 1887; *NYT*, Oct 24, 1887; Harriott Bulloch to Nannie Caskie Dawson, Jun 29, 1887, Hutchison-Dawson Papers, MS 2226, GHS. Box 3, Folder 26; JDB to Elliott Roosevelt, Jul 19, 1883, in Roosevelt, *Hunting Big Game in the Eighties*), 147–148.

105. Toxteth Park Registration District, marriage certificate, Liverpool, Lancashire, s.v., "Maxwell Hyslop Maxwell"; U.K. National Archives, Census Returns of England and Wales, 1891, RG: 12, piece 2941, folio 5, p. 3, s.v. "James D. Bulloch."

106. Passenger list, Ancestry.com, 1888, Arrival: New York, Microfilm roll: M237_518, Line: 11, List number: 488, 18–19; James D. Bulloch, Jr. to Nannie Caskie Dawson, Jan 25, 1888, Hutchison-Dawson Papers, MS 2226, GHS, Box 3, Folder 26.

107. TR to ARC, Jul 1, 1888, bMS Am 1834(111-782), TRC.

108. TR to ARC, May 20, 1888, bMS Am 1834(111-782), TRC.

109. TR to ARC, Jul 1, 1888, bMS Am 1834(111-782), TRC.

110. National Archives, United Kingdom, Liverpool Record Office, ref 362 SAL 7/1; James D. Bulloch, Jr., to Nannie Caskie Dawson, Jan 25, 1888, Hutchison-Dawson Papers, MS 2226, GHS, Box 3, Folder 26.

111. New Orleans *Times Picayune*, Sep 7, 1888; Robert Jones, "Bulloch Family Collection"; National Archives, United Kingdom, Liverpool Record Office, ref 362 SAL 7/1 (quoted material).

112. JDB to Nannie Hutchison Dawson, Jun 26, 1886, Hutchison–Dawson papers, MS 2226, GHS.

113. TR to ARC, Nov 20, 1888, bMS Am 1834, 260.

114. TR to Lodge, Dec 16, 1888, and

Theodore Roosevelt, Elting E. Morison, ed., *The Letters of Theodore Roosevelt*, vol. 1, *The Years of Preparation, 1868–1898* (Cambridge: Harvard University Press, 1951), 150–151.

Chapter 6

1. Summary and biographical note and JDB to Nannie Hutchison Dawson, June 22, 1865, Hutchison-Dawson Papers, MS 2226, GHS, Box 3 Folder 25; General Register Office, *England and Wales Civil Registration Indexes*, London; *Census Returns of England and Wales, 1891*, Kew, Surrey, England: The National Archives of the UK.

2. Rable, *Civil Wars, Women*, 271. JDB to Nannie Caskie Dawson, Mar 25, 1889, and Jul 2, 1892 (quoted material), Hutchison-Dawson Papers, MS 2226, GHS, Box 3, Folder 26.

3. JDB to Nannie Caskie Dawson, May 9, 1889, Hutchison-Dawson Papers, MS 2226, GHS, Box 3, Folder 26.

4. JDB to John Dawson Nov 1, 1893, Hutchison-Dawson Papers, MS 2226, GHS, Box 3, Folder 26.

5. JDB to Nannie Caskie Dawson, May 9, 1889, Hutchison-Dawson Papers, MS 2226, GHS, Box 3, Folder 26.

6. *Evening Gazette*, Cedar Rapids, Iowa, Feb 24, 1909; Henry Rayner, A.R. Urquhart, J. Chambers, eds., *Journal of Mental Science* 55 (London: J. and A. Churchill, 1909), 329–331 (quoted material).

7. Rayner, et al., eds., *Journal of Mental Science* 55, 329–331; *The Shoreditch Observer*, Feb 27, 1909.

8. *The Shoreditch Observer*, Feb 27, 1909 (quoted material); Ruth Hoberman, *Museum Trouble: Edwardian Fiction and the Emergence of Modernism* (Charlottesville: University of Virginia Press, 2011), 1–2; *The London Telegraph*, Feb 3, 2010.

9. Blackman, *Wild Rose*, 6, 182–185; JDB to Davis, Jul 29, 1889, in John Warwick Daniel, *Life and Reminiscences of Jefferson Davis* (Baltimore: R.H. Woodward, 1890), 436.

10. JDB to Davis, Jul 29, 1889, in Daniel, *Life and Reminiscences of Jefferson Davis*, 436–440.

11. Hamilton Basso, *Beauregard, the*

Great Creole (New York: C. Scribner's Sons, 1933), 310.

12. JDB to Varina H. Davis, Dec 7, 1889, MOC, Jefferson Davis Family Collection, Box 30.

13. Cashin, *First Lady of the Confederacy*, 18-19, 23, 26, 111, 169; Rable, *Civil Wars, Women*, 144.

14. Cashin, *First Lady of the Confederacy*, 18-19, 23, 274.

15. Ibid., 308; Public Law 95–466, Oct 17, 1978; Senate Joint Resolution 16, 95th U.S. Congress (1977–1978).

16. Morris, *The Rise of Theodore Roosevelt*, 430-431, 438; Wilson and McKay, *James D. Bulloch*, 263-264.

17. Wilson and McKay, *James D. Bulloch*, 264; JDB to Corinne Roosevelt Robinson, Aug 1, 1893, bMS Am 1785(182), TRC; Passenger list, Ancestry.com, 1891, Arrival: New York, Microfilm roll: M237_573, Line: 11, List number: 1201; Cook, *Eleanor Roosevelt*, vol. One, 66-68.

18. Morris, *The Rise of Theodore Roosevelt*, 445; *Anglo-American Times*, Jan 22, 1892; Ellis Island Foundation, SS *Lahn* manifest, page 740, line 48, *https://www.ellisisland.org/*.

19. NARA, Passport Applications, Ser: M1490; Roll: 1629, s.v. "Corinne Roosevelt Robinson"; Ellis Island Foundation, SS *Teutonic* manifest, page 74, lines 40 and 41; 1892, Microfilm roll: M237_582, Line: 32, Page: 14, *NYT*, Mar 9, 1892; *Anglo-American Times*, Jan 29 and Mar 25, 1892; Wilson and McKay, *James D. Bulloch*, 264.

20. Eleanor Roosevelt, *The Autobiography of Eleanor Roosevelt* (New York: Da Capo, 1992), 3.

21. *NYT* obituary, Dec 9, 1892.

22. Roosevelt, *Autobiography of Eleanor Roosevelt*, 3-13: Wilson and McKay, *James D. Bulloch*, 266.

23. *NYT*, Jun 10, 1893, and Aug 16, 1894; Cook, *Eleanor Roosevelt*, vol. 1, 83-84; James King Gracie to Corinne (Roosevelt) Robinson, bMS Am 1785 (533), TRC (quoted material).

24. New York Society Library, "New York City Marriage and Death Notices: 1857–1868," http://www.nysoclib.org/king/king3.html; *NYT*, Dec 4, 1903; *The Brooklyn Daily Eagle*, Jun 2, 1904; Wilson and McKay, *James D. Bulloch*, 244.

25. JDB to Corinne Roosevelt Robinson, Aug 29, 1894 (quoted material), bMS Am 1785(182), TRC.

26. Wilson and McKay, *James D. Bulloch*, 265; *Anglo American Times*, Dec 23, 1893; *NYT*, Nov 19, 1878; Caroli, *The Roosevelt Women*, 97-99; Morris, *Edith Kermit Roosevelt*, 146; Rixey, *Bamie*, 76.

27. Rixey, *Bamie*, 84-87; Caroli, *The Roosevelt Women*, 102-108.

28. *The London Times*, Nov 18, 1892; Wilson and McKay, *James D. Bulloch*, 269.

29. *Philadelphia Times*, Nov 26, 1895; Ancestry.com, *UK, Incoming Passenger Lists, 1878–1960*. Corinne, Douglas, their four children, a nurse, and maid, had arrived in Liverpool the previous June, but Bamie did not have any bridesmaids.

30. Roosevelt, *Autobiography of Eleanor Roosevelt*, 21, 22, 44 (quoted material).

31. *Philadelphia Times*, Nov 26, 1895. Note: duchesse satin is a lustrous, elegant fabric and a tulle veil is sheer.

32. TR to ARC, May 3, 1896, bMS Am 1834(111–782), TRC.

33. Morris, *The Rise of Theodore Roosevelt*, 128.

34. Rable, *Civil Wars, Women*, 3, 273.

35. Cook, *Eleanor Roosevelt*, vol. 1, 162-169, 199-201, 206, 379; Rable, *Civil Wars, Women*, 145.

36. Roosevelt, *Hunting Big Game in the Eighties*, 158; *NYT*, May 22, 23, 29 and Oct 24, 1887; Cook, *Eleanor Roosevelt*, vol. 1, 48-49; Harriott Bulloch to Nannie Caskie Dawson, Jun 29, 1887, Hutchison-Dawson Papers, MS 2226, GHS; Lash, *Eleanor and Franklin*, 29-30.

37. Lash, *Eleanor and Franklin*, 96-97; Cook, *Eleanor Roosevelt*. vol. 1, 137; Michael Teague, *Mrs. L.: Conversations with Alice Roosevelt Longworth* (Garden City, NY: Doubleday, 1981), 22 (quoted material).

38. Roosevelt, *Autobiography of Eleanor Roosevelt*, 22.

39. Rixey, *Bamie*, v.

40. Rable, *Civil Wars, Women*, x; Caroli, *The Roosevelt Women*, 121-122; Morris, *Edith Kermit Roosevelt*, 98 (quoted material).

41. Roosevelt, *Autobiography of Eleanor Roosevelt*, 44.

42. Rixey, *Bamie*, 165; Roosevelt, *Autobiography of Eleanor Roosevelt*, 20; Wilson and McKay, *James D. Bulloch*, 232-234. Souvestre's boarding school in England was named Allenswood.

43. Lash, *Eleanor and Franklin*, 146-147; Roosevelt, *Hunting Big Game*, 37-38.

44. JSB to Elliott Roosevelt, Jul 19, 1883, Roosevelt, *Hunting Big Game*, 147-148.

45. Wilson and McKay, *James D. Bulloch*, 263; Toxteth Park Registration District, marriage certificate, Liverpool, Lancashire, s.v., "Maxwell Hyslop Maxwell"; U.K. National Archives, Census Returns of England and Wales, 1891, RG: 12, piece 2941, folio 5, p. 3, s.v. "James D. Bulloch"; McCullough, *Mornings on Horseback*, 46.

46. Death Certificate, no. 4, Toxteth Park, Liverpool and Burial Certificate, Toxteth Park, 11 a.m., Jul 6, 1897, s.v. "Harriot Cross Bulloch" (sic), courtesy Bob Jones, Liverpool.

47. JDB to Dawson, Jul 2, 1882, Hutchison-Dawson papers, MS 2226, Box 3, Folder 26, GHS (quoted material); James had Dunnie's remains reburied next to his mother's on Sep 7, 1897.

48. TR to ARC, Aug 17, 1897, bMS Am 1834(111–782), TRC (on Navy Dept. letterhead) (quoted material); *London Times*, Jul 15, 1898.

49. *London Times*, Jul 15, 1898; Death Certificate, no. 163, Conway, Crueddyn, Caernavon and Denbigh, Jul 14, 1898, s.v. "Irvine Stephens Bulloch," courtesy Bob Jones, Liverpool; *Liverpool Mercury*, Jul 18, 1898.

50. Death Certificate, no. 427, Liverpool, Mount Pleasant, Jan 8, 1901, s.v. "James Dunwoody Bulloch," courtesy Bob Jones, Liverpool; *Liverpool Mercury*, Jan 9, 1901, *Liverpool Courier* and *Liverpool Daily Post*, Jan 11, 1901. Also in attendance were Mr. and Mrs. Walter Wilson (no relation to the author).

51. *The West Australian*, Mar 27, 2011, courtesy Dr. Jim Elliott, Perth.

52. Principal Probate Registry, London, England, 323, Oct 26, 1937, s.v. "Maxwell Hyslop Maxwell"; 463, Sep 19, 1941, s.v. "Jessie Hart Hyslop Maxwell"; Principal Probate Registry, London, England, 914, Mar 7, 1947, s.v. "Martha Louise Bulloch."

53. Rable, *Civil Wars, Women*, 236.

54. Faust, *Mothers of Invention*, 4.

55. Jennifer E. Manning, et al. *Women in the United States Congress: Historical Overview, Tables, Discussion* (Washington: Congressional Research Service, Feb 18, 2014), 3-4; Jennifer E. Manning, *Membership of the 113th Congress: A Profile* (Washington: Congressional Research Service, Mar 14, 2014), 7. Note: Despite the newfound equality at the ballot box, the percentage of women in the U.S. Congress did not sustain a rate of over 4 percent until 1981. Twentieth-century female Congressional membership peaked at 12.5 percent in 1999 with 67 members. In 2015, that number had slowly grown to 104 female members (84 in the House and 20 in the Senate). Even with this progress, women still constituted less than 20 percent of the total membership (435 House and 100 Senate).

56. Rable, *Civil Wars, Women*, 288.

Bibliography

Archives, Official Documents, Unpublished Collections

Carter, Robert R. Shirley Plantation *Collection*, John D. Rockefeller, Jr., Library, Colonial Williamsburg Foundation, Williamsburg, VA.

Critchfield, L.J. *Reports of Cases Argued and Determined in the Supreme Court of Ohio*, vol. 6. Cincinnati: Robert Clarke & Co., 1874.

Dodge, Andrew R. *Biographical Directory of the United States Congress, 1774–2005*. Washington, D.C.: GPO, 2005.

Eller, RADM Ernest McNeill, ed. *Civil War Naval Chronology 1861–1865*. Washington: GPO for the U.S. Navy Department, Naval History Division, 1971.

_____, ed. *Dictionary of American Naval Fighting Ships*. Vol. VII. 1963. Reprint. Washington: GPO for the U.S. Navy Department, Naval History Division, 1977.

Geer, Elihu, comp. *Geer's Hartford City Directory and Harford Illustrated*. Hartford: Elihu Geer, 1882.

Georgia Archives. Morrow, GA. Marriage Records, 1828–1978.

Georgia Historical Society, Savannah, GA. Hutchison-Dawson Papers. MS 2226.

Historical Society of Pennsylvania, Historic Pennsylvania Church and Town Records.

Hotchkiss, William A., comp. *A Codification of the Statute Law of Georgia*. Augusta: Charles E. Grenville, 1848.

Huddleston, Connie. "A Social and Economic History of the James Stephens Bulloch Family of Bulloch Hall, Roswell, Georgia." Unpublished manuscript, 2008.

Jones, Reverend John. Family Papers, Hargrett Rare Book and Manuscript Library, University of Georgia Libraries, Athens.

Jones, Robert. "Bulloch Family Collection." Liverpool, Lancashire, England, including photographs and e-mail communications, "King's Rifle Volunteer Brigade, 1882."

Lancashire County, England. Records.

Library of Congress. Theodore Roosevelt Papers, Manuscript Division, *Personal Diary of Theodore Roosevelt, 1881*.

Liverpool, England, Record Office. *Register of Baptisms in the Parish of St. John Waterloo, in the County of Lancaster*. London: Shaw & Sons, 1865.

London Metropolitan Archives, Saint Peter, Belsize Park, Register of Marriages.

Manning, Jennifer E. *Membership of the 113th Congress: A Profile*. Washington: Congressional Research Service, Mar 14, 2014.

_____, Colleen J. Shogan and Ida A. Brudnick. *Women in the United States Congress: Historical Overview, Tables, Discussion*. Washington: Congressional Research Service, Feb 18, 2014.

Mariners' Museum Library, Newport News, VA. James Dunwody Bulloch Collection, 1847–1954, MS0283.

Museum of the Confederacy, Richmond, VA. Eleanor S. Brockenbrough Library,

Confederate Navy and Jefferson Davis Family Collections.

National Archives and Records Administration. RG: 29, Census; RG: 36, U.S. Customs Service; RG: 59, Passport Applications; RG: 109, Confederate Files.

National Archives and Records Administration, Southeast Region (Atlanta), Morrow, GA. *Coastwise Slave Manifests, 1801—1860*, Record Group: *36*.

Principal Probate Registry, London, England.

Probate Court, Liberty County Courthouse, Hinesville, GA.

Sebrell, Thomas. "Persuading John Bull: The American Civil War Comes to Fleet Street." PhD. Diss., Queen Mary: University of London, 2010.

Southern Historical Collection, Wilson Library, University of North Carolina, Chapel Hill.

Stevens, Thomas Holdup, et al. "The Wreck of the Maria Helena," in *Adventures at Sea*. New York: Harper Brothers, 1908.

Theodore Roosevelt Collection. Houghton Library, Harvard University, Cambridge, MA.

Toxteth Park, England, Registration District. Marriage and Death certificates.

U.K. National Archives. Census Returns of England and Wales; Home Office Naturalisation Papers.

U.S. Coast Survey Survey Map. "Anacapa Island in Santa Barbara Channel," 1854.

U.S. Congress. Public Law 95–466, Oct 17, 1978.

U.S. Congress. Senate Joint Resolution 16, 95th U.S. Congress (1977–1978).

U.S. Congress, House of Representatives. *A Biographical Congressional Directory, 1774 to 1903*, 57th Congress, 2d Session, Ex. Doc. 458. Washington: Government Printing Office, 1903.

U.S. Congress, House of Representatives, *Message from the President of the United States*, 31st Congress, 1st Session. Ex. Doc. No. 17. Washington, D.C.: GPO, 1850.

U.S. Congress. House of Representatives. *Report of Lieut. Neil M. Howison, United States Navy*, 30th Congress, 1st Session, Misc. Doc. No. 29. Washington: Government Printing Office, 1867: 1–36.

U.S. Congress, Senate. *Annual Report of the Superintendent of the Coast Survey for the Year Ending, Nov. 1851*. 32d Cong., 1st Sess., Senate Ex. Doc. No. 3. Washington: Robert Armstrong, 1852.

U.S. Interior Department, Census Office. Eighth Census, 1860.

U.S. Navy Department. *Naval War Records, Office Memoranda No. 8, Officers in the Confederate States Navy, 1861–65*. Washington: GPO, 1898.

U.S. Navy Department. *Register of the Commissioned and Warrant Officers of the Navy of the United States, Including Officers of the Marine Corps*. Washington: C. Alexander, 1848 and 1852.

U.S. Treasury Department. *Decisions of the Comptroller of the Treasury, Containing Decisions of Robert B. Bowler, Comptroller, and Edw. A. Bowers, Assistant Comptroller*. Vol. II. Washington: GPO, 1896: 84–89.

U.S. War Department. *The War of the Rebellion: A Compilation of the Official Records of the Union and Confederate Armies*," Ser. 3, Vol. 1. Washington: GPO, 1899.

University of New York Medical Dept. *Annual Announcement of Lectures*. New York: Joseph H. Jennings, 1848.

Vandergriff, Cara, "'Petticoat Gunboats': The Wartime Expansion of Confederate Women's Discursive Opportunities Through Ladies' Gunboat Societies." Master's Thesis, University of Tennessee, 2013. http://trace.tennessee.edu/utk_gradthes/1691.

Watson, E.J., Comm. *Handbook of South Carolina: Resources, Institutions and Industries of the State*, 2d ed. Columbia: State Dept. of Agriculture, Commerce, and Immigration, 1908.

Journal and Periodical Articles

Bulloch, James. S. "Report of Committee on Internal Police and Discipline." *Army and Navy Chronicle* 5, no. 1 (Jul 6, 1837), 4–5.

Ford, Elizabeth Austin. "The Bullochs of Georgia." *The Georgia Review* 6, no. 3 (Fall 1952), 318–331.

Greene, Richard Henry, et al., eds. "William Gaston Bulloch." *The New York Genealogical and Biographical Record Quarterly* 44 (Jan 1913), 232.

Greer, Richard A. "A.G. Abell's Hawaiian Interlude." *Hawaiian Journal of History* 29 (1995), 57–74.

Hacker, J. David. "A Census-Based Count of the Civil War Dead." *Civil War History* 57, no. 4 (Dec 2011), 307–348.

Harden, William. "William McWhir, An Irish Friend of Washington," *Georgia Historical Quarterly* I, no. 3 (Sep 1917), 197–219.

Himes, George H. "Letters by Burr Osborn, Survivor of the Howison Expedition to Oregon, 1846: Reminiscences of Experiences Growing Out of Wrecking of the United States Schooner Shark at Mouth of Columbia on Eastward Voyage of Expedition." *Quarterly of the Oregon Historical Society* 14, no. 4 (Dec 1913), 355–365.

Mallard, John B. "Liberty County, Georgia, An Address Delivered at Hinesville, July 4, 1876." *Georgia Historical Quarterly* II, no. 1 (Mar 1918), 1–21.

McLeod, Mrs. Hugh. "The Loss of the Steamer Pulaski." *Georgia Historical Quarterly* 3, no. 1 (Mar 1919), 63–95.

Neblett, Thomas R. "Major Edward C. Anderson and the C.S.S. Fingal." *Georgia Historical Quarterly* 52, no. 2 (Jun 1968), 132–158.

Owsley, Hariet Chappell. "Henry Shelton Sanford and Federal Surveillance Abroad, 1861–1865." *Mississippi Valley Historical Review* 48, no. 2 (Sep 1961), 211–228.

Pegram, Robert B. "The Cruise of the CSS Nashville: The Report of Lieutenant Robert B. Pegram, CSN." *Virginia Magazine of History and Biography* 66, no. 3 (Jul 1958), 345–350.

Royal National Life-Boat Institution. *The Lifeboat: Journal of the National Life-Boat Institution* 8, 9 and 10 (1873, 1876 and 1879).

Shine, Gregory Painter. "A Gallant Little Schooner." *Oregon Historical Quarterly* 109, no. 4 (Winter 2008): 536–565.

Spettel, Sarah, and Mark Donald White. "The Portrayal of J. Marion Sims' Controversial Surgical Legacy." *Journal of Urology* 185 (Jun 2011), 2424–2427.

Wall, L.L. "The Medical Ethics of Dr. J. Marion Sims: A Fresh Look at the Historical Record." *Journal of Medical Ethics* 32, no. 6 (Jun 2006), 346–350.

Newspapers

Alexandria (VA) *Gazette*
Anglo-American Times, London
Army and Navy Chronicle, Washington, D.C.
Army and Navy Register, Washington, D.C.
Atlanta (GA) *Constitution*
Atlanta (GA) *Atlantic Journal Magazine*
Augusta (GA) *Daily Constitutionalist*
Baltimore (MD) *American and Commercial Daily Advertiser*
Baltimore (MD) *Sun*
(Boston) *Daily Atlas*
Boston Evening Transcript
(Boston) *The Liberator*
The Brooklyn (NY) *Daily Eagle*
(Cedar Rapids, IA) *Evening Gazette*
Charleston (SC) *Carolina Gazette*
Charleston (SC) *City Gazette*
Charleston (SC) *Courier*
(Charleston, SC) *Evening Post*
Charleston (SC) *Observer*
Columbia (SC) *State*
Darien (GA) *Gazette*
The Emancipator (New York)
The Georgian (Savannah)
Harper's Weekly
(Hartford, CT) *The Times*
(Honolulu) *The Friend*
The Illustrated London News
Liverpool Courier
Liverpool Daily Post
Liverpool Mercury
London *Sun and Central Press*
The London Telegraph
London Times
Macon (GA) *Weekly Telegraph*
Milledgeville (GA) *Reflector*
Mobile (AL) *Register*
New Bedford (MA) *Whaleman's Shipping List and Merchants Transcript*
New Orleans Times-Picayune
New York *Commercial Advertiser*
New York *Evening Post*
New York *Spectator*
New York Times
New York Tribune
New York *Weekly Herald*
(Newbern, NC) *Weekly Progress*
Niles Weekly Register (Philadelphia)
Oregon Spectator
Philadelphia Public Ledger
Philadelphia Times
(Richmond) *Enquirer*

Richmond *Times-Dispatch*
Richmond *Whig*
(San Francisco) *Californian*
Savannah (GA) *Daily Advertiser*
Savannah (GA) *Republican*
The Shoreditch Observer (UK)
Southern Banner (Athens, GA)
Sun and Central Press (London)
Washington (DC) *Daily National Intelligencer*
Washington (DC) *Daily Union*
The West Australian
Wilmington (NC) *Journal*

Online Resources

Ancestry.com.
Ancestry.com. Passenger Lists, *http://ancestry.com/*.
Biographical Directory of the U.S. Congress, s.v., "Elliott, John" *http://bioguide.congress.gov/scripts/biodisplay.pl?index=E000124*.
City of Savannah, "A List of Mayors and Aldermen of the City of Savannah, Georgia, 1790—2012," *http://www.savannahga.gov/DocumentCenter/View/1971*.
Ellis Island Foundation, "Ellis Island/Port of New York Records," *https://www.ellisisland.org/*.
Erie Maritime Museum, www.flagshipniagara.org.
Find a Grave, *www.findagrave.com.* "Stuart Elliott."
Genealogy Bank, www.Genealogybank.com.
Green-Wood Cemetery, *www.green-wood.com*.
Holcomb, Brent. "Senator John Elliott." *http://www.quarterman.org/who/senelliott.html*.
Hyslop-Maxwell Family, *http://hyslopmaxwell.com/*.
Liberty County Historical Society, *www.libertyhistory.org*.
National Park Service, Theodore Roosevelt Birthplace, *www.nps.gov/history/history/online_books/presidents*.
National Society of the Colonial Dames of America in the State of Georgia. "The Andrew Low House." *http://nscdaga.org/about-us/*.
NavSource Naval History, http://www.navsource.org/.
New Georgia Encyclopedia. "Daniel Stewart (1761–1829)." *www.newgeorgiaencyclopedia.org*,
New York Society Library. "New York City Marriage and Death Notices: 1857–1868." *http://www.nysoclib.org/king/king3.html*.
Pride of Liberty. "Sunbury, by Kate Jones Martin"; "Reverend William McWhir and the Sunbury Academy." *www.prideofliberty.com*.
Roosevelt, Theodore. Speech, Apr 23, 1910, Sorbonne, Paris, France, "Citizenship in a Republic." http://design.caltech.edu/erik/Misc/Citizenship_in_a_Republic.pdf.
Rose O'Neal Greenhow. *European Diary, http://www.onealwebsite.com/RebelRose/*.
Roswell Historical Society. "Roswell's Historic Founder's Cemetery," *www.roswellgov.com/DocumentCenter/Home/View/2026*.
U.S. Naval Historical Center. "Dictionary of American Fighting Ships." *DANFS Online*, http:// www. history.navy.mil/danfs/.
Washington and Lee University. *On the Fringe of Fame: The Career of Richard Bland Lee II in the South and West, 1797–1875,* by Elizabeth Fleming Rhodes. Pasadena, CA: Castle, 1990. *http://leearchive.wlu.edu/papers/books/fringe/08.html*.

Published Primary Works

Anderson, Edward C. *Confederate Foreign Agent: The European Diary of Major Edward C. Anderson.* Edited by William S. Hoole. Tuscaloosa, AL: Confederate, 1976.
Bailey, Candace. *Music and the Southern Belle: From Accomplished Lady to Confederate Composer.* Carbondale: Southern Illinois University Press, 2010.
Bigelow, John. *France and the Confederate Navy, 1862–1868: An International Episode.* New York: Harper & Brothers, 1888.
Brooke, John M. *Ironclads and Big Guns of the Confederacy: The Journal and Letters of John M. Brooke.* Edited by George M. Brooke, Jr. Columbia: University of South Carolina, 2002.
Bulloch, James D. *Secret Service of the Confederate States in Europe, or How*

the Confederate Cruisers Were Equipped. Vols. I and II. New York: G.P. Putnam's Sons, 1884.

Chesnut, Mary Boykin Miller. *A Diary from Dixie*. 1949. Reprint. Cambridge: Harvard University Press, 1994.

Converse, Frank H. *Adventures at Sea*. New York: Harper & Brothers, 1908.

Cook, Blanche Wiesen. *Eleanor Roosevelt, Vol. One, 1884–1933*. New York: Viking, 1992.

Cowles, Anna Roosevelt, comp. *Letters from Theodore Roosevelt to Anna Roosevelt Cowles, 1870–1918*. New York: Charles Scribner's Sons, 1924.

Cox, Connie M., and Darlene M. Providence Walsh. *Providence: Selected Correspondence of George Hull Camp*. Macon, GA: Indigo, 2008.

Dana, Richard H. *To Cuba and Back: A Vacation Voyage*. London: Smith, Elder, 1859.

Daniel, John Warwick. *Life and Reminiscences of Jefferson Davis*. Baltimore: R.H. Woodward, 1890.

Davis, Jefferson. *Jefferson Davis, Constitutionalist: His Letters, Papers, and Speeches*, Vols. 8 & 9. Edited by Rowland Dunbar. Jackson: Mississippi Dept. of Archives and History, 1923.

_____. *Jefferson Davis Private Letters, 1823–1889*. Edited by Hudson Strode. 1966. Reprint. New York: Da Capo, 1995.

_____. *The Papers of Jefferson Davis*, Vols. 10 & 12. Edited by Lynda Lasswell Crist. Baton Rouge: Louisiana State University, 1999.

_____. *The Rise and Fall of the Confederate Government*. Vol. II. New York: D. Appleton and Co., 1881.

Dix, Morgan. *Memoirs of John Adams Dix*. Vol. I. New York: Harper & Brothers, 1883.

Ellyson, Moses. *The Richmond Directory, and Business Advertiser, for 1856*. Richmond: H.K. Ellyson, 1856.

Forrest, Douglas F. *Odyssey in Gray: A Diary of Confederate Service, 1863–1865*. Edited by William N. Still, Jr. Richmond: Virginia State Library, 1979.

Galloway, Tammy. *Dear Old Roswell: Civil War Letters of the King Family of Roswell, Georgia*. Macon: Mercer University Press, 2003.

Gould, George M., ed. *The Jefferson Med-ical College of Philadelphia: A History, 1826–1904*, Vol. II. New York: Lewis, 1904.

Harden, William. *Recollections of a Long and Satisfactory Life*. 1934. Reprint. New York: Negro Universities Press, 1968.

Harvard Law School. *Catalogue of the Students in the Law School of the University at Cambridge from the Establishment of the School to the End of the Year 1858*. Cambridge: Welch, Bigelow, & Co., 1859.

Hayes, Rutherford Birchard. *Diary and Letters of Rutherford Birchard Hayes*: vol. 1, 1834–1860. Columbus: Ohio State Archæological and Historical Society, 1922.

Kell, John McIntosh. *Recollections of a Naval Life: Including the Cruises of the Confederate States Steamers Sumter and Alabama*. Washington: Neale, 1900.

Larkin, Thomas Oliver. *The Larkin Papers*, Vol. VIII, 1848–1861. Edited by George P. Hammond. Berkeley: University of California Press, 1962.

Louisiana Writer's Project, comp. *Louisiana: A Guide to the State*. 1941. Reprint. St. Clair Shores, MI: Somerset, 1973.

Mars, James. *Life of James Mars, a Slave Born and Sold in Connecticut*, 6th ed. Hartford: Case, Lockwood & Co., 1868.

McLeod, Mrs. Hugh (Miss Rebecca Lamar). "The Loss of the Steamer *Pulaski*." *Georgia Historical Quarterly*, vol. 3, no. 2 (Jun 1919), 63–95.

Merrell, Henry. *Autobiography of Henry Merrell*. Edited by James L. Skinner. Athens: University of Georgia Press, 1991.

Morse, Sydney E. *System of Geography for the Use of Schools*. New York: Harper & Brothers, 1844–1850.

Munn, Henry B., and Alfred Martien, comp. *Class of 1847: The Centennial Class, College of New Jersey, Princeton, N.J., Now Princeton University: Consisting of Brief Biographies of Its Members from 1847 to 1907*. Philadelphia: Patterson and White, 1907.

Myers, Robert Manson. *The Children of Pride: A True Story of Georgia and the Civil War*. 1972. Reprint. New Haven: Yale University Press, 1984.

Nolan, Edward J. ed. *Proceedings of the Academy of Natural Sciences of Philadelphia*, Vol. 62. Philadelphia: Academy of Natural Sciences, 1910.

Pennsylvania University. *Biographical Catalogue of the Matriculates of the College, 1749–1893.* Philadelphia: Society of the Alumni, 1894.

Pennsylvania University. *Catalogue of the Trustees, Officers, and Students, Session 1860–61.* Philadelphia: Collins, 1861.

Philadelphia College of Physicians. *Transactions*, 3rd Ser., Vol. 9. Philadelphia: Dornan, 1887.

Robinson, Corinne Roosevelt. *My Brother, Theodore Roosevelt*. New York: Charles Scribner's Sons, 1921.

Roosevelt, Eleanor. *The Autobiography of Eleanor Roosevelt*. New York: Da Capo, 1992.

Roosevelt, Elliott. *Hunting Big Game in the Eighties: The Letters of Elliott Roosevelt Sportsman*. Edited by Eleanor Roosevelt. New York: Charles Scribner's Sons, 1933.

Roosevelt, Theodore. *Letters from Theodore Roosevelt to Anna R. Cowles, 1870 to 1918*. New York: Charles Scribner's Sons, 1924.

_____. *The Letters of Theodore Roosevelt*, Vol. 1, *The Years of Preparation, 1868–1898*. Edited by Elting E. Morison. Cambridge: Harvard University Press, 1951.

_____. *Theodore Roosevelt: An Autobiography*. New York: Macmillan Co., 1913.

_____. *Theodore Roosevelt's Diaries of Boyhood and Youth*. New York: Charles Scribner's Sons, 1928.

Semmes, Raphael. *Memoirs of Service Afloat, during the War Between the States*. Baltimore: Kelly Piet & Co., 1869.

Sever, Catherine Elliott (with introduction by Monroe F. Cockrell). "A Memory of the South." *After Sundown*, Vol. VIII (Dec 1957).

Sherman, William Tecumseh. *Memoirs of Gen. W.T. Sherman*, Vol. 1. Edited by James Gillespie Blaine. New York: C. L. Webster & Company, 1891.

Smith, Roswell C. *Smith's Atlas Designed to Accompany the Geography*. New York: Cady & Burgess, 1849.

_____. *Smith's Quarto Geography*. New York: Cady & Burgess, 1848–1850.

Taylor, Thomas E. *Running the Blockade*. London: John Murray, 1896.

Telfair, Mary. *Mary Telfair to Mary Few: Selected Letters, 1802–1844*. Athens: University of Georgia Press, 2011.

Vandiver, Frank E. *Confederate Blockade Running through Bermuda, 1861–1865*. Austin: University of Texas Press, 1947.

Waddell, James I. *CSS Shenandoah: The Memoirs of James Iredell Waddell*. Edited by James D. Horan. New York: Crown, 1960.

Walker, Georgiana Gholson. *The Private Journal of Georgiana Gholson Walker, 1862–1865: With Selections from the Post-War Years, 1865–1876*. Edited by Dwight Franklin Henderson. Tuscaloosa, AL: Confederate, 1963.

Walpole, Frederick. *Four Years in the Pacific in Her Majesty's Ship "Collingwood." From 1844 to 1848*. London: Richard Bentley, 1849.

Watson, Henry Bulls. *The Journals of Marine Second Lieutenant Henry Bulls Watson, 1845–1848, Occasional Papers*. Edited by Charles R. Smith. Washington, D.C.: History and Museums Division Headquarters, U.S. Marine Corps, Government Printing Office, 1990.

Webb, Isaac. *Catalogue of the Pupils of Isaac Webb and Julius S. Shailer's Family School, Maple Grove*. Middletown, CT: William Starr, 1841.

_____. *Catalogue of the Pupils of Isaac Webb, Esq., Private Barding School*. Middletown, CT, 1839.

Williams, John Rodgers, ed. *Academic Honors in Princeton University, 1748–1902*. Princeton: C.S. Robinson & Co. University Press, 1902.

Published Secondary Works

Abbott, Karen. *Liar, Temptress, Soldier, Spy: Four Women Undercover in the Civil War*. New York: Harper, 2014.

Basso, Hamilton. *Beauregard, the Great Creole*. New York: C. Scribner's Sons, 1933.

Beecher, Catharine E. *A Treatise on Domestic Economy*. Boston: T.H. Webb & Co., 1842.

Blackman, Ann. *Wild Rose: Rose O'Neale Greenhow, Civil War Spy*. Westminster, MD: Random House, 2005.

Bowcock, Andrew. *CSS Alabama:*

Anatomy of a Raider. London: Chatham, 2002.

Brands, H.W. *TR, the Last Romantic.* New York: Basic, 1997.

Braynard, Frank O. *S.S. Savannah, the Elegant Steam Ship,* Athens: University of Georgia Press, 1963.

Breed, Rev. William P. *West Spruce Street Presbyterian Church of Philadelphia: 1856–1881.* Philadelphia: Sherman & Co., 1881.

Bulloch, Joseph Gaston Baillie. *A Biographical Sketch of the Hon. Archibald Bulloch, President of Georgia, 1776–77.* Privately published, 1900.

_____. *A History and Genealogy of the Families of Bellinger and De Veaux and Allied Families.* Savannah: The Morning News Print, 1895.

_____. *History and Genealogy of the Stewart, Elliott and Dunwody Families.* Savannah: Privately published, 1895.

_____. *A History of the Glen Family of South Carolina and Georgia.* Washington, D.C.: J.G.B. Bulloch, 1923.

Calonius, Erik. *The Wanderer: The Last American Slave Ship and the Conspiracy that Set Its Sails.* 2006. Reprint. New York: St. Martin's, 2008.

Campbell, Jill. *Natural Masques: Gender and Identity in Fielding's Plays and Novels.* Stanford: Stanford University Press, 1995.

Caroli, Betty B. *The Roosevelt Women.* New York: Basic, 1999.

Cashin, Joan E. *First Lady of the Confederacy: Varina Davis's Civil War.* Cambridge, MA: Belknap Press, 2006.

Caskie, Jacquelin A. *The Caskie Family of Virginia.* Charlottesville: Conway, 1928.

Chaffin, Tom. *Sea of Gray: The Around-the-World Odyssey of the Confederate Raider Shenandoah.* New York: Hill and Wang, 2006.

Clarke, Erskine. *Dwelling Place: A Plantation Epic.* New Haven, CT: Yale University Press, 2005.

Clinton, Catherine. *The Other Civil War: American Women in the Nineteenth Century.* New York: Hill and Wang, 1984.

_____. *Tara Revisited: Women, War, & the Plantation Legend.* New York: Abbeyville, 1995.

Cullum, George W. *Biographical Register of the Officers and Graduates of the U.S. Military Academy from 1802 to 1867.* 1879. Reprint. Bedford, MA: Applewood, 2009.

De La Pedraja, Rene. *A Historical Dictionary of the U.S. Merchant Marine and Shipping Industry: Since the Introduction of Steam.* Westport, CT: Greenwood, 1994.

Edgeworth, Maria. *Tales of a Fashionable Life, Chapter IV, The Absentee.* 1823. Reprint. Boston: Samuel H. Parker, 1826.

Fair, John D. *The Tifts of Georgia: Connecticut Yankees in King Cotton's Court.* Macon: Mercer University Press, 2010).

Farnham, Christie Anne. *The Education of the Southern Belle: Higher Education and Student Socialization in the Antebellum South.* New York: New York University Press, 1994.

Faust, Drew Gilpin. *Mothers of Invention: Women of the Slaveholding South in the American Civil War.* New York: Vintage, 1997.

Finkelman, Paul. *An Imperfect Union: Slavery, Federalism, and Comity.* 1981. Reprint. Union, NJ: Lawbook Exchange, 2000.

Gamble, Thomas Jr. *A History of the City Government of Savannah, Ga., from 1790 to 1901.* Savannah: City Council, 1900.

Graham, Eric J. *Clydebuilt: The Blockade Runners of the American Civil War.* Edinburgh: Birlinn, 2005.

Green, A., and Company. *Directory for Liverpool and Birkenhead, 1870.* London: A. Green & Co., 1870.

Gross, Alexander, James B. Scouller, et al. *A History of the Methodist Church, South: The United Presbyterian Church; The Cumberland Presbyterian Church and the Presbyterian Church, South, in the United States.* New York: The Christian Literature Co., 1894.

Gunning, Martha House. *Historical and Genealogical Collections of the Martha Stewart Bulloch Chapter, Vol. 592.* Roswell, GA: Martha Stewart Bulloch Chapter, NSDAR, 2001.

Hagedorn, Hermann. *The Boys' Life of Theodore Roosevelt.* New York: Harper and Brothers, 1918.

Harper, Judith E. *Women During the Civil War: An Encyclopedia.* New York: Routledge, 2004.

Harris, Julia Collier. *The Life and Letters of Joel Chandler Harris.* Boston: AMS, 1918.

Hedrick, Joan D. *Harriet Beecher Stowe: A Life.* New York: Oxford University Press, 1994.

Heidler, David S., and Jeanne T. Heidler. *Encyclopedia of the American Civil War: A Political, Social, and Military History.* 2000. Reprint. New York: W.W. Norton, 2002.

Hitt, Michael D. *Bulloch Hall.* Roswell, GA: Self- published, 1995.

Hoberman, Ruth. *Museum Trouble: Edwardian Fiction and the Emergence of Modernism.* Charlottesville: University of Virginia Press, 2011.

Hoole, William S. *Four Years in the Confederate Navy: The Career of Captain John Low on the C.S.S. Fingal, Florida, Alabama, Tuscaloosa, and Ajax.* Athens: University of Georgia, 1964.

Howard, Michael. *The Franco-Prussian War: The German Invasion of France, 1870–1871.* 1961. Reprint. London: Routledge, 2001.

Howland, S. A. *Steamboat Disasters and Railroad Accidents in the United States,* 2d ed. Worcester: Dorr, Howland & Co., 1840.

Huse, Caleb. *The Supplies for the Confederate Army.* Boston: T.R. Marvin & Son, 1904.

Hussey, John. *Cruisers, Cotton, and Confederates.* Wirral, UK: Countryvise, 2008.

Iglehart, Ferdinand Cowle. *Theodore Roosevelt, the Man as I Knew Him.* New York: Christian Herald, 1919.

Jabour, Anya. *Scarlett's Sisters: Young Women in the Old South.* Chapel Hill: University of North Carolina Press, 2007.

James, Lawrence. *The Rise and Fall of the British Empire.* 1994. Reprint. London: Abacus, 2004.

James, Wilbur D. *The Confederate Rams at Birkenhead.* Tuscaloosa, AL: Confederate, 1961.

Johnson, Charles J., Jr. *Mary Telfair: The Life and Legacy of a Nineteenth-Century Woman.* Savannah: Frederic C. Beil, 2002.

Jones, Charles Edgeworth. *Education in Georgia.* Washington: U.S. GPO, 1889.

Kelley, Mary. *Learning to Stand and Speak: Women, Education, and Public Life in America's Republic.* Chapel Hill: University of North Carolina Press, 2006.

Kinnaman, Stephen Chapin. *Captain Bulloch: The Life of James Dunwoody Bulloch, Naval Agent of the Confederacy.* Indianapolis: Dog Ear, 2013.

Knight, Lucian Lamar. *Georgia's Landmarks, Memorials, and Legends,* vol. II. Atlanta: Byrd, 1914.

Lash, Joseph P. *Eleanor and Franklin.* New York: W.W. Norton, 1971.

Lester, Richard I. *Confederate Finance and Purchasing in Great Britain.* Charlottesville: University of Virginia, 1975.

Le Vert, Octavia Walton. *Souvenirs of Travel,* Vol. I. New York: S.H. Goetzel & Co., 1857.

Lovell, Caroline Couper. *The Light of Other Days.* Macon, GA: Mercer University Press, 1995.

Maffitt, Emma Martin. *The Life and Services of John Newland Maffitt.* New York: Neale, 1906.

Marchant, Anyda. *Viscount Mauá and the Empire of Brazil.* Berkeley: University of California Press, 1965.

Martin, Clarece. *A Glimpse of the Past: The History of Bulloch Hall and Roswell Georgia.* 1973. Reprint. Roswell: Lake, 1987.

McCullough, David. *Mornings on Horseback.* New York: Simon and Schuster, 1981.

McKay, Gary. *The Sea King: The Life of James Iredell Waddell.* Edinburgh: Birlinn, 2009.

Melton, Maurice. *The Best Station of Them All: The Savannah Squadron, 1861–1865.* Tuscaloosa: University of Alabama Press 2012.

Merli, Frank. *The Alabama, British Neutrality and the American Civil War.* Bloomington: Indiana University Press, 2004.

_____. *Great Britain and the Confederate Navy: 1861–1865.* Bloomington: Indiana University Press, 1970.

Michael, Chris. *Lelia.* Birkenhead, UK: Countryvise, 2004.

Milton, David H. *Lincoln's Spymaster: Thomas Haines Dudley and the Liverpool Network.* Mechanicsburg, PA: Stackpole, 2003.

Mitchell, Margaret. *Gone With the Wind.*

1936. Reprint. New York: Simon and Schuster, 2007.

Mode, Peter George. *Source Book and Bibliographical Guide for American Church History.* Menasha WI: George Banta, 1921.

Morgan, Philip. *African American Life in the Georgia Lowcountry: The Atlantic World and the Gullah Geechee.* Athens: University of Georgia Press, 2011.

Morris, Edmund. *The Rise of Theodore Roosevelt.* New York: Coward, McCann, and Geoghegan, 1979.

Morris, Sylvia J. *Edith Kermit Roosevelt: Portrait of a First Lady.* New York: Coward, McCann, and Geoghegan, 1980.

Mottelay, Paul F., and Thomas Campbell-Copeland, eds. *Frank Leslie's Illustrations: The Soldier in Our Civil War,* Vol II. New York: Stanley Bradley Publishing Co., 1893.

Nepveux, Ethel Trenholm Seabrook. *George Alfred Trenholm and the Company that Went to War,* 2d ed. Anderson, SC: Electric City, 1994.

Nevin, Alfred, ed. *Encyclopædia of the Presbyterian Church in the United States of America.* Philadelphia: Presbyterian Encyclopædia Publishing Company, 1884.

Old Etonian Association. *The Eton Register, Part II, 1853–1859.* Eton: Spottiswoode, 1905.

O'Toole, G.J.A. *Honorable Treachery: A History of U.S. Intelligence, Espionage, and Covert Action from the American Revolution to the CIA.* New York: Atlantic Monthly, 1991.

Owsley, Frank L., Jr. *King Cotton Diplomacy: Foreign Relations of the Confederate States of America.* Chicago: University of Chicago, 1931.

Patterson, James. *The Old School Presbyterian Church on Slavery.* New Wilmington: Vincent, Ferguson & Co., 1857.

Putnam, Carlton. *Theodore Roosevelt: The Formative Years, 1858–1886.* Vol. I. New York: Charles Scribner's Sons, 1958.

Rable, George C. *Civil Wars, Women and the Crisis of Southern Nationalism.* Urbana: University of Illinois Press, 1991.

Rayner, Henry, A.R. Urquhart and J. Chambers, eds. *Journal of Mental Science* 55. London: J. & A. Churchill, 1909.

Richards, Roger C. *History of Southern Baptists.* Bloomington, IN: CrossBooks, 2012.

Rixey, Lilian. *Bamie: Theodore Roosevelt's Remarkable Sister.* New York: David McKay, 1963.

Roosevelt, Theodore. *The Naval War of 1812.* Vol. 1, 3d ed. New York: G.P. Putnam's Sons, 1900.

Scharf, J. Thomas. *History of the Confederate States Navy.* 1887. Reprint. New York: Gramercy, 1996.

Scott, Mary Wingfield. *Houses of Old Richmond.* Richmond: Valentine Museum, 1941.

Settle, Raymond W., ed. *The March of the Mounted Riflemen.* 1940. Reprint. Lincoln: University of Nebraska, 1989.

Slick, David. *Graveyard of the Atlantic: Shipwrecks of the North Carolina Coast.* Chapel Hill: University of North Carolina Press, 1952.

Spann, Edward K. *Gotham at War: New York City, 1860–1865.* Wilmington, DE: Scholarly Resources, 2002.

Spencer, Warren. *The Confederate Navy in Europe.* Tuscaloosa: University of Alabama, 1983.

Sprunt, James. *Chronicles of The Cape Fear River, 1660–1916.* 1916. Reprint. Wilmington: Broadfoot, 1992.

Stacy, James. *History of the Midway Congregational Church, Liberty County Georgia.* Newnan, GA: S.W. Murray, 1899.

Stern, Philip Van Doren. *When the Guns Roared.* Garden City, NY: Doubleday, 1965.

Stiles, Henry Reed. *The History and Genealogies of Ancient Windsor, Connecticut,* Vol. 2. Hartford: Case, Lockwood & Brainard Co., 1892.

Swift, David E. *Black Prophets of Justice: Activist Clergy Before the Civil War.* Baton Rouge: LSU Press, 1989.

Teague, Michael. *Mrs. L.: Conversations with Alice Roosevelt Longworth.* Garden City, NY: Doubleday, 1981.

Thompson, Samuel Bernard. *Confederate Purchasing Operations Abroad.* Chapel Hill: University of North Carolina Press, 1935.

United States Military Academy Association of Graduates. *Tenth Annual Reunion of the Association of the Graduates of the United States Military*

Academy, at West Point, New York. June 12, 1879. New York: D. Van Nostrand, 1879.

Wawro, Geoffrey. *The Austro-Prussian War: Austria's War with Prussia and Italy in 1866.* New York: Cambridge University, 1996.

Whittelsey, Charles Barney. *The Roosevelt Genealogy, 1649–1902.* Hartford: Charles Barney Whittelsey, 1902.

Williams, David. *The Georgia Gold Rush: Twenty-Niners, Cherokees, and Gold Fever.* Columbia: University of South Carolina, 1993.

Willson, Beckles. *John Slidell and the Confederates in Paris.* New York: Minton, Balch, 1932.

Wilson, Adelaide. *Historic and Picturesque Savannah.* Boston: Boston Photogravure Co., 1889.

Wilson, Walter E., and Gary L. McKay, *James D. Bulloch: Secret Agent and Mastermind of the Confederate Navy.* Jefferson, NC: McFarland, 2012.

Wise, Steven R. *Lifeline of the Confederacy: Blockade Running During the American Civil War.* Columbia: University of South Carolina, 1988.

Index

Abell, Alexander G. 55
Abell, Sarah 55
Adams, Charles F. 112, 135, 138
Adelphi Hotel *see* Liverpool
Africa 33, 97, 132, 137
African Americans 25, 26, 32–34, 105
Alabama (AL) 44, 87, 102; *see also* Mobile; Montgomery
CSS *Alabama* 109, 113, 123, 124, 128–132, 137, 138, 156, 164, 165, 190, 199; *see also* *Enrica*; *No. 290*
Albany (NY) 171
Alexander, Adam L. 198
American Education Society 203*n*33
Anderson, Edward C. 110, 111, 113
Anderson, Henry M. 199
Andover Theological Seminary (MA) 27
SS *Annie Childs* 114, 118, 150
Arctic (Sea) 179
SS *Arctic* 84
Ascot (UK) 151, 152
Ashton, J. Hubley 164
Astor, Helen Schermerhorn 185, 197
Astor, John Jacob (Jack), IV 197
Atlanta (GA) 1, 44, 47, 88
CSS *Atlanta* 123, 145; *see also* SS *Fingal*
USS *Atlanta* 145; *see also* SS *Fingal*
SS *Atlantic* 83, 84
Atlantic Ocean 16, 53, 71, 93, 150, 153, 175, 180, 191
Augusta (GA) 17, 19, 66
SS *Augusta* 94
Australia (AS) 3, 192, 193
Austria (AU) 153, 182, 207*n*24; *see also* Vienna
Auteuil (FR) 130
Azores (PO) 132

Bahamas (BF) 106, 123; *see also* Nassau
Ball, Willis 206*n*10
Baltimore (MD) 39, 67, 117, 157, 158
Barhamville Female Collegiate Institute (SC) 72, 153

Barney, Hiram 111
Barrington Hall *see* Roswell
Bavaria 156, 200
Bay of Wrecks *see* Christmas Island
Bayard, Nicholas J. 68, 75
Bayard, Sarah Glen 75
Bayard, Florida 75, 197, 212*n*12, 213*n*25
Beard, Edward (freedman) 203*n*47
Beard, Joseph (freedman) 203*n*47
Beaufort (NC) 118
Beauregard, Pierre G. T. 133, 180
Beaver Meadows (PA) 106, 118, 216*n*17
Beecher, Catharine Esther 27, 28, 72, 197, 204*n*57
Beecher, Harriet *see* Stowe, Harriet Beecher
Belgium (BE) 153
Benjamin, Judah P. 101, 102, 139
Bermuda (BD) 106, 112, 113, 117, 126, 132–135, 138
SS *Bermuda* 109, 110, 112, 117
Bess (slave) 51, 96
Bible *see* Holy Bible
SS *Bienville* 101, 102, 164
Bigelow, John 110
SS *Black Warrior* 86, 87, 90, 91, 92, 93, 94, 95, 213*n*34, 213*n*43
blockade 5, 49, 59, 90, 106, 108–110, 112–114, 118–120, 123, 126, 127, 130, 132–134, 137–139, 143–145, 150, 167, 180, 190, 191, 198, 199
Bonaparte, Louis-Napoléon 113, 135, 136, 156, 198
Bordeaux (FR) 135
Boston (MA) 33, 74, 80, 163, 203*n*33
Boyd, Belle 220*n*115
Boyd, Priscilla (freed slave) 25, 203*n*47
Boyd, Sam (freedman) 203*n*47
Brazil (BR) 49, 52, 65, 137, 163, 164; *see also* Pernambuco; Rio de Janeiro
Breed, William P. 96
Brest (FR) 135
Bright's disease 171

239